# INSIDE INSIGHT

# INSIDE INSIGHT

## Worley's Identity Discovery Profile
## (WIDP)

**John W. Worley, Ph. D.**

ELM HILL

A Division of
HarperCollins Christian Publishing

www.elmhillbooks.com

## Inside Insight

### Worley's Identity Discovery Profile (WIDP)

Published in Nashville, Tennessee, by Elm Hill, an imprint of Thomas Nelson. Elm Hill and Thomas Nelson are registered trademarks of HarperCollins Christian Publishing, Inc.

Elm Hill titles may be purchased in bulk for educational, business, fund-raising, or sales promotional use. For information, please e-mail SpecialMarkets@ThomasNelson.com.

Scripture quotations marked KJV are from the King James Version. Public domain.

Scripture quotations marked NASB are from New American Standard Bible˚. Copyright © 1960, 1962, 1963, 1968, 1971, 1972, 1973, 1975, 1977, 1995 by The Lockman Foundation. Used by permission. (www.Lockman.org)

Scripture quotations marked NIV are from the Holy Bible, New International Version˚, NIV˚. Copyright © 1973, 1978, 1984, 2011 by Biblica, Inc.˚ Used by permission of Zondervan. All rights reserved worldwide. www.Zondervan.com. The "NIV" and "New International Version" are trademarks registered in the United States Patent and Trademark Office by Biblica, Inc.˚

### Library of Congress Cataloging-in-Publication Data

Library of Congress Control Number: 2018966880

ISBN 978-1-400306862 (Paperback)
ISBN 978-1-400306909 (eBook)

# DEDICATION

*Love of my life, Barbara, who sacrificed her time without me so I could be in my study writing, for long periods at a time. I missed you. I am forever grateful.*

*To my four daughters Angela, Sherri, Melaney, and Christina; who have always been an inspiration in my endeavors towards WIDP and this book. I have been blessed to have them with me on this journey and in my life.*

*To God, who gave me life and intelligence, and a relationship with him. And, to my blessed family. God has given me, thirty-four-members so far, who I love and adore. I thank God for being able to be part of their lives.*

*I dedicate this book to those that will read it. Because your life will be changed.*
***Surefire!***

# ACKNOWLEDGMENTS

I wish to acknowledge the following:

- God, for his grace, love, and forgiveness!
- My friend Stephen Engman, who has been a long-time friend, and a loyal supporter of WIDP, Steve has provided immeasurable insight and constant encouragement over the years.
- All WIDP Associates and Affiliates. I am grateful for your constant praise for WIDP.
- To all the professionals; Corporations, Clinicians, Educators, Pastors, and Family members that have encouraged me to write a book about WIDP.
- Now, with the knowledge of WIDP, your "Inside Insight" about people development will be reinforced, and your quality of life improved!

# CONTENTS

## Inside Insight
## WIDP

# FOREWORD

## November 2, 2018

It's not often that an opportunity presents itself to write a foreword to a book that illustrates what a great friend and brother's life work represents, a real breakthrough in how we consider ourselves, view others, determine our rightful goals, and ultimately empower ourselves to be more of our natural self. This is such an opportunity. To foreshadow with just one word, consider the term "characterize," as I will return to this word and how the ability to characterize ourselves is of value and benefit.

My friend John, the distinguished Dr. John Worley is one of my all-time best friends. I have, and have had many great friends, but John remains at or near the top in the 20 plus years I have known him and his wife, Barbara. But, more than that, he's an inspiration to me and to most people whom he meets.

John is the wealthiest person whom I know, blessed with four beautiful daughters who have married and presented an unquantified number of grandchildren and great-grandchildren. I lost count since the number seems to increase with high frequency. My count is guaranteed to be out of date by the time I write this forward. Stands to reason John was and is a great and accomplished father. Of course, John married well. Barbara, whom I admire and respect, really couldn't be a better match for John.

John is also a pastor, and easily the most knowledgeable person whom I have ever known in the domain of the evangelical. Have a question about beliefs, history or underlying theological concepts? John can give you several opinions from any one of dozens of viewpoints. If that weren't enough, of all the readers whom I have ever known, John is the most voracious. He consumes books as we consume air or food. I could probably think of a comparably insatiable reader or two whom I have known in my life, and indeed, a few come to mind, but in all cases, I would have to say John would have the edge.

These facts and many of the other points I mentioned here may not be relevant to John's book or his ideas. They may not apply to how John ever developed his assessment concepts. If they are not, I find it interesting that so much background could be removed from the overall picture, and yet the image of John's profile and assessment would remain.

Before we proceed to John's ideas, and their value, the reader might benefit from a brief description of me, some of my professional experiences, my axiology, and as a result, my point of view. Some may even find a few credentials listed here.

I have spent many, many years of my professional life as an executive recruiter. I entered what at that time was referred to as the "personnel" industry in the late 1970's. I'm fond of recalling for people that in those times, and before, we were certainly not viewed as a key component of a company, and frequently were not viewed as a key member of executive staff. We just were more of a catch-all, hiring, firing, training sometimes, but nowhere near where the industry has evolved in current times. We were almost an afterthought or a necessary evil. It's not an exaggeration to state how many "personnel" offices were right next door to the restrooms, literally. There is a metaphor here.

Since those early days in the industry, which I would view as being the post-war, the 1950s to the 1970s, the industry evolved. It started to be referred to as the Human Resources field. It became a center of excellence within many companies and reflected the overall trend toward a better knowledge of and more in-depth valuation for the individual employee. It later evolved further to the Human Capital Management field we have today, which, according to many analysts, is valued as a multi-billion dollar market.

A new name reflected this evolution. In the 1980's or so, we all got a promotion and big upgrade in stature when we became "Human Resources." We still weren't taken all that seriously at that time, certainly not as a line management position in manufacturing, operations, engineering or marketing, but a step in the right direction. We were moving on up and increasing our legitimacy, and our "seat at the table" where executive decisions were concerned. Of course, this was particularly true in companies where the presence of labor unions was a factor.

Organizationally, where you might previously have found a Vice President of Personnel, you would now find a Vice President of Human Resources. That individual would have several specialists working for him or her to complete the HR functions. The functional areas were generally Staffing and Recruiting, Compensation and Benefits Administration, Labor or Employee Relations, depending on whether there was a labor union or not, and Training and Development.

During the 1980's and 1990's, I personally was immersed in industry roles other than HR, mostly with responsibilities in direct product and services sales, marketing, channels management and distribution, generally with Fortune 500 companies such as Honeywell, which was running at about $2.0 Billion of annual sales in the early to mid 1980's, Loral Aerospace and others. These companies were squarely in the industrial or Aerospace and Defense markets or enterprise level computing markets.

My responsibilities to help these companies grow also meant I hired and fired teams of other sales and marketing contributors, presales and applications engineers, and product marketing and product management professionals. In order to win multimillion-dollar level contracts to solve a client's problems and satisfy their requirements, an entire business acquisition team would need to be assembled, generally inclusive of engineering, development, management, marketing, and other areas. So, in my non HR career, I still was responsible for HR related functions such as identifying, qualifying and recruiting talent to join a specific project team. It was a great background to have and certainly served me well as I reentered the HR world in the mid-1990's as an executive recruiter.

By the time the late 1990's arrived, the US economy was essentially in "full employment." Hiring bonuses became the norm, even for new college graduates with unproven commercial experience. What we were observing was the gradual case being developed for an elevation of the HR industry into something more. Companies recognized they might succeed based upon their employees. Previously, engineering companies particularly prided themselves on their intellectual property, inventions, designs and their ability to manufacture. As technical and engineering parity became more commonplace, companies really had to find other areas to gain competitive advantage. I believe these were the circumstances that ushered in the era of valued employees.

It was around that time in the early 2000's that our industry was promoted again. We received a shiny new title. We became Human Capital Management professionals. What we all know as the "people" industry, really emphasized great employment and vocational fit, personal development, and of course, leveraging people as a company's competitive advantage. If our products and pricing were generally comparable, how will a consumer's business be earned? Enter Human Capital Management as we now know it.

I reentered the executive recruitment industry in early 1996. Knowing the value of each individual, I opened a boutique shop that focused on low volume, high touch executive recruiting that emphasized a broader than usual sense of the personal dynamics of a team and the new individuals that would be hired. I took pride in the fact that my clients enjoyed a 100 % voluntary employee retention ration in my first two years of operation. It was at that time that I formed *iGoHire* ®, an entity I own to this day, as well as the registered trademark. It was also around that time that John and I first met.

For many years after I assisted growing companies to attract top-level talent, I also applied my skills to Executive and Career Coaching. I opened many doors for candidates who wanted to improve themselves professionally, and started off with an executive assessment, a fresh definition of how they would optimally deploy themselves professionally, what their evaluation criteria ought to be as they consider various options, and a development of a list of prospective employers, targeted mailer to the CEO, and then follow up phone calls to secure personal interviews for my client, the candidate. When the right door was opened for a candidate, it was really like a major revelation. Of course, the hiring manager would think the candidate was a gift.

Over the course of my career, both in the industry as well as in the Human Capital Management field I interviewed thousands of individuals and hired hundreds, both for my own teams as well as client companies. It's with some conviction that I can attest to the value of having the kind of personal and professional insights into oneself and into everyone on a team or in a given environment.

We all have our view of the promise of assessment tools in general, and John's tools in particular. The reader can well imagine the frustration and cost of really not being in tune with oneself, and what we seek in the areas of people interaction, professional initiative, and personal relationships. John's breakthrough is really in a few different areas. John can best explain his ideas himself, but a significant breakthrough lies in how all three are tied together.

People and companies do incur the cost of frustration and lost productivity when they are not optimally deployed. While I will leave the measurement of that frustration and lost productivity to professional and forensic sleuths, we can all agree that this cost is high. Turnover and lost productivity are chief among them, but there are other costs. It's also unnecessary to incur this cost in this day and age.

On the positive side, we have all lived in the groove, or seen other people in the groove, really just enjoying their jobs more than anyone should be generally allowed. We've also seen companies that are really in the groove, with employees who are genuinely excited to be a part of their work. As a musician and guitarist, I have yet to enter a guitar store or the shop of a guitar builder and see anything less than an entirely enthusiastic, happy and apparently stress-free individual eager to assist me. Smiles abound.

I suppose this can occur naturally. I suppose it could occur accidentally. Sometimes companies such as Apple or Starbuck's develop their esprit de corps from day one, and the excitement of their employees may occur regardless of what corporate mantras and mission statements may exhort. But, we may agree on how unlikely this all is when companies and hiring are left to their own devices. It generally is by design.

In the case of people, either in or out of the context of their careers, those who have the benefit of an assessment will simply have insights that others will never enjoy. Of course, my background in the career and employment domain means I focus on the value of John's assessment tools in that area, be it for an individual or a hiring entity. But, that's really not the entire benefit profile.

Let's proceed to John's book and ideas on personal assessment. John does indeed explain and describe his ideas, and his thoughts are indeed breakthroughs compared to what is otherwise available on the market with the current state of the art in assessment tools.

At the outset, I promised to elaborate on the term "characterization." It's my word, possibly more than it's John's word. John tends to allude to the term "profile." While we may think we know ourselves, that's a far cry from having an independent, psychometric analysis of what we're made of, who we are, and what we're all about. In short, we benefit from a "characterization" of ourselves.

This characterization could come in many forms, clinical, verbal, artistic, musical, intellectual or even physical. As a great Boston Bruins fan, the photograph of Bobby Orr flying horizontally in the air after scoring the winning goal of a Stanley Cup championship has been worth many thousands of words. Did it characterize Bobby Orr? Arguably yes. Of course, you could watch hours of highlight reels, but for one moment in time, that photograph characterized Bobby Orr.

The reader may benefit from two specific, real-life applications assessment and characterization that I have personally and professionally deployed in the course of my operation as an HCM professional. I will allude to the application and benefit in two different but similar and related realms, one in the "hiring" world for corporations, and one in "career management."

When companies want to attract and retain talent, they frequently have a discernible and distinct core with which new hires must be in harmony. That core may be based upon the founder's own persona and background and may also be based upon the persona and backgrounds of the leadership of that company. It may include an image. It may include core values. It may include style. It may include academic pedigree. It may consist of socio-economic orientation. It may include technical or business perspective and point of view. It may include a relative amount of entrepreneurialism and proclivity to prosper in a startup environment, or may gravitate more toward a mature and well established or "blue chip" environment. Years ago, we executive recruiters knew well the "IBM" image or persona, down to the dress code of IBM executives. Nowadays, we might refer to Apple or Starbuck's, and we tend to conjure images in our minds of the kind of folks whom we believe might fit well within those environments.

We executive recruiters, prior to the advent of advanced assessment tools, justified our fees to a large extent based upon our ability to save a hiring entity's time by insulating them from time-consuming consideration of candidates who really do not fit the "mold" of what they are looking for in a candidate. We did well, by the way, because the better recruiters did take the time to develop a thorough and comprehensive perspective of their client.

I personally developed two applications for WIDP suitable to my HCM world. The first application I developed for WIDP was to "characterize" the executive staff of my client, the hiring entity, and many of their top producers. I would also assess the candidates and receive an independent perspective on where specifically might fit in well, and where the candidate may not. I have been able to increase the confidence level of my recommendation and referral of a candidate for hire.

Of course, any good recruiter will always have confidence in their own training, experience, knowledge of their own client, wisdom, judgment, and intuition, even without formal assessment tools.

The more visionary amongst us, however, develop even more confidence in our "read" on individuals with the use of tools such as WIDP.

The second application which I developed pertains to the career management and guidance field. For many years, I put my executive recruiter skills to use in a different application; I put them to work for individuals seeking to manage their career, maximize their earnings, and capitalize on all their skills and attributes.

Without elaborating on all the arcane details associated with how a great career coach will help a candidate maximize their opportunity, it should be noted that lacking formal and professional guidance, many of us tend to fail or underachieve. This is not because we're not smart or accomplished or self-promoting enough, but rather because we don't really know our true and best ways of deploying ourselves, what specifically we want to do, and even how we ought to assess an opportunity when it does present itself. If you can imagine the true cost of failing to optimally deploy yourself over the several working decades that you will likely work, you can appreciate the true cost of non optimum use of your given talents, skills, capacities and inclinations.

In over 50 cases that I can recall, I used WIDP to first characterize and assess an individual prior to dispensing advice on how to optimally manage their career. Of course, a "resume" would ultimately be developed, but it would not be anything like what is seen in the traditional world because it would be forward-looking and include the results of information that could only have been discovered in the course of a formal survey with WIDP.

In addition, we all know the value of interviewing well, and successfully managing the personal interview or batteries of personal interviews that one might expect in the course of interacting with a prospective employer. I have always said that my favorite part of the entire recruitment and hiring process was the interview strategy. I can offer much wisdom on interview strategy, but so much of it is based upon the insights and discovery enabled by the use of advanced assessment tools such as WIDP.

Very directly, most of us, lacking the insight of thorough assessment, tend to respond rather than direct. Of course, the candidate may still receive an offer however they would be less effective and may be offered less than a more effective candidate. I applied the WIDP insights to enable a candidate to interview far more "proactively" It may be said that my use of the tool enabled candidates to interview the hiring entity at least as much as the hiring entity interviewed them. Given my interview strategy recommendations and the insight, my candidates received as a result of their assessment, which party do you suppose was more effective during the interview process, the hiring entity or my candidate?

In today's world, it seems like discovering one's true identity may be more nuanced, more elusive and less clearly defined than in previous times. As an Executive and Career Coach and Executive Recruiter, I certainly see that and the cost of that problem. But as a parent, do we not want our kids to have every advantage and be clued in as much as possible to who they are? And of course, as they consider their prospective marital partners, is it not of value to be able to characterize their potential partners as well?

As a teenager in the 1960s and seeing how the world has evolved, life appears to be much more fluid now, perhaps more relativistic, less absolute. I don't have a view of whether that's good or bad, but I do have a belief that we have a benefit to having some access to our basics. Those basics could be a return to our hometown, the home in which we were raised, a visit to our old college or high school or a class reunion. It's who we are. In John's world, he has a God-given ability to help people characterize themselves and help them discover who they are, not who society or life or friends or guidance counselors or media have told them that they are. It can be a huge difference. We need to know, and we can use some help in the discovery process. John and his profiling capability can help.

I know the virtue of profiling in the employment and career domain, but I will never lose my appreciation for the value of that profiling in all walks of life. We all benefit from knowing our profile as individuals, as human beings, as family members, marital partners, and social people. I see the virtue of this in the employment domain, and of course, I urge readers to embark on this assessment journey for their purposes, either personally or to reap maximum shareholder value for their entity.

My hope is this book broadens the reach well beyond the narrow confines of the career and employment domain, into the human field. We will manage life better, as well as relationships and career. It's a great and worthy endeavor to assess oneself. Let's embark on this journey with John, and know ourselves better, and live better.

Michael P Athas / Founder *iGoHire* ®

# PREFACE

You!

That is why I wrote this book!

Because I care about you and your future and the quality of your life, I choose the BEST for you and want to show you how valuable you are as a creation of God.

As a clinical psychologist, I found a massive gap in the lack of understanding flaws of humanity and the challenging remedy of cognitive behavioral therapy and quality assessment instruments. After spending years as a clinician, I became increasingly burdened with the single question as to a missing link. **"Why aren't the systemic processes taught working?"** The formal education, licensures, certifications, diplomas, and degrees plus being certified on the most popular assessments instruments available in the markets left me feeling like knowledge betrayed me.

Or were they deficient assessment instruments initially; personality, character, and behavior! Perhaps? You cannot have confidence in any of the assessments—they will betray logic.

I saw the same companies, businesses, professionals, individuals, and families returning time after times with the same problems and getting the same results—which amounted to short-term fixes. However, there was never any permanent positive results, primarily because none of the available "tools" addressed the fundamental, underlying problems that were causing these people mental pain. I spent thousands of dollars in becoming certified on multiple personalities, and behavioral instruments. They all let me down, in the end, providing no long-lasting solutions to life's complicated issues that clutter the mind, distort the truth, and rob individuals of their quality of being emotional, spiritual and physical. I was frustrated, to say the least, that I could not provide more answers for them. I knew there was more to offer.

So, I created Worley's Identity Discovery Profile (WIDP), aka Worley's ID Profile. It is a sixty-question questionnaire that only takes 10–15 minutes to complete. That data entered a software program, and a 16–18-page assessment of the individual WIDP Profile generated, printed, and emailed to you from www.WIDP.org.

- I have trained hundreds of individuals on the use and application of WIDP for every life; application for: corporations, executive development, pastors, leadership development, sales management, marketing, upward mobility, change agent developer, people developers, new hire assessments, are being transformed using WIDP every day in every area of human resource and management.

- I have presented seminars on WIDP at the National Association of Sports Psychologists three years in a row.
- Conducted a research project at the Lowell, MA Public School on a class of second grade students (thirty-four), their teachers, teacher aids, assistant principal, and principal all participated.
- A college senior conducted a high school WIDP survey at a Christian School Academy in New Hampshire.
- We held a seminar to over 100 pastors from Portugal and Spain in five days using an interpreter.
- Workshops and presentations conducted throughout America.
- Wall Street—one of the Twin Towers Tycoons, purchased WIDP Profiles and software in a five-minute conversation!
- There are no cultural barriers to WIDP!

For years, people had been challenging me to write a book about Worley's ID Profile (WIDP) because of the positive impact it had on their lives in the areas as mentioned above. Why, might you ask, Write another book? The short answer: Because they had experienced long-term healing by understanding who they were created to be by seeing who they are today based upon their unremarkable temperament makeup revealed to them by their unique found knowledge from experiencing WIDP.

As I considered whether to write such a book, I began to ask myself a series of questions. My thinking went something like this:

- Why should I undertake writing a book on a subject that is very misunderstood by most people yet is simple to understand?

  - Well, you write the book because of the burning desire in your heart to help people out of their misery of doom and gloom. You write the book because you are compelled to "once again" climb the mountain trying to free people from bondages that have held them captive for years, decades, even *lifetimes*. You write a book because you know it is needed because only the "tip of the truth" exposed to the person is understood about themselves.

- How do you share with someone the idea that by understanding their temperament, their quality of life will change forever, whether it be in the corporate world or personally?

  - You take the time to teach them in a natural way that connects with their inner being, their thoughts about themselves, and their idea of who they are or who they think they are. You show them the goodness and uniqueness of who they are and that there will never be another person like them. Help them understand that they *are* extraordinary because of their unique temperament design.

- Why write *another book* about temperament?

  - Because for the most part, society does not realize what temperament is or where it comes from—and to live successful lives, you need to know what their temperament is and how to function knowing that information. By writing a book about Temperament (WIDP), I could help more people [understand this] than I could ever reach through one-on-one sessions or in a seminar setting.

So, I decided to write the book—but it's about ***TEMPERAMENT***—not character, personality, or behavior! If you will permit yourself and take the time to grasp the concept of being a unique person that you are as you read this book, your life will be transformed by the time you reach the end. Your quality of life will improve as you understand your correct temperament. Your relationships with others will improve as you begin to understand others based on their unique temperament designs. You will become spellbound with their unique design as well as your special temperament design.

But wait a minute! The success of your Christian life depends on two critical things:

1.  How well you understand yourself and your temperament and take time to educate yourself about your unique
2.  How ***successfully*** you learn to analyze everything about your temperament design.

Becoming a Christian does not end the decision-making process of life. You still have choices to make, but if by force of habit your determination is based on self-will, you will be miserable. We all need guidance about our unique God designed temperament. That understanding will change your world and give you "Inside Insight."

**Writing this book about Worley's Identity Discovery Profile (WIDP) has been an exciting. journey.**

**If you do not have your personal profile do it now. Go to www.WIDP.org and complete the WIDP Questionnaire online. Only takes a few minutes.**

**Get your life changing results immediately!**

# WHO IS DR. WORLEY?

## John W. Worley, Ph.D.

## President and Founder of Worley's ID Profile

Dr. Worley, a clinical psychologist, has earned a Ph.D. in Marriage and Family Therapy and a Master of Divinity. He also studied at the Institute of Holy Land Studies, Jerusalem, Israel. Dr. Worley has thirty-four years' experience in organizational, educational, ministry, executive coaching, and leadership development, seminar presentations, and teaching.

Dr. Worley is a native of Ohio and has been a resident of Massachusetts since 1974. He and his wife Barbara have been married for fifty-seven years and have four daughters, three sons-in-law, seven granddaughters, and one grandson and seven great-grandchildren. He has been a leader in many capacities.

- Currently, he is Director of Worley's ID Profile (WIDP)
- An Executive Coach developing people.

Dr. Worley has been granted two professional licenses in the Commonwealth of Massachusetts, Mental Health Clinical Counselor (MHCC) and Marriage and Family Therapist (M&FT); they are currently not active.

Dr. Worley is a fifteen-year United States Army veteran wounded in Vietnam. He has many years of personal experience in dealing with problems that plague corporations, educational institutions, professional counselors, ministries, families, and individuals. This personal experience, coupled with his extensive educational backgrounds, has earned him the reputation of being one of the best-qualified consultants and trainers in the trade today. Any individual or corporation who seeks reliable consulting or training will receive the best professional services available from Worley's ID Profile.

As a clinical psychologist with thirty-four years combined pastoral, consulting, and counseling experience, Dr. Worley has tried virtually every psychological, behavioral, temperament, and personality questionnaires available in today's market. As a professional consultant, Dr. Worley feels obligated to his clients, individual or corporate, to meet their needs as quickly as possible.

Much time is spent during the initial interview process assessing corporations, individuals, HR Departments, and managers before an effective plan are in place. Dr. Worley was searching for a comprehensive profile that would help him assist corporations, educational institutions, professional counselors, ministries, families, and individuals to understand themselves as individuals better a new understanding of their team members, coworkers, or new hires. The WIDP assessment requires completion of a simple questionnaire that measures their temperament needs and desires in three areas—social, leadership, and relationships. Dr. Worley could not find any psychological, temperament, behavioral, or personality profile anywhere that would accomplish the task of assessing these specific areas of an individual.

What Dr. Worley got from all the tests, profiles, instruments, and questionnaires he tried were complex graphs, charts, and minimal benefit to his clients. Every test certainly had its good points, but who wants to administer ten different assessments to everyone with little to no results?

The frustrations that Dr. Worley encountered during the last three decades were that most assessments and profiles measure external behavior. The exact response approach is acceptable for focused therapy, behavioral modification, or application in a vocational setting, whether it is a megacorporation, a private individual practice, or workplace. When one is actively dealing with observable behavior that is contrary, emotional, or intellectual, the necessary changes for improvement that need made within that person's behavior are evident. In these situations, behavioral modification required in most cases will produce acceptable results, although the behavioral change will only be temporary. Interim results realized because the root needs and desires of the individual have not been dealt with appropriately or entirely. Therefore, adverse behavior and conflict with coworkers and friends remain without permanent changes. Instead, constant interruptions dealing with the manifestation of the adverse reactions continue to cost corporations, large or small, billions of dollars annually. And the relationships of the individual continue to spiral into chaos.

When individuals produce unacceptable behavior because of their needs and desires not met, an objective behavioral profile is not adequate in identifying those problem(s). The solid pattern that defines one's personality based upon the immediate environmental focus of the individual answering the questions is defective because of the natural concentration is based on behavior and not temperament. The focus could be as a spouse, significant other, boss, friend, coworker, employer, relative, or the local service station attendant. This discussion leads one away from the real issue(s), causing the personal turmoil. Subjective behavior determined by a profile: a profile that subjectively measures the foundational needs and desires of the individual. When those needs and wants are identified and fulfilled, the personality or behavior of the person becomes healthy and acceptable instead of being always in conflict with others. Dr. Worley could not find a profile which measured a person's needs and desires based on a person's temperaments.

It is essential to realize that social interaction will be is influenced by the temperament of those involved in the conversation. Your emotional display is going to reflect your preferences based on your needs and desires according to your temperament. So, you are going to react differently in a community setting than you do in your work or home setting, as are the other people participating. And so are the other people involved. Why? Because we allow people in our space to form our thoughts and opinions based on how we feel and what we perceive in those situations. Therefore, we may put on a mask and present what we want them to see, not the real reflection of who we are. We don't see the real person. Instead, we see their character, personality, or behavior, frustrating, to say the least.

After years of research, beginning with the traditional behavioral patterns and moving through a process of evaluating the most popular instruments on the market, Dr. Worley decided to develop Worley's ID Profile (WIDP). The need for a pattern of this nature became apparent after years of counseling and consulting. Dr. Worley feels that the most significant behavioral problem existing today is the people's lack of understanding of their primary needs and desires based on their temperament makeup.

The intent and objective of Worley's ID Profile are not to measure intelligence or mental disorders, but to gauge needs and desires that are fundamental to the individual profiled. There are many other excellent instruments for measuring intellect, psychological illness, and personality types. However, there is lack of tools which will establish getting to the heart of the individual and identifying their needs based on who they are foundational. Assisted by consultants, counseling professionals, and computer programmers, Dr. Worley asked the question,

## "What would the ideal profile look like?"

Months later, the creation of a temperament profile was complete, and the answer to the above question proclaimed. Its name: Worley's ID Profile!

Worley's ID Profile (WIDP) is the answer. WIDP stands for

| Worley's | W | | |
|---|---|---|---|
| | I | Identity: | Identify Your Inner Needs and Desires |
| | D | Discovery: | Dare to Become All You Can Be |
| Profile | P | | |

Once you experience the WIDP temperament profile, you immediately see the tremendous benefits of the assessment printout the software program produces. It's fast, easy, economical, reliable, and dependable. Corporations and individuals benefit equally. Worley's ID Profile surpasses assessment instruments like;

- Meyers Briggs Type Indicator (MBTI)
- Taylor Johnson Temperament Analysis (TJTA)
- Preventive Index
- Caliper
- Fundamental Individual Relational Orientation-Behavior (FIRO-B) (FIRO-BC)
- Temperament by Tim LaHaye and Florence Littauer.
- Personal Profile Survey (PPS) (aka DiSC)

Worley's ID Profile is the most reliable and innovative temperament profile of the twenty-first century.

### Try it today and see for yourself!

The WIDP Questionnaire is available in three languages: English, Spanish, and Portuguese. Both for adults and youth (ages six–sixteen). Visit www.WIDP.org to get your personal profile.

# CHAPTER 1

# WHAT IS WIDP?

It was a bright, beautiful fall day when Frieda stepped out of her shiny red Mustang into the sunshine, tossed back her long, blonde hair, and waved at a small group sitting at a picnic table beneath three large oak trees. "Hiya, Sam!" she exclaimed, running over to the tall, middle-aged man dressed in smartly pressed khakis and a dark blue polo shirt. "How're the kids? Oh, hi Jill, I didn't see you," she added, noticing a short, plump brunette sitting on a lawn chair. "Hey, Pete!"

"Kids are fine," Sam replied. "Um, Frieda, you did remember the grill, didn't you?"

Frieda's face quickly went white, then blossomed red. "Oh, golly," she said, "I *knew* I forgot something. I mean, I made sure to bring the paper cups, napkins, and foil; however, you know, Sam, you can't expect me to remember *everything*."

"Oh, great," said Pete, a thin, dark-haired man leaning against the oak. "Sam, you should've known better than to leave it to *her*." He turned his back on the group and stared out across a small creek that lined the edge of the picnic area. "Now, what're we supposed to do?"

"Frieda dear, at a cookout, the grill *is* everything. Well, I guess we'll make our fire." He turned to Jill. "Hon, you gather some wood while I get the matches and the chicken."

"Aw, C'mon, Sammie," Jill whined. "Frieda forgot the grill, let her get the sticks. I don't want to eat chicken cooked on a smoky wood fire—it'll taste awful. Besides, there's nobody, even here. Where is Dan and Sallie and Rob?"

"Dan's down by the creek fishing," said Pete. "Said to call him when the food's ready. Sallie and Rob aren't coming. They said these reunions always turn out disastrous."

"Guess they were right," mumbled Jill.

"Geez, I'm sorry, guys." Frieda clapped her hands together. "I know, I'll drive back to town, and buy a bucket of Kentucky fried …then we won't have to worry about cooking! C'mon, Pete, wanna take a ride?"

"And what about the chicken we brought—it'll get worse," Jill said. "Besides, I hate Kentucky fried chicken. It's too greasy and salty."

"Wait," said Sam. "We can get a fire going if you'll all just help me gather some wood."

"Forget it, Sam," exclaimed Frieda. "C'mon, Pete, let's go get the Kentucky fried."

"Okay," said Pete. "I'm game!"

"Sam, take me home," said Jill. "This isn't what I had in mind at all."

"No, Jill. Oh, okay, fine," Sam said, shaking his head. "Frieda, when you pass by Dan, tell him you, me, and Pete will be back in a little while."

What went wrong? The short answer is "Everything!" While the actual scene described above is fictitious, the same type of scenario is played out millions of times each day across the world. The reasons? People with different temperaments are thrown together in a myriad of situations, people who haven't learned to understand their own needs and desires, let alone recognize it when their needs and wants conflict with another person's. Then they are expected to experience complete harmony between all of them? Unrealistic.

In this example, the one person who could have helped resolve the situation was Dan, whose temperament type Phlegmatic includes attributes that make him a natural peacemaker. Unfortunately, the same characteristics that make Dan a peacemaker also cause him to avoid conflict altogether. Because Dan doesn't fully understand his potential to serve as a mediator, he succumbs to his tendency to run away from the battle and focuses on fishing, while the cookout falls apart. After all, he had experienced so much conflict at group gatherings in the past that he disengaged, to begin with, and went fishing to avoid the dispute.

How do we get to the point where we (1) understand our own needs and desires, (2) recognize other people's needs and desires, and (3) know how to act to maintain peace and harmony in our relationships? Now is where understanding the principles of temperament will change your life. Let me give you a brief explanation of temperament:

All around us, we see chaos in various relationships and sometimes within our relationships. We see conflict, devastations, family destructions, corporate meltdowns, leadership failure, and in many cases mental fatigue and institutionalization. We look around us and realize there is something muddled in our world. Well, you see we are all inherent with built-in qualities, which determine the way we pick out others based on who we are and our present emotional conditions, which define our responses to the situations in our lives and relationships. These qualities are inherently built-in attributes that do not change throughout our lives. They are individual qualities that make each of us extraordinary and one-of-a-kind person.

Moreover, there will never be another "you" in this world. Many people live simple lives because they do not ever get the opportunity to "discover or know themselves." Once we become sensitive of and identify with our own set of unique, vital qualities and also determine the drive that is within us or lack of it, we can begin to confidently impact our performance and proceedings in a very positive manner. These conditions that are particular to our genetic coding determine our unique temperament. Understanding our temperament, as well as the temperament of others, brings to the forefront various opportunities for improvements in every area of life whether it is in your experience, family, or in a corporate environment. Understanding temperament brings experience and success to the individuals who are willing to be determined in understanding the unfound mysteries of temperament.

To begin with, we need to understand that **temperament is neither character nor personality**. Instead, temperament, character, and personality are three entirely different aspects of our being that we need to know if we are to get along peacefully with others. The following chart shows how temperament influences character—and how nature shapes our personality (i.e., our behavior).

| *Temperament* | Our *temperament* is determined while we are still in our mother's womb. Temperament is intrinsic to our being—that is, we were born with our genetic nature, and there is nothing we can do to change it. We can learn to recognize what our temperament is, and we can learn to modify our behavior, so we get along with people who have differing attitudes, but we cannot change our temperament. |
| --- | --- |
| *Character* | Our *character* depends on (1) our temperament and (2) our environment—that is, our family of origin and the influence of people as well as the experiences we encounter. Although we can learn to change our character, it is not easy. Once we learn to believe certain things and act on our beliefs, it's hard for us to turn. |
| *Personality* | Our *personality* is how we manifest ourselves to the world. In many ways, personality is self-selected. We only reveal what we want others to see. We may exhibit several different types of personalities at different times, manifesting the one we believe best suits our present circumstance. Although the behavior that we choose to demonstrate may not be real action, nevertheless it is what we decide to display. Therefore, we cannot determine the correct temperament because personality is the mask and not the real person. So, who is the real person? |

**Temperament vs. Personality**

Many people mistake personality for temperament and most psychological profiles available on the markets today focus on personality. For example, the accessible DiSC Profile and the MBTI Profile focus on personality. As a result, the DiSC and the MBTI only reveal the objective (observable) side of a person's personality. However, as the chart above makes clear, personality does not necessarily represent the real person. Personality is a ***chosen mask*** an individual present to the world and, is on what the person wishes to reveal about themselves at that moment. Five minutes later in another conversation with another person, the chosen mask changes again because of the nature of the discussion or the person you are in communication with is of another authority.

Worley's ID Profile (WIDP) focuses on temperament, which is not alterable or fluid-like character and personality. A person's temperament is stationary despite his or her environmental focus. Therefore, individuals who understand their temperament can understand themselves and others more effectively. Each person is extraordinary and unique based on their natural temperament makeup. God uniquely designs people at conception. Some prefer to call it genetic makeup or their "core, id, or ego." I prefer the term *temperament*.

Let's take a closer look at some of the differences between personality and temperament.

## An Overview of Personality

Personality training is designed to identify individual styles of personality in a particular setting or environmental focus. In other words, your personality changes depending on your current environment.

The Personal Profile Survey (PPS), also referred to as the DiSC, is designed to increase understanding, acceptance, and respect for individual differences in the work or social environment. Based on the DiSC model of behavior developed by William Moulton Marston and John Geier, this model identifies four distinct types of behavioral tendencies ("personalities") people use to meet their needs and desires. All people could use all four of these trends to some extent. However, individuals use some behaviors more than others.

Here are brief definitions of the four behavioral tendencies:

| D | Dominance | People with a high **D** behavioral tendency seek to meet their needs by controlling their environment through direct, forceful action, often overcoming opposition in hostile or antagonistic situations. |
|---|---|---|
| i | Influencing | People with a high **i** behavioral tendency seek to meet their needs by persuading others to work with them to accomplish results. They function efficiently in favorable, supportive environments. |
| S | Steadiness | People with a high **S** behavioral tendency seek to meet their needs by cooperating with others to carry out their respective tasks. They function efficiently in favorable, supportive environments. |
| C | Cautiousness | People with a high **C** behavioral tendency seek to meet their needs by working with existing circumstances to provide quality and accuracy. They strive to achieve their standards for results, even in hostile environments. |

Personality training deals with the real side of the person based on an environmental focus during evaluation. Persons answering the behavioral profile may respond one way as an employee, another as a spouse, another at the family picnic, another way in a conflict situation, and Another way in an intimate relationship with someone close.

As a result, using the DiSC assessment, you can end up with several different personality profiles for the same person. Nevertheless, each pattern requires the individual to fill out another separate questionnaire to evaluate each of the environmental focuses that are influencing them.

In the example above, a person can potentially exhibit up to multiple different personalities depending on how they are functioning in an environment:

- As an employee
- As a spouse
- At a family picnic
- In a conflicted relationship
- In an intimate relationship
- In a business meeting
- At a social gathering

The mask approach mentioned previously, in which a person only reveals what they want other people to see, is a self-selected mask. As a result, the person only allows you to observe certain facets of their personality. What you do not understand is the individual's actual temperament. Even with those various assessments, you still don't know who the person is because of the fluctuating **"mask"** that is always changing based on what the person wants you to see or know about them. Therefore, you still never know who the real people are or what is right or false about them. You are dealing with the mask the person is presenting to you, and then you make your decisions based on your observations. Observations of the mask you see. Bad choice.

## Temperament

The temperament approach is designed to identify an individual's demonstrated side (observable behavior) and their desired side (inner needs and desires), which is stable and unchanging. It is not fluid like the various personality and character assessments available on the market today, including the DiSC, MBTI, Keirsey, Cleaver, Preventive Index, Caliper, Cattell's 16 Personality Factor, and others.

Most authors who write about temperament have categorized individuals as being made up of one primary and one secondary character. Through research and observation, I believe people are much more complicated. Therefore, WIDP compartmentalizes an individual's temperament profile into three distinct areas: social/vocational, leadership, and relationship. Individuals may have a different temperament in each of the three regions or a combination of temperaments, called a blended temperament, in one or more of the three sectors. WIDP further parses each of the three areas into two different segments:

- *Demonstrated behavior*—behavior directed toward others, and
- *Desired behavior*—behavior desired or not desired by others toward them.

## Here are the five Temperament Types as defined under WIDP:

### *Introverted Sanguine (IS)*

The Introverted Sanguine will process the facts and then not do anything with them for fear of rejection. People who possess this temperament also will set about questioning those they trust to verify that their interpretation of information or situations is correct. This inability to act is entirely in line with the other aspects of the Introverted Sanguine. Introverted Sanguine is not dense in cognitive skills—they are unable to initiate action. They are very loyal servants and like to be included with others and appear to be introverts. However, when "invited in," they respond like the Sanguine (see below). (Remember Pete from the vignette at the beginning of this chapter? Once he was invited to get the Kentucky fried chicken, he perked right up and began to act just like Frieda, a true Sanguine.) When, rejected, whether real or imagined, they will withdraw into isolation—emotionally, mentally, and physically. They are extremely compassionate and are always looking for rejection or disapproval from others.

The Introverted Sanguine motto: *"Will someone, please recognize me?"*

## Sanguine (S)

The Sanguine will process information in a simplified form and manner. For them, nothing is all that complicated. This short attention span allows them the opportunity to act quickly and move on to other people and situations very quickly.

The Sanguine is more people-oriented than task-oriented. The Sanguine are excellent speakers, and have a unique ability to rally people together and inspire them onward. The Sanguine bring life to the forefronts for the more severe and task-oriented temperaments, such as the Choleric and the Melancholy. The Sanguine have excellent people skills and succeed in any environment that requires interaction with individuals or groups. The Sanguine never get enough socializing, recognition, or approval; to them, anything that involves people is fun. They like to be "on stage" and to be the center of attention whenever possible. They make life worth living and exciting, and they want you to enjoy life as much as they can at the moment. They feel it is their job to make you laugh.

The Sanguine motto: *"Let's play and have fun."*

## Phlegmatic (P)

The Phlegmatic will take their time and think about and dissect a situation. After they scrutinize it, they can be detail-oriented perfectionists and will make the necessary decisions, and they are quite capable of doing so—but don't expect a sudden change. Once the Phlegmatic mind is made up, it's hard for them to change. They are team players and expect everyone to carry their weight. They make great diplomats and function well as introverts or extroverts. Henry Kissinger, Colin Powell, and Condoleezza Rice are Phlegmatic. Phlegmatic people are beautiful peacemakers; they are experts at disarming personality conflicts, and they make great comedians. They can tell jokes and never show emotion about them. That is partially what makes them funny. The Phlegmatic has a higher tolerance for social interaction than the Choleric or Melancholy but will retreat to their privacy once they reach their saturation point with people.

The Phlegmatic motto: *"Let's not move too quickly on this!"*

## Melancholy.

The Melancholy is very intellectual and needs time and space to analyze incoming facts. They will retreat into their private world and explain the situation over and over. After this assimilation, they are ready to make up their mind and usually have a clear understanding of the situation. Most Melancholy make vital decisions effectually. Melancholy individuals are extraordinarily shy and prefer to be alone, and tolerate very little socialization unless (1) the socialization involves something or someone in which they have an interest or (2) are on a task assignment that includes many people. They are self-sacrificing, will work around the clock to meet deadlines, and are very economically conscious. Money is significant to them. (Remember Jill from the vignette? She was more interested in taking the chicken home to the freezer than socializing with the group.) Criticism of a Melancholy is a sure way of creating a direct conflict with them. The Melancholy does not appreciate constructive criticism. When it comes to blaming, the Melancholy needs approached with "kid gloves."

The Melancholy motto: *"Let's think about this for a while."*

### Choleric (C)

The Choleric is quick to receive and process information. They devour facts and are swift to conclude. Their fast decisions are not to be confused with "jumping to conclusions," for the Choleric who will need to process all the data that is available. This characteristic can cause people who possess other temperaments lots of fear and frustration because the Choleric can produce more work than the other four temperaments. If they are not careful, the Choleric can overwhelm those around them. They are very powerful and make good leaders; in fact, Choleric will always rise to the top as leaders. Their focus is still on the tasks at hand or the visions and goals they have set for themselves. Their people skills make them appear to be people oriented. However, they are only people-oriented and visionary about needing and assimilating people to assist them in completing their tasks or their vision. Once the work/image is complete, they neither want nor require much socialization and quickly become introverted. (Remember Sam from the vignettes? At first, he tried to organize everything so the picnic could continue despite having no grill, but once Frieda and Pete decided for fast-food chicken, Sam was quick to move on—i.e., take Jill home then gets back to eat the Kentucky Fried Chicken.

The Choleric motto: *"Lead, follow, or get out of the way."*

### The Three Areas of WIDP

The three areas of Worley's ID Profile System are social/vocational, leadership, and relationship. Here are descriptions of each:

### Social/Vocational

The first area of temperament in Worley's ID Profile System is the social/vocational profile. To understand this pattern, think of it as *socialization.* Socialization/Vocation is the area that dictates how people will interact with the world in general—for example, in situations such as parties, at work, while shopping, and other conditions that bring people into contact with other people. The area of social/vocational does not involve the deep, intense emotions of intimate relationships (found in the temperament area of Relationship) but with the surface, relations encountered in daily social situations. Social/Vocational temperament needs can range from involvement with many people or connect with only a few select individuals.

## *Leadership*

The next area of the temperament in WIDP is leadership. Our leadership profile determines how we lead others, influence people and situations, take the initiative or power (control) of people in various conditions—and how we allow individuals and situations to impact or change us. In general, it is the *decision* part of a person's temperament that dictates whether they will be a leader or a follower in life. Depending on an individual's temperament, leadership will prescribe how he or she makes decisions and who will be dominant in the relationship between them. The temperament needs in leadership can range from total dominance in a relationship to preferring to be dominated by the other party. To get an accurate picture of a person's temperament, we must understand how his or her leadership profile dovetails with both the social/vocational profile and the relationship profile.

Leadership is crucial to comprehend because people are either leading or being led, in a Social/ Vocational environment or leading or being led, in a close intimate Relationship. There are times in the workplace when individuals will permit their emotional involvement with coworkers and friends to influence how they interact with them. Leadership in the area of vocation can be very inappropriate and cause great conflict and destroy relationships and injure the functionality of the organization. It is called the **Good Old Boy (GOB)** system. We hire or promote friends into positions of authority and responsibility that they are not qualified for only to cripple that position. Then six months into the job management find that they do not have the skills or experience to perform. We will talk more about this later.

## *Relationship*

The third area of the WIDP profile is the relationship profile. This area of the temperament determines how involved an individual wants to be in their relationships, and the degree of affection and approval they (1) want from others and (2) want to give to others. Unlike the social/vocational and leadership profiles, which determine how an individual interacts with groups of people, the relationship is the area of the temperament that deals with one-on-one interactions. Whereas the social pattern covers general social situations, the relationship profile involves the deeper relationships individuals have in life, such as family member relationships or close intimate relationships. These relationships may be with only one or two people, or it could be with many people. Of course, the number of close intimate relationships Individuals have been determined by their temperament preferences. Having many close relationships or only a few close intimate friends do not decide whether individuals are "normal." Individual choices determine the number of close ties. Either option is okay if it is what the person wants.

In a nutshell:

- The *social* profile determines:      *who is in or out of the relationship,*
- The *leadership* profile defines:      *who maintains the power and makes the decisions for the relationship*
- The *relationship* profile determines:      *how emotionally close or distant the relationship is.*

## Demonstrated vs. Desired Behavior

Each of these three areas of temperaments—social/vocational, leadership, and relationship—divide into two reaction areas: the **demonstrated** and the **desired.**

The first area is how we *demonstrate* ourselves in that area of our temperament, whether it be social, leadership, or relationship. The leadership profile gives us an excellent example of this: the demonstrated area of leadership determines how an individual will want to control others and how much control over those around one will exert. People with a high demonstrated score in leadership will need to dominate those people around them.

The *desired* area determines how much an individual will allow others to affect them in this field. Again, the leadership profile gives us a good example: the desired score of leadership determines how an individual will allow others to make their decisions and control their behavior. People who let little outside control will have a low desired score. If the individual's desired count is high on leadership, this indicates the need to be dominated by others.

WIDP helps each learn about their unique needs in these subcategories:

- social needs and desires
- independence needs and desires
- relationship needs and desires
- criteria for relationships
- perception of self
- perception by others
- perception of others
- intellectual orientation
- emotional orientation
- work orientation
- motivation
- rejection/acceptance profile
- probable strengths
- probable weaknesses

## In Summary

To summarize this chapter, we have discovered the following facets of temperament:

There are five temperaments:

1. Introverted Sanguine
2. Sanguine
3. Phlegmatic
4. Melancholy
5. Choleric

These five temperaments assessed in three areas:

1.   social/vocational
2.   leadership
3.   relationship

***Important Note:*** People can be any one of the temperaments in any of the three areas of social/vocational, leadership, or relationship. In other words, a person can be a combination of temperaments depending upon which area of the temperament they are looking. An individual could be a Melancholy in the social/vocational environment, Choleric in leadership, and Sanguine in a relationship.

These three areas of social/vocational, leadership, and relationship are further broken down into two behavior areas:

1.   demonstrated behavior
2.   desired behavior

Here's an analogy that may help: temperament is like playing a mixture game of chess where each person has six chessmen:

Each chessman has his characteristics, which determine how he will respond in various circumstances. In other words, the way a person will react will depend on their type of situation. For example, imagine a person openly challenges something you say. You may feel (and act) one way if the case you are in is social and feel (and work) precisely the opposite if you are in a relationship situation—even though on the surface the circumstances are identical.

We will explore all the interesting nuances of temperament in the chapters that follow.

# CHAPTER 2

# WHY DO WE NEED THE WIDP TEMPERAMENT PROFILE?

Humans are experiencing significant levels of emotional and psychological pain. The most highly prescribed drugs are for anxiety and depressive disorders. Sharply rising are the numbers of psychologists, psychiatrists, psychics, astrologers, gurus, and the 900 telephone services, Face Book, Instagram, IM, YouTube, personality typing, behavior profiles, self-talk therapy, self-help books, and whatever might offer relief from the confusion and discomforts associated with emotional conflict. People from all walks of life, which include denominational leaders, pastors, elders, deacons, trustees, lay leaders, corporate managers, human resource personnel directors, consultants, educators, trainers, families, and individuals are seeking cures for damaged relationships, identity crises, career indecisions, confusion, and conflicts. Worley's Identity Discovery (WIDP) temperament profile offers an insightful summary in determining an individual's specific needs, desires, and interpersonal behaviors. The WIDP temperament profile identifies three major life areas: social profile, leadership profile, and relationship profile, which accurately demonstrates that varying temperament needs and desires are not right or wrong but merely individual temperament differences and preferences. By teaching the individual about their unique needs, the individual can utilize Worley's ID Profile to help them restore balance and peace in their lives and relationships.

Relationships include, for many individuals, differing areas of life, in which the individual is called upon to interact with various personalities and situations. WIDP helps people to better comprehend themselves and others about their temperament makeup within the following three areas.

| | |
|---|---|
| **Social Profile** | identifies the individual's temperament needs and desires for socialization, work, school, and other superficial relationships. The social profile helps answer the question, **who is in or out of relationships with this individual?** |
| **Leadership Profile** | identifies the individual's temperament needs and desires for influencing others, making decisions, and assuming responsibilities. Needs may range from independence to dependence. The leadership profile helps answers the question, **who maintains the power and makes decisions in relationships with this individual?** |

**Relationship Profile**     identifies the individual's temperament needs and desires in close relationships with family and friends. Needs may range from relationships with expressions of love with many people to isolation. The relationship profile answers the question, **how emotionally open or closed to relationships is this individual?**

# Worley's Identity Discovery Profile

John 10:10 The thief comes only to steal and kill and destroy; I have come that they may have life and have it to the full. (NIV)

John 10:10 The thief cometh not, but for to steal, and to kill, and to destroy I am come that they might have life and that they might have it more abundantly. (KJV)

4053 perissos {perissos'}from 4012 (in the sense of beyond); TDNT - 6:61,828; more, beyond measure, more abundantly, exceeding abundantly above, exceeding some number or ratio or rank or need, over and above, more than is necessary, super-added, supremely, something further, much more than all, superior, extraordinary, surpassing, uncommon, superiority, more eminent, more remarkable, more excellent

Abundantly! Is there anyone reading this today who wants life more **abundantly**?

I do not know about you, but I want all that God has in store for me. I want all his promises, all his mercy, all his grace, and all of his unconditional love.

I not only prefer the fatted calf spoken of in Luke 15 slaughtered for the prodigal son.

I also prefer the cattle on a thousand hills talked about in Psalm 50:10.

I prefer the riches spoken of in Psalm 112:1–3.

I prefer godliness with great contentment mentioned in 1 Tim. 6:6.

I prefer all these things spoken of in Matthew 6:33, "But seek first his kingdom and his righteousness, and *all these things* will be given to you as well." (NIV)

I prefer "The peace of God, which passes all understanding, shall keep your hearts and minds through Christ Jesus." Phil 4:7

"It is the glory of God to conceal a matter,

To search a matter is the glory of *kings*." (Proverbs 25:2, NIV84)

To search out 02713 chaqar {khawkar'} a primitive root; TWOT - 729 1) to search, search for, search out, examine, investigate a matter 01697 dabar {dawbaw'} from 01696; TWOT speech, word, speaking, thing, saying, utterance, business, occupation, acts, matter, case, something, is the glory of kings. Proverbs 25:2.

John 10:10 "The thief cometh not, but for to steal, and to kill, and to destroy I am come that they might have life, and that they might have it more abundantly." (KJV)

Do you want **abundant** marriages?

Do you want **overflowing** relationships?

Do you want a better understanding of why you:

    Like to socialize or do not want to socialize?

    Think the way you do?

    Act the way you do?

    Interact with or don't interact with people?

    Lead or don't want to lead?

    Initiate or do not initiate in intimate situations?

Jeremiah 1:5 "Before I formed you in the womb I knew you, before you were born I set you apart; I appointed you as a prophet to the nations." (NIV84)

Psalm 139.13–16:

[13] For you created my inmost being;

    you knit me together in my mother's womb.

[14] I praise you because I am fearfully and wonderfully made;

    your works are wonderful,

    I know that full well.

[15] My frame was not hidden from you

    when I was made in the secret place.

    When I was woven together in the depths of the earth,

[16] your eyes saw my unformed body.

    All the days ordained for me

    were written in your book

    before one of them came to be. (NIV)

Ephesians 2:10: "For we are God's workmanship, created in Christ Jesus to do good works, which God prepared in advance for us to do."

As a man or woman of God, you have an obligation to yourself and more importantly to God if you believe this passage of Scripture.

Do you believe it? Yes?

Do you believe that God called you and knew you before the foundations of the world were laid?

Do you believe that He knew you before you were formed in your mother's womb?

If you believe this, then you need to have understanding, wisdom, and knowledge, about who you are is based on the intrinsic design of your temperament!

Why are you so unique that God called you into existence?

Why did He give you the temperament you have?

What are you supposed to do or be doing with your talents and gifts?

What are you to do with your mind, your emotions, your feelings?

What are you supposed to do with who you are?

Each of us is a very, very, unique person. God himself chooses you for a reason and this period. Why?… Why? Do not look at your outward appearance; consider your heart, emotions, feelings, and that burning compassion within you. God has designed you the way you are for Himself. To serve Him.

It is the glory of God to conceal a matter,

To search a matter is the glory of *kings*. (Proverbs 25:2)

He is not looking for an Isaiah, Jeremiah, Peter, or Paul. He is looking for you to be who you are as he created you. There will never be another person on the face of this earth like you. Never!

You are the only person who knows the experiences of your childhood, teen years, young adult years, adult, relationships, classmates, teams, college, feelings, and memories, good and evil.

- No one has ever looked at the world through your eyes.
- No one has ever thought your thoughts.
- No one has ever experienced your personal needs and desires.
- Only two people know who you are: God and you!
- (Perhaps you are not all that reliable either.)

Then perhaps you are. I prefer to go with the positive because I know the value of your temperament. Know this: your temperament is valuable and needs to be understood to enhance your quality of life. I can't tell you, but I know God's design has tremendous value. You are his design. Study your WIDP Temperament Profile for a few hours as it will change your life.

You can put on a mask for others and present to them what you want them to see, not the real you, just a fabrication, lie, but hey, they don't know. After all, you got your mask in place. And quite smug about it too.

On and on it goes and the more you think about it, the more you begin to realize that you indeed are very different from everyone else on this planet. Begin to look at yourself through a new set of eyes. You will benefit.

I need your attention:

> ***Begin to look at yourself through a new set of eyes. Your temperament eyes! Your design at creation-conception. Your soul-body-mind were all determined at conception.***

At that point, God called you into existence, fashioned you in your mother's womb, and numbered your days so that you might serve Him. You must search out a matter(s) about yourself and life. Find out who you are! WIDP is a powerful resource to assist in bringing quality and quantity into your life.

As a Christian, you need to spend the rest of your life, identifying why you were called. What does God want to do with you? His Word says:

Hebrews 12:1–3 [1] Therefore, since such a great cloud of witnesses surrounds we (you), let us (you) throw off everything that hinders and the sin that so easily entangles, and let us (you) run with perseverance the race marked out for us (you). [2] Let us fix our eyes on Jesus, the author, and perfecter of our faith, who for the joy set before him endured the cross, scorning its shame, and sat down at the right hand of the throne of God. [3] Consider him who endured such opposition from sinful men, so that you will not grow weary and lose heart. (NIV84)

Be encouraged by Peter's reassuring voice.

2 Peter 1: **Greeting 1** Simeon Peter, a servant and apostle of Jesus Christ, **To those who have obtained a faith of equal standing with ours by the righteousness of our God and Savior Jesus Christ:** 2 Peter 1:1 (ESV)

CHAPTER 3

# TRIANGLE

**THE BUILDING BLOCKS**

Temperament is your genetic coding at conception. You <u>can't</u> determine a person's temperament by observation alone.

Don't forget the triangle concept below, because it is one of the most critical issues in understanding what's the actual temperament of an individual.

What is temperament? We must look at the concept of the triangle below as representing the whole makeup of an individual. Let's call these various levels of the triangle to be the building blocks.

So, starting with the empty triangle as the frame of an individual.

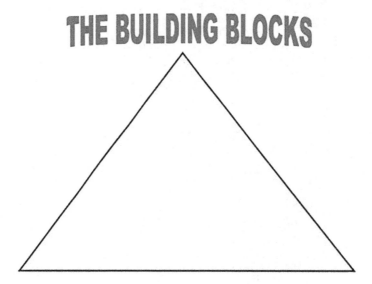

We have talked about understanding the various pieces in the game of chess as being like temperament—especially regarding the number of the different facets or parts of one's temperament and gaining an understanding of those various aspects of a person's temperament. In the game of chess, you have the pawn, rook, knight, bishop, queen, and king. They all have different moves they can make, and some are stronger than others. When you consider the synonyms for "temperament," you will get the following: nature, **character, personality**, disposition, temper, spirit, outlook, and makeup. Thesaurus lists the terms as similar or the same and uses the words as being exchangeable. They are not interchangeable, nor are they the same. Not when it comes to understanding temperament.

As we had stated above, understanding your temperament is similar to playing chess. Like chess, you have six (6) different components of your temperament that are considered to know the total person and also when interrelating with others. Moreover, these parts are:

| | | |
|---|---|---|
| Social Profile | 1. | Demonstrated Socializing |
| | 2. | Desired Socializing |
| Leadership Profile | 3. | Demonstrated Leadership |
| | 4. | Desired Leadership |
| Relationship Profile | 5. | Demonstrated Relationship |
| | 6. | Desired Relationship |

We discussed these six different parts of temperament in the chapter "The Three Domains of Temperament."

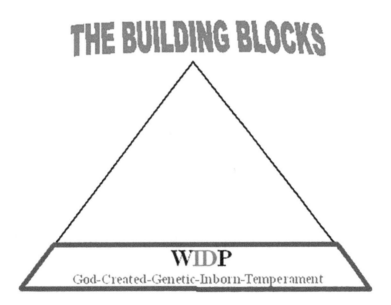

Let me show you a significant difference between them. The illustration of the triangle will be used to describe temperament, character, personality, and behavior. The triangle will concretely give you a solid understanding of each of these four components. There will be no confusion as to their meanings after this illustration.

At the bottom of the triangle, which is the broadest and fullest part of the triangle that supports everything above the base, is what I call the Worley's Identity Discovery Temperament (WIDP).

## TEMPERAMENT: God-Created, Genetic, Innate, Temperament

Adding the first section of the triangle, this is called the temperament. Your temperament is who you are "genetically" or "inborn" (God-created) and this part of you, your temperament, is fixed and does not change regardless of your character changes or personality and behavior differences. Your temperament is the real you. Your temperament is the "identity" that you became at conception. Temperament is your different impression for life! Your ID (identification) ego (id) of who and what you are as a person. It is the part of you that you cannot escape from, remove, alter, or disguise or oppose. It is called "temperament."

That is what WIDP is all about, discovering your temperament, your real self without a personality (mask), the "Worley Experience." Getting and reading your WIDP Profile is like being introduced to yourself in a way that you have never experienced before. Most people think they know who they are until completing a WIDP questionnaire, and then they get back their WIDP Profile, a six to eight page Class A Profile, and twelve to seventeen pages for the Class C WIDP Profile report.

Moreover, it is **all about you** this time. At that point, the majority of people are astonished at what they read in their profiles and what they find out about themselves.

For the first time in their lives, they see in black and white on paper that they are who it says they are in the WIDP profile report. A real, stunning discovery of oneself. For many people it is liberating, exhilarating; for others awe-inspiring, comforting; for some, it is confirmation of who they already knew about themselves but could not put their finger on it or describe it to someone. A few people do not like what they read about themselves and want to be someone else or have a different temperament. That, folks, is not an option. What you see is what you get.

Reading your WIDP Profile is like reading an exceptional report about yourself that is accurate to the point of being an "instruction manual" for you. The Profile is a manufactured diagram of all your features and functions. Moreover, we did not forget and leave anything out, and there are no spare parts.

Your temperament is unalterable by you or anyone else. However, you could have been **"tampered"** with or **"molded"** into being something or someone other than who you are. Even then your temperament has not been changed; it's been damaged to the point you cannot see the actual identity of the individual nor can the injured person experience their correct intrinsic temperament. Tampered or molded with, known as codependency will cause an enormous amount of anxiety and inner turmoil within that individual.

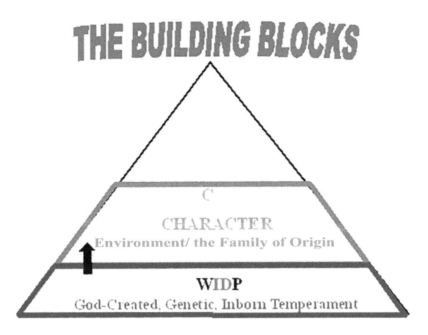

# THE BUILDING BLOCKS

**CHARACTER: family of origin, environment, culture make up the middle section of the triangle.** Definition of Character is:

The character traits described as being determined by "influence, shaping, and molding by our environment, their family of origin, and culture." Your parents, siblings, relatives, neighbors and neighborhood friends, teachers, family, and culture will have an impact on the shaping of your character and who you are as a person. This shaping begins to occur when our intellectual skills start to develop, somewhere between the ages of eighteen to twenty-four months old, we can process information and come to conclusions on the data we process. Then from that age on into the middle to late teens and early twenties, our character is continually shaped and determined by our environment, family of origin, and our culture.

If you lived in a rural area of Maine and moved to Manhattan, NY your lifestyle would change dramatically, and your character will take on a different presentation because of your new environment. Right? Likewise, if you move from the hills of West Virginia and rent an apartment on Beacon Hill in Boston, MA or the suburb of any metropolitan city that new environment will affect your character immensely? Right!

You see, since our childhood—various facets of our life have molded our character:

- Our family
- Our environment
- Our neighbors
- Our friends
- Our teachers
- Our culture

We were not what and who we are now, but our character has affected us through the years.

Can we change our character by choice? Yes, we can, but it takes an active person to swim against the tides of family and the culture of where you lived, and all the other people mentioned above that directly affected your life. The list is endless as to who had a significant influence in your life as far as shaping your character is concerned. Think about it for a moment. Who had a substantial impact in developing your character as it is today? A real question is not it?

Yes, the family of origin, culture, and geographical relocation can change your character. Example: the person mentioned above who lived in a rural community moves to Manhattan, NY. Their character is going to experience "culture shock" at first, and then they will begin to take on their new community's character. Moreover, in a couple of years, the people from the rural community where the individual originally came from will not recognize the new "metropolitan" person who used to be like one of them. What happened? Their new environment changed its character. They evolved from being a rural community person to becoming a contemporary person. What happened? Their new surroundings influenced their character, and they "took on" the characters of that environment.

Have you ever heard someone say, "You can tell who a person is based on the character of the individuals they spend most of their time with." Well, there you have it. The character is changed by the "character," whether it be good or bad, of those you live with, socialize with, or are your closest friends.

Their intellect determines most people's character and what they allow themselves to believe is factual about them. Just because they think "this or that" doesn't mean it is right about them. It just so happens that that is who they are at that moment in time. Since we have only the intellect and experiences in life to draw from, our age and exposure to life significantly limit us. Unfortunately, our understanding is very superficial when it comes to knowing ourselves. The intrinsic part of us has all those feelings and emotions that we cannot describe. We know we have them but are not aware of their origin. Oh, we have a good idea, or at least we think we do, but our character is still determined by what and how we were fashioned by our family of origin, environment, and the culture. So, we may go in and out of several different character definitions of ourselves during our formative years. However, sooner or later our role is defined. Moreover, unless there is a significant family of origin, environment, or cultural change, we will remain to be who we are as that environment fashioned us.

We have nothing else to guide us except our consciousness, which keeps us on somewhat of a guided pathway of life "if" we listen to our conscious and if we were not fashioned inappropriately by our family of origin, environment, and culture.

Most relationships based on temperament needs and desires fulfilled and the compatibility of those two individuals are usually not understood without understanding temperament. Two people can get along fine if they meet each other's temperament needs and desires. However, without an understanding of each other's temperament that superficial relationship wears thin quickly, and then there is nothing left but an unfulfilled couple. So they try finding happiness in many different ways that can fulfill their temperament needs and desires through their character as they're fashioned: gain wealth, vocational aspirations, materialism, sex, children, alcohol, geographical relocation (to fix their problems), and hobbies of all kinds. Not until they understand themselves—you know, meet their private person, their temperament, their unique design conceived in your mothers' womb. You know, temperament! Until this happens, there will be a void in your life. It is like probing into the night trying to find something that does not even exist. You know there is something inside of you that you cannot explain, but logically you cannot tell what it is, but it does cause you to feel different at times. Moreover, you're lost for answers and keep living in a world of bewilderment about some of your thoughts and behaviors.

Chasing your character or the development of your character only leads to a dead end. Your character is not who you are, and that is why you need to get to the foundational level temperament so that you can see clearly and understand who you are by experiencing your true self, your temperament. It is at this point of agreement for the first time, where you honestly see the difference between your temperament and your character. Then at that point, you begin to separate your temperament from your character, and suddenly you have a new understanding that sheds light on your true self.

So now let's look at personality and define how it plays out in our lives and see the difference personality has with temperament and character.

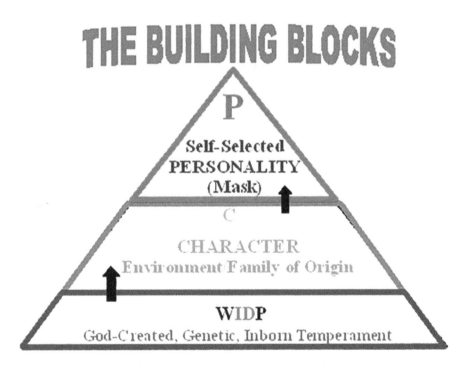

## PERSONALITY: Self-Selected PERSONALITY

**Mask/Personality** So, located at the top of the triangle, we have a **personality** which is **self-selected,** and is a **mask/personality** for most people.

What we mean by mask/personality is that what you see is not automatically the real person. Most people allow you to see what they want you to know about them. Therefore, they put on their mask/personality. All the temperaments **except** the Sanguine put on a mask/personality. The purpose of people putting on a mask/personality is so that you cannot see the real person behind the mask/personality. You can only see what they let you see or what they want you to know about them.

For example, let's say individual interviews for a job. Well, to start with, it is common practice for people to write a different resume for each position they are interviewing so they can leverage themselves in with that potential employer. They do all their research on the company and their history, product, size, net worth, and upward mobility opportunity. The resume they present to one group will be different than it was for another employer, although it may be the same position because they want you to see them as the person for that job. Therefore, they will present to you all their strengths for that particular job, and they will tweak their resumes to reflect their compatibility for that specific job. That is called showing a "mask/personality" for that company. They are telling you, the potential employer, what they think you want to see, not who they are. So, in effect, the company is interviewing a "mask/personality." What happens next?

The company hires the individual based on the "mask/personality" presented to them during the interview. The company spends several thousands of dollars processing that person into their business and getting them acclimated to the new position and understanding the vision and goals of the enterprise. The people settle into the job and within sixty–ninety days, the company begins to realize that the person is not producing the quality of work nor do they have the proficiency that they presented during their hiring interview. Now the company is saddled with having someone in the organization which is neither qualified nor competent for the position hired. Now, what are they going to do, start over again? They do not have any choice. What happened? They hired a "mask/personality" and not the real person, which is significant today in "Corporate America." How are they going to remove that individual and find an individual who is the right fit for the position with the right skills?

Even if they interviewed the individual based on their previous training, experience, accomplishments, and also talked them from competency-based interviewing, they could still have significant problems. Why? The company did not take into consideration the individual's temperament needs and desires during the hiring process for the position hired.

Now, what has happened here? The "mask/personality" was determined out of their character and they presented themselves as they wanted you to see them, and now you are stuck with the problem (mask/personality).

Today most companies are using "personality" instruments to screen and hire people based on their "mask/personality." I hear comments like, "I use the MBTI (Myers-Brigs Type Instrument), the DiSC, the professional analysis, Kersey, FIRO-B, 16 PF, and on and on they go naming "mask/personality" instruments, and they wonder why they are having such conflicts within their organizations.

It is a proven fact that if an individual's inner/natural needs and desires are not being met positively, they will get them fulfilled in an unhealthy way. Here the company believes they are connecting with the "actual person." They are joining with a "mask/personality," and one that is false at that, and they are determining the future of their organization based on a "mask/personality" that is fabricated and is wrong, and they are hiring that person? That becomes a severe mistake that will cost that organization uncompromisingly.

As you get to know individuals, the **"mask/personality"** will change. Remember that everyone puts on their best "mask/personality" initially. However, over time the actual person hid behind the "mask/personality" will come out and you will see changes in that individual's day-to-day performance and behavior and then you will wonder who the real person is?

The "mask/personality" is presented by the individual as their choice as to what or who they want to reveal to others about themselves. Finally, it is through their "behavior" that you see the person. So, let's ask the question: is this the real person? No, it is not! You will never really know the actual person until you have them complete a WIDP Questionnaire and you process it and have a WIDP Profile in your hands. Then you will know the real person and their WIDP intrinsic designed.

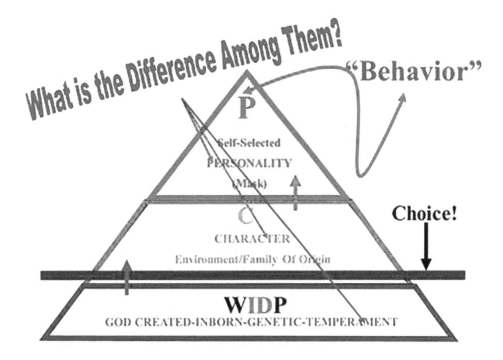

There is one more critical point in the development of the triangle. I call it **The choice**! The choice is the burgundy bar found in the Character section in the above chart.

There comes the point in everyone's life when they will come face-to-face with Jesus Christ and Calvary. At that point, they will choose to follow Jesus Christ, or they will not. That choice will determine the quality of life they live.

So, let's sum up. Your temperament is who you are "genetically" or "inborn (God-created)" and is fixed and does not change regardless of your character personality or behavior. Your temperament is the real you all six parts.

The character is going to reflect the family of origin, environment, and the culture in which you have lived or are now living and your character shaped by that environment, people, and the culture within that environment.

The personality is a person's mask/personality that you may or may not see behind, which will be determined based upon your relationship with that person. It is complicated to define what a person's temperament is by observation because people only reveal what they want you to see about them.

The behavior is the visible manifestation of the person's mask/personality and is not necessarily the actual person either. Remember they can behave the way they want to base upon what they want you to see about them.

Out of all of the building blocks, temperament, character, and personality, they determine their behavior based on the shaping of their character and personality. Those two will change, but their temperament will never vary, and the only way to identify the actual person is using the WIDP assessment.

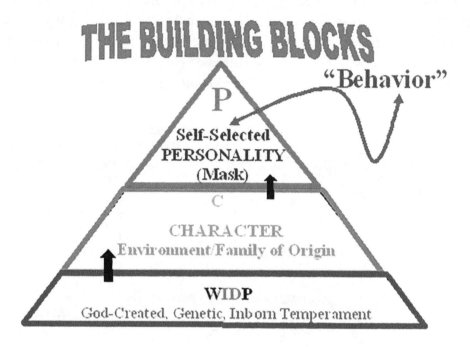

So, the bottom line for precise identification of an individual is indeed the bottom of the triangle, which is their WIDP temperament.

*For the educator, the WIDP eliminates the potential for reduced classroom behavior. For the counselor, it pinpoints motivators that regulate psychological patterns of clients.*

*Dr. Worley's training sessions are equally as valuable. They are casual, informative, and practical. I was most impressed by the diverse range of professionals who attended.*

*Only by comparing the WIDP with other programs out there can one truly appreciate its value!*

**KAREN DUDE, HIGH SCHOOL TEACHER, NEW HAMPSHIRE PUBLIC SCHOOLS**

# CHAPTER 4

# THE INTROVERTED SANGUINE

**What is an introvert?**

So, what does this book define as an introvert? If you are an introvert, you are born with a temperament that craves to be alone, delights in a few meaningful connections, thinks before speaking, and observes before approaching. If you are an introvert, you thrive in the inner sanctuary of the mind, heart, and spirit, but shrink in the external world of people, parties, noise, drama, and chaos. As an introvert, you are loyal, sensitive, perceptive, gentle, and reflective. You prefer to operate behind the scenes, preserve your precious energy, and influence the world in a quiet but powerful way. Most of all, you want to be left alone so you can think, dream, regenerate, watch nature programs, "Nat-Geo," "Naked and Afraid!" If this is how you think, feel, and behave, you're an *introvert!* Introverts are beautiful people; they make the world happen in every corner of the globe. There are no cultural barriers to WIDP and understanding temperament because everyone has temperament preferences that need to be identified for them to improve their quality of life. Introverts are special!

But once someone takes the initiative and starts talking to him or invites him into an interview, he can go on for hours—well, not hours, but for a good long while. Of course, sooner or later Pete will grow tired of the conversation or lose interest in the subject matter, then Pete will give one excuse or another and slip back into inconspicuousness, watching the real players work the room. The reason he will move back into obscurity is that he was not getting the personal attention he desired. Perceiving that as rejection, whether it is real or imagined, Pete withdraws. And he will not come out socially until someone invites him. Unfortunately, Pete lives in a very lonely world and thinks that people do not like him. Of course, this is not true; it is just a misunderstanding on Pete's part of not knowing nor understanding his temperament makeup.

At work, Pete's a hard and very devoted and loyal worker. No matter what his boss asks, Pete exhibits a can-do attitude and will work long hours, always willing to go the extra mile. He resents it when his boss fails to recognize his contributions, but that only makes Pete more determined to do a better job next time. Pete does so much better when he gets regular "pats on the back" or "praises of his work," and that makes him want to do a better job. Pete loves attention and needs a lot of validation.

In his relationships, Pete is guarded yet loyal and giving. He needs constant reassurance from people close to him, though he always questions it when they show him, unconditional love. He is still wondering if their reassurance is genuine or not. Pete is the kind of person that always puts the responsibility on the other person in the relationship to maintain the relationship. Pete is the kind of person that gets confused in relationships because he doesn't know his real value to other people. When someone tells him something confident about himself, he will doubt the sincerity of their statement and expect them to prove it through their behavior toward him. However, once that honesty showed, Pete becomes a real trusted and loyal friend to the end. He is a "one-man dog" and is faithful and loyal in his relationship.

Pete is an Introverted Sanguine. As such, he longs to take center stage. Though Pete could be the life of the party, he never will be. And that's okay—he has many gifts and has a lot of exceptional principles. For example, the Introverted Sanguine is people-oriented, gentle, diligent, loving, compassionate, supportive, and loyal—not a bad list of qualities. The problems occur when the Introverted Sanguine lets these positive attributes get out of balance and they do not get their needs met, and they become passive, inward, awkward, and withdrawn. They shrink away from the people they need because of their fear of rejection. And the denial is 99 percent false and they perceive it as absolute truth and rejection.

## The Introverted Sanguine – Demonstrated vs. Desired Behavior

The Introverted Sanguine by nature has a very intricate social orientation. As the chart shows, in the extreme they *demonstrate* introverted behavior but *desires* that others respond to them like an extrovert.

| Introvert | 0 | 1 | 2 | 3 | 4 | 5 | 6 | 7 | 8 | 9 | Extrovert |
|---|---|---|---|---|---|---|---|---|---|---|---|
| | | | | | | | | | | | |
| **Social** | | | | | | | | | | | |
| • *Demonstrated* | X | | | | | | | | | | |
| • *Desired* | | | | | | | | | | X | |
| **Leadership** | | | | | | | | | | | |
| • *Demonstrated* | X | | | | | | | | | | |
| • *Desired* | | | | | | | | | | X | |
| **Relationship** | | | | | | | | | | | |
| • *Demonstrated* | X | | | | | | | | | | |
| • *Desired* | | | | | | | | | | X | |

Because of this dichotomy, the Introverted Sanguine can appear very snobbish, as if he doesn't care. He can seem aloof and independent and act like an outsider. He will not initiate interaction with others and instead go off by himself or works as if he is not interested in socializing; then, when nobody approaches him, he wonders why. The behavior he demonstrates is interpreted by others as "Leave me alone … I'm not interested in talking to you." And guess what? People do leave him alone—which is the opposite of what he wants!

What the Introvert Sanguine want and need are inclusion socially. Their significant lack is recognition and approval. That's why it's hard for the Introverted Sanguine to say no to someone without feeling guilt or shame for doing so. He will always say yes, they become weighed down trying to be the do-gooder. The irony is that he then finds it harder and harder to say no when asked to do even more—he wants inclusion and fears rejection if he says no. As a result, he always feels overwhelmed—or *is* overwhelmed in with his workload. It should be obvious by now that one important lesson the Introverted Sanguine needs to learn is that it's okay to say "No."

Introverted Sanguine self-esteem is typically low. If Introverted Sanguine don't feel good about himself and feels unworthy of deserving recognition and approval, Introverted Sanguine will disengage emotionally and physically. That's the reason Introverted Sanguine don't have the right to refuse anyone.

If he is invited into a social setting or invited by an individual to lunch, shopping, or a trade show, he feels very exceptional for that occasion. However, he will need to be asked the next time again. He needs inviting. He evaluates himself from incident to incident as to his value and always places the burden of responsibility for validating him on the other person.

Let's look at the three areas of the WIDP profile—social/vocational, leadership, and relationship—to see what makes the Introverted Sanguine tick.

## The Social/Vocational Profile—Introverted Sanguine

| Introvert | | 0 | 1 | 2 | 3 | 4 | 5 | 6 | 7 | 8 | 9 | Extrovert |
|---|---|---|---|---|---|---|---|---|---|---|---|---|
| | | | | | | | | | | | | |
| • *Demonstrated* | | X | | | | | | | | | | |
| • *Desired* | | | | | | | | | | | X | |

In considering the Introverted Sanguine social/vocational profile, we need to look at some factors, beginning with social needs and desires.

## INTROVERTED SANGUINE IN SOCIAL

| Temperament (out of 3,449 people) | # People | Social | # People | Leadership | # People | Relationship |
|---|---|---|---|---|---|---|
| Introverted Sanguine | 202 | 5.86% | 82 | 2.38% | 243 | 7.05% |
| Introverted Sanguine Compulsive | 13 | 0.38% | 26 | 0.75% | 0 | 0.00% |

*Social Needs and Desires.* The Introverted Sanguine expresses himself as an introvert but is relationship-oriented, which means he has a high need for acceptance and socialization with people. Individuals in this temperament tend to remain introverted until others initiate contact. When others welcome him into a relationship, the Introverted Sanguine will respond as an extrovert.

## A Note about the Social Profile

The social profile outlines your needs and desires for light friendships, work/career associations, and other casual relationships. By comparing the social profile with your current life situation, you can understand conflict areas and achieve a comfortable level of interpersonal contact in work or social environment. For helpful hints on overcoming potential barriers.

**Remember:** The social profile should be applied only to the individual's casual social/career contacts. To determine the individual's needs and desires in close personal relationships, please consult the relationship profile.

This characteristic is called an approach/avoidance conflict, which means such an individual has a strong need and desire for socialization but is unable to express his needs because of severe fear of rejection. The Introverted Sanguine requirement is to be accepted and included by people but is dependent on others to take the initiative in establishing and maintaining friendships.

The Introvert Sanguine also needs repeated assurances of approval in established relationships, and has a strong need for security in his life. Although he is loving and kind in relationships where his needs are recognized and met, the Introverted Sanguine may experience different conflicts caused by his dependence on others and his inability to express and meet his needs. And whereas he has many talents and excellent character qualities to contribute to relationships, he may frequently encounter difficulties caused by being nonassertive in a hostile world. As he gains self-understanding and confidence, the Introverted Sanguine can begin to ensure that his needs are expressed and met. An Introverted Sanguine married to someone who is Choleric in the social profile will experience a lot of internal conflict in that relationship. The Choleric in social orientation will show a lot of attention to people with handshakes, hugs, and touch. They do this for their agenda of getting from those people what they want from them. Therefore, they act very kindly to them. The Introverted Sanguine will perceive that kind of demonstrative behavior as being "too relational" and mistake it more intimate relationship behavior. However, to the Choleric, it is only to get their needs met by using other people to extract information from them or to get them to assist them in accomplishing their mission. Once the socializing is over and they go home, the Choleric will have forgotten who even spoke to or showed any attention to them, unless they have made a mental note of how a person could be an asset to them for something they have that the Choleric needs. The Introverted Sanguine will have their feelings hurt because they want that "perceived affection" their spouse shared with strangers directed towards them, and they expect their spouse and friends to know this about them as if they were mind readers. Introverted Sanguine tend to be very jealous of their spouse and spend a lot of their life in depression because of it. Unfortunately, the Introverted Sanguine is unable to confront the strong Choleric for fear of rejection and will continue to do a slow burn internally. This lack of communication about his interaction with others causes constant anger and frustration in the relationship. Both must understand the temperament needs and desires of each other's temperament, Otherwise, they will live in constant turmoil and conflict, and the marriage could be in jeopardy because of this misunderstanding.

***Criteria for Friendships.*** The Introverted Sanguine has a high need for inclusion in social relationships but does not express this need. As a result, they may remain socially isolated unless people reach out to them. He is very responsive when others initiate socialization and will become friendly and outgoing. The Introverted Sanguine relates well to people who are close, supportive, and sensitive to them. Loving and committed when trust established, he needs frequent reassurance that he is accepted and needed— even in longstanding friendships. Once they're "invited in" they become full-blown Sanguine and can be quite active, colorful, and lively towards individuals or groups. It is like they become another person. But social inclusion for the Introverted Sanguine is like being freed from a prison of isolation.

*Perception of Self.* The Introverted Sanguine tends to be self-protective because of his low self-esteem and poor self-image. He may perceive himself as worthless in comparison to others and readily takes the blame for problems even when he is not responsible. The Introverted Sanguine tends to project his negative self-image onto others and fear their rejection; in fact, his reluctance to initiate relationships may be a defense against possible hurt and rejection. This low self-esteem and fear of rejection create barriers to the Introverted Sanguine's ability to express his skills and foster his compassionate, people-oriented nature. Working toward a more positive self-concept will help him achieve his full potential in life.

*Perception by Others.* In social situations, the Introverted Sanguine often appears passive and quiet, and will remain alone until personally invited to join the group. Often his behavior is indirect, and he may express an action that is the opposite of what he desires. While the Introverted Sanguine may appear uninterested in pursuing friendships, he is very responsive when included and encouraged by others. Gentle and kind, he is loving and self-sacrificing with people who have earned his trust. And, because he is nonassertive, he may be used or taken for granted by more aggressive people.

*Perception of Others.* The Introverted Sanguine feels a strong need to assist people and make them happy. Sensitive to their problems, he is very willing to serve and support them. He may have difficulty refusing their requests and can become exhausted trying to meet the claims and demands of others—all while neglecting his own needs. The Introverted Sanguine may expect others to know what he needs and wants; at the same time, he has a strong desire for other people to recognize his efforts. He tends to be suspicious of people and may distrust their motives until they earn his trust, or he believes they sincerely accept him. The Introverted Sanguine usually tries to maintain peace at any cost. As a result, he is very susceptible to peer pressure and may seek approval by following the crowd—even if the behavior conflicts with his values. He will often ask friends for advice and assistance in decision-making and may become dependent on those close to him. They ask, "Are you coming to my promotion party, cook-out, housewarming, marriage, etc.?" because they don't know if you are coming or not, and it is important to them. But if you show up on your own, then they think you do like them and care about them.

*Intellectual Orientation.* The Introverted Sanguine possesses high intellectual capacities. Their talents and abilities are hidden by their low self-esteem, which prevents them from expressing their ideas and achieving their potential. They want support and assistance from others in assuming responsibilities and making decisions; when given a choice, the Introverted Sanguine prefers mutual accountability and decision-making. Introverted Sanguine is unable to make decisions and prefers that someone else make their decisions for them. However, they want to be part of the decision-making process. There is a very unusual thing that takes place in this decision-making process with the Introverted Sanguine. Once an individual has asked the Introverted Sanguine their opinion, the Introverted Sanguine does not care what the final determination is as long as they are taken into consideration in the process. It is the strangest thing, but it is true. They do not care about what the final decision is, just being considered already satisfies them.

*Emotional Orientation.* Although the emotionally guarded Introverted Sanguine can be quite expressive in established relationships, at the same time, they can be reluctant to share negative emotions under any circumstances. Because of the inner conflict caused by their unmet needs, they may struggle with emotional difficulties such as fear, stress, guilt, feeling unloved, feeling unappreciated, etc. They require assistance to assert them and express their needs directly. As a result, even though they may experience much-internalized anger and resentment, they avoid confrontation and rarely shows passion. They may feel frustrated when their aberrant behavior is not interpreted accurately by others or when they do not receive needed attention and approval. He is reluctant to acknowledge the anger and may describe his passion as "hurt feelings," but deep inside, he's filled with rage. One serious problem with this is that unresolved anger leads to more dangerous conditions that may manifest as moodiness, depression, withdrawal, and further isolation from people. The Introverted Sanguine can become vengeful toward those who hurt him. As he learns to express anger and deal with it appropriately, he will experience a marked increase in emotional stability and inner peace. The Introverted Sanguine needs to know that is a natural part of their temperament for them to have internalized and externalized anger. It is not hurt feelings. Call it what it is, anger. The key is for them to be able to learn to express their disappointments in life, anger, and not let people take advantage of them. They need to know that it is all right for them to say no to people when people want them to say yes, and it is all right to say "yes" when people want them to say "no." Introverted Sanguine does not need to permit themselves to be "run over" by the stronger temperaments of the Choleric and the Melancholy. It is all right for them to say, "I do not like for you to talk that way to me" or "Please don't treat me like I don't count; I count just as much as you do." When it comes to socializing, and they want to be involved, they need to be able to say "Hey, I would like to participate in the reunion committee too" or "May I join the group for lunch too?" If anything, the Introverted Sanguine needs to acknowledge that the label they have given of "hurt feelings," is real "anger" internalized or externalized, in a burst of emotional outbreaks, and they need to gain an understanding that this is a significant issue in their life.

***Work Orientation.*** The Introverted Sanguine is a diligent and dependable worker. Careful and accurate in his work, he maintains a steady pace as he works tirelessly to meet deadlines and achieve goals. He relies on supervisors for direction and encouragement and is usually most comfortable in structured, no leadership positions. Efficient and supportive of others, the Introverted Sanguine works well as part of a team and readily volunteers his assistance. Relationship-oriented rather than task-oriented, he functions best in work situations that include opportunities to interact with people. He needs recognition and appreciation from others for his work and performs tasks accurately to gain approval. The Introverted Sanguine exhibits a high need for security in his career. They make great employees and are very loyal and trustworthy. They do need emotional stroking occasionally to know that they are doing a good job and are necessary. In the work setting, they need to learn to speak the truth if they feel that they are mistreated in any way by other coworkers or by their employer. Since they do not like confrontation, they are prone to permit themselves to be abused and not say anything about it because they do not want to offend anyone. Therefore, they continue to stay in abusive situations.

***Motivation.*** The Introverted Sanguine stirred by the threat of punishment and may be highly responsive to emotional punishment such as guilt, rejection, and loss of recognition. Introverted Sanguine also can be driven by the reward of approval and appreciation for accomplishments and is willing to modify their behavior to avoid negative consequences or to gain support. The most excellent motivator for the Introverted Sanguine is individual recognitions publicly or privately. They will beam when approval is shown them. For most Introverted Sanguine, they would rather have proper support and recognition than a pay raise. They are the only temperament that feels this way. The rest of the temperaments would say, "Show me the money."

***Rejection/Acceptance Profile.*** Much of the Introverted Sanguine behavior is born out of severe fear of rejection and the need to avoid rejection and gain recognition. Introverted Sanguine need frequent reassurances of love and affection from those close to him. To others, his indirect manner may appear that he is rejecting of others when he is very accepting of people. Unfortunate for the Introverted Sanguine, they live behind the unwanted mask of appearing as though they do not want others approaching them. Then people don't approach them because they look like they don't want to contact with others because of their body language. Then the Introverted Sanguine perceive R42ejection, whether it is real or imagined and act on it as though it were real. This body language causes a significant loss for the Introverted Sanguine. But they can improve their quality of life by understanding that they are all right, and that people do want to be around them and that people do like them regardless of their temperament. Introverted Sanguine is entertaining people once they feel accepted.

## The Leadership Profile—Introverted Sanguine

| Introvert | 0 | 1 | 2 | 3 | 4 | 5 | 6 | 7 | 8 | 9 | Extrovert |
|---|---|---|---|---|---|---|---|---|---|---|---|
|  |  |  |  |  |  |  |  |  |  |  |  |
| • *Demonstrated* | X |  |  |  |  |  |  |  |  |  |  |
| • *Desired* |  |  |  |  |  |  |  |  |  | X |  |

In considering the Introverted Sanguine leadership profile, we need to look at some factors, beginning with leadership needs and desires.

## INTROVERTED SANGUINE IN LEADERSHIP

| <u>Temperamen</u>t (out of 3,449 people) | <u># People</u> | <u>Social</u> | <u># People</u> | <u>Leadership</u> | <u># People</u> | <u>Relationship</u> |
|---|---|---|---|---|---|---|
| Introverted Sanguine | 202 | 5.86% | 82 | 2.38% | 243 | 7.05% |
| Introverted Sanguine Compulsive | 13 | 0.38% | 26 | 0.75% | 0 | 0.00% |

***Leadership Needs and Desires.*** The Introverted Sanguine usually does not accept responsibilities or make decisions independently. Instead, he depends on others for assistance in directing his life while wanting little control over the lives and behaviors of others. Rarely expressing his dependency needs directly, he is most comfortable when people recognize and meet his needs. The Introverted Sanguine tends to lack confidence in his ability to successfully fulfill responsibilities or make decisions. As a result, he needs support and encouragement to achieve his goals, most often from a few close friends/coworkers to share his decision-making and responsibilities. However, the Introverted Sanguine **can lead** if they are in a number two (2) position. The second in command always received instructions from the number one leader as to what to do. Therefore, the Introverted Sanguine can lead if they are driving as a second in command and are not required to make the initial decision. They can be very good at implementing someone else's choices and function very well in that position. Let me share a story of an Introverted Sanguine in leadership titled "The Unwanted Promotion."

***Criteria for Relationships.*** While the Introverted Sanguine expresses himself as an introvert, they are relationship-oriented and has a high need for acceptance and interaction with people. He tends to remain introverted until others initiate contact or welcome him into a relationship, after which he responds as an extrovert. The Introverted Sanguine exhibits an approach/avoidance conflict: that is, he has a strong need and desire for socialization but is unable to express his needs. Inhibited by a severe fear of rejection, he has a strong need to be accepted and included by people but is dependent on others to take the initiative in establishing and maintaining friendships. He needs frequent assurances of approval in established relationships, have a strong need for security in his life and is loving and kind in relationships where his needs are recognized and met. He may experience different conflicts caused by his dependence in others and his inability to express and meet his needs. Although he has many talents and excellent character qualities to contribute to relationships, he may frequently encounter difficulties caused by being nonassertive and feel powerless in a hostile world. As he gains self-understanding and confidence, he can begin to ensure that his needs can be articulated and met.

***Perception of Self.*** The Introverted Sanguine tends to be self-protective because of his low self-esteem in and poor self-image when it comes to assuming leadership. He may perceive himself as worthless in comparison to others and readily takes the blame for problems, even when he is not responsible. He tends to project his negative self-image onto others and fears their rejection; his reluctance to initiate relationships may be a defense against possible hurt and rejection. The low self-esteem and fear of rejection are barriers to the expression of his abilities and his compassionate, people-oriented nature. Working toward a more positive self-concept will help him achieve his full potential in life and reduce the internal conflict he has of himself because he perceived himself as a nobody.

## A Note about the Leadership Profile

The adult leadership profile identifies the individual's ability to provide leadership, make decisions, and assume responsibilities. This profile outlines the individual's needs and desires for independence, achievement, and recognition. Because leadership needs and desires are expressed through socializing with people, the leadership profile should not be evaluated alone. They should be interpreted with either the social profile or the relationship profile.

– Evaluated together, the leadership profile and the social profile help determine the individual's career needs. By comparing the results with the individual's current employment situation, you can target conflict areas and help the individual maximize career skills.

– Evaluated together, the leadership profile and the relationship profile help determine the individual's independence-dependence needs in close relationships. By comparing the results with the individual's current life situation, you can target conflict areas and help the individual enhance relationships.

***Perception by Others.*** Often appearing passive and quiet in social situations, the Introverted Sanguine will remain alone until he is personally invited to join the group. His behavior often is indirect; in fact, he may express an action that is the opposite of what he desires. For example, he may appear uninterested in pursuing friendships even though he will be very responsive when included and encouraged by others. He is compassionate when others initiate friendships and become friendly and outgoing. Gentle and kind, loving and generous with people who have earned his trust, the Introverted Sanguine relates well to people who are supportive and sensitive to him. At the same time, he is nonassertive and may be used or taken for granted by more aggressive people. This no assertiveness makes him vulnerable to the stronger temperaments when it comes to providing leadership and managing people.

***Perception of Others.*** The Introverted Sanguine has a strong need to assist people and make them happy. Sensitive to other peoples' problems, he is very willing to serve and support them. He may have difficulty refusing requests and can become exhausted trying to meet the requests and demands of others while neglecting his own needs. He has a strong desire for other people to recognize his efforts and may expect them to know what he needs and wants. Therefore, Introverted Sanguine makes great employees because of their loyalty and commitment. They will work around the clock to get the job done, but they do need validation for the great work he is doing. He tends to be suspicious of people until they earn his trust; even then, he may distrust other peoples' motives or have difficulty believing they sincerely accept him. The Introverted Sanguine usually tries to maintain peace at any cost. As a result, he is susceptible to peer pressure and may seek approval by following the crowd even if the behavior conflicts with his values. He checks with friends for advice and assistance in decision-making and may become dependent on those close to him.

***Intellectual Orientation.*** Although the Introverted Sanguine has high mental capacities, their talents and abilities are hidden by their low self-esteem. Low self-esteem can prevent them from expressing their ideas and achieving their potential as a leader or managing people. They want support and assistance from others in assuming responsibilities and making decisions.

***Emotional Orientation.*** While the Introverted Sanguine is emotionally guarded and reluctant to share negative emotions, they can be emotionally expressive in established relationships. Because of the inner conflict caused by their unmet needs, they may struggle with emotional difficulties such as fear, stress, guilt, feeling unloved, feeling unappreciated, and so on. Introverted Sanguine need assistance to assert themselves and express their needs directly. Because Introverted Sanguine avoids confrontation and rarely shows anger, they may experience much-internalized rage and resentment. Introverted Sanguine may feel frustrated when their aberrant behavior is not interpreted accurately by others or when the Introverted Sanguine does not receive needed attention and approval. At the same time, the Introverted Sanguine is reluctant to acknowledge the anger and may describe their passion as "hurt feelings." Unresolved outrage may manifest as moodiness, depression, withdrawal, and further isolation from people and his temper can become vengeful toward those who hurt him. As the Introverted Sanguine learns to express anger and deal with it appropriately, he will experience a marked increase in emotional stability and inner peace.

***Work Orientation.*** The Introverted Sanguine is a diligent, dependable worker, careful and accurate in his work. An efficient worker, he works tirelessly to meet deadlines and achieve goals, maintaining a steady pace all the while. Usually most comfortable in structured, no leadership positions, he works well as part of a team and relies on supervisors for direction and encouragement. Quite supportive of others, he readily volunteers his assistance. Because he is relationship-oriented rather than task-oriented, he functions best in work situations that include opportunities to interact with people. He needs recognition and appreciation from others and performs tasks accurately to gain approval. The Introverted Sanguine has a strong need for security in his career.

*Motivation.* Motivated by the threat of punishment, the Introverted Sanguine may be highly responsive to emotional punishment such as guilt, rejection, and loss of recognition. Introverted Sanguine also can be motivated by the reward of approval and appreciation for accomplishments and are willing to modify their behavior to avoid negative consequences or to gain support.

*Rejection/Acceptance Profile.* The Introverted Sanguine has a severe fear of rejection, and therefore, directs much behavior toward avoiding rejection and gaining acceptance. Introverted Sanguine need frequent reassurances of love and affection from those close to him. His indirect manner may appear rejecting of others when he is very accepting of people.

**The Relationship Profile – Introverted Sanguine**

| Introvert | 0 | 1 | 2 | 3 | 4 | 5 | 6 | 7 | 8 | 9 | Extrovert |
|---|---|---|---|---|---|---|---|---|---|---|---|
| | | | | | | | | | | | |
| • *Demonstrated* | X | | | | | | | | | | |
| • *Desired* | | | | | | | | | | X | |

In considering the Introverted Sanguine relationship profile, we need to look at some factors, beginning with relationship needs and desires.

## INTROVERTED SANGUINE IN RELATIONSHIP

| Temperament (out of 3,449 people) | # People | Social | # People | Leadership | # People | Relationship |
|---|---|---|---|---|---|---|
| Introverted Sanguine | 202 | 5.86% | 82 | 2.38% | 243 | 7.05% |
| Introverted Sanguine Compulsive | 13 | 0.38% | 26 | 0.75% | 0 | 0.00% |

### A Note about the Relationship Profile

The adult relationship profile identifies the individual's preferences for emotional involvement and shared affection on a one-to-one basis. This profile outlines the individual's needs and desires for emotional sharing and relationships. For most people, the relationship profile is the dominant pattern that influences behavior in the social and leadership areas.

By comparing the relationship profile with the individual's current life situation, you can target conflict areas and help the individual meet fundamental needs that are not met.

## *Relationship Needs and Desires*

A criterion for a relationship indicates the individual's preferences in developing and establishing relationships; may identify types of people who are compatible and incompatible with the individual's temperament.

Although the Introverted Sanguine expresses himself as an introvert, he is relationship-oriented, and has a high need for acceptance and interaction with people. He tends to remain introverted until others initiate contact and then responds as an extrovert when others welcome him into a relationship.

He possesses a strong desire for close personal relationships and needs to receive high amounts of love and approval. The Introverted Sanguine suffers from approach/avoidance conflict: that is, he has a strong need and desire for love but is unable to express his needs. Inhibited by a severe fear of rejection, he needs to be accepted and included by people but is dependent on others to take the initiative in establishing and maintaining relationships. He is loving and kind in relationships where his needs are recognized and met, but still needs frequent assurances of approval in established relationships. The Introverted Sanguine may experience different conflicts caused by his dependence on others and his inability to express and meet his needs. Although he has many talents and excellent character qualities to contribute to relationships, he may frequently encounter difficulties caused by being nonassertive in a hostile world. As he gains self-understanding and confidence, he can begin to ensure that his needs are expressed and met. The Introverted Sanguine is exceptionally loyal to their significant other, their family, and their close friends. They are committed to the relationship and will endure a considerable amount of conflict to remain faithful to the relationship. However, they do expect to get their needs and desires met by their significant other, family members, and close friends. They are always there for you, and they also hope you to be there for them and to understand their needs and desires.

***Criteria for Relationships.*** The Introverted Sanguine has a strong need for inclusion in social interactions but does not express this need. Introverted Sanguine rarely attempts to establish or maintain a close relationship and may remain socially isolated unless people reach out to him. Responsive when others initiate socialization, he becomes friendly and outgoing and relates well to close people, supportive, and sensitive to him. Loving and committed once trust established, he needs frequent reassurance that he is accepted and needed, even in longstanding relationships. Internally, the Introverted Sanguine responds like a dog wagging his tail when its master comes home. But the tail wagging is all internal and not visibly seen by the master, family, or friends. They must feel comfortable and safe that you will not reject them first before they display any emotion, touch, or communications that they are happy to see you. Inside they are very excited and say things like, "Oh, boy, here comes my mate! I'm so excited they are home, and I have missed them so much because…," "I can hardly contain myself. I am so excited to see them and…," "I hope they are happy to see me too."

***Perception of Self.*** The Introverted Sanguine tends to be self-protective because of his low self-esteem and poor self-image. He may perceive himself as worthless in comparison to others and readily takes the blame for problems even when he is not responsible. He tends to project his negative self-image onto others and fears their rejection; in fact, his reluctance to initiate relationships may be a defense against possible hurt and rejection. The low self-esteem in and fear of rejection are barriers to the expression of his abilities and his compassionate, people-oriented nature. Working toward a more positive self-concept will help him achieve his full potential in life.

***Perception by Others.*** Often appearing passive and withdrawn, the Introverted Sanguine remains alone until personally invited to participate. His behavior often is indirect, and he may express an action that is the opposite of what he desires. Although he may appear uninterested in being close to others, he is very responsive when included and encouraged. His nature is to be gentle and kind, and he is loving and self-sacrificing with people who have earned his trust. He is by nature, also nonassertive; as a result, he may be used or taken for granted by more aggressive people. When other temperaments first see the Introverted

Sanguine, they are quite taken back by their non-display of emotions and behavior. They seem to appear that they don't care whether or not you are even there. Introverted Sanguine causes another temperament to stay away from the Introverted Sanguine although that is the last thing the Introverted Sanguine wants from them.

***Perception of Others.*** The Introverted Sanguine genuinely loves those who have earned his trust and may show his love by performing tasks rather than by open expressions of love. He has a strong need to assist people and make them happy, is sensitive to their problems, and is very willing to serve and support them. He may have difficulty refusing their requests and can become exhausted trying to meet the claims and demands of others while neglecting his own needs. He may expect others to know what he needs and wants and has a strong desire for recognition for his efforts. He tends to be suspicious of people until they earn his trust and may distrust their motives or have difficulty believing they sincerely accept him. The Introverted Sanguine usually tries to maintain peace at any cost. He is susceptible to peer pressure and may seek approval by following the crowd—even if the behavior conflicts with his values. He checks with friends for advice and assistance in decision making and may become dependent on those close to him.

***Intellectual Orientation.*** Although the Introverted Sanguine possesses high mental capacities, their talents and abilities can be hidden by their low self-esteem, which prevents them from expressing their ideas and achieving their potential. Diligent and dependable in their work habits, they want to support and assistance from others in assuming responsibilities and making decisions.

***Emotional Orientation.*** The Introverted Sanguine is emotionally guarded but can be emotionally expressive in established relationships and responds well to love and affection. They are reluctant to share negative emotions and, because of the inner conflict caused by their unmet needs, may struggle with emotional difficulties such as fear, stress, guilt, feeling unloved, feeling unappreciated, etc. They need assistance to assert and express their needs directly. Although they avoid confrontation and rarely shows anger, they may experience much-internalized rage and resentment. They may feel frustrated when their erratic behavior is not interpreted accurately by others or when they do not receive needed attention and approval. The Introverted Sanguine is reluctant to acknowledge the anger and may describe his passion as "hurt feelings." He can become vengeful toward those who hurt him, and his unresolved anger may manifest as moodiness, depression, withdrawal, and further isolation from people. As he learns to express anger and deal with it appropriately, the Introverted Sanguine will experience a marked increase in emotional stability and inner peace.

***Motivation.*** The Introverted Sanguine is motivated by the threat of punishment and can be highly responsive to emotional punishment such as guilt, rejection, and loss of recognition. At the same time, Introverted Sanguine is motivated by the reward of approval and appreciation for accomplishments. They are willing to modify their behavior to avoid negative consequences or to gain support.

***Rejection/Acceptance Profile.*** The Introverted Sanguine possesses a severe fear of rejection and directs much behavior toward avoiding rejection and gaining acceptance. Introverted Sanguine need frequent reassurances of love and affection from those close to him. His indirect manner may communicate rejection to his loved ones when, in reality, he is very accepting of people and incredibly loving and faithful in secure relationships.

# Help for the Introverted Sanguine

## Characteristics of the Introverted Sanguine

### *Probable Strengths*

- Relationship-oriented – is highly relational and responsive to people but must be personally invited into relationships. Body language says, "Don't approach me," but that's because of the fear of rejection.
- Kind, gentle, and loving to others – is the most natural, kind, soft, and loving of all the temperaments.
- Diligent – is a very hard, determined, and dependable worker if praised, recognized, and appreciated.
- Compassionate – is highly sensitive to people's needs and problems.
- Supportive – has a natural servant's heart and is very willing to assist people.
- Loyal – is faithful to family and friends.

### *Potential Weaknesses*

Dependent/independent conflict – appears withdrawn like an introvert yet desires to be an extrovert.

- Low self-esteem – exhibits many insecurities and is often depressed and very sensitive to rejection from others. Often feels that "nobody likes me."
- Nonassertive – likes for others to take the lead in the decision-making process. Is reluctant to refuse requests from others.
- Isolated – is unwilling to initiate friendships but becomes depressed about being alone. Often ends up alone because of their lack of confidence.
- Manipulative and controlling – will often use indirect behavior to get people to do what they want.
- Internalized anger – becomes anxious or depressed when he is not acknowledged. Can become bitter and resentful for the same reason.

### *Decisions for the Introverted Sanguine*

Unable to make decisions and prefers that someone else make decisions for him. However, he does want considered as part of the decision-making process.

As we have seen in the preceding pages, the Introverted Sanguine is a complex individual with a considerable amount of potential. The chart shows a summary of *potential* weaknesses and *probable* strengths.

The good news is that the Introverted Sanguine doesn't have to resign himself to allowing his inherent weaknesses to rule him. There are many things he can do to improve his life.

The Introverted Sanguine needs to evaluate his intentions and determine the reasons for his actions and speech. For example, he needs to ask himself:

- Why do I always feel I need to isolate myself from others?
- Why do I feel as though I'm not as good as other people?
- Why am I fearful of initiating relationships toward others?

- Why do I always think that they do not like me or want to be involved with me?
- Why do I always say yes when I don't want to?
- Why do I still find myself alone and very lonely?
- Why won't others initiate relationships toward me?
- Why can't I insert myself and ask others if I can join them in their activities?
- Why do I always try to accommodate others at my own expense?
- Why can't I express myself and stick up for myself with more dominant people?

## Do's and Don'ts for the Introverted Sanguine

| Do | Don't |
|---|---|
| Grow up and try to remember your obligations | Interrupt or add to others' stories |
| Face reality; life isn't always a party | Shirk everything off |
| Aim for the quiet dignity | Expect others to protect, care for you forever |
| Get organized | Walk into a room unemotional |
| Make schedules | Overcommit yourself emotionally |
| Make lists | Be too aloof |
| Find someone who will hold you accountable | Always be on the sideline |
| Enhance conversation limit details | Control by manipulation |
| Plan people on your calendar each day | Become debt-laden |
| Be on time | Make always make yourself scarce |
| Concentrate on truth and honesty | Become socially distant |
| Finish what you start | Be a con artist |
| Be sensitive to others' needs | Overbuy to compensate loneliness |
| Listen more, talk less | |
| Ask questions | |
| Seek a job that can give you a sense of recognition | |
| Put things back in the same place | |
| Keep track of spending | |
| Choose one time per week to clean/arrange | |
| Improve your volume of communication | |

Here are some other things the Introverted Sanguine can do.

***To overcome his shyness, he can:***

- Learn to initiate conversations with others first
- Get into the limelight yourself
- Approach others for what you want
- Enter groups and become a part

***To avoid being a "hidden servant," he can:***

- Let his desires to serve others be made known
- Announce his interest to participate in
- Invite himself to groups or social activities

***To become more decisive, he can:***

- Learn to make his own decisions
- Learn to stop counting on other people to make decisions for him

***Accept the fact that he does not want to lead will help him avoid:***

- Letting others abuse or manipulate him
- Allowing others to drive him where he does not want to go

***Learn to say no to others!***

# BASIC INTROVERTED SANGUINE TEMPERAMENT DETAILS

The Introverted Sanguine

I.   Potential Strengths of the Introverted Sanguine Temperament

   A.  Relationship-Oriented
      1.  Likes to go to parties and church events but must be personally invited.
      2.  Does not initiate the connection, although they genuinely want one.
      3.  Has a high need to be recognized.

   B.  Gentle Spirit
      1.  No other temperament is kinder or more sensitive.
      2.  Naturally, have the "Fruit of the Spirit."

   C.  Servant
      1.  Tries to accommodate others at their own expense.
      2.  Usually, it runs them ragged.

D. Diligent
1. Can be very persistent if they believe that their attention to a task will bring them praise or recognition.
2. Can be very task-oriented if they think that this will help them build a deep personal relationship.

II. Potential Weaknesses/Shortcomings of the Introverted Sanguine Temperament

A. Withdrawn and Downbeat
1. They are an introvert, yet they desire to be an extrovert.
2. Has many interests and concerns yet does not express them.
3. Characterized by low-voiced behavior and high responsive behavior.
4. Usually suffers from poor or low self-esteem.
5. Very insecure.
6. The Introverted Sanguine does not speak or stand up for their rights, therefore; are quickly taken advantage of by more aggressive and dominant temperaments.

B. Isolated
1. Often alone and isolated because they are nonassertive.
2. They expect others to "read their mind" or guess their need to be accepted and included.

C. Dependent
1. Doesn't like to make decisions or choices on their own.
2. Weak-willed.
3. Wants others to take care of them and tell them what to do.
4. Has a difficult time making decisions independently or taking on responsibilities individually.

D. Anxiety—If they do not receive the desired response or recognition, they will begin to manufacture bitterness and resentment, which leads to severe stress.

E. Anger—can manifest cold, calculating violence, which can explode after they cannot take the abuse anymore.

F. Depression
1. Very sensitive to rejection.
2. Often has a hard time differentiating between what is real and imagined.
3. Often suffers from neurotic depression.
4. Volatile temperament.

G. Manipulative
1. Uses erratic behavior as a tactic to employ people.
2. Will check out all the advice you suggest to someone else before doing what you have indicated. Whether the individual disagrees with your counsel, they will tend to do what the other person says.

## Shy Introverted Sanguine

Shy Introverted Sanguine is shy

- Learn to initiate conversations with others first
- Get into the limelight yourself
- Approach others for what you want
- Enter groups and become a part

Shy Introverted Sanguine are hidden servants

- Let your desires to serve others be made known
- Announce your interest to participate
- Invite yourself to groups or social activities

Shy Introverted Sanguine are indecisive

- Learn to make decisions on your own
- Don't count on others for your decisions

Shy Introverted Sanguine cannot lead

- Learn to accept this fact
- Don't let others abuse you or manipulate you
- Don't let others lead you where you do not want to go
- Learn to say no to others

# STRENGTH AND WEAKNESSES
## of the
# INTROVERTED SANGUINE

| | STRENGTHS | WEAKNESSES |
|---|---|---|
| **EMOTIONS:** | Highly relational | Not demonstrative in relationships |
| | Naturally gentle and kind | Easily abused by others |
| | Has a servant's heart | Will work beyond expectation |
| | Diligent worker | Need praise and recognition for work |
| | Very accommodating | Does not speak up for themselves |
| | Everything to everyone | Significant burnout pleasing people |
| | Party-spirited people | Perceives rejection easily |
| | Emotional | Appears withdrawn and alone |
| | Sincere at heart | Nonassertive |
| | Loyal | Indecisive |
| | The dependable | Easily taken advantage of |
| | Trustworthy | Becomes anxious easily |
| | Committed to relationships | Can become bitter and resentful |
| | Serious | Can be very manipulative |
| | Innocent | Uses much indirect behavior |
| | Devoted | Expects others to make their decisions |
| | Tender | Often depressed |
| **WORK:** | Good worker | Would instead talk |
| | Creative | Forgetful |
| | Great appearance | Weak follow-through |
| | Colorful | Lacks self-confidence |
| **RIGHT ATTITUDE** | Friendly | Slow-moving |
| | Dependable workers | Forgetful |
| | Excellent team member | Decides by feelings |
| | Very relational | Wastes time talking |
| **FRIENDS:** | Thrives on friendships | Hates to be alone |
| | People-oriented | Needs recognition |
| | Thrives on compliments | Wants to be invited in |
| | Loyal to friends | Can be manipulative |
| | Accepts others easily | Hides hurt feelings |
| | Likes many friends | Pouts easily |
| | Likes social activities | Does not make the first move |

## Temperament Weaknesses
## of the Introverted Sanguine

| | |
|---|---|
| Appears withdrawn | Bodily appearance looks like they do not want to approach, but they do |
| Rejection fears | Perceive rejection whether real or imagined and act on it as though it is real |
| Isolationist | Can isolate from people and cloister away emotionally, and no one will ever know |
| Passive aggression | They can become unreceptive in their responsibilities to job and relationships if they feel jilted |
| Nonassertive | They have difficulty with emphasizing themselves into a situation with people |
| Laid-back | Their laid-back demeanor permits stronger temperaments to take advantage of them |
| Quiet spoken | Their soft mannerisms elicit exploitation |
| Underdog | Not being active in desires for leadership causes them ending up in places they do not want to be due to their inability to speak up when needed |
| Apprehensive | They can get very nervous when tensions rise, or thing go wrong for them |
| Depression | Can become downcast due to lack of recognition |
| Offended | If not recognized for their quality of effort, can become very nasty and annoyed |
| Calculating | Can be very cunning and begin scheming if feeling rejected or unliked |
| Decisions | Making decisions is a challenging task for them. Pronouncements for them are hard and very infrequently |
| Life Directions | They welcome instruction guidance on life's issues, and they like others to help them with decisions |
| Pouting | Can be a grouch and go around moping with a scowl on their face showing their unhappiness |
| Non-initiator | Have a tough time engaging in conversation with anyone due to their fear of rejection and not being accepted |
| Breakdown | They are susceptible to burning themselves out due to mental or physical exhaustion |

## Temperament Strengths
## of the Introverted Sanguine

| | |
|---|---|
| Dependable workers | You can give them a job, and it will get done on time; if overtime is needed to complete the task, they will be there |
| Team players | They are great team players and participate as required however they can assist |
| Optimistic | Right attitude and pleasant to be around |
| Presence | Their appearance is always neat, and they are very colorful and bright |
| Loyalty | Trustworthiness is their strong suit and qualifies them for essential tasks |
| Innocent | They maintain comportment of innocence |
| Relationship Commitment | Relationship commitment is fundamental to who they are, a friend or employee |

| | |
|---|---|
| Accommodating | They will go out of their way to assist friends and coworkers |
| Relational individuals | They love to be with and around people that accept them without judging |
| Transparent | They are genuinely see-through individuals and are openly honest |
| Sincere at heart | They are soft and tender |
| People-oriented | They love people and being with people anywhere and anytime |
| Acceptance | Accepts most people without interrogation |
| Friendly | Has many friends and always has room for more |
| Diligence | For them, it is about prioritizing work and relationships and putting them at the center of life |
| Thoughtful | Will still be where they are supposed to be at the correct time |
| Social | Enjoys community functions and being. with energetic people |

*"I have been an instructor on the MBTI for years. After fifteen (15) minutes of evaluating Worley's ID Profile, I recognized the superiority of WIDP over the MBTI. Corporate America will rapidly be replacing the MBTI and the DiSC and other instruments with the WIDP when they experience the validity and reliability of WIDP. Every MBTI trainer and corporate user need to consider WIDP!"*

CARL ERICKSON, MBTI TRAINER, THE
BEACON GROUP, NORTHBRIDGE, MA

# CHAPTER 5

# THE SANGUINE

For as long as anyone can remember, Barb has been full of high energy. She can't sit still to save her life, and bounces from one thing to the next with the power of a rocket. She is always the life of the party, and can carry on several conversations at once while helping people get drinks, find a place to put their coats, prepare snacks—you name it. She is always the first one at any social event—church, concerts, parties, etc., and the last one to leave, often volunteering to help clean up or plan the next gathering. Sometimes she attends functions she hasn't even been invited to, telling herself that it was just an oversight that she wasn't on the list. As far as Barb is concerned, the world is her oyster, and everyone else is there to talk and laugh with—whether they wanted to speak or not! And wherever she goes, she brings laughter and fun.

At work, Barb loves her job and about everyone she works with loving her. She loves to chat with her coworkers and frequently wanders the halls looking for someone to talk to about anything. No matter who needs help with a project—subordinates, peers, and superiors alike—Barb is right there pitching in. She will always go the extra mile to make sure everyone is happy with her work, even if it means staying at the office all night. As a result, she is always juggling her work and family life and trying to make sure things at home doesn't fall apart because she has overcommitted herself. Then, when her husband or children complain that she's not there for them, she feels defeated but only momentarily. Next time she tells herself, *I'll work harder and faster, so everything will be perfect.*

In her relationships, Barb is loving, warm, and compassionate, always going the extra mile to help friends, acquaintances, and strangers alike—and she can never understand it when others don't do the same. She loves showering people with attention and will drop whatever she is doing to go to places and be with people. She loves to buy flowers and gifts for others; sometimes the gifts she buys are expensive, extravagant, and whimsical. She often finds herself saying or doing things that go against the grain of her moral fabric. Of course, she justifies her behavior by telling herself that she's only acting that way, so she doesn't offend anyone.

Barb is a Sanguine. Unlike the Introverted Sanguine, she has no qualms about taking center stage anytime, anywhere—in fact, it's about impossible to get the Sanguine *off* the stage! The exciting thing about the Sanguine is that her positive qualities—outgoing, people-oriented, enthusiastic, responsive, talkative, loving, and compassionate—are also what tends to get her into trouble. That is because; she is continually talking with someone or doing something, she leaves little time for herself to recharge. Then, when she becomes fatigued, she is susceptible to losing her temper or acting in ways that she ordinarily wouldn't even consider. She needs to be accepted so high that at times, she will do things she knows are morally and legally wrong.

She will flare up over the smallest issue and explode. Then, twenty minutes later, she will forget what made her angry. She forgives easily and wants to be forgiven the same way. She can't understand, "What the big deal is—everything is okay now." Of course, that's not the way other people see it. Her anger can push other people away from her, which will cause her additional stress because she *always needs people to accept her*. When she does externalize her rage, it affects her physically, emotionally, and spiritually:

*Physically.* She may self-indulge by going on eating or drinking binges, taking drugs, etc. She also may neglect her body by not bathing or wearing dirty clothes. They even may bite their nails. Finally, she may hurt herself by punching walls and other objects—that is, if there is no one around to take the punches. All these are examples of wrong ways of dealing with rejection after her outburst of anger has alienated her from friends and loved ones.

*Emotionally.* Sanguine may swing and become down, depressed, and moody. When the Introverted Sanguine is down; no one can pull them up until they are ready to be pulled up. The Introverted Sanguine will be so down that no one will want to be around her. Her emotions are like a pendulum swinging back and forth from a depressed mood to boosted with enthusiasm. When she turns the other way and becomes happy, she will go out and talk to anyone who will listen to her; if she's not careful, she will "wear out her welcome" with her remaining friends. In some cases, isolation becomes their solution for a short period as they cannot be away from people very long. They need social interaction, it's their lifeline.

*Spiritually.* When the Sanguine is downhearted, they will not be able to focus on God. They are relationship-oriented and needs someone with "flesh and bones" to talk about anything. To come back up spiritually time alone with God and in prayer is the best solution. Praying and reading Scripture or sharing with a close friend and praying with them is comforting and reassuring. Sanguine need to get out and be with other people. If she is spiritually on top, then the world around her is just beautiful in her eyes and the world is their playground and all people their friend.

## The Sanguine – Demonstrated vs. Desired Behavior

The Sanguine is by Nature, outgoing, people-oriented, and enthusiastic. She is very talkative and responsive to people as well as loving and compassionate. As the chart shows, in the extreme he or she both *demonstrates* and *desires* highly extroverted behavior.

| Introvert | 0 | 1 | 2 | 3 | 4 | 5 | 6 | 7 | 8 | 9 | Extrovert |
|---|---|---|---|---|---|---|---|---|---|---|---|
| | | | | | | | | | | | |
| **Social** | | | | | | | | | | | |
| • *Demonstrated* | | | | | | | | | | X | |
| • *Desired* | | | | | | | | | | X | |
| **Leadership** | | | | | | | | | | | |
| • *Demonstrated* | | | | | | | | | | X | |
| • *Desired* | | | | | | | | | | X | |
| **Relationship** | | | | | | | | | | | |
| • *Demonstrated* | | | | | | | | | | X | |
| • *Desired* | | | | | | | | | | X | |

Let's look at the three areas of the WIDP profile—social/vocational, leadership, and relationship—to see what makes the Sanguine tick.

## The Social/Vocational Profile – Sanguine

| Introvert | 0 | 1 | 2 | 3 | 4 | 5 | 6 | 7 | 8 | 9 | Extrovert |
|---|---|---|---|---|---|---|---|---|---|---|---|
| | | | | | | | | | | | |
| • *Demonstrated* | | | | | | | | | | X | |
| • *Desired* | | | | | | | | | | X | |

In considering the **Sanguine Social/Vocational Profile**, we need to look at some factors, beginning with social needs and desires.

| Temperament (out of 3,449 people) | # People | Social | # People | Leadership | # People | Relationship |
|---|---|---|---|---|---|---|
| Sanguine | 345 | 10.00% | 26 | 0.75% | 362 | 10.50% |
| Sanguine Compulsive | 55 | 1.59% | 4 | 0.12% | 71 | 2.06% |

*Social Needs and Desires.* The Sanguine possesses excellent social skills and is outgoing and friendly. She feels an intense need to be with people and may feel compulsively *driven* to socialize and interact with others. She has great difficulty being alone for extended periods and avoids individual activities. The Sanguine needs to give and receive affection and uses touches, hugs, and other physical demonstrations of love toward others. She is highly energetic and prefers to maintain an active, fast-paced lifestyle. Always seeking attention and approval, she has a strong desire to be popular with everyone.

## A Note about the Social Profile

The social profile outlines your needs and desires for light friendships, work/career associations, and other casual relationships. By comparing the social profile with your current life situation, you can understand conflict areas and achieve a comfortable level of interpersonal contact in work or social environment. For helpful hints on overcoming potential barriers, see page xx.

*Remember:* The social profile should be applied only to the individual's casual social/career contacts. To determine the individual's needs and desires in close personal relationships, please consult the relationship profile.

*Criteria for Friendships.* The Sanguine is exceptionally enthusiastic about life and prefers to associate with those who share their need for energetic, fun-filled activities. She values people who share her excellent communication abilities and is attracted to people who express the immense love, and approval she craves. While she usually avoids hostile or rejecting people, she is accepting of all types of people, and may have unlimited numbers of friends and acquaintances. The Sanguine frequently initiates friendships and organizes social events, and is usually the center of attention. She is attracted to stable people for in-depth or long-term relationships.

***Perception of Self.*** Optimistic and enthusiastic about life, the Sanguine tends to focus on her successes in and ignore her failures. She projects self-confidence but fears rejection and loss of approval in her struggle against low self-esteem and insecurities. She needs constant reassurance that she is approved and accepted and uses her strong social skills and regular activity to defend against her fear of rejection. The Sanguine possesses a high need to project the "right" image to others and gain their approval. She may unconsciously assume different roles to please people and be unaware of her inner needs and desires. Often responding to environmental stimuli rather than inward convictions, the Sanguine stays active consistently, often because people contact allows her little time for self-introspection.

***Perception by Others.*** Friendly and open, even with strangers, the Sanguine exhibits contagious excitement about life and attracts many people by her warmth, empathy, and readily expressed approval of others. She possesses an innate ability to make people feel loved and valued. They are just naturally attracted to about everyone. Usually, the center of attention, in most settings, she uses her excellent verbal communication skills and sense of humor to dominate conversations. She has a strong need to please and assist people and is willing to listen, do favors, and encourage anyone who needs help. Her high energy level and enthusiasm may be overwhelming to less extroverted people. At times, the Sanguine may unintentionally exaggerate and appear demanding and manipulative.

***Perception of Others.*** The Sanguine genuinely likes and accepts people and is responsive to their needs, focusing on their positive qualities rather than their faults. She is compassionate, identifying easily with the feelings of others. She gives many positive reinforcements to people, freely expressing praise and compliments, even to strangers. The Sanguine needs constant verbal feedback that her behavior is correct and is alert to verbal cues indicating acceptance or rejection by others. She can be susceptible to peer pressure and may go along with an individual or group even if the behavior conflicts with her values. She may allow herself to be depleted and exhausted by the demands of others.

***Intellectual Orientation.*** Although the Sanguine possesses good mental abilities, they understand people better than ideas and concepts. She has a short attention span and is very responsive to outside stimuli; as a result, her environment may easily distract her. The Sanguine decision-making can be impulsive, and is based on emotions and people's needs rather than on consequences. Sanguine do not have to put a lot of time into analyzing things or situations to decide. They don't complicate when it comes to making decisions. For them, life is quite simple and straightforward. She lives in the present, may not learn from past Mistakes, and may postpone goal setting and plan for the future.

***Emotional Orientation.*** The Sanguine is emotionally open and expressive with most people and can become "high" and excited by contacts with others. Usually cheerful and optimistic, she laughs, and cries easily and may appear emotionally volatile at times. She may be hot-tempered and expresses anger verbally, but she quickly forgives and forgets and rarely internalizes rage or holds a grudge. Sanguine is jealous when attention is shown to someone else and not them. If their needs for consideration and approval are frustrated, she may become bitter and hostile. Although she prefers recognition for good behavior, she can use negative behaviors crying, pouting, and tantrums to get attention or even adopt destructive habits. The Sanguine is rarely depressed and can improve her mood by a change of environment. She often expresses the desire to enhance behaviors but may lack the self-discipline to implement her good intentions. She may become anxious through forced inactivity or if she is required to spend much time alone.

***Work Orientation.*** Relationship-oriented with an excellent ability to inspire and motivate people, the Sanguine has an outstanding promotional capacity and excellent verbal skills. She excels in communication and interpersonal relationships but is easily bored with tasks, systems, and routine work. She can assume many responsibilities and be generous for others. At the same time, she may have difficulty directing energies toward task completion and tends to be impractical and disorganized. The Sanguine has excellent leadership abilities and is a strong motivator as part of a team. Sanguine possesses differing needs for *independence* and *dependence* when it comes to their vocation. She is influential in groups, valued by others for her ability to help people work together. She has a high energy level and needs constant activity. Always seeking recognition for her accomplishments, the Sanguine needs frequent opportunities to interact with people in her employment setting. Note, however, that she may have difficulty working under authoritarian leadership or in a highly structured environment. She will have trouble staying out of close relationships, and often she will make her leadership decisions based on the level of the relationship with that particular person. Sanguine need affirmation and are quick to have their friendlier coworkers positioned to work with them.

***Motivation.*** Motivated by the need for approval, above all the Sanguine craves to be recognized and loved just for being herself. Sanguine have little desire to be rewarded with money or possessions. Their most important motivation is having people around her like her. That is their biggest motivation. She also is motivated by her fear of losing recognition or approval and as a result, adjusts her behavior to meet people's expectations. Motivation, of course, can cause significant complications in her job and career.

***Rejection/Acceptance Profile.*** The Sanguine exhibits an intense fear of rejection and needs extensive social interaction to meet the constant need for approval. She is unwilling to hurt others by rejecting them and conveys unconditional love and acceptance. She will even come to the defense of others if you talk negatively about them in their absence and she will offer alibis for them or corrections to your statements about them. She reacts as if you are talking about her, but she is defending the person that you are speaking to at the moment. If anyone rejects her at any time, she quickly forms new friendships and moves on in life and dismissed the former relationship. She may have hurt feelings and feel terminated for a period but promptly adjusts and gets involved in a new relationship.

## The Leadership Profile – Sanguine

| Introvert | | 0 | 1 | 2 | 3 | 4 | 5 | 6 | 7 | 8 | 9 | Extrovert |
|---|---|---|---|---|---|---|---|---|---|---|---|---|
| | | | | | | | | | | | | |
| • *Demonstrated* | | | | | | | | | | | X | |
| • *Desired* | | | | | | | | | | | X | |

In considering the Sanguine leadership profile, we need to look at some factors, beginning with leadership needs and desires.

## SANGUINE IN LEADERSHIP

| Temperament (out of 3,449 people) | # People | Social | # People | Leadership | # People | Relationship |
|---|---|---|---|---|---|---|
| Introverted Sanguine | 345 | 10.00% | 26 | 0.75% | 362 | 10.50% |
| Introverted Sanguine Compulsive | 55 | 1.59% | 4 | 0.12% | 71 | 2.06% |

### A Note about the Leadership Profile

The adult leadership profile identifies the individual's ability to provide leadership, make decisions, and assume responsibilities. This profile outlines the individual's needs and desires for independence, achievement, and recognition. Because leadership needs and desires are expressed through socializing with people, the leadership profile should not be evaluated alone. It's interpreted with either the Social profile or the Relationship profile.

– Evaluated together, the leadership profile and the social profile help determine the individual's career needs. By comparing the results with the individual's current employment situation, you can target conflict areas and help the individual maximize career skills.

– Evaluated together, the leadership profile and the relationship profile help determine the individual's independence-dependence needs in close relationships. By comparing the results with the individual's current life situation, you can target conflict areas and help the individual enhance relationships.

***Leadership Needs and Desires.*** The Sanguine possesses differing needs for *independence* and *dependence.* As a result, her behavior may vary as she tries to satisfy both extremes of needs. Her independence needs include a strong desire to please other people and seek their recognition and approval. To meet these requirements, she can assume many responsibilities and decision-making tasks as well as function as a confident, productive leader. If she does not receive the approval and recognition, she desires, however, she may begin to feel deprived by unmet dependency needs and temporarily abandon her responsibilities, becoming self-indulgent with social activities, hobbies, or avoidance behaviors. Eventually, however, feelings of guilt and worthlessness will drive her back to independence, and she will assume responsibilities until the dependency needs again become overwhelming. The good news is that as she gains an understanding of her needs and behavior patterns, these inconsistencies can change.

I know an individual who, being a Sanguine in leadership, experienced tremendous difficulty in leading because of the **independent vs. dependent** modes of driving. He was with a talent for fifteen years and never really was successful. His peers, as well as the team he was leading, had difficulty with him. The problems were that he would take charge and drive, and then someone or something would challenge him, and he would swing to the dependent side of the Sanguine. When in the dependent mode he would sulk, pout, and disengage from responsibilities and people. Once he was over his adult temper tantrum, he would swing back into his independent mode and retake charge. Emotional swinging causes significant confusion to those serving under him. Being informed of this "swing" characteristic to his temperament, he immediately became angry and said: "Well, I might as well go to work for a rubbish company. That is all I can do, and all I am worth doing is riding on the back of a garbage truck and pick up trash all day long where I don't lead anybody except throw trash cans around." Then he swung back to the independent side and said: "I can't think like that because I do like to lead." He was swinging in that conversation. Sanguine make challenging leaders. It becomes complicated for them as well as those under them. And to top it off, Sanguine are great caring people, and this emotional component even compounds the problem and takes it to a higher level of complexity.

*Criteria for Relationships.* Outgoing and friendly, the Sanguine needs and desires to be with people and may feel *driven* to socialize and interact with others. Enthusiastic about life and accepting of all types of people, she may have an unlimited number of friends and acquaintances—although she prefers those who share her need for energetic, fun-filled activities. She has difficulty being alone for extended periods and avoids initiating individual actions with others. The Sanguine is attracted to people who express the boundless love and approval she craves and shuns hostile or rejecting people. She values individuals who share her excellent communication abilities. In her independent mode, she's drawn to people she can influence, and motivate. In her dependent manner, she wants others to meet her needs and make decisions for her. So, her criteria for relationships in leadership are going to be based on either her independent or her dependent mode. And if you are not in tune with her temperament, then you are not going to understand her.

*Perception of Self.* Optimistic and enthusiastic about life, the Sanguine tends to focus on her successes in and ignore her failures. She projects self-confidence but fears rejection and loss of approval and struggles in with low self-esteem and insecurities. She needs constant reassurance that she is approved and accepted in and uses her strong social skills and regular activity to defend against her fear of rejection. The Sanguine feels a strong need to project the right image to others to gain their approval. She may be unaware of her inner needs and desires and, as a result, unconsciously assume different roles to please people. She often responds to environmental stimuli rather than inward convictions, and her craving for constant activity and population contact allows her little time for self-introspection. She may at times express concern about her cycle of behaviors as she attempts to meet her conflicting needs for independence and dependence—especially when this cycle causes others to disapprove of her. At this point, she becomes despondent and non-productive and withdraws from the relationships and takes a nosedive. She then perceived herself as unwanted and rejected which cause tremendous emotional pain for her.

*Perception by Others.* Friendly and open even with strangers, the Sanguine possesses a contagious excitement about life. She attracts many people by her warmth, empathy, and readily expressed approval toward them. Her innate ability to make people feel loved and valued, coupled with her excellent verbal communication skills and a sense of humor, make her the center of attention in most settings. She tends to dominate many conversations and may unintentionally exaggerate; the Sanguine invented fish stories. She has a strong need to please and assist people and is willing to listen to, do favors for, and encourage anyone who needs her. Sanguine do have a servant's heart if they feel accepted. She also has a strong urge to make people laugh. She thinks that one of her assignments in life is to make people laugh. If she feels that she has something funny to say and gets a laugh out of you the first time telling the story, she will say it a couple more times with just a little different slant to get another laugh out of you. If you are laughing at her jokes, to her that is a sign of acceptance, and she needs approval from everyone if she can get it. Her high energy level and enthusiasm may be overwhelming to less extroverted people—to the point of her appearing demanding and manipulative at times. The less extroverted can only handle so much of her, and then they have to get away from her. Her friends and coworkers may be confused when she alternates between independence and dependence and have hard feelings about assuming the responsibilities she abandons.

***Perception of Others.*** The Sanguine genuinely likes people and is responsive to their needs. She conveys acceptance and focuses on their positive qualities rather than on their faults. Loving and compassionate, she identifies easily with the feelings of others and provides constant positive reinforcement to people. She freely expresses praise and compliments, even to strangers. The Sanguine is keenly alert to verbal cues indicating acceptance or rejection by others and conforms her behavior to please them. If she determines that others are being insensitive, mean, or unfair to another person, present or absent, she will step in and defend them based on her desire to accept everyone. The perception of the group may ventilate toward their leader in a group discussion or at lunch, and the Sanguine will step in and defend the leader. Even if the leader is wrong, the Sanguine will find something good about the leader to share with the group even if she doesn't like the leader herself. She needs frequent verbal feedback that her behavior is "correct" and may cave to peer pressure; if challenged, she may conform to a group's values—even if the action conflicts with her values. This "team's value" type of behavior can become a serious issue of her violating her moral and ethical foundations to the point of jeopardizing her character. Also, she may allow herself to be depleted and exhausted by other people's demands.

***Intellectual Orientation.*** The Sanguine possesses good mental abilities and understands people better than ideas or concepts. They do not respond well to an academic setting and most generally avoid educational settings. Responsive to outside stimuli and often easily distracted by her environment, she has a short attention span. Her decision-making can be impulsive, based on emotions and people's needs rather than on consequences. This, of course, will cause significant conflict for the Sanguine in leadership. The Sanguine lives in the present, may not learn from the past mistakes and may postpone goal setting and plan. These are not good characteristics for the Sanguine in a leadership position.

***Emotional Orientation.*** Emotionally open and expressive with most people, the Sanguine laughs and cries easily and at times may appear emotionally volatile. But while she expresses anger verbally and is hot-tempered, she quickly forgives and forgets and rarely internalizes rage or holds grudges. Then she cannot understand why others still are angry and can't get over the issue. The way she sees it is that they had a clash and now it is over and let's move on. What the Sanguine does not realize is that their temperament is the only one that can "get over" an issue so quickly. Unfortunately, the other four temperaments cannot adjust so soon, and therefore the Sanguine feels rejected even when she has forgiven or agreed to be over the conflict. She can become jealous of the attention given to others, and if her needs for consideration and approval is frustrated, she may become bitter and hostile. If she feels unappreciated, she may slide into the dependent phase of the cycle, where she may feel guilty and worthless. These negative feelings will drive her back to independence. While she prefers recognition for good behavior, she can use negative behaviors (crying, pouting, and tantrums) or adopt destructive habits to get attention. She often expresses the desire to improve her behavior but may lack the self-discipline to implement her good intentions. The Sanguine may become anxious through forced inactivity or if she is required to spend too much time alone.

***Work Orientation.*** The Sanguine is highly relationship-oriented and possesses an excellent ability to inspire and motivate people. With her unique promotional capacity and excellent verbal skills, she excels in communication and interpersonal relationships and can function as an energetic leader and make good decisions. She is influential in groups, valued by others for her ability to help people work together. She has a high energy level and needs constant activity. And although she can assume many responsibilities and be generous for others, she tends to be impractical and disorganized, is easily bored with tasks, systems, and routine work, and may have difficulty completing tasks. The Sanguine needs frequent opportunities to interact with people in her employment setting as well as constant recognition for her accomplishments. If she is criticized or deprived of attention, she may abandon all her projects, and temporarily become dependent. She also may have difficulty working under the authoritarian leadership or in a highly structured environment. Sanguine make excellent "up front" people and have excellent social skills that make them successful in selling, marketing, and motivating people. High cheerleaders. One of their greatest talents is that they do very well in a situation where they do not know anyone present. They have an uncanny way of making everyone they encounter as if they have known them forever.

*Motivation.* Highly motivated by the need for approval, the Sanguine seeks to be recognized and loved only for being herself. And while she has little desire to be rewarded with money or possessions, she is motivated by her fear of losing recognition or approval and quickly adapts her behavior to meet people's expectations. In leadership, this can cause the Sanguine significant problems of permitting their relationships with employees to sabotage the work or goals to gain approval.

*Rejection/Acceptance Profile.* The Sanguine fears rejection and needs extensive social interaction to meet the requirements for adoption. Unwilling to hurt others by rejecting them, they will convey unconditional love and acceptance. Although she remains independent and productive when her efforts produce support and appreciation from people, rejection or criticism by others may trigger her dependent behavior. Rejection causes her to withdrawal and becomes despondent.

**The Relationship Profile - Sanguine**

| Introvert | 0 | 1 | 2 | 3 | 4 | 5 | 6 | 7 | 8 | 9 | Extrovert |
|---|---|---|---|---|---|---|---|---|---|---|---|
| | | | | | | | | | | | |
| • Demonstrated | | | | | | | | | | X | |
| • Desired | | | | | | | | | | X | |

In considering the Sanguine relationship profile, we need to look at some factors, beginning with relationship needs and desires.

## SANGUINE IN RELATIONSHIP

| Temperament (out of 3,449 people) | # People | Social | # People | Leadership | # People | Relationship |
|---|---|---|---|---|---|---|
| Sanguine | 345 | 10.00% | 82 | 2.38% | 362 | 10.50% |
| Sanguine Compulsive | 55 | 1.59% | 26 | 0.75% | 71 | 2.06% |

## A Note about the relationship profile

The adult relationship profile identifies the individual's preferences for emotional involvement in and shared affection on a one-to-one basis. This profile outlines the individual's needs and desires for emotional sharing and relationships. For most people, the relationship profile is the dominant pattern that influences behavior in the social and leadership areas.

By comparing the relationship profile with the individual's current life situation, you can target conflict areas and help them meet their inner needs that are not satisfied.

### Relationship Needs and Desires

A criterion for a relationship indicates the person's preferences in developing and establishing relationships; may identify types of people who are compatible and incompatible with the individual's temperament.

Outgoing and friendly, the Sanguine possesses excellent social skills. She has a strong need and desire to be with people and may feel compulsively driven to socialize and interact with others. Sanguine can become so involved in developing relationships that they wear themselves out physically. They end up "crashing" and can sleep well into the day recovering from the social activities, the social marathon; they just come off. She has difficulty being alone for extended periods and avoids individual actions. The Sanguine needs warm personal relationships with many people and readily initiates and responds to closeness. She has a strong need to give and receive affection and uses many touches, hugs, and other physical demonstrations of love toward others. Enjoying a high energy level, she prefers to maintain an active, fast-paced lifestyle. And, with a great need for attention and approval and an intense craving to be popular with everybody, she needs constant reassurances of love from her close relationships.

**Criteria for Relationships.** Enthusiastic about life and accepting of all types of people, the Sanguine values highly individuals who share her excellent communication abilities and prefers those who share her need for energetic, fun-filled activities. Frequently initiating friendships and organizing social events, she is usually the center of attention and may have unlimited numbers of friends and acquaintances. Being very popular can be a problem area for those other temperaments that become involved with a Sanguine. The Sanguine will have many friends, and this can cause jealousy in the relationships if the Sanguine is in a relationship with someone other than a Sanguine. Sanguine are so open in their dealings that they seem flirtatious, manipulative, and deceiving to the different temperaments. Sanguine are perceived as being promiscuous when, they are just who they are, Sanguine. What you see is what you get. They are transparent individuals who speak the truth, and most people do not understand them because they do not understand people who are so real.

The Sanguine are attracted to supporting individuals who express the unconditional love and approval she craves and usually avoids hostile or rejecting people. She has a strong need to know she is valued by those she loves and are stable, loving people for in-depth or long-term relationships.

**Perception of Self.** Optimistic and enthusiastic about life, the Sanguine tends to focus on her successes in and ignore her failures. She projects self-confidence but struggles with low self-esteem and insecurities and needs constant reassurance that she is approved and accepted. To counter her fears of rejection and loss of approval, she uses her strong social skills to remain active continuously while projecting the "right image" to others. One consequence of her constant activity and people contact is that she has little time for self-introspection so that she may be unaware of her inner needs and desires. Instead, she often responds to environmental stimuli rather than inward convictions and may unconsciously assume different roles to please people.

***Perception by Others.*** Friendly and open even with strangers, the Sanguine exudes a contagious excitement about life and attracts many people by her warmth, empathy, and readily expressed approval toward them. She has an innate ability to make people feel loved and valued. Possessing excellent verbal communication skills as well as a keen sense of humor, she is usually the center of attention and tends to dominate conversations, sometimes unintentionally exaggerating. She has a strong need to please and assist people and is always willing to listen to, do favors for, and encourage anyone who needs her. At the same time, her high energy level and enthusiasm may be overwhelming to less extroverted people, and she can seem manipulative and demanding. Her high need for love and approval may cause tension in close relationships. She can also be perceived as being excessive and exaggerated in many areas of her life. Here is a typical note that a Sanguine would write:

Dear Melaney,

You should never have gone away to school this last year because there has been something new and exciting going on every day. We had a great organization rally in June in the latest addition to the corporate office that has the most beautiful and colorful art pieces I have ever seen. My boss picked it out and asked me my advice before purchasing it. Just after the dedication, we had refreshments and enjoyable social time. Everyone was there.

You and Julie know how I feel about her, tripped and fell and broke her nose. Isn't that funny, Julie with a broken nose. The Ambulance came, and they took her to the hospital, and I followed in my new red Honda that I like. So, will you. At the hospital, I got to meet her doctor. WOW, is he ever a hunk and I think he is single too. I am thinking about asking him for a date. What do you say?

Oh, yea, Billy passed, and I attended his memorial service. His brothers Joe and Phillip were there. I can't remember the other one's name.

Then Kathy found out she had breast cancer and only has a maximum of three years of living. Of course, this is after her father just remarried that woman that everyone is talking about all around town. She is the one we met at the mall last time we went shopping.

I attended Christina's wedding in October, and it was so beautiful. All the people were fashionably dressed and attractive, and the ceremony was breathtaking and the food delicious you would have loved it. Marie even wore a dress instead of blue jeans. Imagine that! I signed your name in the guest book at the wedding because I know how much you wanted to be there. There were so many people they will never know you weren't there. The wedding was the best I've ever been to, with handsome men everywhere. Oh, how I loved flirting with all of them. I even got to dance with the most handsome one there. Bet you can't guess who that was? I will give you a clue. He was our classmate that had the "you know what." Isn't that awesome? I can't wait until you come home so I can fill you in on all the details. It will take me days to "catch you up" on all that has happened while you were away. Got to go, I must get my hair done, polish my nails, and buy a new dress at the "Fashion Bug" for this weekend. See you, Angela

***Perception of Others.*** The Sanguine genuinely likes people and is responsive to their needs. She conveys acceptance of others, focusing on their positive qualities rather than their faults. Highly compassionate, she identifies quickly with the feelings of others. She gives constant positive reinforcement to people, and freely expresses praise and compliments, even to strangers. She may allow herself to become exhausted and exhausted by the demands of others. Alert to verbal cues indicating acceptance or rejection by others, she will alter her behavior to please them. Although she needs frequent verbal feedback that her response is correct and daily reassurances that she is loved, she can be susceptible to peer pressure and may conform to a group's values—even if their behavior conflicts with her values.

***Intellectual Orientation.*** Possessing excellent mental abilities, the Sanguine understands people better than ideas and concepts. She has a short attention span, is responsive to outside stimuli, and can be easily distracted by her environment, often postponing goal setting and planning for the future. Her decision-making can be impulsive, based on emotions and people's needs rather than on consequences. The Sanguine lives in the present and may not learn from her past mistakes. Therefore, she repeats the same mistakes repeatedly. But to them, it is no big deal. They pass it off and say, "So what? Are you perfect in everything you do?" Not accepting responsibility for their repeated negative behavior catches up with them and cause broken relationships and the problem at work.

***Emotional Orientation.*** Emotionally open and expressive with most people, the Sanguine laughs and cries easily and may appear emotionally volatile at times. She honestly expresses her inner needs and emotions and expects others to be emotionally open with her, requiring deep emotional sharing in close relationships. She is usually cheerful and optimistic but may be hot-tempered, expressing anger verbally. The Sanguine rarely internalizes rage or holds grudges but quickly forgives and forgets. At the same time, she may become bitter and hostile if her needs for attention and approval are frustrated or she feels jealous of the attention given to others. Rarely depressed, the Sanguine can improve her mood in by merely changing her environment. She can become "high" and excited by contacts with people, and may become anxious through forced inactivity or if she is required to spend much time alone. While she needs recognition for good behavior, she can use negative behaviors crying, pouting, and tantrums to get attention; she also may adopt destructive habits. She often expresses the desire to improve her practices but may lack the self-discipline to implement her good intentions.

***Motivation.*** Highly motivated for approval, the Sanguine seeks to be recognized and loved for being propelled herself. When she is in a close relationship with someone, and they have a conflict between them, the best thing the significant other can do to stimulate the Sanguine is to tell them they love them regardless of the offense and to hug them and hold them for a time. Once they feel you're genuine toward them, they will emotionally move right back into a good mood. And while she has little desire to be rewarded with money or possessions, she is motivated by her fear of losing recognition or approval from close relationships and quickly adapts her behavior to meet people's expectations.

***Rejection/Acceptance Profile.*** The Sanguine fears rejection by others and needs extensive social interaction and daily assurances of love from her close relationships to meet her constant need for approval. The Sanguine never gets too much love and attention from her close friends and relatives.

If her needs are frustrated, she usually tries harder to win approval; if she feels rejected, she quickly forms new relationships. Unwilling to hurt others by dismissing them, she conveys unconditional love and acceptance.

## Help for the Sanguine
### Characteristics of the Sanguine

#### *Probable Strengths*

- Compassionate – is sensitive, gentle, kind, warm, and friendly; has a great need to give and receive love and attention; cries and forgives easily; make people feel accepted and likes to give and receive hugs and handshakes.
- Outgoing – is the life of the party, warm, friendly; loves to cheer people on and make them laugh; is the most emotional and extroverted of the temperaments.
- Skilled communicator – uses very descriptive and colorful language; is an excellent conversationalist and a great encourager.
- Creative – is talented in developing new projects; loves the arts, music, and entertainment industries.
- Optimistic – lives one day at a time; is enthusiastic and brings experience and humor to the other temperaments.
- Transparent – "what you see is what you get;" is open and honest with thoughts and feelings and tries to help others do the same

#### *Potential Weaknesses*

- Undisciplined – is disorganized and has a short attention span (unless tasks are people-oriented).
- Emotionally volatile – experiences mood swings; when upset can be verbally caustic or use indirect behavior to manipulate or control others
- Impractical – the inability to function as an extrovert or focus their compassion, spontaneity to people, and a great need to give and receive affection and approval can cause them to become impractical or disruptive.
- Egotistical – needs to be the center of attention; use of negative behaviors to gain attention; can become annoying by dominating conversations; tends to exaggerate; pretty color with their adjectives and explanations.
- Unfocused – usually not academically or administratively oriented; don't like to concentrate for extended periods on "things"; prefers "people-oriented" tasks.
- Insecure – has a severe fear of rejection; tends to care about others too deeply, which causes a lot of pain and overreactions.
- Complex – struggles with competing needs for dependence/independence.

## *Decisions for the Sanguine*

Decision making for Sanguine is a straightforward process. They do not need to put a lot of time into making decisions. Issues of life for the Sanguine are quite simple; they don't complicate them.

By now you should have a pretty good idea of what makes a Sanguine tick. People, excitement, colorful attire, fun, and laughter. You also should know that even though the Sanguine is outgoing, upbeat, and confident, she can suffer from a complex of insecurities that, when her needs and desires are left unmet, can make her say things or act in ways that are less than desirable. If you are a Sanguine, here are some things to keep in mind that will help you avoid these pitfalls:

1. ***You are upbeat, open, and friendly.*** It is okay to be confident and transparent with people. As a Sanguine, God created within you a compelling need to be with people. You are like a ray of sunshine when you come into the room. However, you do need to learn to become sensitive to those around you. You need to know that not all people are people-oriented; some people are task-oriented, and cannot relate to you. In your social/vocational relationships, you are regenerated by being with people; individuals with different temperaments may be transformed by quiet, alone time. Learning this will help you become more sensitive to other people's needs and not just focus on your own needs.

   When you cannot be with other people, talking on the phone, listening to the radio, watching television, or reading a romance story will lessen the stress of being alone.

2. ***You will tend to take on the morals of the crowd.*** It is okay to adopt the morals of the group you are with—if the mob has good morals. To keep from being rejected, you will be tempted severely to take on bad morals and say and do things you do not want to say and do, so it is essential that you associate with people of good morals.

   As a Sanguine, you are very emotional, and your emotions will tend to run from high to low. There is no middle of the road. You are either happy as a lark or as depressed as a person stranded on an island by themselves. To remain comfortable, you need to swing and self-indulge—but this needs to be Godly self-indulgence. You must remember that when people reject you, you do not have to say and do things you know are wrong. God's love is consistent, and He will never deny you.

3. ***You are talkative.*** It is okay to be verbose; however, you need to learn that you cannot always be the center of attention. You need to get to share the spotlight. Other temperaments can only take so much of your enthusiasm and "limelight," and if overwhelmed by your constant activity they will get angry, frustrated, and then figure out how to get away from you. Then they will avoid you in the future, and this will be ultimate rejection, which you do not want. So, you must be sensitive and "give" when others can receive and do not overload them with too much of your "bright and cheerful" self. Watch for signs of people's body language that says, "I've had enough of her." Then quietly disengage, and let someone else have the floor for a while and get the attention off you.

   When you are on the job, you should not keep others from doing their work. You tend to want to tell every little thing that happens to you to anyone that is around—whether they listen or not. You need to learn self-discipline and remember that there are a time and a place for socializing, but it is not on company time. That is not being fair to your employer or fellow workers, and it discredits you as a person and as a faithful employee. And it could cost you a job or your promotion.

4. ***You get angry.*** It is okay to get angry, but it is *not* okay to be hot-tempered and fly into a rage. You need to learn to discipline yourself and stop and think before you "fly off the handle." Now that you understand that getting angry is a "temperament tendency," you also need to accept responsibility for managing that trend—it is not okay to smash your fist into a wall or another person or throw a temper tantrum. By understanding your temperament, you now can be more responsible than ever in dealing with your anger in a way that is acceptable to other people and pleasing to God.

## Do's and Don'ts for the Sanguine

| Do | Don't |
| --- | --- |
| • Grow up and try to remember your obligations | • Interrupt or add to others' stories |
| • Face reality; life isn't always a party | • Laugh everything off |
| • Aim for the quiet dignity | • Expect others to protect you forever |
| • Get a personal calendar and keep an updated schedule | • Walk into a room, "talking." |
| • Make easy-to-follow schedules | • Overcommit yourself to too many projects |
| • Learn to make lists | • Be too loud |
| • Find someone who will hold you accountable | • Always be "on stage." |
| • Get to the point; in conversation, limit details | • Control by charm and wit |
| • Plan variety each day | • Become debt-laden |
| • Be on time, aim to be early | • Make a fool of yourself |
| • Concentrate on truth and honesty | • Become a party animal |
| • Finish what you start or delegate so that you can keep commitments | • Become a con artist |
| • Develop sensitivity to others' needs | • Compulsively become a shopaholic |
| • Listen more, talk less | |
| • Draw others out with questions | |
| • Seek a job or have a hobby that can give you a sense of recognition | |
| • Put things back in the same place every time | |
| • Keep track of spending so that you won't become a shopaholic | |
| • Choose one time per week to clean/arrange | |
| • Tone down your volume of speech and laughter | |
| • Realize that talking too loudly and using wild gestures appears foolish | |

Become Aware of Your Natural Strengths and Learn to Use Them Wisely

| Natural Strength | | Strength Carried to the Extreme | | Compulsion |
|---|---|---|---|---|
| | | | | |
| Magnetic personality | | Becomes dependent on charm and wit | | Can become con artist, sociopath |
| | | | | |
| Entertaining storyteller | | Talks constantly | | Must be talking to feel secure |
| | | | | |
| Loves to go shopping | | Buys and charges irrationally | | Becomes debt-laden "shopaholic" |
| | | | | |
| Life of the party | | Too loud, too wild | | Makes a fool of self; becomes party animal |

## How to Recognize Whether Your Child Is a Sanguine?

| Strengths | Weaknesses | Emotional Needs |
|---|---|---|
| *Baby* | | |
| They are bright and wide-eyed; acts curious; gurgles and coos; wants company; shows off; is responsive | Know they are cute; screams for attention | Constant care and affection |
| *Child* | | |
| They are daring and eager; acts innocent; is inventive, imaginative, cheerful, and enthusiastic; is fun-loving; chatters constantly; bounces back; energized by people | Does not follow through; is disorganized and easily distracted; has a short interest span; experiences emotional ups and downs; wants credit for everything he does; tells fibs; is forgetful | Constant attention; approval; |
| *Teen* | | |
| Active cheerleaders; charms others; gets daring; joins clubs; is popular, the life of the party; is creative; wants to please; apologizes frequently | Deceptive; gives creative excuses; is easily led astray; craves attention; needs peer approval; is a "con-artist"; won't study; acts immature; gossips; avoids dull tasks and routines; can't handle criticism; doesn't pay attention to details; has lofty goals | Constant attention; approval; affection; acceptance; the presence of people and activity |

# The Sanguine

- Potential Strengths of the Sanguine Temperament
  - Outgoing
    - Super extrovert
    - Loves the limelight and excels at communication
  - Responsive
    - Very touchy – likes to give hugs and handshakes.
    - Has the ability and capacity to make the person they are talking to feel important.
  - Warm and Friendly
    - They are the life of the party
    - A people-person
    - Appears to be more confident than they are
  - Talkative
    - A good conversationalist
    - Uses many adjectives in conversation, making the discussion colorful
  - Enthusiastic
    - Have no problem starting projects
    - Often in a lively mood
    - A morning person
    - Usually doesn't do much preparing but live for the day and doesn't often learn from mistakes
  - Compassionate
    - A compassionate heart and cries easily
    - Sanguine forgive people easily
- Potential Weaknesses/Shortcomings of the Sanguine Temperament
  - Undisciplined
    - Great appeal for the opposite sex and consequently faces temptations more than others
    - The most significant weakness is a lack of discipline
    - Rarely profits from past mistakes and seldom looks ahead
    - Usually disorganized – garage, bedroom, closet, and office are disaster areas.
    - Usually not a good student because it is hard for them to concentrate for extended periods
    - If not in the limelight, can be a great procrastinator
    - Terrible record keeper
  - Emotionally Unstable
    - The only temperament more emotional than the Sanguine is the Melancholy (but they are not as expressive)
    - Cries when watching a sad movie on TV
    - Discouraged easily and can drift into a pattern of excusing their weaknesses or feeling sorry for themselves
    - Lack of emotional consistency usually limits him vocationally, and it indeed destroys him spiritually

- Unproductive
  - Often impractical and disorganized
  - Easily excited and tends to run off half-cocked in the wrong direction
  - Very active, but their activity usually produces little results.
- Egocentric or Egotistical
  - Sharp dresser
  - Can become obnoxious by dominating not just the significant part of the conversation but all of it
  - Tends to talk more and more about themselves and are occupied with the things that are of interest to them and think others are equally interested in them
  - Every human is plagued with egotism, but the Sanguine has a double dose of the problem
  - Exaggerates – Fish stories were invented by the Sanguine

## Popular Sanguine

Popular Sanguine talks too much

- Let another talk also
- Talk less
- Watch for signs of boredom
- Condense your comments
- Stop exaggerating

Popular Sanguine are self-centered

- Be sensitive to other people's interests
- Learn to listen to

Popular Sanguine has uncultivated memories

- Pay attention to names
- Don't repeat so often
- Write things down
- Don't forget the children

Popular Sanguine are unpredictable and inclined to forget the friendship

- Read the body language of others and their needs for relationship
- Put others needs first
- Realize that people like you
- Don't ignore your commitments

Popular Sanguine interrupt and answer for others

- Don't think you must always fill the gap
- Give others time to speak for themselves

Popular Sanguine are disorganized and immature

- Pull your life together
- Grow up

## STRENGTH AND WEAKNESSES
### of the
### SANGUINE

| STRENGTHS | WEAKNESSES |
|---|---|

**EMOTIONS:**

| STRENGTHS | WEAKNESSES |
|---|---|
| Appealing personality | Compulsive talker |
| Talkative, storyteller | Exaggerates and elaborates |
| Life of the party | Dwells on trivia |
| Good sense of humor | Cannot remember names |
| Memory for color | Scares others off |
| Physically holds on to listener | So happy for some |
| Emotional and demonstrative | Has restless energy |
| Enthusiastic and expressive | Egotistical |
| Cheerful and bubbling over | Blusters and complaints |
| Curious | Naïve gets taken in |
| Right on stage | Has a loud voice and laugh |
| Wide-eyed and innocent | Controlled by circumstances |
| Lives in the present | Get angry easily |
| Changeable disposition | Seems phony to some |
| Sincere at heart | Never grow up |

**WORK:**

| STRENGTHS | WEAKNESSES |
|---|---|
| Volunteers for jobs | Would rather talk |
| Thinks up new activities | Forgets obligations |
| Looks great on the surface | Does not follow through |
| Creative and colorful | Confidence fades fast |
| Has energy and enthusiasm | Undisciplined |
| Starts in a flashy way | Priorities out of order |
| Inspires others to join | Decides by feelings |
| Charms others to work | Easily distracted |
|  | Wastes time talking |

**FRIENDS:**

| STRENGTHS | WEAKNESSES |
|---|---|
| Makes friends easily | Hates to be alone |
| *Loves people* | Needs to be center stage |
| Thrives on compliments | Wants to be popular |
| Seems exciting | Looks for credit |
| Envied by other | Dominates conversations |
| Doesn't hold grudges | Interrupts and doesn't listen |
| Apologizes quickly | Answers for others |
| Prevents dull moments | Fickle and forgetful |
| Likes spontaneous activities | Makes excuses |
|  | Repeats stories |

## Temperament Strengths of the Sanguine

| | | |
|---|---|---|
| Animated | – | Full of life, active use of the hand, arm, and face gestures. |
| Playful | – | Full of fun and good humor. |
| Sociable | – | One who sees being with others as an opportunity to be cute and entertaining rather than as a challenge or business opportunity. |
| Convincing | – | Can win you over to anything through the sheer charm of his personality. |
| Refreshing | – | Renews and stimulates or makes others feel good. |
| Spirited | – | Full of life and excitement. |
| Promoter | – | Urges or compels others to go along, join, or invest through the charm of his personality. |
| Spontaneous | – | Prefers all of life to be impulsive, unpremeditated activity, not restricted by plans. |
| Optimistic | – | Sunny disposition who convinces himself and others that everything will turn out all right. |
| Funny | – | A sparkling sense of humor that can make virtually any story into a hilarious event. |
| Delightful | – | A person who is upbeat and fun to be around. |
| Cheerful | – | Consistently in good spirits and promoting happiness in others. |
| Inspiring | – | Encourages others to work, join, or be involved, and makes the whole thing fun. |
| Demonstrative | – | Openly expresses emotion, especially affection, and doesn't hesitate to touch others while speaking to them. |
| Mixes Easily | – | Loves a party and can't wait to meet everyone in the room, never meets a stranger. |
| Talker | – | Constantly talking, telling funny stories, and entertaining everyone around, feeling the need to fill the silence to make others comfortable. |
| Lively | – | Full of life, vigorous, energetic. |
| Cute | – | Precious, adorable, center of attention. |
| Fashionable | – | Life of the party and therefore much desired as a party guest. |
| Bouncy | – | A bubbly, lively personality, full of energy. |

## Temperament Weaknesses of the Sanguine

| | | |
|---|---|---|
| Brassy | – | Showy, flashy, comes on strong, too loud. |
| Undisciplined | – | A person whose lack of order permeates almost every area of his life. |
| Repetitious | – | Retells stories and incidents to entertain you without realizing he has already told the story several times before, is always needing something to say. |
| Forgetful | – | Lack of memory, which is usually tied to a lack of discipline and not bothering to record things that aren't fun mentally. |
| Interrupts | – | A person who is more of a talker than a listener, who starts speaking without even realizing someone else is already talking. |
| Unpredictable | – | Maybe ecstatic one moment and down the next, or willing to help but then disappears, or promises to come but forgets to show up. |
| Haphazard | – | Has no consistent way of doing things. |

| | | |
|---|---|---|
| Permissive | – | Allows others (including children) to do as they please to keep from being disliked. |
| Anger Easily | – | One who has a childlike flash-in-the-pan temper that expresses itself in tantrum style and is over and forgotten instantly. |
| Naive | – | Childlike and straightforward perspective lacking sophistication or comprehension of what the deeper levels of life are. |
| Wants Credit | – | Thrives on the creditor approval of others. As an entertainer, this person feeds on the applause, laughter, and acceptance of an audience. |
| Talkative | – | An entertaining, compulsive talker who finds it difficult to listen. |
| Unsystematic | – | Lack of ability to ever get life in order. |
| Inconsistent | – | Erratic, contradictory, with actions and emotions not based on logic. |
| Messy | – | Living in a state of disorder, unable to find things. |
| Show-Off | – | Needs to be the center of attention, wants to be watched. |
| Loud | – | A person whose laugh or voice can be heard above others in the room. |
| Scatter-Brained | – | Lacks the power of concentration or attention, flighty. |
| Restless | – | Likes constant new activity because it isn't fun to do the same things all the time. |
| Changeable | – | A child-like, short attention span that needs a lot of change and variety to keep from getting bored. |

*Wow! No more worrying about whom to hire! Is this the right person or is that the right person? WIDP hit the nail right on the head. It told me precisely who the right person was to fill the job. It worked.*

*What a cost saver. What a time, saver. Never again will I go through the anguish of not being sure. WIDP has made a believer out of me.*

*MARTIN ANDERHOLM, PRESIDENT,
ANDERHOLM PRESS, INC., ORANGE, MA*

# CHAPTER 6

# THE PHLEGMATIC

David has always been able to get along with everyone. He is confident, well spoken, and an excellent conversationalist, equally comfortable talking or listening. David is patient, kind, and an excellent listener who empathizes with other people's problems. At parties and social events, he carries on just as quickly with the dominant, outgoing types as he does the quiet "wallflowers." If things stay on an even keel, David will participate in the conversation. If a conflict arises, however, he will use his dry wit and sarcastic sense of humor to smooth things out; if he is unsuccessful, he will quickly leave the area of the conflict and, if necessary, the entire social event. In a nutshell, David is the kind of person everyone likes to have around. Why, might you ask? Because David is a peace-loving person and he will not cause conflict, thus everybody likes to be around them. They are light and humorous and like to tell good stories and jokes. Phlegmatic make great comedians and politicians.

At work, David keeps his nose to the grindstone most of the time. Meticulous and systematic, David produces quality work consistently. He is not what you would call a "take-charge" guy, and usually, prefers to reach consensus rather than make decisions on his own. While he has personally developed some processes that have improved efficiency in his office, David does not like it when he is forced to adopt new procedures or change his behavior. When it comes to change in anything, "time" is a significant component to David. He does not like quick change and can be extremely resistant to change of any kind. The best way to get agreement from the Phlegmatic when it comes to change is to give them plenty of advanced notice and give them time to think it through. Change to them means work, and they do not want more work, nor do they want you doing more work for them. Remember! It has to do with their physical and mental energy resources. In his relationships, David is very committed and trustworthy. Although he rarely goes overboard when it comes to showing his emotions—that is, he does not "come on strong" or "shower" anyone with affection—he does give and will receive moderate amounts of love from his close relationships. While David has a lot of acquaintances and casual friends, they have very few close friends. It is not that Phlegmatic does not have people in his life that could be and would be close friends; it is a lack of energy. Phlegmatic people have deficient energy levels, and they are always protecting their involvement as it may require them to expend more power than they want.

"Moderation" is a keyword for the Phlegmatic. Phlegmatic is the only temperament that does not have extremes, or as we say, "they are not compulsive" like the other four temperaments can be. However, it has been said about the Phlegmatic that they are "compulsive about not being compulsive!"

In other words, they are not going to be excessively outgoing and expressive, nor are they going to isolate themselves from people and social activities for extended periods. They will "moderately" express themselves socially, and then they will "moderately" disengage from individuals and social events and head for their quiet place. They are like chameleons: they change personalities based on the environment of and the people around them. They are like a pendulum in a clock. They swing back and forth from being an introvert and not wanting to be around people to be an extrovert and need to be around people. It all depends on their level of energy at the time that determines which "mode" they will be in where people are concerned.

David is a Phlegmatic. Calm, friendly, humorous, and dependable, he will tend to avoid conflict at all cost. Usually, this means using his objective, practical, peaceful nature to solve issues with other people diplomatically. If diplomacy fails, however, the Phlegmatic will either clam up—or turn and run.

In general, the Phlegmatic does not become angry quickly or express much anger. When they do become angry, they tend to minimize it, so they do not have to deal with it. If pushed to the limit by someone trying to motivate him to do something he does not want to do, he will dig in his heels and will not budge. As a side note on the Phlegmatic not budging—well, it is worse than that. When a Phlegmatic decides they are not going to yield, they come to a place where Phlegmatic cannot choose to change their mind because they are so entrenched. Anger is a very unusual characteristic of the Phlegmatic, but they are the only temperament having this feature. They also will use his dry sense of humor or witty remarks to "block the demands" of others. Everyday life is draining to a Phlegmatic, and they do not want to deal with anything more than what is necessary—including anger, which is at the top of their list.

When the Phlegmatic does become angry, it affects him physically, emotionally, and spiritually.

*Physically.* The Phlegmatic will expend energy at this point to negotiate a peaceful solution or motivate someone else to handle the situation. Frustration may cause them to overeat as a way of dealing with the pressures that others try to exert over them. He would rather sit and eat than expend precious energy. This inappropriate response to anger makes the Phlegmatic susceptible to heart problems, high blood pressure, and anxiety. They need downtime to rest, recuperate, and rebuild their physical strength. Recovery could take several days depending on the level of physical strength lost.

*Emotionally.* The Phlegmatic "feathers are not easily ruffled," so they express few emotions. Phlegmatic do not get angry, not often. I am not saying that they do not get mad because they do get upset. When a Phlegmatic gets angry, their anger intensifies because they are crazy that they are being forced into a corner to become inflamed. To the Phlegmatic, getting angry "causes too much-expended energy for them." So many times, what happens to the Phlegmatic is that their depression drives them to seek medical assistance. Hence, they end up taking some depressive medication(s). Taking medication only exacerbates the situation and causes them to function outside of the normal range of emotions because their true feelings are clouded because of the effects of the drugs.

*Spiritually.* The Phlegmatic may tend to rest and sleep to reserve their low energy rather than to spend time studying Scripture and praying. Once the Phlegmatic is angered, they require a considerable amount of time to regroup spiritually and get their spiritual equilibrium back. They feel "out of touch" with their spiritual side.

Applicable Scriptures:

*The Lord will give strength unto his people; the Lord will bless his people with peace. (Psalm 29:11, NASB95)*

*The Lord is my strength and my shield; my heart trusted in him, and I am helped: therefore, my heart greatly rejoiceth; and with my song will I praise him. (Psalm 28:7, NASB)*

Because the Phlegmatic can usually negotiate their way through anger and thus they do not have to expend substantial energy to deal with it, of the five temperaments Phlegmatic is the least prone to experience stress because of anger. As stated above, whatever weight they do have will influence them to overeat or sleep excessively. During this period, when they are recovering from the wrath, they are prone to displaying characteristics of depression. They need to give themselves time to recover from that last anger bout. This passion may take a couple of days or a couple of weeks. In the meantime, they will do their best to avoid the person who made them angry for fear of another bout of emotional expression causing them more distress. They become gun-shy of the person or persons that made them angry.

## The Phlegmatic – Demonstrated vs. Desired Behavior

The Phlegmatic is a very even-keeled individual. As the chart shows, they are very moderate in both *demonstrated* and *desired* behavior. In other words, they are neither highly introverted nor extroverted, and desires to (1) give moderate amounts to others and (2) receive moderate amounts from others in all three of the three areas of the WIDP profile.

| Introvert | 0 | 1 | 2 | 3 | 4 | 5 | 6 | 7 | 8 | 9 | Extrovert |
|---|---|---|---|---|---|---|---|---|---|---|---|
| | | | | | | | | | | | |
| **Social** | | | | | | | | | | | |
| • *Demonstrated* | | | | | X | X | | | | | |
| • *Desired* | | | | | X | X | | | | | |
| **Leadership** | | | | | | | | | | | |
| • *Demonstrated* | | | | | X | X | | | | | |
| • *Desired* | | | | | X | X | | | | | |
| **Relationship** | | | | | | | | | | | |
| • *Demonstrated* | | | | | X | X | | | | | |
| • *Desired* | | | | | X | X | | | | | |

Let's take a look at the three areas of the WIDP profile—social/vocational, leadership, and relationship—to see what makes the Phlegmatic tick.

## PHLEGMATIC IN SOCIAL

| Temperament (out of 3,449 people) | # People | Social | # People | Leadership | # People | Relationship |
|---|---|---|---|---|---|---|
| Phlegmatic | 133 | 3.86% | 65 | 1.88% | 318 | 9.22% |
| Phlegmatic Compulsive | NA | NA | NA | NA | NA | NA |

### Phlegmatic in Social

We are studying some of the actions and motives of the five social/vocational areas. In the last issue, we explored the Sanguine. At this point, we will examine the Phlegmatic in social/vocational— Identifying the Actions/Motives for Meeting Temperament Needs of a Phlegmatic in Social/Vocational. In the next issue, we will be studying the actions/motives of the Melancholy in social/vocational.

The social/vocational area encompasses the mental energies and surface relationships.

The following words describe a Phlegmatic in social/vocational:

In review, social/vocational is the need to establish and maintain a satisfactory relationship with people in the area of casual relationships, association, and socialization. This area also encompasses a person's mental energies.

### Phlegmatic in Social

P eacemaker

H omebody

L ow-energy

E ven-keeled

G uarded

M ediator

A damant

T eammate

I ndependent

C apable

A Phlegmatic in social/vocational does not express lots of anger because they are not easily angered. When they do become angry, they tend to minimize it, so they do not have to deal with it.

If Phlegmatic are pushed to the limit by someone who is trying to motivate them to do something, they do not want to do, they will dig in their heels and will not budge. Also, they will use their dry sense of humor/witty remarks to "block the demands" of others, then obstinance surfaces followed by passive aggression. Everyday life is draining to a Phlegmatic in social/vocational, and they do not want to deal with anything more than what is necessary especially anger. But remember this: if you push the Phlegmatic to far, they can explode on you and the situation in a manner that will cause havoc. Don't cross a Phlegmatic! They are normative individuals; keep them sane and peaceful—Phlegmatic are friendly people.

The Phlegmatic in social/vocational will not mind going out and socializing with the Choleric in social/vocational because the Phlegmatic in social/vocational does not want to expend the energy to carry the "weight" of socializing.

The only problem that the Phlegmatic and the Choleric in social/vocational would have is when the Choleric was trying to inspire the Phlegmatic to undertake socializing.

The Phlegmatic would hold off the Choleric in social/vocational by using their sense of humor. The Phlegmatic would irritate the Choleric (who likes to be in control of the situation), and the Choleric would "punish" the Phlegmatic in social/vocational. He would punish the Phlegmatic by withholding himself and being "cool." However, in time, the Choleric would realize that this did not bother the Phlegmatic in social/vocational as much as it would any other temperaments. The Phlegmatic is the only temperament that can "ruffle the feathers" of a Choleric in social/vocational.

To save from being embarrassed when socializing with the Phlegmatic in social/vocational, the Choleric must learn that the Phlegmatic cannot be manipulated.

The Phlegmatic are task-oriented, slow-paced, calm, relaxed going, observers, tolerant of people, have "dry" sense of humor, are selfish, incredibly stubborn, and efficient.

A definition of motive is an incentive to action.

**The Phlegmatic's primary need in social/vocational is to protect their low energy level.**

In determining how these significant needs get met, we need to ascertain:

What is the action?
What is the apparent motive?
What is the real purpose?

**One:**     **What is the action?** This noninvolvement with life.
They would rather stay at home and not get involved in most social events. Sometimes they will procrastinate until it is too late to rsvp or attend.

**Apparent Motive:** They do not like to be with people.

People send them invitations to attend social functions, and many times, they do not respond. They will procrastinate, hoping the people would forget they invited them.

**Actual Purpose:** To preserve their low energy level:

They have a shallow energy level, and they try to protect it. They are "tired" before most of the other temperaments get started!

**Two:**     **What is the action?** They use their "dry" sense of humor.

When they are asked to do something, they do not want to do, they can hold people off by using their humor. When we say "dry" humor, we mean little remarks that seem to be automatic responses. It is their way of warding off a yes or no answer. In other words, they use their humor as a way to avoid committing.

**Apparent Motive:** They do not want to be with people.

It is not that they do not want to be with people; it is just that interacting with people taps their energy reserve.

**Actual Purpose:** To preserve their low energy level.

If they do for others, they have no energy left for themselves. Attending a social function, after a day at work, will further drain their already low energy supply. They need to learn how to maintain balance in this area—taking on social functions on the weekend when they do not have to get up and go to work.

**Three:** **What is the action?** Negotiating peace—at all cost.

If a problem arises, their first thought is, "Let's work this out now so that we do not have to call a meeting."

**Apparent Motive:** To help people solve their problems.

People will come to them with their problems because they know they will have a solution.

**Actual Purpose:** To preserve their low energy level.

By being a negotiator, they can help resolve conflicts before they become a significant problem. This way, they can reserve their energy level.

A Phlegmatic in social/vocational needs to evaluate their motives; they need to ask themselves:

1. Am I doing this for self?
2. Am I doing this for the Lord?

PHLEGMATICS IN SOCIAL/VOCATIONAL ARE "You-I" PEOPLE: They like the concept of "you do it' I will tell you how" syndrome – They like to tell people "how to" so that they do not "have to."

You make the most sales; I will tell you how…
You deal with the problem; I will tell you how…
You attend the social event; I will sit at home…

Scripture: Blessed are the peacemakers; for they shall be called the children of God. (Matthew 5:9, KJV)

Applicable Scripture: And let us not be weary in well doing: for in due season we shall reap, if we faint not, (Galatians 6:9, KJV)

**IN CONCLUSION:**

Phlegmatic in social/vocational need to learn to maintain balance in this area; they can be so protective of their low energy levels that they become noninvolved. They need to put forth an effort to attend a minimal amount of functions—not for themselves as much as for their family and friends; otherwise, they will tend to pull away from everyone.

Phlegmatic in social/vocational need to come to the knowledge that God loves them. He does not expect them to attend all functions they are invited to, but God does need them to stay involved in life. Just like all the other temperaments, they are a vital part of the Body of Christ.

Please remember these are temperament tendencies and, as always, while you are counseling the Phlegmatic in social/vocational, you must take into consideration their walk with the Lord, learned behavior, personality and birth order.

## The Social/Vocational Profile – Phlegmatic

| Introvert | | 0 | 1 | 2 | 3 | 4 | 5 | 6 | 7 | 8 | 9 | Extrovert |
|---|---|---|---|---|---|---|---|---|---|---|---|---|
| | | | | | | | | | | | | |
| • *Demonstrated* | | | | | | | X | X | | | | |
| • *Desired* | | | | | | | X | X | | | | |

In considering the Phlegmatic social/vocational profile, we need to look at some factors, beginning with social needs and desires.

***Social Needs and Desires.*** The Phlegmatic possesses excellent social skills and a keen ability to interact well with all types of people. They are flexible and can adapt quickly to being alone or having a moderate interaction with people. They have a strong need to maintain a peaceful, nondemanding lifestyle, and is comfortable with or without social interaction. The Phlegmatic is content with whatever situation he encounters and tends to accept the status quo in life. They are conservative in their attachments and expectations of people. Because the Phlegmatic possesses a low energy reserve, they choose to expend their available energy on tasks rather than relationships. They need a quiet lifestyle and structured daily routine and may direct much of their behavior toward avoiding fatigue.

## A Note about the Social Profile

The social profile outlines your needs and desires for light friendships, work/career associations, and other casual relationships. By comparing the social profile with your current life situation, you can understand conflict areas and achieve a comfortable level of interpersonal contact in work or social environment.

***Remember:*** The social profile should be applied only to the individual's casual social/career contacts. To determine the individual's needs and desires in close personal relationships, please consult the relationship profile.

***Criteria for Friendships.*** Friendly and sociable, the Phlegmatic genuinely likes people and is free from urgent needs, fear of rejection, low self-esteem, and other barriers to relationships. Because people tend to drain their energy, they avoid extensive social interaction and remains uninvolved in life, preferring to be a spectator instead of an active participant. While they depend on others to initiate social interactions and friendships and maintain relationships with them, they readily participate when invited and is faithful and committed to friends and coworkers.

*Perception of Self.* Confident and self-contained, the Phlegmatic possesses good self-esteem and a healthy self-image. He is usually satisfied with his abilities and accomplishments and remains secure in believing his own opinions and perceptions are correct. He maintains a practical approach to life and people and is calm and complacent and rarely introspective. Despite his ideas and abilities, however, his need to protect his energy reserve may cause him to be an underachiever, unconcerned about reaching his potential in life.

*Perception by Others.* The Phlegmatic appears calm and stable, even under pressure. Others usually perceive them as friendly and understanding, one who finds humor in most situations. Their ability to relate well to people, including hostile or difficult personalities, makes them an accomplished diplomat and a natural negotiator who can often bring objectivity and peace into troubled situations. At the same time, while they are skilled in helping people resolve conflicts, they avoid personal involvement in any conflict situation. They are nonassertive and nonconfrontational and uses their excellent verbal skills, especially sarcastic humor, as a defense. Their ability to make people laugh is an intrinsic natural gift that assists them in keeping out of trouble or conflict with others within their environment. They can hold an audience in stitches very quickly, and they will never crack a smile. Therefore, they are perceived by others as very friendly and funny and easy to be around.

*Perception of Others.* The Phlegmatic is an empathetic listener, compassionate, and understanding of others. He is usually very patient, willing to assist and encourage other people. He is accepting of people and views others positively, remaining tolerant of their faults and mistakes. He avoids overinvolvement in the lives and activities of others and maintains some distance even in close relationships. He may become critical of those who attempt to change or control him and needs recognition and appreciation for his efforts from those people in his environment.

*Intellectual Orientation.* Possessing high mental abilities, the Phlegmatic carefully gathers facts and considers options before deciding; they rarely change their mind once they have formed an opinion. Remember, a critical issue with the Phlegmatic is that they need time to adjust to any change. You cannot "spring" an idea on them and expect them to endorse whatever the plan may be. It is essential to give them time to process the idea of change before they make the transition, and even then, you may experience resistance from them. Why? Because change takes energy and they are all set with expending their energy on your ideas. Objective, practical, highly self-disciplined, consistent, and dependable, the Phlegmatic quickly identifies problems and inequities and inspires others to develop solutions. They have strong principles of correctness and accuracy. Phlegmatic is well thought out, a matter of fact, and severe in their proceedings.

*Emotional Orientation.* Emotionally stable, the Phlegmatic usually remains cheerful and calm, avoiding extremes of emotional expression and using a sense of humor as a defense. They are not prone to moodiness or depression and, while they experience strong emotions, they do not express them easily. They rarely become angry or suffers "hurt feelings" and usually avoids confrontation, attempting to maintain peace in every situation. They may become anxious or fearful when faced with change, when people make excessive demands on him, or when placed in conflict situations—even if he is not directly involved. The stress of any kind will rob the Phlegmatic of their energy. They need to learn to replenish their energy by taking "power naps" when they have no energy left. If only for ten or fifteen minutes, it will restore them and get them back on track emotionally.

*Work Orientation.* The Phlegmatic is task-oriented rather than people-oriented. Phlegmatic is organized, and often they are very good at their job; he thinks things through very thoroughly in his approach to tasks, is accurate and precise in his work, and a perfectionist about details. He handles routine or tedious assignments efficiently, maintains a slow, steady work pace, and consistently produces excellent results. The Phlegmatic is disciplined and efficient and draws his excellent self-concept from his successful job performance. While the Phlegmatic ideal career involves tasks, not people, he relates well to people for periods, is willing to accommodate coworkers, and readily assists when asked. He adapts well to those in authority and can be a capable leader, although he does not often seek leadership roles, and may prefer to work independently or as part of a team. The Phlegmatic needs reassurance from others before assuming responsibilities and is both conservative in his approach and unlikely to take risks. He functions best in a stable, controlled work environment, where his relaxed style brings harmony to his work area and provides stability to teams composed of varied work styles. He may procrastinate when faced with decision-making and can be stubborn and resistant to change, even if the changes will bring improvement. Because he is so meticulous about his performance and spends a considerable amount of energy in adhering to strict requirements, he may be exhausted by the end of the day. He is an 8:00 AM to 4:30 PM employee and will punch in at 7:59 AM and punch out at precisely 4:30 PM. Overtime is not in his vocabulary unless everyone is working overtime with him. He is the kind of employee that will stay in the same job for thirty to forty years doing the same thing every day and look forward to his gold watch and retirement.

*Motivation.* The Phlegmatic is self-motivated but needs to be convinced intellectually before acting. They have a strong desire to avoid conflict or change and is seldom motivated by outside influences to change. They may change his behavior to avoid conflict (punishment) or achieve peace (reward). The best way to describe a Phlegmatic is that they are deliberate and have only one pace, and they determined what that speed will be.

*Rejection/Acceptance Profile.* The Phlegmatic does not fear rejection or need acceptance by others, and rarely uses dismissal against others. They do not take rejection personally and possesses an excellent ability to make people feel accepted. Put bluntly; they do not care what or how you think about them, and will not let how you feel or think to determine their value. They are not moved by what you believe and reason.

### The Leadership Profile – Phlegmatic

| Introvert | | 0 | 1 | 2 | 3 | 4 | 5 | 6 | 7 | 8 | 9 | Extrovert |
|---|---|---|---|---|---|---|---|---|---|---|---|---|
| | | | | | | | | | | | | |
| • | *Demonstrated* | | | | | X | X | | | | | |
| • | *Desired* | | | | | X | X | | | | | |

In considering the Phlegmatic leadership profile, we need to look at some factors, beginning with leadership needs and desires.

## PHLEGMATIC IN LEADERSHIP

| Temperament (out of 3,449 people) | # People | Social | # People | Leadership | # People | Relationship |
|---|---|---|---|---|---|---|
| Phlegmatic | 345 | 10.00% | 26 | 0.75% | 362 | 10.50% |
| Phlegmatic Compulsive | NA | NA | NA | NA | NA | NA |

### A Note about the Leadership Profile

The adult leadership profile identifies the individual's ability to provide leadership, make decisions, and assume responsibilities. This profile outlines the individual's needs and desires for independence, achievements, and recognition. Because leadership needs and desires expressed through socializing with people, the leadership profile should not be evaluated alone. Compare it with either the social profile or the relationship profile.

– Together, the leadership profile and the social profile help determine the individual's career needs. By comparing the results with the individual's current employment situation, you can target conflict areas and assist the individual.

– Evaluated together, the leadership profile and the relationship profile assist in determining the person's independence-dependence needs in close relationships. By comparing the results with the individual's current life situation, you can target conflict areas and help the individual enhance relationships.

*Leadership Needs and Desires.* The Phlegmatic is independent and desires only a moderate amount of influence and control over other people. As a result, they allow others to have reasonable authority over their life. While they possess excellent decision-making skills and the ability to assume responsibilities, they usually prefer to share tasks instead of carrying the burden alone. You will not find too many Phlegmatic, leading a company. They prefer to be a team player. However, you will see them in leadership when blended with another temperament such as the Phlegmatic Choleric (PC)/Choleric Phlegmatic (CP) or the Phlegmatic Melancholy (PM) or the Melancholy Phlegmatic (MP). In these cases, their leadership is one of leading by diplomacy not by force, strength, or power. Individuals that fall into these categories are referred to as the "soft leaders."

In some cases, whenever you find a Phlegmatic blend of leadership, the organization will be the "status quo" "Good Ole Boy: kind of an organization. They will not be setting any records but just plodding along and producing day after day what is required to be going forward. The Phlegmatic has a strong need to maintain a peaceful, nondemanding lifestyle with a structured daily routine. They have an excellent ability to be content with whatever situation he encounters and tends to accept the status quo in life. Because they possess a low energy reserve, they have a strong need to avoid fatigue and chooses to expend available energy on tasks, not relationships. Much of their behavior is directed toward meeting this requirement.

*Criteria for Friendships.* Friendly and sociable, the Phlegmatic genuinely likes people. They possess excellent social skills and can interact well with all types of individuals. They are content with or without social interaction and is free from urgent needs, fear of rejection, low self-esteem, and other barriers to relationships. Because people tend to drain their energy, the Phlegmatic avoids extensive socialization and maintains an attitude of noninvolvement in life, usually preferring to be a spectator rather than an active participant. They often depend on others to initiate social interactions and friendships, but will readily participate when invited. At the same time, they are faithful and committed to friends and coworkers. They need friends to encourage their plans and decisions and motivate them to get more involved in life.

***Perception of Self.*** Confident and self-contained with a positive self-image, the Phlegmatic is satisfied with his abilities and accomplishments and secure in believing their own opinions and viewpoints are correct. To help alleviate concerns about criticism or failure, they seek to share responsibility. Despite their ideas and abilities, their need to protect their energy reserve may make them seem unconcerned about reaching their potential in life; as a result, they may be an underachiever. Calm, complacent, and rarely introspective, the Phlegmatic maintains a practical approach to life and people.

***Perception by Others.*** Calm and stable even under pressure, the Phlegmatic is perceived as friendly and understanding. They can find humor in most situations and possesses the ability to relate well to people, including hostile or difficult personalities. A natural negotiator and diplomat, the Phlegmatic often brings objectivity and peace to troubled situations. Despite their skill in helping people resolve conflicts, however, they are nonassertive and non-confrontational and avoids personal involvement in any conflict situation. They use their excellent verbal skills, especially sarcastic humor, as a defense. The Phlegmatic may appear indecisive because of his tendency to procrastinate.

***Perception of Others.*** The Phlegmatic is patient, compassionate, and understanding of others. He is an empathetic listener and sets realistic expectations of others. He views other people positively and accepts them for who they are, is tolerant of their faults and mistakes, and is willing to assist and encourage. At the same time, he avoids overinvolvement in the lives and activities of others and maintains some distance even in close relationships. He needs recognition and appreciation for his efforts but does not call attention to his achievements. The Phlegmatic may become critical of those who attempt to change or control him.

***Intellectual Orientation.*** The Phlegmatic will not be seeking out leadership positions, although he does possess high mental abilities. Objective, practical, and highly self-disciplined, he is excellent at identifying problems and inequities but low on energy to make it happen. He carefully gathers facts and considers options before deciding. Although he seeks input and support from others and often inspires others to develop solutions, he does not necessarily change his mind if people disagree with his decision.

***Emotional Orientation.*** The Phlegmatic is emotionally stable, is not prone to moodiness or depression, and usually remains cheerful and calm. He avoids extremes of emotional expression and uses his sense of humor as a defense. Although he experiences strong emotions, he does not express them easily, and rarely becomes annoyed or undergoes "hurt feelings." The Phlegmatic usually avoids confrontation, and tries to maintain peace in every situation. He may become anxious or fearful when faced with change when people place excessive demands on him, or in conflict situations—even if he is not directly involved. As a leader, the Phlegmatic will always maintain a low profile and avoid conflict at all cost to functions without emotional stress. If there is an issue to deal with and there is the potential for conflict, they will delegate the matter, or they will avoid the situation and, in many cases, ignore the problem. If they are forced to face a situation, they will make decisions and sometimes promises that get them out of the situation but do not address the problem. In other words, they will "go around" the problem without addressing it directly.

***Work Orientation.*** Task-oriented rather than people-oriented, the Phlegmatic is well organized in his approaches to tasks. Disciplined and efficient, he is accurate and precise in his work and is a perfectionist when it comes to details. He is very dependable and can be relied upon to be at work and always be on time. He can handle routine or tedious assignments efficiently and maintains a slow, steady work pace that consistently produces excellent results. Because he draws his excellent self-concept from successful job performance, the Phlegmatic ideal career involves tasks, not people. He possesses the ability to relate very well to people for short periods, is willing to accommodate coworkers, and adapts well to those in authority and readily assists when asked. He can be a capable leader but needs reassurance from others before assuming responsibilities; as a result, he does not often seek leadership roles, and usually prefers to work independently or as part of a team. Conservative in his approach and unlikely to take risks, the Phlegmatic functions best in a stable, controlled work environment. Their laid-back style brings harmony to his work area and provides stability to teams composed of varied work styles. He may procrastinate when faced with decision-making and can be stubborn and resistant to change, even if the changes will bring improvement. Because he spends a considerable amount of energy adhering to strict requirements and ensuring that he performs well, he may be exhausted by the ends of the day.

***Motivation.*** The motivation for the Phlegmatic to assume or take a leadership position is not all that common. Phlegmatic prefers to function as part of a team and will do regular responsibilities but will not seek out leadership positions. The Phlegmatic is self-motivated but, because of their strong desire to avoid conflict or change, they need to be convinced intellectually before acting. They are seldom motivated by outside influences to change and may change his behavior to avoid conflict (punishment) or achieve peace (reward). The most exceptional reward/motivation for the Phlegmatic is money and working in a relaxed environment with no overtime.

***Rejection/Acceptance Profile.*** The Phlegmatic can make people feel accepted and does not fear rejection or need acceptance by others. He does not take rejection personally and rarely uses denial against others. So as a leader, the Phlegmatic will let minor conflict roll off their back like water off duck's back. They do not permit dismissal to affect their emotions.

## The Relationship Profile – Phlegmatic

| Introvert | 0 | 1 | 2 | 3 | 4 | 5 | 6 | 7 | 8 | 9 | Extrovert |
|---|---|---|---|---|---|---|---|---|---|---|---|
|  |  |  |  |  |  |  |  |  |  |  |  |
| • *Demonstrated* |  |  |  |  |  | X | X |  |  |  |  |
| • *Desired* |  |  |  |  |  | X | X |  |  |  |  |

In considering the Phlegmatic relationship profile, we need to look at some factors, beginning with relationship needs and desires.

## PHLEGMATIC IN RELATIONSHIP

| Temperament (out of 3,449 people) | # People | Social | # People | Leadership | # People | Relationship |
|---|---|---|---|---|---|---|
| Phlegmatic | 345 | 10.00% | 26 | 0.75% | 362 | 10.50% |
| Phlegmatic Compulsive | NA | NA | NA | NA | NA | NA |

### A Note about the Relationship Profile

The adult relationship profile identifies the individual's preferences for emotional involvement in and shared affection on a one-to-one basis. This profile outlines the individual's needs and desires for emotional sharing and relationships. For most people, the relationship profile is the dominant pattern that influences behavior in the social and leadership areas.

By comparing the relationship profile with the individuals' current life situation, you can target conflict areas and help the person meet essential needs not fulfilled.

## *Relationship Needs and Desires*

A criterion for a relationship indicates the individual's preferences in developing and establishing relationships; may identify types of people who are compatible and incompatible with the individual's temperament.

Conservative in his attachments and expectations of people, the Phlegmatic is usually content with a few close relationships; in those links, he needs to express and receive moderate amounts of love and affection. He has balanced needs for communicating realistic gestures of respect to others and does not require repeated assurances of love. In their close relationships, they may expect the other person to expend more effort than they do to maintain the relationship and initiate expressions of love. This conduct is because of their low energy, and they do not want to spend what power they do have sustaining a relationship. Possessing an excellent ability to be content with whatever situation they encounter, the Phlegmatic tends to accept the status quo in life and has a strong need to maintain a peaceful, nondemanding lifestyle. Because they have a low energy reserve, they have a strong need to avoid fatigue and may direct much of their behavior toward meeting this requirement. They prefer a quiet lifestyle and structured daily routines and may choose to use their available energy on tasks rather than relationships.

**Criteria for Relationships.** The Phlegmatic is friendly and sociable, and genuinely likes people. Phlegmatic is free from urgent needs, fear of rejection, low self-esteem, and other barriers to relationships. At the same time, because people tend to drain their energy, including those they are close to, he needs a predictable routine in his life and avoids extensive social interaction. They prefer quiet time at home instead of participation in social events and maintains an attitude of noninvolvement in life, usually preferring to be a spectator instead of an active participant. The Phlegmatic rarely initiates social interactions or friendships, depending on others to start and maintain relationships with them. However, they readily participate when invited and is faithful and committed to friends and loved ones.

**Perception of Self.** Confident and self-contained, the Phlegmatic is satisfied with their abilities and accomplishments, secure in believing his own opinions and viewpoints are correct. He maintains a practical approach to life and people. Calm, complacent, and rarely reflective, they have healthy self-esteem and a positive self-image, confidence that they are loved and accepted by those close to them. Despite their ideas and abilities, the Phlegmatic need to protect their energy reserve may make them seem unconcerned about reaching their potential in life and cause them to be an underachiever. Most Phlegmatic feel very comfortable with the lifestyle that they carve out for themselves. They will always try to be in an environment that is hassle-free from stress, anxiety, and commotion.

**Perception by Others.** The Phlegmatic is calm and stable even under pressure and usually perceived as friendly and understanding. He relates well to most people, including hostile or difficult personalities, often bringing objectivity and peace into troubled situations and viewed as a peacemaker. As a result, they are a natural diplomat and negotiator, skilled in helping people resolve conflicts. Nonassertive and nonconfrontational, he usually avoids personal involvement in any conflict situation. Able to find humor in most cases, the Phlegmatic uses their excellent verbal skills, especially sarcastic fun, as a defense. Their loved ones may feel neglected at times, wanting more attention and expressions of love that they can give.

**Perception of Others.** Patient, compassionate, understanding, and usually accepting of others, the Phlegmatic is an empathetic listener willing to assist and encourage. They view others positively and is tolerant of their faults and mistakes. At the same time, they need recognition and appreciation for their efforts and avoids overinvolvement in the lives and activities of others, maintaining some distance even in close relationships. They may become critical of those who attempt to change or control them. They will avoid people who are cantankerous or possess disruptive behavior. They sometimes will prevent the stable characteristics of a Choleric or Melancholy because they are so driven and focused. That aggressive approach to life or in the work setting is just too much for the Phlegmatic. So, they are always on the lookout so that they can avoid such situations.

**Intellectual Orientation.** Conservative in the approach to life, the Phlegmatic is unlikely to take risks. They possess high mental abilities, carefully gathering facts, and considering options before deciding. Although they may procrastinate when faced with decision-making and prefers shared responsibility, they rarely change their mind once they have formed an opinion. Objective, practical, and highly self-disciplined, the Phlegmatic are well organized, accurate, and precise in their work. He is excellent at, identifying problems and inequities and inspiring others to develop solutions. Phlegmatic position themselves so they can delegate or suggest others to correct the issues they have identified. Of course, this becomes a stumbling block in the personal environment and can have a very negative impact on his close relationships.

**Emotional Orientation.** Emotionally stable and usually cheerful and calm, the Phlegmatic avoids extremes of emotional expression. He is not prone to moodiness or depression and uses his sense of humor and sarcasm as a defense. In some situations, he will become the "clown" in a group of friends to deflect criticism or conflict. He experiences strong emotions but does not express them easily, even in close relationships, and has difficulty verbalizing his love for others. The Phlegmatic rarely becomes angry or experiences "hurt feelings." He avoids confrontation and tries to maintain peace in every situation. He may become anxious or fearful when faced with change or when close relationships place excessive demands on him. He also may feel anxiety in conflict situations, even if he is not directly involved. Of course, you must remember that the Phlegmatic does have a breaking point emotionally and they can explode if pushed too far. Of course, if they are thrust into a conflict situation, that will deplete their energy immediately. The best thing for them at that point is to take a nap. Power naps are very beneficial for the Phlegmatic.

**Motivation.** While the Phlegmatic is self-motivated, he possesses a strong desire to avoid conflict and change and needs to be convinced intellectually before acting even in close relationships. Phlegmatic can be stubborn and resistant to change even if the changes bring improvement within intimate relationships. The resistance can be a stumbling block for the connection to mature. He is seldom motivated by outside influences to change and may modify their behavior to avoid conflict (punishment) or achieve peace (reward). The most important thing to remember about the Phlegmatic is that they need time to change regardless of what the issue may be about; they will need a chance to digest and come to their conclusions evaluating if the change is right for them.

**Rejection/Acceptance Profile.** The Phlegmatic usually does not fear rejection, take rejection personally, or need acceptance by others. Phlegmatic easily makes other people feel accepted and rarely uses dismissal against others. Although he does not deliberately reject loved ones, they may perceive his lack of involvement as rejection. Always remember it is an energy issue and not necessarily that they do not like you or are not interested. They must pace themselves and get through the day with what energy they do have.

# Help for the Phlegmatic
## Characteristics of the Phlegmatic

### *Probable Strengths*

- Calm, quiet, and stable – is "easygoing," cheerful, and rarely agitated by people or situations
- Sociable and friendly – the most likable of the temperaments; is sympathetic and kind to people
- Objective and fair – is a born diplomat; a natural peacemaker in conflicts
- Dependable and consistent – remains faithful to people and responsibilities; is not prone to sudden change
- Humorous – enjoys a good joke; sees the lighter side of life
- Practical – is highly organized and efficient; pragmatic in his approach to tasks and life in general

### *Potential Weaknesses*

- Slow-paced – appears to lack motivation; rarely does more than is expected
- Procrastinates – tends to ignore responsibilities more than the other temperaments
- Self-centered – protects himself from pain and avoids involvement whenever possible
- Stubborn – refuses to change his mind; is highly resistant to change
- Fearful and indecisive – avoids situations that require confrontation, action, or involvement
- Frugal – can make him come across as cheap
- Sarcastic – uses cynicism and dry humor as a defense

*Decisions for the Phlegmatic*

He avoids and fears to make decisions as it may require his involvement, and he does not want to be involved in creating more work for himself.

He may see what needs to be done but will tell someone else and expect them to do it.

Now that we have considered the three areas of the WIDP profile, you should have a pretty good understanding of the Phlegmatic and their fundamental needs and desires. The chart also shows some unique characteristics of the Phlegmatic, including probable strengths and potential weaknesses.

# IT IS OK SERIES – PHLEGMATIC

I am highlighting the Phlegmatic in social/vocational. The following are some things about which they should not feel guilty.

*A Phlegmatic in Social/Vocational*

When you tell a Phlegmatic in social/vocational:

**1.  That they are slow-paced, tire quickly, and tend to be an observer—**

You also need to say to them:

It is **okay** to be slow-paced: **it is okay** that they tire quickly and tend to be observers. They do not have to feel guilty because of this; however, you do not want them leaving your sessions with the idea that they can drift through life because of what you told them.

They must not use this as an excuse to do nothing. Phlegmatic need to put forth an effort to become involved in life; otherwise, they will tend to preserve their low energy to the point that they are not using any at all.

They need to learn to think of others and not just themselves; others will tend to think of them as being selfish—and they can be—if they get too wrapped up in reserving their energy to the point where they will not get involved at all. The Phlegmatic in social/vocational can do this without realizing what they are doing.

**2.  That they have a "dry" sense of humor –**

You also need to tell them:

Having a dry sense of humor is **okay**. You need to explain what a dry sense of humor means and why they have it. It means making quick, witty, sometimes cutting remarks. These remarks can be, to those around the Phlegmatic in social/vocational, totally unexpected and sometimes unwanted. The Phlegmatic in social/vocational does this to keep others at a distance—if you get too close to someone, they might expect them to get involved in a project that might cause them to expend energy they do not have.

You need to inform them that their remark can be cutting and offensive and can hurt others. You need to make them aware of the fact that they can use this humor in a gentle, straightforward way. Many times, they do not realize that their remarks can be cutting and offensive—their only thought is to reserve their energy.

They need to understand why they use this dry sense of humor—because, if Phlegmatic is good at it, no one will want them involved and they will expend no energy at all!

As with the other temperaments, the Phlegmatic needs to learn to maintain balance in their life. Enlightenment is the key!

If you are a Phlegmatic, there's a good chance you spend much time feeling guilty about the way you think and act. Here are some things you may want to keep in mind that will help you better understand yourself and spend less time feeling guilty about who you are:

### 3. *You are slow-paced, you tire quickly, and you tend to be an observer.*

It is okay to be slow-paced, and it *is* okay to tire quickly and be an observer. You do not have to feel guilty because of this—it is part of your temperament.

At the same time, you should not merely drift through life or use this as an excuse to do nothing. You need to put forth an effort to become involved in life; otherwise, there's a good chance you will tend to preserve your energy to the point that you are not using any at all. You need to learn to think of others and not just yourself. If you do not, other people will believe that you are selfish.

Procrastination can stop progress entirely if you let it run according to you your needs. How about the needs of your organization you work for or your relationships? Procrastination will drive them away. Think about their needs too.

Self-Centeredness: Be aware of the needs of those around you and don't always be protecting yourself. It is not all about you; others count too.

Stubbornness: Try not being so stubborn occasionally. You will find that there are rewards for involvement.

Fearful and indecisive: Often, your fears are something you conjured up in your mind to protect yourself, and they do not even exist.

Frugal: Buy someone a cup of coffee or lunch occasionally. People take notice of your lack of financial participation during "pay up" time at lunch or outings.

### 4. *You have a "dry" sense of humor.*

It *is* okay to have a dry sense of humor—that is, you make quick, witty, and sometimes cutting remarks. To those around you, these statements can be totally unexpected and sometimes unwanted. You may do this to keep others at a distance or to avoid getting too close to someone. You see, if you allow another people to get too close, they might expect someone to get involved in a project that will cause you the Phlegmatic to expend energy you do not have. The problem is that while you may be successful in, preserving your power, you also may end up alienating yourself from everyone and end up without any friends!

You need to realize that sometimes your remarks can be cutting and offensive and can hurt others. That does not mean you should not use your sense of humor—but you need to use it in a gentle, natural way. As with all things in your life, the key is to maintain balance.

Sometimes, Phlegmatic will use sarcasm or humor as a defense mechanism. However, sometimes they will pawn their insecurities off using irony or humor. The real issues are due to their low self-esteem, and therefore, they use sarcasm and fun to build themselves up in front of others.

Decisions: Not deciding is a decision. A decision not to choose. That kind of thinking can be a stop blocker and cause all sorts of problems in work and relationships.

# Humor in the Workplace

### Humor in the Workplace Helps Build Teamwork, Manage Stress

Rush! Produce! Collaborate! Produce! Compete! Produce! Sometimes a day at the office feels like *Alice in Wonderland's* **Mad Hatter's Tea Party:** "No time, no room, clean plates, move down!" When the pace overwhelms you, tame the whirlwind with humor!

### Why does humor work?

A good sense of humor lets you deal with others' imperfections and gives you the ability to take yourself lightly and your job seriously. It does not mean leaving your peers rolling in the aisles, but it does suggest using laughter and fun to bring out the best in workday situations. People let off steam in several ways. The passive approach creates a calm and collected outside, but leaves you churning on the inside. Others choose to be outwardly angry, but that can lead to other problems! However, using humor acts like the valve on the top of a pressure cooker—it lets off steam and makes that funny noise, besides! Appropriate use of humor helps relieve stress, develop harmony with peers, and create goodwill. Moreover, guess what? It is free!

### Practice makes perfect!

Like everything else we are good at, education and practice account for the skillful use of humor. However, remember you are at work. Know that joking is a diversion issue. Never use it at the expense of another person and understand that offensive humor—whether it be cultural or sexual—in the workplace creates stress and ill will. Make humor meaningful, keep it fresh, and help your clients flex their mood muscles!

### Do's and Don'ts for the Phlegmatic

| Do | Don't |
| --- | --- |
| • Speak up and enter the conversation | • Let resentment build. It comes out as sarcasm in your "one-liner" humor. |
| • Move into action with enthusiasm | • Procrastinate and expect others to do your work |
| • Say what you mean | • Always say "I do not care"; make a choice |
| • Be willing to take a risk | • Be a wet blanket on others' ideas |
| • Involve yourself in others' lives | • Be so stubborn all the time |

| | |
|---|---|
| • Start with proper nutrition and exercise to help gain energy | • Take advantage of everyone else when it comes to paying for coffee, donuts, or lunch |
| • Trust your abilities | |
| • Recognize your tendency toward laziness and realize how it affects others | |
| • Model a winner's attitude | |
| • Find your real interest and pursue it | |
| • Finish three projects you have started and set dates for others | |
| • Practice the etiquette of "rejoicing with those who rejoice." | |
| • Learn some phrases to encourage others | |
| • Show you heard and did care | |
| • Develop a plan to keep heading toward growth | |
| • Plan to do several jobs in one day and do them | |
| • Communicate your feelings so that people will relate to you | |
| • Love yourself for who you are | |
| • Focus on your strengths instead of your weaknesses | |
| • Write down problems that need a decision | |
| • If necessary, seek help for possible solutions and choose one | |
| • Remember—it is only the first time you do something new that is frightening—next time will be easy | |

## Become Aware of Your Natural Strengths and Learn to Use Them Wisely

| Natural Strength | | Strength Carried to the Extreme | | Compulsion |
|---|---|---|---|---|
| | | | | |
| Low-key emotions | | Hides emotions | | Blocks out all feeling |
| | | | | |
| Easygoing and adaptable | | Lets others decide | | Can't make any decisions |
| | | | | |

85

| Cooperative and pleasant | | Compromises standards | | Easily becomes a pawn |
|---|---|---|---|---|
| | | | | |
| Mellow | | Becomes lazy and laid back | | Refuses to budge |

## How to Recognize Whether Your Child Is a Phlegmatic

| Strengths | Weaknesses | Emotional Needs |
|---|---|---|
| **Baby** | | |
| Easygoing, undemanding, happy, adjustable, good with other children, not easily angered | Slow, can be shy or indifferent | Moderate attention, praise, loving and gentle motivation |
| **Child** | | |
| Watches others, easily amused, little trouble, dependable, lovable, agreeable | Selfish, teasing, avoids work, fearful, quietly stubborn, lazy, retreats to TV | Peace and relaxation, attention, praise, self-worth, loving motivation, and sleep |
| **Teen** | | |
| Pleasing personality, witty, good listener, mediate problems, hides emotions, leads when pushed, casual attitude, good with helping other students with their emotional issues, good at saving money, others flock to them for counsel, make excellent team members | Indecisive, unenthusiastic, too compromising, unmotivated, sarcastic, uninvolved, procrastinate, will of iron; avoid conflict, confrontation, initiative, decisions, extra work, responsibility, chores, keeping room in order, tension, quarrels | Peace and relaxation, attention, praise, self-worth, loving motivation, good night's sleep, conflict-free environments |

**Strengths of a Phlegmatic**

Steady, not moved easily
Patient
Free from stress, tends to worry
Lives a balanced life
Meek, most gentle people on the planet
In control of themselves
In control of their environment
Comfortable with themselves
Stays focused on the project, gets it done
Dry sense of humor
Very witty
Dependable

**Weaknesses of a Phlegmatic**

Introvert
Watcher, not doer
Meets requirements, then stops
Must be restarted after a project
Unenthusiastic
Can be very stubborn
Not always a team player
Lazy, gets tired easily
Struggles with self-motivation
Tormented by fear
Indecisive about the next step
Avoids responsibilities, extra burdens

Practical and efficient conserves energy

Calm, cool, collected

Brings peace to the workplace

Makes a perfect parent

Takes quality time with their children

Family comes first

Durable leaders

Peaceful and agreeable

Excellent administrative skills

Good salespeople

Good mediators

Tough projects do not worry them

Excellent under pressure

Self-sufficient

Has the gift of moderation

Gets involved when they feel needed

Has the gift of help

Easy to get along with

Does not offend others

Walks away from arguments

Good listeners

Predictable

Hides real feelings, emotions

Can be selfish, want their way

Can be too compromising

Self-righteous, everyone else is wrong

May think they do not need God

Not involved in demanding relationships

Do not discipline well

Not goal oriented

Discourage others

Stay uninvolved

Must be nudged to participate

Last one to get involved

Hard to get excited

Tendency to judge others

Teases extroverts—they annoy them

Resists change

Can be sarcastic

Procrastinates

Critical of people who get-up-and-go

Hold grudges

Unworried

Possessive

*As a professional clinical psychologist, I have used many psychological instruments in the last forty (40) years. I have not seen such a powerful apparatus that is so quick and easy yet provides so much critical data on my clients. Worley's ID Profile is indeed the tool of the 21st century. I will be recommending WIDP to my professional clinical associate's entire nationwide.*

RAYMOND DANIELS, PH.D.,
PRESIDENT, INSTITUTE OF BEHAVIORAL
SCIENCES, DERRY, NH

# CHAPTER 7

# THE MELANCHOLY

Ask Jill's friends and acquaintances and they'll tell you she's a loner who spends most of her time at home alone. She has always been okay with small groups but forgets about parties, concerts, and other venues where they are expected to interact with lots of people. Most of the time, you might as well not even invite her.

Ask Jill's work associates, and they'll tell you they don't know how they'd get along without her. Everything she does is flawless. Oh, she may take her time doing her work and ask a lot of questions, and once in a while she may even miss a deadline, but the finished product is well worth the wait. The only reason she would blunder a timeline is that she is searching for more data so her finished product will be "perfect." She is just thorough, and she is not procrastinating. She likes to work by herself most of the times with no pressure, but you give her enough freedom and time to get the job done, you can be sure it'll be done and done right. Jill will work around the clock to make sure she gets everything just right. If anyone suggests that her work is incorrect or incomplete, she will feel rejected to the point of becoming depressed. Even when people praise her effort, however, Jill is rarely satisfied with the results and feels she could have done a better job.

Ask Jill's close friends and loved ones and they'll tell you that nobody is more faithful or committed than her. She will bend over backward for them, to the point of exhaustion, and complete everything she starts no matter how long it takes and regardless of the cost, regarding time and energy. At the same time, Jill is very frugal with her money and rarely if ever spends frivolously or takes financial risks. Economic security is high on her list of dos.

Jill's closest friends also know that even though she often appears exceptionally confident, she is very fearful of criticism, which is one of the main reasons she prefers to be alone or with one or two others. "Competency" is key to the understanding of a Melancholy work ethic. She will work until she has "mastered" the subject matter whatever it may be. It can be fixing a gourmet dinner or remodeling their home, whatever she takes on as a task will always be prefaced by her being competent at the JOB first. She will research, study, read, practice, and practice, until she has satisfied her expected level of performance. Many Melancholy will be so focused that they will isolate themselves from everyone, including their immediate family so that she can perfect herself or improve whatever project or task she has taken on. She is the "midnight cowboy" who stays at work late "getting the project completed" even at the expense of her family and close relationships. She MUST come across as a competent and qualified individual.

## Melancholy

They are very gifted, creative, and work hard to make the most of their talents. They are extraordinarily analytical and will work tirelessly to understand every facet of a problem before creating the solution. The ironic thing about the Melancholy is, like the Sanguine, their positive qualities are also what tends to get them into trouble. Often, they are so faithful, diligent, and generous that they end up neglecting her own needs. Then, when criticized or if their hard work isn't noticed or appreciated, they feel rejected, so they end up getting hurt on both sides of the equation.

I know a chiropractor who is so intense in her professional life that she only endorses the color beige. She has no time to "**think**" about other colors. Everything that she has is beige—beige exterior home, beige clothes, beige paint in every room of her house, beige carpeting, beige furniture, beige car, down to and including her professional dress. She has no color in her life other than beige. Talk about compulsive! And she, of course, is Melancholy in all three areas of her temperament: social/vocational, leadership, and relationship.

*Physically*: They can hurt themselves from pushing too hard at physical activities such as weightlifting, rock climbing, whitewater rafting, etc. They may suffer from severe headaches, are prone to irritable bowel syndrome (IBS), back pain, and can suffer from too much weight loss too fast if they undertake projects that are just physically too much for them. But they must show you how much they can do. And it is at this point where they overdo and physically are prone to harming themselves. However, on the other hand, the Melancholy will also be the overachievers and are the ones who bring home the gold medals at the Olympics. If you want to see a Melancholy in action, watch an ice skater, diver, runner, or any other Olympic contender, and most of them will be Melancholy. The perfectionist!

*Emotionally:* They are very speedy to isolate and disengage from people due to them feeling criticized or judged and then become very moody and angry. They do not like being around people, and when they are because they must because their vocation requires it, they can be cold and indifferent to individuals within that environment. It's not that they do not like people; it's that being around people requires them to interact with the people, and that interferes with their need to think and analyze. Besides, they are also busy reliving in their mind all the events that led up to their anger stemming from their being criticized or judged. The results are that they then hurt others by becoming too self-centered, cynical, and critical themselves. But there is an upside to the emotional makeup of the Melancholy. They are the ones who make up the most significant percentage of being faithful and loyal friends or significant others. You can depend on them to be there when the times get rough. And believe me, time does get rough when we need someone to lean on for emotional support. If you have a Melancholy friend or significant other, you can bet your bottom dollar they will be there for you through thick and thin.

*Spiritually:* They can hurt themselves and others by blaming God for their troubles and be so consumed with their anger that they make no room for God in their lives. They become angry at God and blame him for allowing the conflicts and problems of life that have happened to them in the past or sensitive issues that are currently happening to them. They are the people who may say they feel that He has left them because they are so angry. While they are filled with this anger and blaming God, there is no room for unconditional love or forgiveness within them. They cannot seem to get over the anger and may stay in that state for days and in some cases weeks. God's love cannot flow through a vessel filled with rage; therefore, it is essential that the Melancholy in social/vocational learns how to **forgive** and **forget**.

Jesus Christ is the perfect example. He freely pardoned our sins and forgave us and continues to forgive us daily, providing we ask according to 1 Jn. 1:9. Because he has freed us, we can free others from the chains of our anger and resentment, and the feelings of hostility. Forgiving someone does not mean that your relationship healed as though nothing happened. Reconciliation comes first which is immediate. Then restoration is a process that takes time and may take days, weeks, months, and in some cases years.

## The Melancholy – Demonstrated vs. Desired Behavior

The Melancholy is by nature shy, introspective, and extremely sensitive. Although they are very compassionate and faithful to those they allow to be close to her, they usually choose to remain isolated and alone. As the chart shows, in the extreme they both *demonstrate* and *desire* highly introverted behavior.

| Introvert | 0 | 1 | 2 | 3 | 4 | 5 | 6 | 7 | 8 | 9 | Extrovert |
|---|---|---|---|---|---|---|---|---|---|---|---|
| | | | | | | | | | | | |
| **Social** | | | | | | | | | | | |
| • *Demonstrated* | X | | | | | | | | | | |
| • *Desired* | X | | | | | | | | | | |
| **Leadership** | | | | | | | | | | | |
| • *Demonstrated* | X | | | | | | | | | | |
| • *Desired* | X | | | | | | | | | | |
| **Relationship** | | | | | | | | | | | |
| • *Demonstrated* | X | | | | | | | | | | |
| • *Desired* | X | | | | | | | | | | |

Let's look at the three areas of the WIDP profile—social/vocational, leadership, and relationship—to learn more about the Melancholy.

## The Social/Vocational Profile – Melancholy

| Introvert | 0 | 1 | 2 | 3 | 4 | 5 | 6 | 7 | 8 | 9 | Extrovert |
|---|---|---|---|---|---|---|---|---|---|---|---|
| | | | | | | | | | | | |
| • *Demonstrated* | X | | | | | | | | | | |
| • *Desired* | X | | | | | | | | | | |

In considering the Melancholy's social/vocational profile, we need to look at some factors, beginning with social needs and desires.

## MELANCHOLY IN SOCIAL

**Temperamen**t (out of 3,449 people)     # People   Social   **# People  Leadership  # People   Relationship**

| | # People | Social | # People | Leadership | # People | Relationship |
|---|---|---|---|---|---|---|
| Melancholy | 1355 | 39.29% | 1084 | 31.43% | 800 | 23.20% |
| Melancholy Compulsive | 303 | 8.79% | 839 | 24.33% | 22 | 0.64% |

### A Note about the Social Profile

The social profile outlines your needs and desires for light friendships, work/career associations, and other casual relationships. By comparing the social profile with your current life situation, you can understand conflict areas and achieve a comfortable level of interpersonal contact in the work or social environments.

*Remember:* The social profile should be applied only to your casual social/career contacts. To determine your needs and desires in close personal relationships, please consult the relationship profile.

*Social Needs and Desires.* The Melancholy has a high need for privacy and usually prefers to be alone. As a result, they rarely initiate friendships, socializes with very few people, and tends to avoid social events. Although they need acceptance and approval from others, they prefer not to be approached by others, and her fear of rejection prevents her from becoming involved with people. Although they have difficulty understanding people, they do appreciate tasks and may, in fact, view life as a series of jobs to perform. At the same time, the Melancholy has a strong family orientation and considers their home a sanctuary from the world. They are far more comfortable relating to one-on-one or in small groups than in large gatherings and needs daily time alone to counter the stress of interaction with people. The Melancholy need for privacy dictates their lifestyle of noninvolvement with people. As seen above in the demonstrated and desired scale, you can see that the Melancholy temperament falls into the introverted sides of the scale. However, do not forget that some Melancholy will fall in the 2 or 3 range on the scale. The range of 2 or 3 does indicate that these Melancholy are introverted individuals and are very rational people **who need very little socialization** and spend most of their time thinking out issues. So, remember some Melancholy do fall into the range of desiring a few relationships. Those who have either a zero to one (0–1) on the scale that is very low and that this "individually rarely expresses this behavior and compulsively avoids this behavior." But the individual who has a two or three (2–3) on the scale that is low and that this "individual **may occasionally express this behavior**." Of course, the little socialization that the Melancholy does participate in let them see themselves as a person who does "socialize."

*Criteria for Friendships.* Loyal and committed to the few people she chooses for friends; the Melancholy allow themselves to become vulnerable only with these carefully selected people. On the one hand, they are dependable, quick to make sacrifices for their friends, and willing to get involved in humanitarian causes that benefit humanity. On the other hand, they may have impossibly high expectations for themselves and others and tends to evaluate people intellectually rather than emotionally, valuing those who share their logical and rational approach to life. They avoid conflict in interpersonal relationships and usually prevents aggressive or domineering people.

***Perception of Self.*** Although the Melancholy is intellectually gifted and talented in many areas, the Melancholy are hindered low self-esteem and fear of rejection. They tend to be reflective and self-critical and may endlessly analyze their behavior and perceived faults. They focus on their thoughts rather than on people or events. They can be pessimistic about their abilities and may be unaware of their potential in life to the extent of feeling inferior in comparison to others. They tend to be a perfectionist and may set such impossible standards for themselves that they become depressed when they fail to attain them. Unfortunately, the Melancholy will establish a level of perfection that is impossible to accomplish. Therefore, they are always judging themselves too harshly, and this contributes to their being easily depressed or very negative toward themselves.

***Perception by Others.*** Although the Melancholy is adept at hiding their insecurities and projects an image of competence and confidence, they fear criticism and making mistakes. They can be friendly and outgoing with people who have earned their trust. Although they are compassionate and sensitive to other people's needs, their logical outlook may give the impression that they are cold or indifferent. As a result, they may be perceived as unfriendly or a "loner." They are careful and precise in their communications in and has difficulty with small talk or casual conversations. The Melancholy is reluctant to share their knowledge with others, especially in large groups.

***Perception of Others.*** Because of their fear of rejection, the Melancholy may be suspicious of other people's motives and may project their negative self-perception onto others. They usually evaluate other people's words and behavior to determine whether they are being rejected and may become silent or withdraw if they perceive rejection. They are easily hurt, sometimes by the innocent comments or actions of others. The Melancholy rarely shows their emotions and avoids interpersonal aggression; in fact, they are nonassertive even when their opinion is correct. They may apply their high standards to others, and can become critical of those who fail to measure up.

***Intellectual Orientation.*** The Melancholy is intellectually gifted and a creative thinker. They may score in the genius range on intelligence tests and has unlimited capacity to acquire new knowledge and skills. They are logical and analytical in their approach to life, collects data before making decisions, and frequently asks questions to get all the facts. Very observant of people and their environment, they are always thinking, evaluating, and wondering. Able to see vivid, detailed pictures in their mind, they can be very creative. If they learn to control their thoughts, they can be highly productive and maintain a positive attitude. If their ideas are uncontrolled, they may experience emotional mood swings, and often revisit adverse events in their mind. They will even plan revengeful tactics in their minds, but very seldom act on those thoughts. Some Melancholy are sensitive to the concept that they will plot revenge in their minds. However, there are a couple of things that you must consider for this statement. The Melancholy who has a "less than desirable" work ethic and has come out of an environment in constant conflicts and or hostility will plan revenge in their minds. But of course, we are not using an absolute here such as "always plans revenge."

***Emotional Orientation.*** Although the Melancholy is compassionate, the most compassionate of all the temperaments, and empathetic toward others, they may equate emotional expression with loss of control and therefore remains emotionally guarded, reluctant to express their emotions. Don't forget the Melancholy is known as the "people of the mask," so they are professionals at disguising their real feelings and you will never know the difference. They often feel anger at themselves or others, but internalize rather than express it, allowing anger to build over a period, then exploding over a minor situation. They tend to hold grudges and mentally plan vengeance against the offender depending upon their work ethic and principles; as a result, they may tend to be moody and pessimistic, struggle with depression, and be prone to stress-related physical ailments. They can become anxious if they are required to socialize frequently or for long periods, or if deprived of daily time alone. They prefer to avoid situations that require emotional openness instead of intellectual analysis. The Melancholy possesses a strong need to avoid making mistakes and may feel anxiety if criticized. It is a grave offense toward a Melancholy if you reveal "anything" about them in front of other people. Do not talk about them without first getting their permission to speak about them, whether it be about their work ethic or their personal life. Very seldom will they permit you, and if you do not heed this warning you will violate them, and then you will have an enemy because they "don't forget" and are very good at holding grudges for extended periods.

***Work Orientation.*** The Melancholy is task-oriented rather than people-oriented. However, some Melancholy will disagree with this statement, but it is true. They perceive that interaction with people in the work setting is people-oriented, but it is not: it is task oriented. They are analytical and approach functions in a logical and determined organized manner. They can visualize projects from start to finish, and work tirelessly to achieve the goals and meet deadlines. Self-disciplined, they work well independently and resist authoritarian leadership. To avoid making mistakes, they gather facts before making decisions and may appear indecisive at times. The appearance of indecisiveness is no more than allowing for more time to collect data or refine the product. While they are perfectionists and check work down to the smallest detail to ensure that it is error-free; they are rarely satisfied with the results. Possessing excellent leadership abilities (see leadership profile for a detailed description of leadership skills) in standard areas of responsibility, the Melancholy needs to gather and evaluate data before moving into unknown areas or responsibilities. But once the Melancholy attain their desired level of competency in a field, they have no problem stepping in and functioning very well, and they will produce quality results. They work well in a structured daily routine.

***Motivation.*** Independent and self-motivated, the Melancholy needs to perform well to meet their high standards. They are strong-willed and can be stubborn. They are not usually motivated by the promise of reward or the threat of punishment but may have an intense, healthy fear of economic failure; this can be a first self-motivator in the workplace. Financial security is of utmost importance to the Melancholy, and they will always be doing everything they can within their scope of responsibility so that their employment is secure, thereby ensuring their economic security.

***Rejection/Acceptance Profile.*** Because the Melancholy has a severe fear of rejection, they are defensive, avoiding people and situations that cause them to feel rejected. They are very concerned about appearing incompetent and being criticized for their mistakes.

## The Leadership Profile – Melancholy

| Introvert | 0 | 1 | 2 | 3 | 4 | 5 | 6 | 7 | 8 | 9 | Extrovert |
|---|---|---|---|---|---|---|---|---|---|---|---|
| | | | | | | | | | | | |
| • *Demonstrated* | X | | | | | | | | | | |
| • *Desired* | X | | | | | | | | | | |

In considering the leadership profile for the Melancholy, we need to look at some factors, beginning, with leadership needs and desires.

## MELANCHOLY IN LEADERSHIP

**Temperament (out of 3,449 people)**

| | # People | Social | # People | Leadership | # People | Relationship |
|---|---|---|---|---|---|---|
| Melancholy | 1355 | 39.29% | 1084 | 31.43% | 800 | 23.20% |
| Melancholy Compulsive | 303 | 8.79% | 839 | 24.33% | 22 | 0.64% |

### A Note about the Leadership Profile

The adult leadership profile identifies your ability to provide leadership, make decisions, and assume responsibilities. This profile outlines your needs and desires for independence, achievement, and recognition. Because leadership needs and desires expressed through socializing with people, the leadership profile should not be evaluated alone but interpreted with either the social profile or the relationship profile.

– Together, the leadership profile and the social profile help determine your career needs. By comparing the results with your current employment situation, you can target conflict areas and maximize job skills.

– The leadership profile and the relationship profile evaluated together help determine your independence-dependence needs in close relationships. By comparing the results with your current life situation, you can target conflict areas and enhance relationships.

*Leadership Needs and Desires.* The Melancholy is very independent, wanting minimal influence and control over people's lives and behavior; they also resist attempts by others to control their life. Because they have a high need to appear competent and avoid criticism, they prefer to avoid assuming responsibility and making decisions and may be strongly influenced by fear of failure. While they have excellent leadership abilities and functions well in common areas of responsibility, they avoid assuming new duties until they feel comfortable with them. Competency in their job skills and self-confidence is the winning combination for the Melancholy. When these two characteristics are in place, there is relatively nothing they cannot accomplish. It is at this point they make great leaders. When these two are in place, job skills, and self-confidence, they will rise to the top of the leadership ladder and excel as leaders.

*Criteria for Relationships.* Possessing a high need for privacy, the Melancholy rarely initiate friendships. Their fear of rejection prevents them from becoming involved with people. While they allow their self to become vulnerable only with carefully selected people, they are loyal and committed to the few people they choose for friends. Drawn to people with similar high needs for independence, the Melancholy is dependable, quick to make sacrifices for their friends, and willing to become involved in humanitarian causes that benefit humanity. They tend to evaluate others intellectually rather than emotionally and values those who share their logical and rational approach to life. The Melancholy avoids aggressive people as well as the conflict in interpersonal situations, resisting the leadership of oppressive people. However, they will expect the same level of commitment and loyalty that they practice out of those they lead. They are hard workers and hope everyone on their team to be just as hardworking and diligent. And if you do not measure up to the standards of the Melancholy leader, you will find yourself standing in the unemployment line.

***Perception of Self.*** Although they are intellectually gifted and talented in many areas, the Melancholy are hindered by low self-esteem and fear of rejection. Of course, low self-esteem is due primarily to the environments that the Melancholy came out of, particularly the family of origin, where the character and personalities are developed and shaped. If that was a healthy environment, then the Melancholy will be of good self-esteem and self-worth. On the flip side, if the family of origin, character, and personality developed in an unhealthy environment, this will cause the Melancholy to be predisposed to having low self-esteem. They tend to be reflective and self-critical, often feels inferior in comparison to others, and may endlessly analyze their behavior and perceived faults. Their perception themselves can defeat them do to their high need to be perfect in everything they do. Since being perfect is not possible, they will then perceive themselves as inferior while at the same time be outproducing everyone around them in but not meeting their expectations of themselves. They focus on their thoughts rather than on people or events. Therefore, they live in her mind. A perfectionist, they may set impossible standards for themselves and become gloomy, doomed, or depressed when they fail to attain them. Confident in common areas of responsibility, she may doubt their ability to excel in new areas of responsibility and avoids or resists the unknown to prevent making mistakes. As a result, the Melancholy needs to be permitted to assume new responsibilities at their own pace. Give them time to acclimate to the new tasks and responsibilities and provide proper guidance; in the end, you will have a good leader who produces.

***Perception by Others.*** Fearful of criticism and making mistakes, the Melancholy projects an image of competence and confidence and is adept at hiding their insecurities. They can be friendly and outgoing with people who have earned their trust. Although they are compassionate and sensitive to people's needs, their logical outlook may make her seem cold or indifferent. As a result, they are perceived as an unfriendly loner. Careful and precise in their communications, they have difficulty with small talk or casual conversations and is reluctant to share their knowledge with others, especially in large groups. Perceived as distant and emotionally disconnected.

***Perception of Others.*** Because of their fear of rejection, the Melancholy may be suspicious of people's motives and project their negative self-perception onto others. They usually evaluate other people's words and behavior to determine whether they are being rejected and may become silent or withdraw if they perceive rejection. The Melancholy values people with excellent intellectual abilities, especially those who share their highly analytical approach to decision-making. They relate best to authority figures who are their intellectual equals or superiors. They are nonassertive even when their opinion is correct and avoids interpersonal conflict and aggression. They may apply their high standards to others and can become critical of those who fail to measure up.

***Intellectual Orientation.*** The Melancholy is intellectually gifted, a creative thinker who may score in the genius range on intelligence tests. They possess the unlimited capacity to acquire new knowledge and skills. As a leader, they will always be reading about or researching ways in which they can improve their leadership skills. Logical and analytical in her approach to life, the Melancholy views leadership as a series of tasks to be performed that in the end, will show real leadership. They collect data before making decisions or beginning new jobs and is very observant of people and their environment. Always thinking, evaluating, and questioning, they see vivid, detailed pictures in their mind and will be way ahead of others envisioning their approach and refining their skills as a leader. If they control their thoughts and don't get bogged down in negative thinking, they can be highly productive, and maintain a positive attitude. If their feelings are uncontrolled, they may experience emotional mood swings, often reliving adverse events in their mind, which will undermine their ability to function as kind leaders.

***Emotional Orientation.*** Compassionate and empathetic toward others, the Melancholy can remain emotionally guarded and is reluctant to share their emotions, often equating emotional expression with loss of control. And as a leader, in their mind, cannot subject themselves to the scrutiny of emotional expressions around their employees or much less around their peers. They may tend to be moody and pessimistic or struggle with depression if they do not keep their thinking out of the negative and always, if possible, end their thinking process on a positive note. They often feel anger at themselves or others, but internalize rather than express it. As a result, they may allow anger to build over a period then explode over a minor situation. They tend to hold grudges and mentally plan vengeance against the offender. The Melancholy can become anxious if required to interact with people frequently or for extended periods if they are deprived of daily quiet time alone. They have a strong need to avoid making mistakes and may become anxious if criticized. She also experiences stress if another person is their sole responsibility or if people pressure or attempt to control them.

It is essential here for the Melancholy to understand the "stinking thinking versus healthy thinking." Melancholy always go to the negative side of the ledger first in anything that they approach as being Melancholy. Negative thinking is not a bad thing, but what must be understood is the good and the evil of this kind of thinking. If I ask a Melancholy what they think of a new hire's resume, they will tell me everything negative about the person. Why? Because they are looking for perfection and to end up with perfection, they must first remove the **whole negative aspects**. Put simply, how do you get perfections? Eliminate the imperfections! That is the Melancholy approach to about everything in life. Want to sell them a new car? Give them the owner's manual, let them take it home and read it and then return with their unanswered questions. Don't try to tell them how beautiful, fast, and good-looking the car may be. They already know that as they have been on the Internet looking up data on the vehicle they are interested in and you must, as a salesperson, let them sell themselves the car by satisfying their need for data about the car. Same way with the possible new hire. The Melancholy leader wants to know everything there is about the prospective new hire, starting with the bad and ending up with the right real asset. The problem is that sometimes the Melancholy leader will end their assessment of the individual on a "stinking thinking" note and then ponder those negative thoughts over and over until they have beaten it to death. They will be depressed or gloomy because of spending so much time in the negative mode. It is crucial for the Melancholy to try to always, if possible, end in a positive note. Understanding this prevents gloom and doom and speeds up new hire evaluation. So, all you Melancholy get this understanding entrenched in your knowledge. It will improve your quality of leadership and your quality of life.

*Work Orientation.* Task-oriented rather than people-oriented, the Melancholy is highly analytical and approaches tasks in a logical, organized manner. They can visualize projects from start to finish and works tirelessly to lead their team to achieve goals and meet deadlines. They are outstanding in maintaining quality control in a work setting and views quality as more important than quantity. A perfectionist who leads, and checks work down to the smallest detail to ensure that it is error-free, they are rarely satisfied with the results. Self-disciplined, the Melancholy leader works well independently and resists authoritarian leadership from their superiors. To avoid making mistakes, they gather facts before making decisions; as a result, they may appear indecisive at times. They have excellent leadership abilities in common areas of responsibility but needs to gather and evaluate data before moving into unknown areas or responsibilities. They prefer not to take risks and will procrastinate or rebel if pushed into unfamiliar areas before they feel competent. They may perceive specific authority figures as demanding and will rebel to avoid being controlled by them but at the same time be an outstanding leader herself. The Melancholy functions well in a structured daily, highly organized routine. They know where they are going and who and what they need to get there.

*Motivation.* Independent and self-motivated as a leader, the Melancholy needs to lead and perform well to meet their high standards. They are strong-willed and can be stubborn and very tenacious. While they are usually not motivated by the promise of reward or the threat of punishment, they may have an intense fear of economic failure, which can be a first self-motivator in the workplace. A bonus for leaders with good results is always a motivating factor for the Melancholy

*Rejection/Acceptance Profile.* Because the Melancholy has a severe fear of rejection, they avoid people and situations that cause them to feel rejected. They can become defensive if criticized or corrected, and are very concerned about appearing incompetent as a leader, drawing self-esteem from the accuracy and practical application of their leadership skills and performance.

## The Relationship Profile - Melancholy

| Introvert | 0 | 1 | 2 | 3 | 4 | 5 | 6 | 7 | 8 | 9 | Extrovert |
|-----------|---|---|---|---|---|---|---|---|---|---|-----------|
|           |   |   |   |   |   |   |   |   |   |   |           |
| • *Demonstrated* | X |   |   |   |   |   |   |   |   |   |           |
| • *Desired* | X |   |   |   |   |   |   |   |   |   |           |

In considering the Melancholy's relationship profile, we need to look at some factors, beginning with relationship needs and desires.

# MELANCHOLY IN RELATIONSHIP

| Temperament (out of 3,449 people) | # People | Social | # People | Leadership | # People | Relationship |
|---|---|---|---|---|---|---|
| Melancholy | 1355 | 39.29% | 1084 | 31.43% | 800 | 23.20% |
| Melancholy Compulsive | 303 | 8.79% | 839 | 24.33% | 22 | 0.64% |

## A Note about the Relationship Profile

The adult relationship profile identifies your preferences for emotional involvement and shared affection on a one-to-one basis. This profile outlines your needs and desires for emotional sharing and relationships. For most people, the relationship profile is the dominant pattern that influences behavior in the social and leadership areas.

By comparing the relationship profile with your current life situation, you can target conflict areas and meet essential emotional needs that are not being met.

*Relationship Needs and Desires.* The Melancholy is independent and has a high need for privacy. They express a minimal amount of love and affection in close relationships and prefer minimal demonstrations of respect by others; in fact, they may feel smothered by too much physical affection. Although they may establish only a few close relationships in a lifetime, they are faithful and committed to those they love, depending on them to meet all their needs for love. They need acceptance and approval from others, but fear of rejection prevents them from becoming involved with most people. They view life and relationships as a series of tasks performed, and while they understand responsibility and duties, they may have difficulty recognizing people. For the Melancholy, display of affection can and is demonstrated in by "doing things" for their significant others. To the Melancholy, doing tasks for their inner circle of relationships is their way of showing affection. Even in close ties, they do not want sole responsibility for another's happiness or well-being. They are more comfortable relating to one-on-one or in small groups than in large gatherings. Possessing a strong family orientation, the Melancholy considers their home a sanctuary from the world and needs daily quiet time alone to counter the stress of being with people. Fewer people meet the relationship needs, whereas other temperaments need many people to satisfy their relationships needs. Not the Melancholy. They expect to get their needs met by one or two individuals and seldom if ever will have a lot of close friends. However, their own family is an exception, and most always Melancholy will get their inner needs and desires fulfilled by the family members. They may have one or two close friends outside the family, but seldom will there be more.

*Criteria for Relationships.* Socializing with very few people, the Melancholy tends to avoid social events. Because they have a strong need to develop trust in the other person before becoming emotionally involved, intimate relationships tend to grow too slowly and then allow themselves to become vulnerable only with carefully selected people. At the same time, with the few people they choose for friends, they are loyal, committed, and dependable, quick to make sacrifices for those they love. They tend to evaluate people intellectually rather than emotionally and may have impossibly high expectations for themselves and others. They avoid conflict in interpersonal relationships, valuing those who share their logical and rational approach to life; as a result, they usually avoid aggressive or domineering people. That doesn't mean they cannot become angered and display conflict. Don't push them because they can explode on you. They prefer not to explode. They get just as angry at themselves for blowing as they become the problems toward the person they blasted.

Parents who are Melancholy and have children who are extroverted such as Sanguine, Phlegmatic, and Choleric have a difficult time raising children. Extroverted children cause emotional disturbances in Melancholy parents because extroverted children are so demanding socially, physically, and they are very demonstrative, causing unrest for the introverted Melancholy parent(s) who are reserved emotionally. With their wanting to be around people most of the time if not always, their Melancholy parent becomes emotionally drained very quickly from all the emotional activity. The older the children get, the more social they become and sooner or later will want people in their home as friends, guest, parties, etc. and this is a major violation to the Melancholy parent(s). Temperament can be identified in early in child-rearing. Temperament can be assessed soon as age six (6) years old, and sometimes, the more mature five-year-old's can be profiled as well. Not knowing the temperament of children can cause far-reaching consequences between the parent and the children. It is not rebellion on the part of the child; it is a lack of temperament understanding on the part of the parent of the children and the parent's temperament differences and preferences. These issues are more likely to be a problem with a Melancholy parent than the extroverted parents because the Melancholy child can escape to their rooms and it is not evident to the parents that a problem exists. However, this can be a problem too if the parents demand that the Melancholy child is socially active and enroll the child in activities that require them to be interacting with other kids regularly. Lack of temperament knowledge is a problem for the Melancholy child and will cause them to be nervous, uptight, and complainers and whiners. Complaining and whining because they do not want to be with other kids all the time and they do not know what the problem is that causes them stress. They know they don't want to go to the local youth centers to be with a bunch of kids. They want to be in their room doing their own thing and thinking and pondering issues of interest and life itself. The child will have very few friends and maybe only one or two close friends that they want to play regularly.

***Perception of Self.*** Although they are intellectually gifted and talented in many areas, the Melancholy may feel inferior to others and hindered by low self-esteem and fear of rejection, and this will cause them to have few close relationships. They tend to be reflective and self-critical and may endlessly analyze their behavior and perceived faults, and this perception will hinder them having relationships. They often focus inward on their thoughts rather than outward on people or events. Lack of communication is a problem as they get no feedback from friends and close family members. They may be unaware of their potential in life and can be pessimistic about their abilities. The adolescent years for the Melancholy are lonely and very intimidating because they realize they don't know that much, and that makes them very uncomfortable. A perfectionist, the Melancholy may set impossible standards for themselves, and becomes depressed when they fail to attain them where relationships are concerned, and they may not realize that it is a temperament issue until later in life and sometimes they never find out because no one ever tells them about temperament. Therefore, they go through life hindered just because of being informed about their unique disposition. They go through life feeling there is something drastically wrong with them. That is not true: they need to understand their uniqueness as individuals.

***Perception by Others.*** Projecting an image of competence and confidence, the Melancholy is adept at hiding their insecurities even though they fear criticism and making mistakes. They can be friendly and outgoings with people who have earned their trust, and although they are compassionate and sensitive to other people's needs, their logical outlook may give the impression that they are cold or indifferent. They will be careful and precise in their communications; they have difficulty with small talk or casual conversations and expresses love by performing tasks for others instead of through verbal or physical demonstrations. As a result, they are not inclined to be romantic and perceived as an unfriendly loner. The Melancholy may become defensive if criticized or demeaned by loved ones. One of the leading causes leading to relationship failures is self-defense

***Perception of Others.*** Because of their fear of rejection, the Melancholy may be suspicious of other people's motives and project their negative self-perception onto others. They usually evaluate their words and behavior to determine whether they are being rejected and may become silent or withdraw if, they perceive rejection. They may fear rejection by those they love, especially if they have suffered hurts in close relationships in the past and can be easily hurt sometimes by the innocent comments or actions of others. As a result, they rarely show their emotions. They are nonassertive even when their opinion is correct and avoid interpersonal aggression. The Melancholy may apply their high standards to others and can become critical of those who fail to measure up. The lack of demonstrative behavior of the Melancholy toward others is a "catch-22" issue. Others perceive them as not wanting to be approached, and the Melancholy perception is that people do not contact them because they are not approachable, likable, or loveable. Therefore, their understanding of others based on the mirrored reflection of what they are projecting on to them. In the end, the Melancholy loses.

***Intellectual Orientation.*** Intellectually gifted, the Melancholy is a creative thinker and may score in the genius range on intelligence tests. They have an unlimited capacity to acquire new knowledge and skills, is logical and analytical in their approach to life, and frequently asks questions to get all the facts before making decisions. This systematic approach can be a "showstopper" where relationships are concerned, because the intellectual orientation of the Melancholy can come across as being "better than you," or "smarter than you." The Melancholy is very observant of people and their environment and is continually thinking, evaluating, and questioning. They see vivid, detailed pictures in their mind and can be very creative. If they learn to control their thoughts, they can be highly productive and maintain a positive attitude and share their gifting of ideas, dreams, and knowledge. If their beliefs are uncontrolled, they may experience emotional mood swings and re-experience adverse events in their mind. This moving swing will make them less tolerable in relationships and cause unwarranted damage to existing relationships. In general, the Melancholy is a self-disciplined, task-oriented, perfectionist and this will come out in the development of their few close relationships

***Emotional Orientation.*** Although they're compassionate and empathetic toward others, the Melancholy is reluctant to share their emotions and remains emotionally guarded, often equating emotional expressions with loss of control. Their compassion is a gift but is concealed by the guardedness of the Melancholy to display their genuine compassion. They are the kind of person who will sit in a movie theater and hold back tears during painful or moving moments. They are defensive about expressing their feelings, even in close relationships. They may struggle with depression and tend to be moody and pessimistic, often with feelings of anger at herself or others but internalizing rather than expressing it. They may allow anger to build over a period and then explode over a minor situation. They tend to hold grudges and mentally plan vengeance against the offender. Sometimes they will voice their revenge, but very seldom will they act on what they say. It is the anger of the moment manifesting in what they say. It is venting for them. As a result, they may be prone to stress-related physical ailments. Melancholy becomes anxious if he is required to socialize frequently or for extended periods or daily time alone is not on their schedule. They also may feel anxiety if criticized and has a strong need to avoid making mistakes. They prefer to avoid situations that require emotional openness instead of intellectual analysis. They are very capable of playing head games. So be careful how you go about developing your relationships as head games can backfire. If they lose a close connection for any reason, they may never wholly recover emotionally from the hurt. And no one will ever know what is going on inside of them. This is a very lonely place for them to be because they cannot express their feeling to themselves, let alone to a friend or a counselor.

*Motivation.* Independent and self-motivated, the Melancholy needs to perform well to meet her high standards. They are strong-willed and can be stubborn. They are usually not motivated by the promise of reward or the threat of punishment; instead, for the Melancholy, an intense, healthy fear of economic failure can be a first self-motivator. They resist controlling and being controlled in close relationships, and may respond in the defensive if challenged or corrected.

*Rejection/Acceptance Profile.* The Melancholy has a severe fear of rejection and is fearful of appearing incompetent or being criticized for their mistakes, especially around those they are in a close relationship. As a result, they are defensive and avoid people and situations that cause them to feel rejected, depending on their few close connections to meet all their acceptance needs.

## Help for the Melancholy
### Characteristics of the Melancholy

*Probable Strengths*
- Intellectually gifted – possesses many creative abilities
- Analytical – is detail-oriented, methodical, and often a perfectionist
- Self-sacrificing – loyal to loved ones; go above and beyond the call of duty
- Diligent – works tirelessly to achieve goals and meet deadlines
- Disciplined –organized; precise in communications
- Faithful in relationships – committed and dependable
- Sensitive and compassionate – is the most human sympathetic of all the temperaments but does not show it

*Potential Weaknesses*
- Moody – tends to be gloomy or depressed; pessimistic
- Indecisive – fears making mistakes; is prone to be negative, causing indecisiveness, for fear of being wrong
- Introspective – self-centered and self-critical; is the most self-centered of all the temperaments

- Critical – high expectations of people; impossible to please; is the most crucial of all the temperaments
- Sensitive – is touchy and "thin-skinned"; needs to be handled with kid gloves and expects to be appreciated
- Introverted – tends to be a loner; is usually unsociable and needs time to warm up to people; is suspicious of people

### *Decisions for the Melancholy*

Decision making for them is a deliberate process as they must always be perfect.
If they lack data, they will stall making decisions until they accumulate enough data to make the right choices.

Now that we've considered the critical features of the Melancholy's social/vocational, leadership, and relationship profiles, you have a good idea of what this temperament is all about. The chart shows some common characteristics of Melancholy, including probable strengths and potential weaknesses.

If you're a Melancholy, you spend a reasonable amount of time alone—so, you have an excellent opportunity to study the following paragraphs to consider some things that will help you better understand yourself:

*You are an introvert.* Being an introvert, a loner, a recluse is okay. There is no reason for you to feel in the wrong about not wanting to meet people and be around people. Plain and straightforward that is who you are. You don't *need* to be with people. You require more detached time away from people, so you can do what you do—think, dream, regenerate, analyze, and ponder issues of life in general. Your mind works 24 hours a day, seven days a week, 365 days a week. Even when you do go to sleep, there's a good chance you have a very active dream life.

There are times when you do need to put forth an effort to be with people; however, you also need to know that *you do not need to socialize*. Socializing is very low on your priorities of things to do in life. At the same time, if you are on a "mission," you *can* socialize and do an outstanding job of it. You can put on the face of an extrovert and go about your assignment communicating with everyone. But to you, you are completing a task and not socializing—you are *working*. Being with people is imperative for you to remember as it will serve as a way of getting exposure when you want to be with people or have identified a particular person or persons that you want to interact. Just put your "task mask" on and take control. No one will ever know what you are doing because they cannot see behind your mask. No one gets to look behind the veil of a Melancholy unless the Melancholy wants them to find who is behind the masks. Isn't that perfect for the Melancholy?

If you were (or are being) raised by one or more Sanguine parents, they may force you into socializing regularly. In this case, you were "tampered with"—that is, your parents tried to "mold" you into being somebody you are not, an extrovert, instead of an introvert that you are; this is called *abuse*. You will tend to feel guilty, or that something is wrong with you because you are not "normal" like the rest of the families. "Normal" to a Sanguine is always socializing; standard to a Melancholy, however, is being alone. You must remember that the key is to maintain balance in your life. You should not shut yourself off from people, but neither should you socialize like a Sanguine. Once you understand your temperament, you can experience the liberation and freedom to be who you are without fear of disapproval from others.

Socializing is a great issue for Melancholy to grasp; once you do, your quality of life will improve dramatically.

***You have a fear of economic failure.*** Being careful with your money is okay. At the same time, you must learn to find and preserve a balance with your finances. Stockpiling cash when your husband, wife, or children need something is not maintaining a balance, but instead causes hardships on your family members.

Your fear of economic failure is real and requires significant consideration by all concerned. People with other temperaments need to be aware that money is not their "god." Your economic security is critical if you are to enjoy and experience an improved quality of life. You need to learn to maintain a comfortable level of financial security while keeping balance with those you interface with daily.

For you to have a tolerable level of financial security, you may need to do one or more of the following:

- Maintain a minimum balance in your checking or savings account.
- Always keep at least several hundred dollars in your purse or pocket.
- Refrain from charging or buying anything on credit—because you are afraid you won't be able to pay it back. Even mortgages and car payments cause enormous stress for the Melancholy. You will always be trying to pay them off as quickly as possible. Make it a priority to use credit cards as a convenience for you to make purchases but make sure you pay the balance off each month, thus avoiding interest and fees. It then becomes an asset to you because you are building proper credit and using their money to do it. Just make sure you pay the balance off each month **before** the deadline of being charged interest.
- Wait until "specials" are running on things you want to buy.
- Sacrifice your wardrobe instead of spending more money on fashionable clothes.
- Buy a car a couple of years old, so you don't lose all that money driving the new car off the lot. Buying a used car will save you thousands of dollars and pay cash if possible.
- Live within a fixed budget that permits funding for all family members. The critical issue here is B-U-D-G-E-T. Resources work, but you must have discipline. So, make your plan and work the plan. It works very well. How do you think I know?

If you do not maintain balance in the financial area, this fear can consume you to the point that others (including your family) will criticize you for being selfish and thinking only of your own immediate needs.

***You are task oriented.*** It's acceptable to be task oriented. You don't have to feel wrong about needing to keep busy doing tasks. If you stopped doing these responsibilities or jobs, you would feel no value and that you are wasting your time.

When relationship-oriented people surround you, you will tend to think that you are letting these people down if you do not stop "working" to socialize. But if you do stay to socialize and not do a task, your self-esteem will become quite depressed because you feel that you are not a responsible individual. Also, you will experience tremendous stress while you are standing there socializing. The longer you are "nonproductive," to the extent that you need to produce, the higher your anxiety will become.

***You tend to live in your mind.*** It's part of being a Melancholy to be a thinker—but you must not always be thinking negative thoughts. Because you tend to think negative or downward reflection thoughts, you push even your loved ones away from you.

Your mind is like a sci-fi amusement area, and you are very creative in your thinking processes. You can see very vivid pictures and scenes that are out of your past, or you can create new ones as you think. You can reexamine past events over and over, examining and revisiting the same experiences.

One of the most common statements you will say is, "I cannot stop thinking." The issue of you're not being able to stop thinking makes you predisposed to having suicidal thoughts. You think you are crazy because you can't stop thinking. Not being able to *stop your thinking is absurd and is not valid at all.* Constant thought is pervasively ordinary for the Melancholy mind and is nothing to be alarmed over. It is usual for your brain to race all the time. Some Melancholy try to commit suicide to stop thinking. You need to learn to do something with your mind to settle down from negative thinking. Negative thinking can be such a massive part of your thought processes because you always want to be right and perfect. You can try various things to relax your thinking, such as studying something interesting or listening to music, the wind or ocean waves. Watching clouds, birds, animals, insects, or exploring your surroundings can bring you peace. Reading a favorite book or just going for a car ride on the country roads can help mellow you out. It is up to you to discover ways to loosen up from thinking.

Remember, negative thoughts do not belong to you until you take hold of the idea and start, concentrating on it for extended periods. You need to learn to reject the negative thoughts and fill your minds with positive ones.

## Do's and Don'ts for the Melancholy

| Do | Don't |
|---|---|
| • Realize no one likes gloomy people | • Look for trouble |
| • Look for the positive | • Get hurt easily |
| • Search out the source of your insecurities | • Spend so much time planning |
| • Listen for evidence of "false humility." | • Procrastinate |
| • Realize that your insecurities are due to your having to be perfect | • Put unrealistic demands on others |
| • Get the "right things" before starting | • Retreat from those who care |
| • Make quicker decisions | • Become addicted |
| • Relax your unrealistic standards for yourself and others | • Focus on the negative things in life |
| • Be grateful you understand your temperament | • Look at life as a drudgery |
| • Realize you will never be perfect | • Take life so fatally |
| • Lighten up and enjoy life | • Expect others to measure up to your perfectionist ways |
| • Focus on the positive things in your life | • Hide who you are behind a mask |
| • Respect other temperaments | • Always be focusing on tasks; people are talented too |
| • Learn from other temperaments | • Forget to have fun along the way |

Become Aware of Your Natural Strengths and Learn to Use Them Wisely

| Natural Strength | | Strength Carried to the Extreme | | Compulsion |
|---|---|---|---|---|
| | | | | |
| Programmed | | Cannot function without a scheduled plan | | Obsessed with promptness |
| | | | | |
| Physical conditioning | | Extreme physical conditioning | | Can become paranoid about physical appearance |
| | | | | |
| Perfectionist | | Expects others to be perfect too | | Always critical and judging of others |
| | | | | |
| Self-sufficient | | Avoidance of socialization | | Becomes narcissistic and egotistical |

How to Recognize Whether Your Child Is Melancholy

| Strengths | Weaknesses | Emotional Needs |
|---|---|---|
| *Baby* | | |
| Likes routine, quiet, and somber | Cries easily adhere to mother or father | Security, stability, and parental nurturing |
| *Child* | | |
| Intellectual, intense, real friend | Bellyacher and irritable | Validation and support from parents |
| *Teen* | | |
| Neat, creative, economically conscientious | Isolated, depressed, critical of others, and a bad attitude | Isolation from people, quiet time, and stability |

## BASIC MELANCHOLY TEMPERAMENT DETAILS

The Melancholy

I. Potential Strengths of the Melancholy Temperament
   A. Gifted-Genius-prone (A higher percentage of geniuses are Melancholy than any other type.) Usually, have a high IQ
   B. Analytical
      1. A hound for detail.
      2. Analytical ability causes them to diagnose accurately.

C. Self-Sacrificing
1. Doesn't like to be in the limelight but wants to work behind the scene.
2. Will work hard to meet deadlines and will work around the clock if necessary.

D. Self-Disciplined
1. Extremely self-disciplined.
2. Usually, know their limitations and will not take on more than they can handle.
3. Typically does not waste words like the Sanguine but is very precise in stating what they mean.

E. Faithful Friend
1. Seldom puts himself forward to meet people, but instead lets them come to them.
2. Most dependable of all the temperaments because of their perfectionist and conscientious tendencies.
3. Has a strong desire to be loved but finds it difficult to express their true feelings.
4. Faithfulness comes naturally.

F. Perfectionist
1. Strong perfectionistic tendencies.
2. Because they are very reflective, they often relive events and decisions made in the past, thinking how much better they would do it if given another opportunity.

G. Sensitive – Most sensitive of the temperaments.

II. Potential Weaknesses/Shortcomings of the Melancholy Temperament

A. Moody
1. Tends to be very gloomy and depressed.
2. Moodiness is often the result of his self-centered thinking pattern.

B. Self-Centered
1. The most naturally self-centered of the temperaments.
2. Inclined to self-examination and mentally dissecting himself.
3. Prone to be suspicious that people are against him, which can lead to a persecution complex.

C. Pessimistic – Prone to be cynical, which makes him indecisive and fearful of making decisions because they do not want to be wrong and fall short of their perfectionist standards.

D. Critical – The most crucial of the temperaments.
1. Tends to be unyielding in their expectations of other human beings and cannot happily take less than their very best.
2. Criticism, if not spoken, is usually given through nonverbal means.
3. Instead of seeing the good, they tend to look at the wrong.
4. Choleric is hard to please, and Melancholy are impossible to satisfy.

E. Touchy – "Thin-Skinned" and usually needs to be handled with "kid gloves."

F. Unsociable
1. An introvert, although sometimes they will appear to be an extrovert.

2. Needs time to warm up to people.
3. Usually has a small group of friends they feel comfortable being around.

G. Negative – because their perfectionism and conscientiousness often carry with them the severe disadvantages of negativism, pessimism, and criticism.

## Perfect Melancholy

Perfect Melancholy Are Easily Depressed

- Realize no one likes gloomy people
- Don't look for trouble
- Don't get hurt easily
- Look for the positive

Perfect Melancholy Have Low Self-Image

- Search out the source of your insecurities
- Listen for evidence of "false humility."
- Realize that your insecurities are due to your having to be perfect

Perfect Melancholy Procrastinate

- Get the "right things" before starting
- Don't spend so much time planning
- Make quicker decisions

Perfect Melancholy Put Unrealistic Demands on Others

- Relax your unrealistic standards for yourself and others
- Be grateful you understand your temperament
- Realize you will never be perfect

# STRENGTH AND WEAKNESSES
## of the
## MELANCHOLY-PERFECT

|  | STRENGTHS | WEAKNESSES |
|---|---|---|
| **EMOTIONS:** | Deep and thoughtful | Remembers the negatives; |
|  | Analytical | Moody and depressed |
|  | Severe and purposeful | Fears hurt feelings |
|  | Genius-prone | Has false humility |
|  | Talented and creative | Off in another world |
|  | Artistic or musical | Low self-image |
|  | Philosophical and poetic | Has selective hearing |
|  | Appreciative of beauty | Self-centered |
|  | Sensitive to others | Too introspective |
|  | Self-sacrificing | Guilt feelings |
|  | Conscientious | Persecution complex |
|  | Idealistic | Tends to hypochondria |
| **WORK:** | Schedule-oriented | Not people-oriented |
|  | Perfectionist, high standards | Depressed over imperfections |
|  | Detail-conscious | Chooses a difficult task |
|  | Persistent and thorough | Hesitant to start projects |
|  | Orderly and organized | Spends too much time planning |
|  | Neat and tidy | Prefers analysis to work |
|  | Economical | Self-deprecating |
|  | Sees the problems | Hard to please |
|  | Finds creative solutions | Standards often too high |
|  | Needs to finish what he starts | Deep need for approval |
|  | Likes charts, graphs, figures, lists | |
| **FRIENDS:** | Makes friends cautiously | Lives through others |
|  | Content to stay in background | Insecure socially |
|  | Avoids causing attention | Withdrawn and remote |
|  | Faithful and devoted | Critical of others |
|  | Will listen to complaints | Holds back the affection |
|  | Can solve others' problems | Dislikes those in opposition |
|  | Sincere concern for other people | Suspicious of people |
|  | Moved to tears with compassion | Antagonistic and vengeful |
|  | Seeks ideal mate | Unforgiving |
|  | | Full of contradictions |
|  | | Skeptical of compliments |

## Temperament Weaknesses
## of the Melancholy

Bashful     –     Shrinks from getting attention, resulting from self-consciousness.

Unforgiving     –     One who has difficulty releasing or forgetting a hurt or injustice done to them, apt to hold onto a grudge.

Resentful     –     Often holds ill feelings because of real or imagined offenses.

Overelaborate     –     Insistent over trivial matters or details, calling for significant attention to insignificant details.

Insecure     –     One who is apprehensive or lacks confidence.

Unpopular     –     A person whose intensity and demand for perfection can push others away.

Hard to Please     –     A person whose standards set so high that it is difficult ever to satisfy them.

Pessimistic     –     While hoping for the best, this person sees the downside of a situation first.

Alienated     –     Easily feels estranged from others often because of insecurity or fear that others don't enjoy his company.

Negative Attitude     –     One whose attitude is seldom positive and is often able to see only the down or dark sides of each situation.

Withdrawn     –     A person who pulls back to himself and needs a great deal of alone or isolation time.

Too Sensitive     –     Overly introspective and easily offended when misunderstood.

Depressed     –     A person who feels down much of the time.

Introvert     –     A person whose thoughts and interests directed inward lives within himself.

Moody     –     Doesn't get very high emotionally, but quickly slips into low lows, often when feeling unappreciated.

Skeptical     –     Disbelieving, questioning the motive behind the words.

Loner     –     Requires a lot of private time and tends to avoid other people.

Suspicious     –     Tends to suspect or distrust others or ideas.

Revengeful     –     Knowingly holds a grudge and punishes the offender, often by subtly withholding friendship or affection.

Critical     –     Constantly evaluating and making judgments, frequently thinking or expressing adverse reactions.

## Temperament Strengths
## of the Melancholy

Analytical     –     Likes to examine the parts of their logical and proper relationships.

Persistent     –     Sees one project through to its completion before starting another.

Self-Sacrificing     –     Willingly give up his being for the sake of, or to meet the needs of, others.

Considerate     –     Having regard for the needs and feelings of others.

Respectful     –     Treats others with deference, honor, and esteem.

Sensitive     –     Intensively cares about others and what happens.

Planner     –     Prefers to work out a detailed arrangement beforehand for the accomplishment of project or goal and prefers involvement with the planning stages and the finished product rather than the carrying out of the task.

| | | |
|---|---|---|
| Scheduled | – | Makes and lives according to a daily plan, dislike his intention to be interrupted. |
| Orderly | – | A person who has a methodical, systematic arrangement of things. |
| Faithful | – | Consistently reliable, steadfast, loyal, and sometimes devoted beyond reason. |
| Detailed | – | Does everything in proper order with a clear memory of all the things that happened. |
| Cultured | – | One whose interests involve both intellectual and artistic pursuits such as theatre, symphony, ballet. |
| Idealistic | – | Visualizes things in their perfect form and needs to measure up to that standard himself. |
| Deep | – | Intense and often introspective with a distaste for surface conversation and pursuits. |
| Musical | – | Participates in or has a sincere appreciation for music, is committed to music as an art form rather than the fun of performance. |
| Thoughtful | – | A considerate person who remembers special occasions and is quick to make a kind gesture. |
| Loyal | – | Faithful to a person, ideal, or job, sometimes beyond reason. |
| Chart maker | – | Organizes life, tasks, and problem solving by making lists, forms, or graphs. |
| Perfectionist | – | Places high standards on himself and often on others, desiring that everything be in proper order at all times. |
| Behaved | – | Consistently desires to conduct himself within the realm of what he feels is proper. |

# CHAPTER 8

# THE CHOLERIC

Steve is what you would call a take-charge kind of guy. Regardless of what needs to get done, he is ready to jump in head first. Here are a few of the phrases that might describe Steve: "Just do it," "Shoot first, ask questions later," "Take no prisoners," "Might make a right," "Do or die...," "Lead, follow or get out of the way"—get the picture? Although Steve prefers to be correct about everything—and he rarely admits it when he's wrong—his primary motivation is merely to *get things done*. If he makes a decision that doesn't get him what he wants, or his choice happens to be the wrong decision, he'll make another decision to fix the problem and move on. For Steve, the end always justifies the means regardless of who gets hurt in the process. Although he can be quite charming when things are going his way when Steve doesn't understand what he wants, his anger can take over, and he can become ruthless and offensive. Here is one example of an angry Choleric.

Frank worked for a huge computer company in the Northeast, with thousands of employees, and he was one of the top six senior leaders in the organization. He had authority and power, and everyone knew it. The company had a facility down south and the director of that institution, with over 600 employees, was not in good standing with Frank. One day in a scheduled meeting, Frank announced he was going south to correct a situation with one of his directors. He commented, "I'll show him who's boss." The following week, I asked him how the meeting went down south. His reply: "Well, I showed him who was boss. I closed his facility." Frank had closed the facility and put over 600 people in unemployment lines to get to one person, the director of the installation, and he was bragging about it and laughing. Talk about being a hard-nosed, insensitive leader—Wow! He is just one example so hold on to your seats: we will discuss other Choleric leaders later in this chapter.

At work, Steve sets high goals for himself and his colleagues, then steamrolls over everyone and everything that gets in his way. He doesn't care who opposes him or what his critics say about him if he meets his objectives. His opinion is the only one that matters, and he even challenges his supervisors when their agendas don't coincide with his.

In his relationships, Steve enjoys the company of people he can lead—or dominate. Because of his task-oriented, in-control attitudes, Steve has few real friends. Do Choleric have real friends? You will find the Choleric very charming and open in their communications, and you will think that "Hey, this is a nice person and seems as though it would be easy to make friends with." Well, "Yes" and "No!" Yes, they can be more fun people and seem to be caring about other people. However, Choleric people are

**always** on the prowl. By saying "on the prowl," I am referring to the fact that they are **always** looking for people to fit in within their scheme, project, organization, team, or whatever it may be that they are trying to accomplish. In other words, whenever you engage a Choleric, always ask yourself the question: how is this person relating to me? Do I have some skill, product, knowledge, or connection that they can benefit? Most generally, but not always, they will be on an assignment to find people to help them fulfill their mission. So, do Choleric have friends? Yes, they do have friends, or should I say many if not most people would classify them as a friend, but the Choleric will have only a few close friends, those who can get into their inner circle. Most generally it is going to be another Choleric or a Melancholy as they are very compatible. But for sure if you are a friend to a Choleric, you can bet your bottom dollar that their relationship is a "relationship of opportunity." So, they are attracted towards each other because they either have an agenda or they see something in the relationship that can assist them in furthering their goals, ideas, or their dreams. In the process of him connecting with others, there is always a possibility that they will become real friends and develop a long-lasting healthy relationship. Most people will admire Choleric individuals just because they always seem to be on top of whatever they are doing or pursuing. And everyone likes to be recognized as a person who is "in the know" or "rubbing elbows" with successful people. So, if you are in a relationship with him, you will be one of those people who, by association, will be blessed by their contribution to your endeavors or just plain recognition of who you are because of the relationship with him. Those with a Choleric temperament are "movers and shakers," and they tend to run with others who think as they do on the grander scale of life rather than the mundane routines of ho-hum daily life. Choleric is as far away from inconsequential as you can get; they thrive on adventure and are great explorers. The world is their playground. Give them a global airline ticket, a rucksack, and a pair of good hiking boots, and they would be thrilled exploring the entire world. Just get out of the way! Now.

Steve is a Choleric. He is independent, visionary, inspiring, and productive. He is very strong-willed and makes decisions quickly—and he is comfortable with the outcome, often defending his position even when it leads to failure. The Choleric exhibits strong leadership abilities and is an innovative problem solver. He sets ambitious objectives for himself and others and will do whatever it takes to accomplish them, even at the expense of the physical, emotional, or spiritual health of himself and those around him. When he is challenged or unsuccessful, he often uses his anger as the primary motivator to "get people in line." The result of this approach is to alienate himself from other people. The Choleric, however, acts as if he doesn't care and remains aloof, projecting an attitude of superiority and confidence. The level of trust of the Choleric can also be the greatest strength of the Choleric, and it can also be their greatest weakness. You have heard the phrase that says, "Your greatest strength is also your greatest weakness." Well, that is an accurate statement.

Look at the champions on television that have those brutal contests to determine who the most muscular men in the world. They pull boxcars on a train track, lift stones that weight two times more than their weight. Not once but several times to put them on top of a pedestal one at a time. Lifting massive loads and each lift gets heavier by several pounds each lift. Or dragging heavy chains use for ships' anchors 100 feet, on and on it goes. These guys are powerful and can do unbelievable feats of strength. **But,** have you ever seen one of them do **more** than their body will accommodate? What happens? They tear a muscle, ligament, and even break bones because they go too far. Why? Because of arrogance, pride, or they plain go more now than they should and as a result, end up severely hurt. Their most significant asset became their greatest weakness, taking them out of the competition and putting them in a rehabilitation program for several months. And in some cases, the damage is so severe that they can never again participate in that sport again.

How about the person who accepts an assignment others will not touch because of the difficulty of the task? They call on the Choleric because they have a reputation for being able to "always come through" and, as a result, the Choleric knows that they have that reputation and want to "look good" in the eyes of those observing them. So, they take the assignment only to find themselves in a situation where they are working eighty (80) hours per week, have no private life. Their family neglected, their mind in overload modes and they become so worn out that they collapse. Why? Because they are known for getting things done, and they want to show everyone that they can "do it." After all, isn't it proper to protect your pride? No—not at the expense of your health and family.

One good example is the office of the president of the United States. Look at any president, current or past, and find a picture of them before they became president and then get another view of them after they left the office of president. They have gray hair, black eyes, and look like they have aged many years beyond their rear calendar age. I would venture to say that most presidents, current, and the past, are strong Choleric. Of course, President Donald J. Trump is no push-over.

**Physically.** The Choleric is usually very active and always on assignment. Hence, they tend to overextend themselves physically regularly. But they validate their actions as necessary for accomplishing the goals. Their ability to expend much more energy than most temperaments—nevertheless, the Melancholy surely will give them a challenge—enables them to physically extend themselves to the point of jeopardizing their health and in some cases their physical well-being and safety. Again, their desire to excel in whatever they do is always at the forefront of the Choleric. They almost must shine to satisfy themselves. Sometimes they even find themselves in competition with themselves. Talk about overdoing it!

**Emotionally.** Emotionally the Choleric is the most challenging core temperament of all the temperaments. The Choleric shows very little emotion and can cast disapproval on those attitudes that do show emotionalisms or any sign of weakness. Consider General George S. Patton when he visited the field hospital tent and reprimanded the soldier who was in the hospital because he was "afraid" of combat. General Patton slapped him with his gloves— it was winter—several times and yelled at them to get him out of his sight. Emotionally the Choleric can be like a brick. Even in relationships, the Choleric can be quite hard and insensitive. We will cover their insensitiveness later in the book when we look at the Choleric in relationship

**Spiritually.** The Choleric is a competent person and therefore depends upon their senses, education, experiences, and their ability to make quick decisions. They do not put much emphasis on their spirituality. However, if they are rooted and grounded in their spiritual journey and are close to God, they can be a significant player in the world of fulfilling the Great Commandment of Matthew 28. They make great pastors, evangelists, teachers, and missionaries. Their biggest problem spiritually is that they will depend on God seventy-five percent (75%) of the time and rely on themselves twenty-five percent (25%) percent of the time. They do get themselves into "hot water" when they rely on themselves and are not "in tune" with God. Sometimes they learn some tough lessons due to this self-centeredness. You cannot call it narcissistic as it is a just precise determination of the Choleric following their set of rules. They almost always will find a way out of their bad decisions, but they can hurt others in the process. If they are functioning in a spiritual capacity and leading others "the sheep," they can lead them down the wrong paths and cause unnecessary injury.

## Choleric – Demonstrated vs. Desired Behavior

Choleric is, by nature, an active leader and not a follower. As the chart shows, in the extreme he *demonstrates* highly extroverted behavior but *desires* that people leave him alone. In other words, he is good at giving orders but don't want told what to do by anyone. However, there is an exception to this rule. The Choleric will submit to another authority but only for a certain length of time. Choleric must either be in leadership or be in a position where they can work their way up the chain until they find they are in a place of leadership. More on this subject discussed in the leadership section.

| Introvert | 0 | 1 | 2 | 3 | 4 | 5 | 6 | 7 | 8 | 9 | Extrovert |
|---|---|---|---|---|---|---|---|---|---|---|---|
| | | | | | | | | | | | |
| **Social** | | | | | | | | | | | |
| • *Demonstrated* | | | | | | | | | | X | |
| • *Desired* | X | | | | | | | | | | |
| **Leadership** | | | | | | | | | | | |
| • *Demonstrated* | | | | | | | | | | X | |
| • *Desired* | X | | | | | | | | | | |
| **Relationship** | | | | | | | | | | | |
| • *Demonstrated* | | | | | | | | | | X | |
| • *Desired* | X | | | | | | | | | | |

Let's look at the three areas of the WIDP profile—social/vocational, leadership, and relationship—to learn more about the Choleric.

## The Social/Vocational Profile – Choleric

| Introvert | 0 | 1 | 2 | 3 | 4 | 5 | 6 | 7 | 8 | 9 | Extrovert |
|---|---|---|---|---|---|---|---|---|---|---|---|
| | | | | | | | | | | | |
| • *Demonstrated* | | | | | | | | | | X | |
| • *Desired* | X | | | | | | | | | | |

In considering the Choleric social/vocational profile, we need to look at some factors, beginning with social needs and desires.

## CHOLERIC IN SOCIAL

| Temperament (out of 3,449 people) | # People | Social | # People | Leadership | # People | Relationship |
|---|---|---|---|---|---|---|
| Choleric | 50 | 1.45% | 415 | 12.03% | 16 | 0.46% |
| Melancholy Compulsive | 0 | 0.00% | 175 | 5.07% | 0 | 0.00% |

### A Note about the Social Profiles

The social profile outlines your needs and desires for light friendships, work/career associations, and other casual relationships. By comparing the social profile with your current life situation, you can understand conflict areas and achieve a comfortable level of interpersonal contact in work or social environment.

*Remember:* The social profile should be applied only to your casual social/career contacts. To determine your needs and desires in close personal relationships, please consult the relationship profile.

*Social Needs and Desires.* Outgoing and personable in social settings, the Choleric appears to want a high degree of socialization with many people; in truth, he needs and wants only a few carefully selected friends but many casual acquaintances. He has a strong need for accomplishment and may choose activities and friendships that will assist him in attaining his goals, not for purely social reasons. The Choleric has a great need to be in control of his destiny. The Choleric in the social profile will compete with other Choleric in a social setting. Both will become and are automatically competitive with each other. They can become assets to each other if they permit themselves not to be threatened by each other. There is an underlying need to achieve and conquer, but they can at the same time put their mask on and looks and sound very charming. Choleric likes to be the center of attention in social gatherings. Choleric needs to learn how to be sensitive to the needs of other temperaments in social settings and learn how to enjoy those people too.

*Criteria for Relationships.* Achievement-oriented rather than people-oriented, the Choleric depends on their knowledge and skills and has minimal need for close interpersonal relationships. The Choleric will be more fun when it is beneficial to them. They always have their vision or goal at the center of everything they do when interacting with others. If the Choleric determines you can be helpful to them in their idea or purpose, they will come off as pleasant to you, but if you do not have the necessary skills, training, or knowledge they need, then they could care less about you or what you think. Sounds hard but that is what makes him a Choleric. When they do develop relationships, they tend to seek out people they can influence, especially those who can help accomplish their personal goals. They're drawn to individuals who recognize and appreciate their accomplishments and may avoid close relationships with other strong-willed people. They can flip a mental switch in a heartbeat and go from being beautiful and comfortable with the people and turn around and demolish another person. Unfortunately, the Choleric has the characteristics of being very cruel and enjoy it. One must be careful when engaging a Choleric as they can treat you with great respect and in a moment become another person. They can "put on" whatever face they need now to accomplish their goal. Remember, for the Choleric it's all about them and not about you. They will do whatever it takes to get the job done and use whoever they can to do it.

***Perception of Self.*** The Choleric projects optimism and self-confidence can be egotistical, and seldom admits to making a mistake. They are confident in their ability to achieve whatever he desires. His high need for control may mask inner fears, including an inferiority complex; you are never going to know this is going on inside of them, and they would rather die than let anyone know that they could feel that way based upon their actions. Thriving on challenges and setting high personal goals, the Choleric maintains an attitude of competence and usually has an answer or solution to problems. Sometimes they are referred to as know-it-alls. He can adapt his behavior to circumstances and fill any role they feel necessary to achieve his goals. He can step into about any vocational arena and take over. They do not not have to be skilled in the vocation as they will learn as they go and will not look back on bad decisions or mistakes. They will adjust and continue with the focus until they become competent in that particular area. Active and involved, they rarely spend time in self-introspection but views themselves only from a positive perspective.

***Perception by Others.*** Possessing natural leadership abilities, they maintain an image of superiority and confidence. They have excellent social skills and can be outgoing and charismatic as well as physically affectionate, or you may call it "charming." They often give the impression that they desire close relationships with many people; in reality, they are very selective in choosing their friends and may have little understanding of people's needs and emotions. They are usually the dominant figure in groups, often intimidating less confident people by his high energy and decisive manner. They may directly confront those who disagree with them and can be critical and argumentative. They may appear to be a braggart or as one who sees himself in a higher light than others do.

But on the other hand, most generally they will be successful, competent, aggressive, and they possess a compelling desire to fulfill their vision. Sometimes they can be perceived as very charming and genuine in their concerns for all humanity, but underneath that charm and influential personality, there is a "velvet-covered brick." So, beware: you've been forewarned!

***Perception of Others.*** The Choleric is individualistic and does not need to please people, meet their expectations, or seek their opinions. They distrust people's motives and abilities and is reluctant to delegate responsibility. They maintain high expectations of coworkers and friends, expects perfection from themselves and others and is intolerant of incompetence and weak individuals. Their priorities usually involve goals, not people; as a result, they may disregard the rights and feelings of others in his quests for success. They also will not remember names quickly, and they will refer to individuals as "the guy with the red car," or "the tall guy with glasses," or "you know, the one that sat at the left of you." They will remember names only if they feel the person is important to them and can be "used" by them. They tend to motivate people by dominating them and rarely uses persuasion or reasoning - choleric value other independent individuals.

***Intellectual Orientation.*** Highly intelligent and possessing excellent problem-solving abilities and excellent communication skills, the Choleric is always envisioning new goals and challenges. They have an ambitious agenda and severe obstacles to match that are ongoing in their minds 24 x 7. They have an innate ability to develop and implement innovative techniques and makes quick, intuitive decisions. They are strong-willed and rarely changes their mind, even when they are proven wrong. They can have several projects going on in their mind, at any given moment. They are very diligent in searching out data that will provide them with an intellectual edge for whatever reason. They read a lot of self-help books and always looks for new and better data that will help them position themselves more effectively for succeeding and being the victor.

***Emotional Orientation.*** Showing a few deep emotions and fearing loss of control over people and their environments. The Choleric can be repelled by emotional displays from others and usually does not verbalize any dark or loving emotions. Their most prominent expressed emotion may be anger, which they tend to use to achieve and maintain control. They can be quick and may carry grudges and seek revenge for wrongs done to them. They may react with anger or hostility when their independence is threatened or if people disagree with or criticize them; in fact, the Choleric has a potential for exhibiting abusive outrage toward people. Under pressure, they may tend to isolate themselves from other people. They are very susceptible to physical abuse when angered if they came from a dysfunctional family of origins. However, you will rarely, if ever, see him cry.

***Work Orientation.*** The Choleric is task-oriented rather than people-oriented. A highly productive, independent workers, they possess excellent leadership abilities and problem-solving skills. They can assume and complete an impressive amount of responsibility and maintains a practical approach to tasks, overcoming obstacles that would discourage other people. They are the kind of person that will go "out on a limb" just for the excitement of the task at hand. You might call them "risk takers." They don't go for the low-hanging fruit—they go to the top where the biggest and best gather. They are after the "prize." A disciplined, well-organized perfectionist, the Choleric is easily bored with routine activities and needs constant challenges. The challenge could be his middle name. They thrive on challenges and finds them entertaining and worthy of their efforts. They are true survivors. They work at a fast, efficient pace and is reluctant to delegate to others, which can lead to fatigue or burnout, a major downfall of all Choleric. They may equate criticism of their work with loss of approval. They resist authoritarian managers and is most productive when permitted to work independently and remain in control of their schedule and activities. The quickest way to cause them great frustration and agony is to micromanage them. Micromanagement of them will cause them to climb to your level or surpass you, or they will find another employer where they have flexibility, freedom, and is not micromanaged. The production of a Choleric is increased many times over when they can "run his own show" and manage their people as they see fit.

***Motivation.*** Self-motivated by needs for accomplishment and recognition, the Choleric may direct many of their behaviors toward maintaining control of their life. They may be capable of changing their expression or adopting harmful practices to maintain control and attain their goals. If threatened with punishment or loss of power, they may respond in anger but will not usually change. Opportunity and challenge motivate most Choleric. But there is a more important motivation, and that is **a vision**. They are great visionaries and can see into the future and around corners where other temperaments only see what is in front of them. Not he, not the Choleric: they see from the beginning to the end, and that can be weeks, months or years away. They know where they are going, and they need you to help them get there. If you want to motivate them, give him the "green light" on his vision, and he is instantly motivated. At that point, all they need are the resources that will enable them to pursue their ideas.

*Rejection/Acceptance Profile.* The Choleric is self-confident and does not fear personal rejection by others or need their acceptance; at the same time, they depend on people for praise and recognition of their accomplishments. They can be rejecting of people who oppose their plans and unaware that people seek their approval; as a result, they may not easily compliment others or recognize their work. They can improve their relationship dynamics with their workforce by giving them recognition for their contribution to the project. Emotional stroking of team members is not manipulation but sound leadership practices. If the team were not there in place doing the mundane issues required to accomplish the mission, they would not be able to pursue their vision. So, they need to learn to take care of them, so they can take care of him and his vision. Their self-confidence and lack of fear of rejection by others make them somewhat of an "island unto themselves." Not a right spot to be in when your success depends entirely on your team's ability to produce.

Leadership Profile – Choleric

| Introvert | 0 | 1 | 2 | 3 | 4 | 5 | 6 | 7 | 8 | 9 | Extrovert |
|---|---|---|---|---|---|---|---|---|---|---|---|
| | | | | | | | | | | | |
| • *Demonstrated* | | | | | | | | | | X | |
| • *Desired* | X | | | | | | | | | | |

In considering the Leadership Profile for the Choleric, we need to look at some factors, beginning with leadership needs and desires.

## CHOLERIC IN LEADERSHIP

| **Temperament** (out of 3,449 people) | **# People** | **Social** | **# People** | **Leadership** | **# People** | **Relationship** |
|---|---|---|---|---|---|---|
| Choleric | 50 | 1.45% | 415 | 12.03% | 16 | 0.46% |
| Melancholy Compulsive | 0 | 0.00% | 175 | 5.07% | 0 | 0.00% |

**A Note about the Leadership Profile**

The adult leadership profile identifies your ability to provide leadership, make decisions, and assume responsibilities. This profile outlines your needs and desires for independence, achievement, and recognition. Because leadership needs and desires expressed through socializing with people, the leadership profile should not be evaluated alone but interpreted with either the social profile or the relationship profile.

– Together, the leadership profile and the social profile help determine your career needs. By comparing the results with your current employment situation, you can target conflict areas and maximize career skills.

– Together, the leadership profile and the relationship profile help determine your independence-dependence needs in close relationships. By comparing the results with your current life situation, you can target conflict areas and enhance relationships.

***Leadership Needs and Desires.*** Independent, self-reliant, self-sufficient, and self-governing, the Choleric accepts little or no control over others but needs much influence and power over people and events in their life. Freedom for them to be who they are, as thoroughly Choleric, is essential for their success. They make intuitive decisions, and are very clever, discerning, and spontaneous, possesses excellent leadership abilities, and assumes and completes many responsibilities. They need and requires promoting themselves and their goals and visions and has a high need for success and recognition for their accomplishments. Just give them a set of guidelines endorsed by the system, and they will operate just fine and produce above and beyond your expectations.

***Criteria for Relationships.*** Achievement-oriented rather than people-oriented, the Choleric depends on their knowledge and skills and has minimal need for close interpersonal relationships. Instead, they tend to develop relationships to help accomplish personal goals and seeks out people who can be influenced by them, especially those who can assist them. They are drawn to people who recognize and appreciate their accomplishments and may avoid close relationships with other strong-willed people, i.e., different Choleric and Melancholy. It is a guarantee that if you put two Choleric on the same project, there will be conflicts as they both have an innate need to lead and be in control. However, with the WIDP Profile, you can predetermine their temperaments and eliminate problems before they start. In some cases, you can put two Choleric on the same team if they have distinct responsibilities that do not bleed over into the other Choleric area of responsibility. However, they will not become best friends because they both are so bent on doing their own thing and they will also always have a feeling of the other Choleric as trying to invade their responsibilities and taking over their area of trust, and this is going to cause inner conflict within both.

***Perception of Self.*** Projecting optimism and self-confidence, the Choleric can be egotistical, and seldom admits making a mistake. They are confident of their ability to achieve whatever they desire even through their high need for control may mask inner fears, including an inferiority complex which you will never see nor hear about from them. Thriving on challenges and setting high personal goals, the Choleric maintains an attitude of competence and usually has an answer or solution to problems. Sometimes their intentions are so far out, in their vision, that most people will not be able to see them. They can see them, and that is all that matters to them. They can adapt his behavior to circumstances and fill any role they feel necessary to achieve their goals. Active and involved, he rarely spends time in self-introspection, and may view themselves only from a positive perspective. Most importantly they see themselves as high achievers, and that gives them great satisfaction in their inner world

***Perception by Others.*** Possessing natural leadership abilities, the Choleric maintains an image of superiority and confidence. And while they have excellent social skills and can be outgoing, charismatic, and physically affectionate, they may have little understanding of people's needs and emotions. They can be very controlling and verbally manipulative to the point of not responding to the feelings and rights of others and, in most cases, they do not care as his focus is 100 percent on the target of accomplishing their vision. Thus, they are perceived as being manipulative or coercive. They are usually the dominant figure in groups, and if they can push their idea, they can overpower others and ensure everyone is listening to their vision. Less confident people can be intimidated by their high energy and decisive manner. They can be offensive to the Introverted Sanguine, Sanguine, and the Phlegmatic. They may directly confront those who disagree with them and can be critical or argumentative.

***Perception of Others.*** Extremely individualistic, the Choleric does not need to please people or meet their expectations. They are reluctant to delegate responsibility, seldom seeks the opinions of others, and distrusts people's motives and abilities. They maintain high expectations of coworkers and friends and is intolerant of incompetence, expecting perfection from himself and others. Their priorities usually involve goals, not people; as a result, they may disregard the rights and feelings of others in their quest for success. They tend to motivate people by dominating them and rarely uses persuasion or reasoning. While he values other independent individualists, they actively resist any control by others and tends to loose respect for weaker people. In some cases, they will use the temperaments that seem weaker to their moods and loathe them at the same time. They perceive them as soft but as being able to contribute to their vision of being fulfilled.

***Intellectual Orientation.*** Possessing high mental abilities, the Choleric is always envisioning new goals and challenges. They have excellent problem-solving skills, is an excellent communicator, makes quick, intuitive decisions, and can develop and implement innovative techniques. Since they are so alert and operates with a secure gift of discernment, they can see the end from the beginning. Hence, they are going to implement strategies that most other temperaments will not understand and therefore, they will give them resistance to their plans. Now, this is where you need to trust and have confidence in their strategies. Most generally they will have left a path of successes behind them, and you can deduce from those accomplishments that they are dedicated visionary who can bring to pass what they start to accomplish. Their intellectual orientation is powerful and productive, and in the end, everyone wins. Strong-willed, they rarely change their mind, even when they are proven wrong.

***Emotional Orientation.*** Showing a few deep emotions and rarely verbalizing any deep or loving feelings, the Choleric can be repelled by emotional displays from others. Remember the story about General George S. Patton. Well, here again, you will only see the determination of the Choleric as they move forward to take the objective whatever it may be. They will be operating from a base of "task orientation" that they will not see the emotions of those around them. Nor will they want to see them display their feelings. They fear the loss of control over people and their environment. They are quick, and the sentiment they express most often may be anger, which they may use to achieve or maintain power. If you hear of someone leading with force and passion, it will be a Choleric who is burnt out or on the edges of burning out, and they have resolved to use his position of authority to control people around them. They may carry grudges and seek revenge for wrongs done to them and has the potential to exhibits abusive anger and foul language toward people. They may react with anger or hostility of their independence is threatened or if people disagree with or criticize them. They need to be nourished by those in leadership over them without them displaying any control maneuvers or domination over them as they will take that as a threat, and they can become very hard-headed and stubborn. But you will not see any tears from them.

***Work Orientation.*** Task-oriented rather than people-oriented, the Choleric is a highly productive, independent workers. Give them a job to do, and the people and financial resources to do it and then steps back and watch them produce. He has excellent leadership abilities and problem-solving skills and can assume and complete an impressive amount of responsibility that will stagger the mind. Their practical approach to tasks enables them to overcome obstacles that would discourage other people.

They are not quitters; they are fighters and will do feats of accomplishment that are unperceived by the different temperaments. A perfectionist, they are disciplined and well-organized. Able to work at a fast, efficient pace, they need constant challenges, and they are quickly bored with routine activities. They may equate criticism of his work with loss of approval and, as a result, resists, or becomes very stubborn authoritarian managers. They produce when permitted to work independently and remain in control of their schedule and activities. At the same time, their reluctance to delegate to others may lead to fatigue or burnout. There is something about them that causes them to accept more responsibilities than anyone people can handle. However, they will give it 100 percent, and delegation is a characteristic that must be a learned skill or newfound knowledge for them to relinquish any authority. However, again with WIDP, it is possible to educate Choleric so they can even do more than before by understanding their temperament strengths. Once a Choleric realizes they can delegate authority, they get excited because to them, that is the "prize" dangled before them, and it creates more vision and attraction to them. Just what they need, more ideas, but they can handle it, and they like the concepts of delegation because that empowers them to take on more responsibility. That in and of itself gets their visionary juices all stirred up and thinking all kinds of new visions. Again, everybody wins, and more jobs created for the new projects.

*Motivation.* Self-motivated by needs for accomplishment and recognition, many of the Choleric behaviors are toward maintaining control of their life. The most significant motivating factor for the Choleric is leadership. Give them more leadership responsibility, and you have just motivated them. Remember what was said earlier about driving him?

Opportunity and challenge drive most Choleric.

But there is a more significant motivator, and that is **a vision**. They are great visionaries and can see into the future and around corners where other temperaments only see what is in front of them. Not them, not the Choleric, no way: they see from the beginning to the end, and that can be weeks, months, or years away. They know where they are going, and they need you to help them get there. If you want to motivate them, give them the green light on their vision, and they are instantly motivated. They may be capable of changing their behavior or adopting contrary practices to maintain control and attain their goals. If threatened with punishment or loss of power, they may respond in anger but will not usually change. At this point, they just become "cobalt steel" and cannot be moved by anything or by anyone.

*Rejection/Acceptance Profile.* Self-confident, the Choleric does not fear personal rejection by others or need their approval. At the same time, they depend on people for praise and recognition of their accomplishments. Unaware that people seek their support, he may not easily compliment others, or recognize their work and can reject those who oppose their plans. For them, leadership is their life. If they can't lead or you-you attack his administration, you lose his recognition, and your attacks roll off their back like water off a duck back. But if you are in a position of leadership over them and you attack them, you will encounter stubbornness that will not move. Not the right situation for them because "leadership" is who they are, and for them, it is all about leadership. Challenge their leadership, and you are challenging the whole person to the core of his existence.

## The Relationship Profile – Choleric

| Introvert | 0 | 1 | 2 | 3 | 4 | 5 | 6 | 7 | 8 | 9 | Extrovert |
|---|---|---|---|---|---|---|---|---|---|---|---|
| • *Demonstrated* | | | | | | | ▓ | ▓ | ▓ | X | |
| • *Desired* | X | ▓ | ▓ | | | | | | | | |

## CHOLERIC IN RELATIONSHIP

| Temperament (out of 3,449 people) | # People | Social | # People | Leadership | # People | Relationship |
|---|---|---|---|---|---|---|
| Choleric | 50 | 1.45% | 415 | 12.03% | 16 | 0.46% |
| Choleric Compulsive | 0 | 0.00% | 175 | 5.07% | 0 | 0.00% |

In considering the Choleric relationship profile, we need to look at some factors, beginning with relationship needs and desires.

### A Note about the Relationship Profile

The adult relationship profile identified your preferences for emotional involvement and shared affection on a one-to-one basis. This profile outlines your needs and desires for emotional sharing and relationships. For most people, the relationship profile is the dominant pattern that influences behavior in the social and leadership areas.

By comparing the relationship profile with your current life situation, you can target conflict areas and meet personal needs not fulfilled.

*Relationship Needs and Desires.* Outgoing and personable in social settings, the Choleric appears to want a high degree of interaction with many people; however, they need and wants close relationships with very few people. You don't find too many individuals who are Choleric in Relationship. Out of a database of 3,349 profiles, only 0.46 or sixteen (16) people were Choleric. There were zero (0) Choleric compulsives out of the same database. As a result, he may have many casual acquaintances in a relationship. They freely express love and affection but needs minimal love shown to them in close relationships. They may define love as people's willingness to perform tasks for them and desires expressions of love on these terms, not with physical manifestations. That is why there are so few Choleric in a relationship. Think about it for a moment. Choleric demonstrate high numbers 6-7-8-9- and they desire 0-1-2-3. We are talking about a close intimate relationship here. A person who demonstrates that they want a 6-7-8-9 and at the same time Desire a 0-1-2-3 doesn't make sense. Everyone needs someone in their life that they consider as a close intimate relationship. So, therefore, the Choleric would be saying "I want to display (demonstrate) a lot of intimacy toward you, but I only wish to have very little from you back toward me (desire). The Choleric has a high need for accomplishment and may choose activities and friendships that will assist them in attaining his goals rather than for purely relationship reasons. They possess excellent leadership abilities and has a strong need to be in control of their destiny in relationships. There is speculation that individuals who score as Choleric in a relationship may have been abused somewhere in their lifetime and may be suffering from a position of dysfunction which could also be called codependency, or sexual assault sometime in their life. Sexual assault is something to consider.

***Criteria for Relationships.*** Highly productive and independent, the Choleric is achievement-oriented rather than people-oriented. They depend on their knowledge and skills and has minimal need for close interpersonal relationships, tending to develop relationships to help accomplish their personal goals. Here again, we must consider the individual who is a Choleric in a relationship. There are Choleric in a relationship, but there is also the possibility that they are emotionally damaged from a previous dysfunctional relationship. They're drawn to people who recognize and appreciate their accomplishments and seeks out people who can be influenced by them, especially those who are content to let them dominate the relationship. Choleric in a relationship can cause problems if they are presiding improperly. Also, they may not understand his temperaments and therefore, be acting on their intrinsic natural makeup as a Choleric, which creates conflict in relationships. It is at this point where WIDP can liberate them from their negative influence on their relationships. Awareness will assist them in avoiding initiating or investing in close relationships with other strong-willed people who are like them in temperament and are very vigorous and independent.

***Perception of Self.*** While the Choleric projects optimism and self-confidence in a relationship, they can be egotistical and seldom admits making a mistake. Confidence can come across as arrogance or pride. But it is the solidity of the Choleric and is not arrogance or pride: it is just the nature of a Choleric. And although they are confident of their ability to achieve whatever they desire, their high need for control may mask inner fears and inferiority of which you will not see manifest in them or come out of their mouth. They thrive on challenges and sets high personal goals. The Choleric maintains an attitude of competence and usually has an answer or solution to problems for all relationship issues. These attributes do not make them right, but as they see it, they are right. They also can adapt their behavior to circumstances and fill any role they feel necessary to achieve their goals. Their self-perception is perceived as manipulation, but it is just the Choleric in action doing what they do best. Pursuing the aims of the vision as they see it. Active and involved, they rarely spend time in self-introspection and may view them self only from a positive perspective.

***Perception by Others.*** Possessing natural leadership abilities, the Choleric maintains an image of superiority and confidence. They have excellent social skills and can be outgoing, charismatic, and physically affectionate. While they often give the impression that they desire close relationships with, many people, they are very selective in choosing intimate friends. They are usually the dominant figures in groups; they can intimidate less confident people with their high energy and decisive manners. They may have little understanding of people's needs and emotions and often directly confronts those who disagree with them. They can be critical or argumentative. The Choleric can be a perfectionist and demanding in close relationships and may cause others to fear their anger and criticism or become discouraged at their inability to please them. They may appear to desire more intimate relationships than they want based on their response to others. They do not seem to let many people into their private world.

***Perception of Others.*** The Choleric is very individualistic and does not need to please people or meet their expectations. While they value other independent individualists, they distrust people's motives in relationships and abilities, seldom seeks the opinions of others and is reluctant to delegate responsibility for the relationship. Quickly bored with routine activities within the relationship, the Choleric needs constant challenges. Intolerant of incompetence, he expects perfection from themselves and others and maintains high expectations of those they are intimately involved and with their friends. Their priorities usually include goals, not people, and they may disregard the rights and feelings of others in their quest for success. So, in relationships, they are going to have to be educated as to the importance of them understanding how others perceive them. That alone will be a great project for them to digest. They rarely use persuasion or reasoning and tends to motivate people by dominating them. Dominance, of course, will not work in a relationship so that they will have many broken relationships due to this approach. Others are going to perceive them unfavorably based on their past track record.

***Intellectual Orientation.*** Possessing high mental abilities, the Choleric continually envisions new goals and challenges in relationships. They have excellent problem-solving skills and often develops, and implements innovative techniques. Here there could be a problem as one seeks to apply innovative procedures that may not be acceptable to those they are in a relationship. So, there needs to be an honest, two-way conversation going on in these relationships. An excellent communicator, they make quick, intuitive decisions. Having to learn to stop and get feedback from the people they are involved with may cause them some anxiety. But they will have to know that others have a different intellectual orientation and their orientations may not line up with theirs. Therefore, there must be give and take. They adopt a practical approach to tasks and can assume and complete an impressive amount of responsibility. But as mentioned above, there must be two-way communications going on for the relationship to get past the difficulties. The Choleric is quite strong-willed and rarely change their mind even when proven wrong, and this is going to further the inner conflict between them and cause external conflict with those they are in a relationship.

***Emotional orientation.*** The Choleric shows few deep emotions, if ever, and can be repelled by emotional displays from others. Rarely verbalizing any deep or loving feelings, their most prominent expressed emotion may be anger. The manifestation of rage in a close intimate relationship will destroy the relationships very quickly. Because they tend to fear the loss of control of the people and situations in their environment, they may use anger to achieve and maintain power. This approach will not work in close intimate relationships. They can be quick-tempered, may even carry a grudge or seek revenge for wrongs done to them. Vengeance is very dangerous and destructive in any relationship. They may react with anger or hostility if their independence is endangered or if people, they are in a relationship with disagree with or criticize them. Taken to the extreme, the Choleric has the potential for exhibiting abusive anger toward those they are in a relationship. Under pressure, they may isolate from them, and disengage because they cannot withstand the emotional stress it puts on the relationship.

***Motivation.*** Self-motivated by the need for accomplishment and recognition, the Choleric has a high need to be approved and admired by those close to them. Also, many of their behaviors will be toward maintaining control of their life and relationships. They may be capable of changing their tone or adopting new habits to maintain control and attain their goals. The motivation for the Choleric is going to be quite a project for them. As it must come from within since they are so much of a "one-man show" and are primarily self-motivated. But for the sake of the relationships, they will have to make some behavior modifications if they are to maintain the relationships. If threatened with punishment or loss of control, they may respond in anger but will not usually change. Anger is going to cause a frequent breakdown of the relationship and will not produce anything positive or productive. The best way to motivate them is to give them goals to achieve and let them work through their limited knowledge base of how important it is to understand the emotional makeup of those they are in a relationship. Their desire for accomplishment and recognition will be the driving force that will maintain a "vision" for them to pursue. Of course, the primary motivating factors again is "vision."

***Rejection/Acceptance Profile.*** Extremely self-confident, the Choleric does not fear personal rejection by those, they are in a relationship with, nor do they need their approval, however, they do depend on people for praise and recognition of their accomplishments. They are not going to get the praise and recognition until they understand those, they are in a relationship with are not just doormats and have genuine needs too. Unaware that people seek their approval, the Choleric can be rejecting of people who oppose their plans and may not readily compliment those they are in a relationship with or recognize their participation in the furthering of the relationship. They are usually unaware that some of their independent behaviors could lead to difficulties in their close interpersonal relationships and this is where they need education to learn that considering the needs of others is just as important as their needs for leadership.

# Help for the Choleric
## Characteristics of the Choleric

### *Probable Strengths*
- Independent – possesses strong leadership abilities
- Strong-willed – is determined; does not vacillate under pressure
- Visionary – challenged by the unknown; goal-oriented
- Practical – is highly organized
- Decisive – judge people and situations intuitively
- Disciplined – highly productive; thrives on activity

### *Potential Weaknesses*
- Unemotional – insensitivity to people's feelings
- Self-sufficient – difficulty delegating to others
- Impetuous – may assume more responsibility than he can handle
- Domineering – can be manipulative
- Angry – hostile; sarcastic; inability to forgive
- Workaholic – tendencies; susceptible to burnout

### *Decisions for the Choleric*

They are swift to decide on anything or any issue.
If they make a wrong decision, they will make another decision to correct the bad one and move on.

As you can tell from the Choleric social/vocational, leadership, and relationship profiles, people with this temperament can be influential individuals. The chart also shows some common characteristics of the Choleric, including probable strengths and potential weaknesses.

If you're a Choleric, you may be quite comfortable in your skin. However, it may be a good idea to consider the following paragraphs, which may help you better understand yourself.

*You are a compulsive worker.* It's okay for you to work hard. That's one of your most valuable strengths. What you need to do, however, is to learn to relax, take time off, and "harness" the feeling you have to be in the driver's seat. Rest will help take the pressure off yourself and those on your team. What the other temperaments do not know about the Choleric is that the Choleric will work circles around the different temperaments they cannot fathom. Accomplishment is a good thing, and that is why most Choleric end up in leadership positions. But remember this: Choleric **always** will move up the ladder of success, unless they have been tampered with and are dysfunctional due to being out of balance. You must learn to control your constant source of energy-driven temperament. Don't let it control you; instead, you must always have your mood under control. The strength of the Choleric is the best asset of their temperament. If harnessed correctly and nurtured, there is nothing a Choleric cannot accomplish once they set their minds toward that goal.

*You feel that you* **must** *be in control.* While it's perceptive for you to feel the need to be in control, acting as if you require to be in control can alienate you from acquaintances, business colleagues, friends, and loved ones. Here are a few things you can do to be more collaborative with other people:

*Respond to other leadership.* While it may be difficult for you to understand, you are not the only one who can lead. When Choleric bump into other Choleric, whether it be in a social setting or work environments, they immediately are drawn to one another. When this happens, there is a significant chemistry that takes place as they do understand each other's driven nature and can talk along the same lines and therefore, will reinforce each other. The collaboration draws leaders closer together because now they have someone whom they can identify with, someone who understands. If you can get comfortable with the other Choleric and not be intimated by them, you can learn a lot from them, and the relationship can be very beneficial to both parties.

*Don't look down on "the other temperaments."* Not everyone can be as quick on their feet as you are, but that doesn't mean other people don't have good ideas. A weakness that the Choleric has is not having respect, as the Choleric would put it, "for weaker temperaments" and, therefore, the Choleric will criticize the other temperaments to the point of not liking them at all. However, if the Choleric will learn to delegate more responsibility and in some case invest time in training and teaching the other temperaments through modeling for them, their productivity will increase. Productivity always pleases the Choleric.

*Appreciate other temperament types.* Those individuals not as fortunate as Choleric is in their temperament makeup as leaders have different strengths that leaders do not have to offer. Like the mundane issues that Choleric have no tolerance to deal with but the different temperaments, are very capable and efficient. Choleric need these temperaments to support and undergird their vision and goals and must capitalize on their temperament strengths.

***Stop manipulating other people.*** You may think you're fooling people when you get them to do things they don't want to do; most people know when they're in a controlled situation—and they resent it. It is much more efficient to *ask* people to do things and then provide practical, constructive criticism of their results. No one likes to be bullied around or controlled, therefore the Choleric, through positive reinforcement and acknowledgment of those they are leading, will be more beneficial to both the leader and those led.

***You don't know how to handle people.*** Because you are driven to get things done, you have a strong tendency to use other people to an end rather than as valuable people who have their own intrinsic needs and desires. And while it is challenging to *make* yourself more compassionate, you will find that by applying a few simple principles, you will get along much better with people:

***Keep advice until asked.*** You may have to bite your tongue but listening to others and their ideas can provide crucial insight and provide direction that the Choleric may have never thought of on their own. Choleric is very prone to make quick decisions on their own without listening to others' input. Choleric will offer information into a situation whether asked or not, and this can very often get them into complicated cases because their advice is not always wanted. Choleric do not have the correct answer to every situation, although they think they have a solution to everything.

***Tone down your approach.*** Chill out! You can be passionate about what you believe in and convey a sense of excitement without bowling everybody over. Being a dynamic leader and misunderstanding the emotions and feeling of others is a significant deterrent to quality results. The better way to lead is being a "velvet-covered brick"; at least the hardness of the Choleric is somewhat subdued and is more palatable. Dictatorial, hardnosed, loud, and angry approach to a team or group is not received well. You can lead without being a bully or unapproachable and unwilling to listen to your people. No one likes treated as subservient.

***Stop arguing and causing trouble.*** Nobody wants to spend time with an argumentative, overbearing dictators. Most Choleric are going to be in a leadership position anyway and if they are not, they soon will be, so why all the critical and judging behavior. It is not necessary because the Choleric needs to figure out a softer way of accomplishing the same goal but without the tension and disruption. No one enjoys a job filled continuously with conflict.

***You are usually right, but you also may be unpopular.*** You may need to learn to be humbler in your approaches. Everyone likes an ordinary person. So, you are the leader or one in control you don't have to be intimidated by anything! Surely you do not want to be unpopular, and it is easier to go forward to when you have the endorsement from those who have the skills to take you to the finish line. So, here are a few things to consider:

- ***Let someone else be right.*** In other words, try sharing the glory for a change. You don't always have to be on center stage getting all the applause. Everyone likes to get a pat on the back occasionally. That pat-on-the-back, however little, will gain you tremendous leverage for future projects. If the Choleric has no one to lead to complete the vision, who is going to do it? Alienating your employees is poor management and leadership. Everyone is valuable to the teams and needs to feel that they contribute and are necessary. Their voice needs to be perceived! Employee suggestion boxes are one of the greatest inventions of all times. Free consulting from inside the circle of those who know what is needed to make improvements to the organization or group. Listen to them.

- *Learn to apologize.* Remember the slogan from the film, Love Story: "Love never has to say you're sorry"? That's pure gibberish. If you do care about someone—and even if you don't—apologizing when you are wrong or have acted dangerously will do wonders for helping you build or repair damaged relationships. It is a proven fact that the most five powerful words in the English language is "Please forgive me, I am sorry." Although that is a tough163 saying for the Choleric, it is very beneficial and will gain tremendous respect from those who asked the questions. Apologizing to someone privately or in an audience shows humility. And everyone appreciates a humble individual.

- *Admit you have some faults.* You may think you are perfect, but nobody else does. It is true that we all have flaws. However, the Choleric very rarely admits they have anything wrong with them. The truth is that they have a way of covering up their errors or making it look like someone else has the faults. Choleric are quick thinkers. They are the fastest thinker of the five temperaments. However, they sometimes move so fast that their actions get ahead of their thoughts. They make decisions before they have thought the issue through to completion. Somewhere in their journey of the tasks they are working on, they find a gross error. They realize the error and must reroute their course of action. They know they made a mistake, but instead of owning the mistake, they make another decision on the spot to change directions to correct the deficiency and move forward. Most of the time no one will know what happens; now it just takes place, and the project moves forward, perhaps leaving a scar somewhere in the fabric of the project. Choleric need to learn to slow down on their "quick" decisions, and take the time to filter out all the pros and cons.

## Do's and Don'ts for the Choleric

| Do's | Don'ts |
| --- | --- |
| • Let people offer opinions without cutting them off or putting them down | • Expect everyone to want to do it your way |
| • Understand that others may have information that you do not have | • Take for granted that you know everything |
| • Listen to what people are saying to you; allow your heart to open. | • Be so insensitive that you do not take other feelings into consideration |
| • Allow others to be who they are and respect them for being that person | • Take for granted that everyone wants to hear your opinion |
| • Learn to put others first and realize they have needs too | • Expect the performance of others equal to yours |
| • Look for ways to encourage the creativity of others | • Bully everyone around like a Drill Sergeant |
| • Learn to compromise and cooperate with others | • Be hard-nosed and insensitive toward others |
| • Lear to receive friendliness and warmth from others | • Take advantage of those less skilled or knowledgeable than you |
| • Learn to slow down so you won't burn out | • Always remain aloof and suspicious |
| • Be first to say that you are sorry | • Get into entanglements with more than you can handle |
| • Show the way and don't drive others like they were cattle | • Be so focused on the future that you miss out on the present |
| • Ask instead for commanding orders to others | • Always pressure yourself to accomplish more and more |
| • Develop a plan for encouraging others | • Take on more than you can do justice to |
| • Wait until advice without shoving your way into their conversations | |
| • Admit the reality of you possibly being wrong | |
| • Issue a request instead of an order | |
| • Practice becoming less rigid | |
| • Greet people with a warm smile | |
| • Fun things with your family | |
| • Schedule time off for enjoyment and relaxation | |
| • If it is not your issue, stay out of it | |
| • Ease up on your cravenness | |

**Become Aware of Your Natural Strengths and Learn to Use Them Wisely**

| Natural Strength | | Strength Carried to the Extreme | | Compulsion |
|---|---|---|---|---|
| Visionary | | Angry if people buck his authority | | Dictatorial and obsessive |
| Decisive | | Makes decisions for everyone | | Becomes very manipulative to get their way |
| Independent | | Reckless | | Ridiculous |
| Productive | | Works way beyond the standard | | Workaholic |

**How to Recognize Whether Your Child Is Choleric**

| Strengths | Weaknesses | Emotional Needs |
|---|---|---|
| *Baby* | | |
| Adventuresome, gregarious, full of life, intelligent | Noisy, loud, strong-willed, challenging, dangerous | Needs validation for achievements, desires a pet, their space |
| *Child* | | |
| Industrious, gung-ho, self-confident, responsible, dynamic | Controlling, unrelenting, taxing, inflexible, adamant, severe, harsh | Opportunity to express them and to be heard |
| *Teen* | | |
| Dependable, in control, forceful, organized, problem solver, an exhorter of others | Critical, rude and offensive, domineering, disliked, know-it-all, unremorseful, recluse | Acknowledgment of their strengths, feelings of being in control of their destiny |

# BASIC CHOLERIC
# TEMPERAMENT DETAILS

## The Choleric

## I. Potential Strengths of the Choleric Temperament

A. Strong-Willed
- Does not sway under the pressure of what others think but takes a definite stand.
- Is very determined in whatever task they do.

B. Independent
- If people do not agree with them, that is a shame—they are going to do it with or without them.
- What others think about them or his projects makes very little difference to him.

C. Visionary
- Is adventuresome to the point of leaving a secure position for the challenge of the unknown.
- Has a pioneering spirit and will scour the earth for adventure.
- When they appraise a situation, they do not see the pitfalls or potential problems, but merely keeps their eye on the goal.
- They do not need to be stimulated by their environment but instead encourages their surroundings with endless ideas, plans, and ambitions.

D. Practical
- Happiest, when engaged in a worthwhile project.
- Has a keen eye for the organization but finds detail work distressing.

E. Productive
- Workaholic tendencies.
- Will produce circles around the other temperaments.
- Choleric thrives on the activity of a challenge doing something new and exciting.
- Singleness of purpose often results in accomplishments.
- Decisive
- Can quickly appraise a situation and diagnose the most practical solution.
- Decisions are reached by intuition more than analytical reasoning.
- A good judge of people.
- Leader
- Strong leadership tendencies.
- Forcefulness will tend to dominate a group.
- Self-disciplined.

## II. Potential Weaknesses/Shortcomings of the Choleric Temperament

A. Cold and unemotional
- Most unaffectionate of all the temperaments.
- Emotional rigidity—seldom shows tears.
- Tends to be insensitive to other's needs and inconsiderate of their feelings.

B. Self-sufficient and very independent.

C. Impetuous
- Tends to start projects that they are sorry for later.
- Hard for them to apologize.

D. Domineering

E. Unforgiving
- Will carry a grudge forever.
- Revengeful.

F. Sarcastic – Can be very blunt and cruel.

G. Angry
- Extremely hostile person.
- Can cause pain to others and enjoy it.

## Powerful Choleric

Powerful Choleric are compulsive workers.
- Learn to relax
- Take the pressure off others
- Let your drive become harnessed
- Learn to take time off

Powerful Choleric must be in control
- Respond to other leadership
- Do not look down on "the dummies."
- Stop manipulating

Powerful Choleric do not know how to handle people
- Practice, practice
- Keep advice until asked
- Tone down your approach
- Stop arguing and causing trouble

Powerful Choleric is right but unpopular
- Let someone else be right
- Learn to apologize
- Admit you have some faults

## STRENGTH AND WEAKNESSES
### of the
## CHOLERIC-POWERFUL

| | STRENGTHS | WEAKNESSES |
|---|---|---|
| **EMOTIONS:** | Born leader | Bossy |
| | Dynamic and active | Impatient |
| | Compulsive need for change | Quick-tempered |
| | Must correct wrongs | Cannot relax |
| | Strong-willed and decisive | Too impetuous |
| | Unemotional | Enjoys controversy and arguments |
| | Not easily discouraged | Won't give up when losing |
| | Independent and self-sufficient | Comes on too strong |
| | Exudes confidence | Inflexible |
| | Can run anything | Is not complementary |
| | Very determined | Dislikes tears and emotions |
| | Visionary | Is unsympathetic |
| | | |
| **WORK:** | Goal-oriented | Little tolerance for mistakes |
| | Sees the whole picture | Does not analyze details |
| | Organizes well | Bored by trivia |
| | Seeks practical solutions | May make rash decisions |
| | Moves quickly to action | Maybe rude or tactless |
| | Delegates work | Manipulates people |
| | Insists on production | Demanding of others |
| | Makes the goal | End justifies the means |
| | Stimulates activity | Work may become his god |
| | Thrives on opposition | Demands loyalty in the ranks |
| | | |
| **FRIENDS:** | Has little need for friends | Tends to use people |
| | Will work for group activity | Dominates others |
| | Will lead and organize | Decides for others |
| | Is usually right | Knows everything |
| | Excels in emergencies | Can do everything better |
| | | Is too independent |
| | | Possessive of friends and mate |
| | | Can't say, "I am sorry." |
| | | Maybe right but unpopular |

## Temperament Weaknesses
## of the Choleric

Bossy   –   Commanding, domineering, sometimes overbearing in adult relationships.

Unsympathetic   –   Finds it difficult to relate to the problems or hurts of others.

Resistant   –   Strives works against or hesitates to accept any other way but his own.

Frank   –   Straightforward, outspoken, and doesn't mind telling you exactly what he thinks.

Exasperated   –   A person who finds it challenging to endure irritation or wait for others.

Unaffectionate   –   Finds it difficult to verbally or physically demonstrate tenderness openly.

Headstrong   –   Insists on having his way.

Proud   –   One with high self-esteem who sees himself as always right and the best person for the job.

Argumentative   –   Incites arguments generally because he is confident, he is right no matter what the situation may be.

Nervy   –   Full of confidence, courage, and sheer guts, often in a negative sense.

Workaholic   –   An aggressive goal-setter who must be continuously productive and feels very guilty when resting is not driven by a need for perfection or completion but by a need for accomplishment and reward.

Tactless   –   Sometimes expresses himself in an offensive and inconsiderate way.

Domineering   –   Compulsively takes control of situations and people, usually telling others what to do.

Intolerant   –   Appears unable to withstand or accept another's attitudes, the point of view or way of doing things.

Manipulative   –   Influences or manages shrewdly or deviously to his advantage, will get his way somehow.

Stubborn   –   Determined to exert his own will, not easily persuaded, obstinate.

Lord Over   –   Doesn't hesitate to let you know that he is right or is in control.

Short-Tempered   –   Has to demand impatience-based anger and a short fuse. Anger expressed when others are not moving fast enough or have not completed what they have been asked to do.

Rash   –   May act hastily, without thinking things through, generally because of impatience.

Crafty   –   Shrewd, one who can always find a way to get to the desired end.

## Temperament Strengths
## of the Choleric

Adventurous   –   One who will take on new and daring enterprises with a determination to master them.

Persuasive   –   Convinces others through logic and fact rather than charm or power.

Strong-Willed   –   One who is determined to have his way.

Competitive   –   Turns every situation, happening, or game into a contest and always plays to win!

Resourceful   –   Able to act quickly and efficiently in all situations.

Self-Reliant   —    An independent person who can entirely rely on his capabilities, judgment, and resources.

Positive   —    Knows it will turn out right if he's in charge.

Sure   —    Self-confident rarely hesitates or wavers.

Outspoken   —    Speaks frankly and without reserve.

Forceful   —    A commanding personality against whom others would wait to take a stand.

Daring   —    Willing to take risks, fearless, and bold.

Confident   —    Self-assured and confident in their ability and success.

Independent   —    Self-sufficient, self-supporting, self-confident, and seems to have little need for help.

Decisive   —    A person with quick, conclusive, judgment-making ability.

Mover   —    Driven by a need to be productive, is a leader whom others follow, finds it difficult to sit still.

Tenacious   —    Holds on firmly, stubbornly, and won't let go until the goal's accomplished.

Leader   —    A natural born director who is driven to be in charge, and often finds it difficult to believe that anyone else can do the job as well.

Chief   —    Commands leadership and expects people to follow.

Productive   —    Must continuously be working or achieving, often finds it very difficult to rest.

Bold   —    Fearless, daring, forward, and unafraid of risk.

| | |
|---|---|
| Practical | Demanding |
| Quick thinker | Heavy-handed |
| Good troubleshooters | Easily Bored |
| Enthusiastic | Straightforwardly annoyed |
| Will not give up | Impatient |
| Great ambition | Bossy and arrogant |
| Fearless and courageous | Quick tempered |
| Passion to winning | Can't relax |
| Warm | Can be icy |
| Thrilled with opposition | Too hasty |
| Yearns for great things | Inflexible |
| Intelligent | Is not harmonizing |
| Does not complain | Unsympathetic |
| Born leader | Dislikes emotions |
| Strong-willed | Little tolerance for blunders |
| Not easily discouraged | Can be discourteous, bad-mannered |
| Independent | Sarcastic |
| Projects confidence | Critical, hard |
| Delegates work well | Must be in control |
| Makes the goal | Pride, has magnified ego |
| Stimulates others | Holds a grudge |
| Excels in emergencies | Revengeful |
| Visionary | Their plan is always the best |

| | |
|---|---|
| Likes pressure | Tends to use people |
| Self-reliant | Decides for others |
| Energetic | Can do everything better |
| Daring, risk-taker | Can't say, "I'm sorry" |
| Decisive | Too independent |
| Determined | Furthermore, busy for family |
| Achiever | May make reckless decisions |
| Direct | Tends to overcontrol |
| Wants results | Enjoys controversy, arguments |
| Likes to accomplish | "Knows everything" |
| Goal-oriented | Can be brutal, cold |

## The DeWalt Challenge
## For
## Joe the Choleric

Even though it is mid-January and the temperature has not hit 20 degrees in the last week here in, Massachusetts, the sweat is pouring off me. The challenge has got me to focus entirely on one task. Every obstacle that would prevent me from being the best at this has to be removed or negotiated away. I wanted to be the next "King of the Drill" for DeWalt Million-Dollar Challenge. The challenge was to drive five 1 5/8" screws into a pine board with a 14.4-volt DeWalt cordless screw gun faster than anybody else. Sounds manageable, but you cannot touch the screw gun or the screws until you hit the timer with the same hand you intend to pick up the gun. After you hit the timer, you can grab the screw gun. Then grab the screws and go to work. When finished, you hit the red timer button with the bottom of the screw gun. Now, try doing this in a hurry, six-seconds! When you put the challenge into the equation, suddenly you begin to fumble the screws. Your hands tremble. You feel the presence of every eyeball that is watching you. Your senses are in slow motion, but your movements are in high gear. The challenge sounds easy but being fast obstacles must be overcome.

It is now 12:30 AM and I am still pushing myself to hit that sub-6 second mark. I have been trying for 4 hours to score ten sub-6 second times. I frustrate myself with the relentlessness my driven nature pushes my body for perfection. Every movement calculated; every step must be flawlessly executed. Every other thought should be kept from distracting me from the goal. If all these parts are not in place, then I end up with another 8-second run: unacceptable.

For me, I am a reserved person. I do not like to be "on stage." The kiosk that DeWalt used for the challenge was two steps up to a 6' 2" diamond plate platform. So just being on that platform was like being on stage. That in of itself gave me a reason to be nervous. I just did not like being up there.

I knew from the first day trying for the challenge that for me to be any good at it I would have to get over that nervous energy the challenge caused every time I stepped up onto that dreaded platform.

In my opinion, DeWalt makes the very best tools for the construction field that I have ever used. I have been working in the construction field for twenty years now and have been sold out to DeWalt tools since I bought my first 9-volt cordless drill in 1994. Whenever I am ready for an upgrade to a device, I compare everything else to what DeWalt has to offer. Guess who wins my comparison tool test—DeWalt.

They do not always win on cost, but indeed the extra expense is worth the longevity, durability, and power the tools provide. Like the time I dropped an 18-volt cordless drill when I was up two stories on an extension ladder. It hit the pavement so hard I thought for sure it was done. I approached it like I was about to give it its last rites. The battery had landed 10' away from the screw gun. It was scuffed and bruised but worked just fine. This type of quality goes into all their tools.

The challenge was equally thought out and planned. The preliminary round of the challenge was held at home improvement centers like the Home Depot, Lowes, and others. Each event allowed anybody to try out one time per game. The contestant with the best time would be declared the winner of that game and would then qualify for the next round, which was the regional match.

Looking back on the day, I qualified for the regional event; I was nervous. My hands were cold. My insides were shaking with fear. I was trying not to look nervous; I approached the DeWalt representative. I thought I was mastering my anxiety well, but I am sure it came through in my body language and expressions. The DeWalt contest was going to be my first official try at the challenge of the competition. Everything in me was telling me to forget about it and go home. However, I could not. There was a nagging drive in me that motivated me forward to accomplish the task regardless of my fear.

I stepped up to the platform, and a shiver went throughout my body. I began to rub my hands to warm them to keep them from trembling. I set up in the ready position as I had planned hours before. When I put my left hand out over the screws, I could see my fingers trembling. I ignored it and tried to appear as I had it together. Without torturing myself any further, I hit the timer with my right hand. The challenge had begun. I had driven myself past my fears; past the thoughts that keep dreams from coming right and past the fear of platforms. Now all I had to do is perform. When I grabbed the screws, I dropped most of them and ended up with two in my hand. The first screws I tried to drive bent over. I drove the other screw, and I now had one completed. I went back to the tray for more screws and managed to fumble a bunch into my hand, and drove four more screws, dropping two or three more in-between. I could hear the disappointing sighs of the people around me. I had quick movements, but my execution was terrible. I finally drove the last screw and hit the timer with the bottom of the gun. I looked up at the time, and it read 15 seconds even. Not what I expected. My time recorded, and the representative said he would contact me if my time held up. I went away thinking that time is not only beatable but also pitiful by my standards. I had to get better.

I spent the rest of that day at work agonizing over my performance. I knew I could do better. I had much practice to do to become the next "King of the Drill."

I did not expect to be contacted by the DeWalt representative that day. I was surprised to read the e-mail that announced that I was the winner of that day's event and I qualified for the regional competition. Now I knew I would see that platform again. My desire to be the best went into overdrive.

I began to visit other local events and inconspicuously started taking notes on the dimensions of the kiosk, timer size, type of drywall screws, and other details I could pick up. I watched other people fumble around up there. I learned what not to do and what things I had to improve on, like the way you pick up the screws are critical to success. I determined initially to survey the screw tray before I started the timer so that I could pinpoint which screws I would pick up first. Rather than picking up a bunch randomly, with some practice picking up two or three screws pointing in the same direction, I improved my time considerably.

Within a month, while the local events were still going on, I improved my time down to the 8–10 seconds range. Again, I was envisioning an unbeatable and unstoppable time of 6 seconds or better. A lofty goal for a nervous, reserved contestant but my driven nature would not allow me to shy away from the challenge.

From the day I qualified in June to the time the regional event would occur in September, I knew I had much work to do.

I built a kiosk to the exact measurements of the DeWalt kiosk, using a DeWalt 14.4-volt cordless drill of course. I even had the platform lined with the diamond plate to resemble their platform. I searched the internet to find a timer and timer button like those I would be competing. I bought one that was quite similar. I built this kiosk with care and attention to detail.

Spending the time and money to build the kiosk had had some rewards, of course. My motivation in was to be the fastest driller in the country. I rarely ever thought of the prize. The regional winner would get a 2003 Chevy Express van filled with DeWalt tools and a round trip to Phoenix, Arizona, for the final competition. That alone was a $40,000 package. The "King of the Drill" or the grand prize winner in Phoenix would walk away with a fresh one million dollars. You can imagine such a prize would motivate thousands of contestants for the local events. Last, I had heard 140,000 people entered the competition. I felt lucky to be one of the few to even qualify for a regional contest.

My kiosk turned out to be a beautiful piece of furniture. It was painted with three coats of soft gloss black paint and adorned with DeWalt logos and signage I manage to get from one of the events. The kiosk was placed neatly in the back corner of my office. There it was during my workday beckoning me to practice! Whenever I wanted a break from work, I would do 20–25 runs and track my times in a notebook. By the end of the day, I would have 150–200 entries. Those entries were the ones that got recorded; there were many more that never made into the notebook because I was practicing technique rather than speed.

I would regularly practice for two hours every evening. On days I had more time, I would sweat at the kiosks for four-plus hours. My drive was so high that it was hard to stop, even when my arms were weary. I just knew one more try could be the one to get me to my goal.

The days before the regional event, I spent three eight-hour days fine-tuning my technique and speed. My times were down in the low 7-second range. A terrific improvement but still not where I wanted to be before the regional. So, I felt unprepared the day I traveled to New Jersey to meet the other thirty-two contestants in the New England Regional event.

I arrived in New Jersey a day early to get acquainted with the territory. I bought a mini version of the kiosks in the trunk of the rental car so that I could practice right up to the last moment.

The next morning I got up early, checked out of the hotel, and had some breakfast. I ordered a bagel with some eggs, but all I could eat was half of the bagel. I was not hungry. All I had on my mind was performing on that platform. The regional event was held at a Chevrolet dealership to promote the fact they were going to give away a Chevy van that day. I got there early. I was the first contestant there. The DeWalt representatives were still setting up. The competition began at 1:00 PM, so I had three hours to get loose and hopefully comfortable with my new surroundings.

I was relaxed leading up to the competition. As soon as the representative took the contestants into a conference room to go over the rules, that ended my relaxation. The first player was called randomly in and was sent up to the platform to get ready. The crowd that gathered was asked to be quiet. The first runs would begin when he pressed the timer. He would be the one to break the ice and set the pace. I think he had the most pressure on us all. He ended up with time in the 12 seconds. A beatable time, I thought. Two contestants later, that time was beaten with an 11.26. My name was pulled as the tenth players to compete. My heart began to race, my hands grew cold, and this was it: all that I practiced for came down to the next few seconds. Escorted to the edge of the platform, I was asked to test the screw gun. I stepped up to the platform. I took a deep breath and felt nervous like I always did. This time, I had practice behind me.

Stepping up to the platform symbolized an excellent deal for me. Most of us end up being spectators in rather than participators. Just look at our stadiums during a big football game. Granted we all can't play football, but we all can step up to the platform in our area of expertise. Until that moment I never had "stepped up" even to try. Fear of failure, I am sure, plagues most of us. Regardless of whether I failed or succeeded that day, I knew it was better to face my fears and fail than not try at all.

I relaxed enough to take an extra moment to study the screws tray for my initial grab. I crouched down into my ready position; my left hand went out over the shelf. I could see it tremble again. Another breath and my right hand acted more by instinct than a command: the timer was pressed. I quickly grabbed three screws perfectly and drove them faster than I ever have. Back to the tray for two more screws—I dropped one of the two and drove the one that was in my hand. The last screw came out of the shelf in a hurry, pulling a few others with it that fell to the ground. I drove the fifth screw and hit the timer. The crowds began its cheering before I could see my time—10.23. I was now in the lead. Two hours and 22 contestants later I was declared the New England regional winner. I won a Chevy Express van filled with DeWalt tools! I was thrilled. It's a feeling I never experienced before. I was moved by the cheering and the sportsmanship of the other contestants lining up to shake my hand. It does not sink in right away but knowing that I had accepted a challenge and worked tirelessly to accomplish it was rewarding enough to me. That's my prize for that day. The van and tools were an added benefit. I was headed to the finals.

The months following were eventful while preparing for the finals. I stepped up my practice times and enlisted the help of my wife, and my father-in-law, who quickly became a valuable resource for my improvement. Within weeks we worked together, and my times fell below seven seconds then down to low six seconds, and just when I did not think it could get any better on a cold January evening, I hit my fastest time ever of 5.29 seconds.

Those nights of extra effort, further determination proved fruitful. I broke through the fear of "I cannot do it" or "It cannot be done." I regularly hit sub-6 second times at least twenty-five times or more in each of my practice sessions.

At the finals in Phoenix, my wife and I had an excellent time compliment of DeWalt. They took care of us. After the second day there, I still hadn't spent any money. We realized how blessed we were. I placed the third fastest time in Phoenix and didn't win the million dollars. Another competitor with the same desire to win did. He deserved it: he performed when the pressure was the greatest.

Later I realized I had used over 200,000 screws in practice. Each one of those screws driven built confidence in me that says you can accomplish anything you set your mind to achieve. I lost the final events, but I know I came out a winner in what I had become in my attempt to conquer the challenge.

Joseph Fodera
January 26, 2005

So, you see how compulsive Choleric can be when they are on a mission.

ON A SIDE NOTE: Since the above Joseph has won several DeWalt contest. His many prizes have consisted of a new contractor's van filled with DeWalt tools, trips for he and his wife, and another new truck last summer, super-cab, and more pallets of DeWalt tools. And that is all just for fun for Joseph the Choleric.

PS: Joseph is my son-in-law married to my third daughter. Joseph is a highly successful man in several areas of his life. He loves God and serves him in many capacities at the senior levels. He is a leading entrepreneurs!   He is as close as a son to me. I love you Joseph!

# CHAPTER 9

# THE THREE DOMAINS OF TEMPERAMENT

## Social Profile – Leadership Profile – Relationship Profile

If you have ever played chess, then you can imagine for a moment playing chess as you consider the various facets of one's temperament that is made up of six different components. So, temperament is like playing with six chessmen whenever you think about your temperament or another person's temperament.

However, before we discuss that, let me tell you something about "labeling" individuals. Most people do not like labels and are offended by them. With temperament, it is essential to understand that you cannot just "label" a person with one temperament unless of course, they happen to have the same temperaments in all three areas of social/vocational, leadership, and relationship. I am not saying that there are not individuals like that because there are quite a few in the Melancholy section. So, these people who happen to have the same temperament in all three areas we call the pure type. For example, "Pure Melancholy" would be someone who is a Melancholy socially/vocationally, Melancholy in leadership, and Melancholy in a relationship Melancholy in all three areas. That person could be labeled as a Pure Melancholy. However, we chose not to refer to people with names. Instead, we address the individual as having a multidimensional temperament.

Now, back to looking at the individual temperament as a chess game and let's give the various dimensions of one's temperament, a structure that we can follow and understand.

**Worley's ID Profile (WIDP)** provides a comprehensive identification of needs, desires, and interpersonal temperaments in three primary areas of life (social/vocational, leadership, and relationship), and those three sectors further divided into two additional categories (demonstrated and desired). So, **Worley's ID Profile (WIDP)** consists of detailed temperament assessments in the following six areas:

| | | |
|---|---|---|
| **Social/Vocational Profile** | Demonstrated | (How they demonstrate toward you socially) |
| | Desired | (How they want you to demonstrate toward them socially) |
| **Leadership Profile** | Demonstrated | (How they demonstrate toward you in leadership) |
| | Desired | (How they want you to demonstrate toward them in leadership) |

**Relationship Profile**    Demonstrated    (How they demonstrate toward you in a relationship)

Desired    (How they want you to demonstrate toward them in a relationship)

So now we have identified the six different facets of an individual's temperament makeup, and they are:

- Demonstrated Socially
- Desired Socially
- Demonstrated Leadership
- Desired Leadership
- Demonstrated Relationship
- Desired Relationship

The above six would be the six chess pieces.

This information enables the consumer, whether it be an individual, family, team, clinician, or an employer to assess the individual's natural makeup quickly. Now, target potential conflicts and develop useful sound strategies for future change to enhance self, development, marriage partners, educational institutions, selection as a prospective employee, progression as an employee, team development, marketing, sales development, or the development of staff and executives.

As an individual gain understanding of self, they will be significantly enhanced, increasing their potential for a fulfilled and balanced life. With improved insight and self-awareness, they will enjoy greater success in interpersonal relations.

As a corporate application, the multifaceted use of WIDP will become an instrument of immense value to the overall operation of the variety of groups mentioned above from many aspects. WIDP becomes a human relations valuable tool in any setting.

**What is the social profile, leadership profile, and the relationship profile?**

I.    Social/Vocational Profile

The social/vocational profile identifies the individual's temperament needs and desires for socialization, work/school associations, and other superficial relationships. Requirements in this area may range from demonstrating and wanting minimal socialization to showing and craving constant socialization. The social profile helps answer the question,

**"Who is in or out of a relationship with this individual?"**

The social profile results should be applied to the individual's social and career contact level of acquaintances **only** and not to family and close friends or intimate relationships.

The social profile indicates the individual's needs and desires in their communication with others; requirements for acceptance and approval identified here.

It's the communication one has with people they meet in their work environment, grocery store, at the gas station, in the mall, at a trade show, conference, or just meeting or being around people in various places. Nothing concrete, just wide-ranging contact with people as one, moves through daily activities not related or targeted people one knows.

Be careful here that you do not include individuals in the work environment as close relationships. However, some people do develop close relationships with their coworkers. At that point, the connection is no longer in the social/vocational arena. It has moved into the relationship side of their preferences. Of course, this link now could cause problems with them in the work environment and become an issue in their dealings with each other. Many relationships are destroyed because of trying to have a close relationship with a coworker. Work-related associations are done regularly throughout the corporate world, but that does not make it functional or actively productive for the organization. Most generally, it causes personal conflict because the individuals involved are trying to make their relationship work in two different environments. Often problems will surface due to some significant issue of authority, promotion, or some organizational point that will put them in very uncomfortable situations that create conflict between them and their employer. Alternatively, it could cause one or both to lose their jobs. Everyone suffers, the couple, and the organization.

## II. Leadership Profile

**The leadership profile** identifies the individual's temperament needs and desires for influencing others, making decisions, and assuming responsibilities. Requirements in this area may range from independence to dependence. The leadership profile helps assess and answer the question of,

**"Who maintains the power and makes decisions in a relationship with this individual?"**

The leadership profile identifies the person's ability to successfully provide leadership whether it be, leading one person or a hundred.

Leadership? Here we must make a distinction between what kind of leadership we are talking about when it comes to leading from a temperament perspective. You see, leadership is not the same in every case, so let's wrap some additional clarifications around this issue of leadership.

We are talking about temperament and remember that temperament is broken down into six components. Right? So, let's back off for a moment and look at the three temperament profiles of social/vocational, leadership, and relationship and disregard the demonstrated and desired factors to explain leadership and how leadership functions.

Let's create a class setting for a moment to illustrate this point. Let's list three individuals, and let's say that we are looking at:

**Jane and her social/vocational profile only**
**John and his leadership profile only (let's say you are John in this illustration)**
**Barbara and her relationship profile only**

Are we illustrating leadership right, John? OK now let's remove Jane and her social profile and eliminate Barbara and her relationship profile. What is left?

**John (you) and his leadership profile only.**

Now John, as a leader, I would like for you to lead. Now, remember since Jane and Barbara are no longer present means that John (leadership) is there all by himself, and I am asking him to lead. Who is he going to lead?

Nobody because there is no one to lead Jane (social/vocational) and Barbara relationship is not present. So, at this point, we have discovered that for John (leadership) to lead, there must be someone to lead. Correct? Okay, let's bring back Jane (social/vocational) and Barbara (relationship) to join John (leadership). Moreover, let's separate Barbara (relationship) from Jane (social/vocational) and John (leadership).

**Jane and her social/vocational profile only**
**John and his leadership profile only (let's say you are John in this illustration)**
**Jane and her social/vocational profile only**

Now, can John lead Jane? Of course, now, he has someone to lead. Moreover, it happens to be that he can either lead Jane in a social or vocational setting. Correct? Remember, evaluated together the leadership profile and social/vocational profile help determine the individual's **social and employment** value.

So, let's say John is attending a convention, and in one of the seminars, they break into groups for a roundtable discussion. John (leadership) is asked to coordinate a group of ten individuals, Jane (social/vocational) is one of them, for debate on a particular topic.

Alternatively, let's say that John (leadership) is the division manager of a corporation and will meet with his division, Jane (Social/Vocational) is in his department, and he is to implement new project goals.

Can John lead in either of these situations? Absolutely! However, he is driving people in the social/vocational area only. He's with the "roundtable group" that he does not know and is leading as the division manager in a corporate setting with people he manages every day.

Well, that seems clear. What about Barbara (relationship) and her participation in this demonstration? What happened to her? OK, let's bring her back:

**Barbara and her relationship profile only**
**John and his leadership profile only (let's say you are John in this illustration)**
**Barbara and her relationship profile only**

Here they are again all three of them. This time let's separate John (leadership) and Barbara (relationship) from Jane (social/vocational) and leave Jane (social/vocational) out of the picture for a moment.

- **Jane and her social/vocational profile only left out for this illustration.**
- **John and his leadership profile only (let's say you are John in this illustration)**
- **Barbara and her relationship profile only.**

What are we looking for with John in leadership and Barbara in the relationship? Can John (leadership) lead Barbara (relationship)? Yes! However, you must remember that now John is driving in the relation and involvement with whom? Relationships with family and friends can be complicated. We have stepped outside of the social/vocational side of John's leadership profile and moved him into leading in close relationships with family and friends. Do you think he will lead differently with his family and close friends than he does at the social/vocational level as he leads the roundtable discussions at the convention? No, he will not. Individuals do not influence the same in close relationships as they do in their work environments. That approach to leading in a close intimate relationship will cause major havoc for the couple.

The main point made here is to understand the concept of leadership. We find out that we lead differently in the social/vocational arena than we lead in relationships. So, the impact of knowing how we drive in these two environments of social/professional versus relationship is significant in understanding and keeping the two separate at all times.

Looking at the three people again:

- **Jane and her social/vocational profile only**
- **John and his leadership profile only (let's say you are John in this illustration)**
- **Barbara and her relationship profile only.**

It is evident that the leadership profile interfaces with the social/vocational profile and that leadership profile also interfaces with the relationship profile. So, the moral of this issue is that if you are a leader, you should always be aware that leading in your social/vocational arena should be entirely different from how you conduct in your related field. If you do not get-up-and-go differently, then you will be sabotaging both your social relationships and your vocational relationships. You cannot and should not try to lead the same way on the job as you do in your close intimate relationships. The ties will dissolve very quickly and on bad terms.

Make sure you grasp this concept because it becomes critical in determining your success as a leader socially/vocationally. Other very critical issues concerning leadership are affected by the relationship profile, which we will discuss next.

## III.   Relationship Profile

**The relationship profile** identifies the individual's temperament needs and desires in close relationships with family and friends. Requirements in this region may range from emotional connections and expression of relationships with many people to isolation from relationships. The relationship profile identifies,

## "How emotionally open or closed to relationships is this individual?"

**Worley's ID Profile (WIDP)** defines these varying needs and desires not as **right** or **wrong,** but as individual differences and preferences. If the person's life situation differs radically from their needs and desires in one or more of their temperament areas, they are experiencing stress, conflict, and anxiety in most relationships. By teaching the individual about their unique needs, you can use **WIDP** to help restore balance and peace to their lives and relationships and positively impact their quality of life and their social/vocation.

The relationships profile outlines the individual's needs and desires for emotional sharing and relationships. For most people, *the relationship profile is the dominant pattern* that influences temperaments in the social/vocational and leadership areas.

**Looking at the three people again:**
**Jane and her social/vocational profile**
**John and his leadership profile only (pretend you are John in this illustration)**
**Barbara and her relationship profile only**

We have just added significant strength to temperament; *the relationship profile is the dominant pattern* that influences temperament in the social/vocational and the leadership areas. The power of the relationships is a BIG issue that plagues corporations of all sizes from a mom-and-pop operation to the corporate organizations that have thousands of employees scattered all over the world. You'll see these problems in organizations everywhere you go, and it is crippling and has crippled success since the beginning of time. It is called the good old boy (GOB) system. Let's look at two different situations in where you can see the concept of the relationship profile is the dominant pattern.

However, before we move on to that, I want to advise you to carefully watch what happens to the leadership profile as we move forward in this illustration. Most people will identify the leadership profile as the strongest of the three patterns. So, let's see what happens in this situation that we have created.

Joseph and Melaney are two people who have never met before, and they met at a social gathering when they both attended the annual town parade. After the ceremony, everyone would gather at the town square for a public picnic that always had many activities going on such as: ringing the bell, basketball challenge, knock the clown off his seat, dart-throwing contest, baseball throwing, and many other competitive and fun activities. They are at a social gathering and don't know each other. They end up with the same top score in the dart-throwing competition, and they must prepare for a tie-breaking contest. Now, this puts them together socially, and they are kidding back and forth, as they are practicing for the final bout, about how they are going to "crush" each other with their superb dart-throwing skills. As it ends up, Melaney won first prize, and Joseph won second. Sorry, Joe!

What just happened? Two people who do not even know each other exist and after a strange "coincident" they meet at a dart-throwing contest competing against each other. Now remember we are considering the power of the relationship profile and don't forget the relationship profile being regarded as the dominant profile, and we are considering that theory of WIDP. Right?

So, what just happened?

## Phase 1    Couple meet at a social gathering Joe and Melaney

Well, Joseph liked what he saw in Melaney, and there seemed to be chemistry between them as they were sweet-talking with each other during their practice for the final dart-throwing playoff between them. Joseph told Melaney that since she won the contest, the least she could do is buy him a cup of coffee so they could celebrate her victory and his defeat. Melaney accepted the invitation.

## Moving on to Phase 2    Couple have coffee together

Now leadership becomes a big issue here because most individuals like to be in control of their destiny and therefore, they determine how much power they will allow someone else when it comes to their personal life. Now for Joseph and Melaney, both agree to have coffee together, there must be some attraction between them. Otherwise, the invitation wouldn't have been completed or the request for coffee accepted. Therefore, both Joseph and Melaney gave up some of their leadership, so they both could allow going for coffee together.

So, what is happening here is that both of them are moving from their social/vocational profile into the relationship profile side of their temperament. There are feeling and or emotions involved in this process as they gravitate towards each other. Both see something in the other person that attracts them.

Now we have completed phase 1, "They meet at a social gathering," and have moved into stage 2, "Couple has coffee together."

Phase 1 Couple meet at a social gathering

## Phase 2    Couple have coffee together

Having a cup of coffee is not the objective; the aim is to get to know each other a little better. During the coffee time together, Joseph becomes more interested in Melaney, and he asks her out for dinner. Now, they have moved out of the social/vocational profile and are into the relationship profile. Now they are moving into phase 3.

Phase 1    Couple meet at a social gathering
Phase 2    Couple have coffee together
Phase 3    Couple have *dinner a few times*

Now, what has happened to the relationship at this point? They have moved into a relationship and are no longer just "social acquaintances": they have moved beyond the social/vocational realm and are into developing a relationship. Remember they both are giving over a certain amount of leadership, so they can have dinner and be together more frequently. If they are to develop their relationship further.

They are moving into each other's space emotionally and physically and giving up their leadership of the relationship bringing them closer together.

After they have had dinner a few times together, they are seen coming out of the restaurant holding hands, hugging each other, and very much in a relationship. So now they have moved into phase 4, "Couple hold hands, hug, and kiss."

Phase 1    Couple meet at a social gathering
Phase 2    Couple have coffee together

Phase 3     Couple have dinner a few times in
**Phase 4     Couple hold hands, hug, and kissing**

So, what comes next in their relationship? Phase 5, "Couple get married."

Phase 1     Couple meets at a social gathering
Phase 2     Couple have coffee together
Phase 3     Couple have dinner a few times
Phase 4     Couple hold hands, hug, and kissing
Phase 5     Couple get married

So, they get married and live happily ever after. Not necessarily right, but it does happen that people stay married for 10–20–30–40–50 or more years. I been married fifty-eight years. If we had only known about temperament at the beginning of our marriage, we could have saved ourselves much pain.

So, there are the five phases of a social/vocational meeting of two people moving through each phase into a relationship to the point of marriage. At the end of dating, both have given over all their leadership for the relationship to mature to the point of meeting each other at the altar. Now, where is the leadership profile in this relationship? When they started, they were both independent and very much in control of their individual lives and didn't even know each other.

Let's look at another set of stages of their relationship dominance and see what happens when leadership enters back into their relationship.

Three of the most challenging issues in marriages that create havoc is; money, children, and sex. If you can keep those three under control, your wedding will be satisfying.

**Phase 1     Couple argue**

Joseph and Melaney are discussing bills: the conversation becomes heated, and they get into an argument. What is the first thing that happens?

The next step in their relationship is phase 2, "Couple take back control":

**Phase 2     Couple take back control**

They both take back leadership (power) of themselves. Joseph slams down his fist on the table, and says he is not going to pay the bills the way Melaney wants him to, and Melaney stands up and insists that he will not speak to her with his angry, demeaning tone and firm, loud voice, and his stubbornness. She walks off bitter, and he goes in the opposite direction just as upset. Now we have a broken relationship, and leadership is at the forefront of both, and they are on nonspeaking terms.

The next step in their relationship is phase 3, "Couple reconcile":

**Phase 1     Couple argue**
**Phase 2     Couple take back control**
**Phase 3     Couple reunites**

Joseph apologizes to Melaney for his loss of control and yelling at and demeaning her and she accepts his apology, and they makeup and together compromise on the issue of paying the bills, and they move back into the relationship. Now everything is OK again. They both give up leadership (control) still for the sake of the relationship. Life is lovely still, and they move forward in their marriage.

Then one day, Melaney comes home from shopping with the kids all day and is so excited to share her purchases with Joseph. She is worn out from handling four children while shopping for clothes for them and she is so proud of her accomplishments, and she is gleaming an excited.

| | |
|---|---|
| **Phase 1** | **Couple argue** |
| **Phase 2** | **Couple take back control** |
| **Phase 3** | **Couple reconcile** |
| **Phase 4** | **Couple argue no reconciliation** |

Joseph does not even look at the clothes. He asks the question; "How much money did you spend?" Melaney tries to explain that she went to Walmart and I got the best buys, end-of-season leftovers, and, all items were 75 percent discounted. Joseph asks again without even considering what the purchases were. "How much money did you spend?" She says $147.00. He immediately goes into a rage and says to her she will have to take the clothes back that he needed that money to pay the rent. Now all four of the children are screaming because mommy and daddy are fighting and they are scared and hungry, and it is past their bedtime. The argument escalates to the point of Melaney having to put the kids in the car and go to her parents' house for the night because she and Joseph cannot get themselves under control. They both are talking divorce toward each other and making hatred remarks to each other, and it is just not a good state for the marriage. They are both fed up with each other; the relationship is nonexistent, and they no longer have feelings for each other and haven't for quite some time.

What just happened? They both took back leadership and moved entirely out of a relationship with each other. Now there is no feeling or emotions for each other, and they are both miserable and do not want to continue in the relationship. They separate, and the next thing is that they move into phase 5, "Divorce."

| | |
|---|---|
| **Phase 1** | **Couple argue** |
| **Phase 2** | **Couple take back control** |
| **Phase 3** | **Couple reconcile** |
| **Phase 4** | **Couple argue no reconciliation** |
| **Phase 5** | **Divorce** |

Unfortunately, the complete reverse of Joseph and Melaney developing their relationship has occurred. Why? Because the relationship profile is the dominant pattern that determines where most relationships end up. Although most people consider leadership to be the strongest of the three profiles of social/vocational, leadership, and relationship, we now conclude that the relationship profile is the dominant pattern.

What does the relationship profile, being the dominant profile, look like in a corporate setting? Again, using the five phases, for illustration purposes, to show the progression of leadership undermined by the stronger relationship profile that is, as we have discussed, the dominant profile

**Phase 1        You are the manager**

Let's say that you are the manager of a division in a large corporation. You have been there for ten years and have established yourself as a successful manager. Your work situation is excellent, and you are very comfortable and secure in your position.
Moving into phase 2

**Phase 2        Work with a close friend**

Philip who came to the company two years earlier and you develop a relationship with him, and he is now your friend. You and Philip have a lot in common and spend a lot of time together golfing, and you both are into rock climbing and visit all the local challenges of rock climbing within a hundred-mile radius of where you live.
Moving into phase 3

**Phase 3        Given authority to promote two of the people in your division**

Philip comes to you and says something like, "I know you are going to give me that promotions since we are such close friends. Right? Now you feel obligated to offer Philip the promotions because after all he is your best friend and you don't want to offend him or sacrifice your relationship.
Moving into phase 4

**Phase 4        Promote your GOB (good old boy), friend**

Now Philip is promoted to the new position (because of his relationship with you). He is happy, you are a fantastic (leadership) friend for supporting him, and things could not be any better for either of you.
Moving into phase 5

**Phase 5        Friend incompetent**

Philip does not have the experience or the necessary skills to adequately handle the responsibility of the position he was promoted As a result, the division suffers and loses valuable production, compounded with frustrated employees over Philip's Inadequacies, and now you, as a manager, are forced into a significant decision. What are you going to do with Philip? Demote him, fire him, give him another position somewhere in the company, or just let the adverse impact continue until the dysfunctional situation cripples the organization. What are you going to do? He is your best friend.

In this illustration, you can see the negative impact that the relationship profile (dominant pattern) can have at the organizational level. Unfortunately, it is a widespread practice that occurs at every level of management throughout our society. Relationship dominance! The organization suffers the loss. Why? Because of the GOB system.

WIDP used correctly and positioned people in places of responsibly is very reliable, efficient, effective, and confident. Remember the rule that you never assign, promote, hire, or employ in any circumstance based on the relationship profile. The proper selections are made from individuals' social/vocational profile and their leadership profile **only.**

Building any successful interpersonal relationship involves moving through the three living areas; social, leadership, and relationship in sequence. People typically begin relationships by setting social issues, to determine if the connection is safe. They then progress to leadership issues, identifying a mutually comfortable way to handle power and control. If the first two areas resolved satisfactorily, people could move into a relationship, an area of emotional closeness with each other. On a side note about this last statement about people entering into relationships: many interpersonal conflicts arise because of social and leadership issues present need to be resolved, yet people are attempting to function in an area of a personal relationship with each other.

Corporately or at any level of business, this is not a correct decision. Corporate relationships are maintained at the social/vocational level, which only includes the social and leadership levels of influence in a person's life on the job and does not contain the relationship profile. **However**, when assigning a position or a team or an individual assignment or hiring someone new, you should always consider their relationship profile because it's a guarantee that it will affect the status of the person in a very critical way.

Now that we have discussed the three profile areas of social/vocational, leadership, and relationship, we will move another level deeper in understanding WIDP in the next chapter.

## CHAPTER 10

# THE TWO DOMAINS OF DEMONSTRATED
# AND DESIRED SCORING

The WIDP Profile report generated for each of the three areas of social/vocational, leadership, and relationship is formed based on two scores: the demonstrated score and the desired score. Each rating may range from zero (0) to nine (9). The individual's results are recorded on the front page of **Worley's ID Profile (WIDP)** and are near the end of the printed profile in a page where all three temperaments are revealed in a graphic format.

In the last chapter, we discussed the three domains of temperament and found that looking at temperament is like looking at six chessmen. Well here again are the six chessmen, and we are going to focus on the demonstrated and desired facets of temperament. The six components are:

| | | |
|---|---|---|
| **Social Profile** | 1. | Demonstrated Socializing |
| | 2. | Desired Socializing |
| **Leadership Profile** | 3. | Demonstrated Leadership |
| | 4. | Desired Leadership |
| **Relationship Profile** | 5. | Demonstrated Relationship |
| | 6. | Desired Relationship |

Demonstrated Score

       **The demonstrated score** indicates:

       *How the individual prefers to act toward other people.*

This behavior can be observed and is the representation that a person presents to others. The demonstrated score in each area is the level of practice the person feels most comfortable in using to

| | |
|---|---|
| **Get together with others** | **Demonstrate socially/vocationally** |
| *Have their way with others* | *Demonstrate leadership* |
| **Be close to others** | **Demonstrate the relationship** |

We must understand the meaning of the numbers. Numbers used in WIDP do not have any value like:

**0 = low/bad**
**9 = high/good**

Numbers used in WIDP indicate the individual's temperament level like:

**0–1–2–3– = Introverted**
**4–5 = Introverted/Extroverted**
**6–7–8–9 = Extroverted**

Let's look at a bar graph that explains the temperament numbering system clearer:

| I | N | T | R | O | V | E | R | T | | I/E | | E | X | T | R | O | V | E | R | T |
|---|---|---|---|---|---|---|---|---|---|---|---|---|---|---|---|---|---|---|---|---|
| 0 | | 1 | | 2 | | 3 | | 4 | 5 | | 6 | | 7 | | 8 | | 9 | | | |

As you can see, it is evident that the temperament numbers only designate where on the bar graph and individuals' temperament falls somewhere between zero (0) and nine (9). They will either be an introvert, introvert/extrovert, or extrovert.

There is no such thing as "good/high" or "low/bad" temperament. It is just who you are as you were coded genetically in your mother's womb at conception. Moreover, your temperament does not change; it stays the same throughout your lifetime.

Yes, your environment and your culture can influence your personality and character, but your natural temperament does not ever change. We will discuss this in depth when we get to the place where we consider the "triangle" concept that explains the difference between temperament, character, personality, and behavior.

Individual numbers in a person's profile mean that whatever area—social/vocational, leadership, and relationship—these figures show up in, they are merely introverted, introverted/extroverted, or extroverted in that area of their temperament. These numbers are in all three areas of one's temperament.

**The introverted** numbers of 0–1–2–3 mean that individuals who have these numbers in one or more of their temperament profile areas are very rational people who need very little socialization and spend most of their time thinking things through.

**The introverted/extroverted** numbers of 4–5 mean that individuals with these figures can function well in either environment as an introvert or extrovert. They are comfortable in both situations.

**The extroverted** numbers of 6–7–8–9 are social and very outgoing people who enjoy being around people most of the time and have a need and desire to be with people frequently if not always.

In this demonstrated score chart, we will, for illustration purposes, be using the social profile for additional explanation. However, we could just as quickly use the leadership profile or the relationship profile.

The WIDP scores are interpreted as follows:

## Demonstrated Score Chart

| 0 – 1 | Very Low | | **The individual rarely expresses this behavior and compulsively avoids this behavior** <br><br> Means that people who score either a zero (0) or one (1) in any of the three profile areas of social/vocational, leadership, or relationship will compulsively avoid that behavior. So, let's say someone scores a 0 in the demonstrated area of their social profile. What does this mean? It means that they will not show at all that they want to socialize with you, nor do they want you inviting them to social events of any kind. Nor do they want you just dropping by to visit them at work or home. They will do everything to keep you away from their private space, and they will be compulsive about avoiding those situations. |
|---|---|---|---|
| 2 – 3 | Low | | **The individual may occasionally express this behavior** <br><br> Means that people who score either a two (2) or three (3) in any of the three profile areas of social/vocational, leadership, or relationship will accept a little socializing and interaction with others. |
| 4 – 5 | Moderate | | **The individual tends towards expressing this behavior** <br><br> Means that people who score either a four (4) or five (5) in any of the three profile areas of social/vocational, leadership, or relationship will function well as an introvert and as an extrovert. However, they will sway back and forth from wanting to socialize to desiring to be by themselves. Too much of either will create stress for them, and they will swing to the opposite. |
| 6 – 7 | High | | **The individual characteristically expresses this behavior** <br><br> A high number of 6 or 7 indicate that individuals with these figures will most often be expressing a desire for socialization in their environment, whether it be social or vocational. |
| 8 – 9 | Very High | | **The individual compulsively expresses this behavior** <br><br> People with very high numbers of 8–9 will always be looking for people and places to socially interact with others. They never get enough socializing, and they draw energy from social activity. |

## Desired Score

### The desired score indicates:
*The individual's preferred behavior from others toward him/her.*

The desired score is the behavioral response an individual does not want. It is not possible to determine the desired score by observation. An individual's desired score is determined through WIDP assessment.

The desired score in each area is the level of behavior the individual prefers others to use in their approaches toward them to

**Get together with them**     *Desired socially/vocationally*
*Have their way with them*     *Desired leadership*
**Be close to them**     **Desired Relationship**

We must again understand the meaning of the numbers. Numbers used in WIDP do not have any value like:

**0 = low/bad**
**9 = high/good**

Numbers used in WIDP indicate the individual's temperament level like:

**0–1–2–3– = Introverted**
**4–5  = Introverted/Extroverted**
**6–7–8–9 = Extroverted**

Let's look at a bar graph that explains the temperament numbering system a little clearer:

## WIDP GRAPHIC
## REPRESENTATION

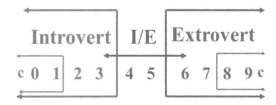

It is an indicator of the individual's inner needs and desires, which may differ significantly from their public image. The desired behavior in each area is action the person prefers others use in their approach to getting together with them (desired social), to get their way (desired leadership) and to be close to them (desired relationship).

In this demonstrated score chart, we will, for illustration purposes, be using the Social Profile for additional explanation. However, we could just as quickly use the Leadership Profile or the relationship profile.

The WIDP scores are interpreted as follows:

**Desired Score Chart**

| 0 – 1 | Very Low | | **The individual rarely wants this behavior demonstrated toward him/her by others and compulsively avoids situations where it may occur** Means that people that score either a zero (0) or one (1) in any of the three profile areas of social/vocational, leadership, or relationship will compulsively avoid that behavior. <br><br> So, let's say someone scores a "0" in the desired area of their social profile. What does this mean? <br><br> It means that they do not desire that you socialize with them, nor do they want to socialize with you. Introverts do not want you to drop by to visit at work or home without an invitation. They will do everything to send you messages telling you that they do not wish to. So, the bottom line is not "Don't approach me," it is "Don't even think about approaching me." |
|---|---|---|---|
| 2 – 3 | Low | | **The individual may occasionally desire this behavior demonstrated toward him/her by others.** <br> The key word here is "occasionally." |
| 4 – 5 | Moderate | | **The individual characteristically wants this behavior demonstrated toward him/her by others.** <br> However, their desire is in "moderation." |
| 6 – 7 | High | | **The individual characteristically wants this behavior expressed toward them.** <br> They have a high need that you demonstrate toward them frequently. |
| 8 – 9 | Very High | | **The individual will compulsively desire to have this behavior demonstrated toward him/her by others.** <br> This person does not ever get tired of you demonstrating toward them, and they will always be wanting more and seem never to get enough. |

We have used the term "compulsive" in discussing the low end of the bar graph the 0–1 and the high end of 8–9. Looking that the bar graph, let's examine the term "compulsive" and what it means.

As you already know the bar graph representing the temperament numbering system, we'll want to understand the word "compulsive" as it relates to temperament. So, let's look at the low-end number of 0–1 and the high-end numbers 8–9. So, let's identify for each temperament their "compulsive" numbers. All numbers that are "compulsive" will be designated with a small c.

# WIDP GRAPHIC
# REPRESENTATION

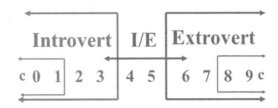

**COMPULSIVE:** (Small c = compulsive)

| | | |
|---|---|---|
| ISc | Introverted Sanguine | Compulsive The compulsive numbers are 08, 09, 19 |
| Sc | Sanguine Compulsive | The compulsive numbers are 89, 99, 98 |
| *P* | *Phlegmatic* | *Has no compulsive numbers* |
| Mc | Melancholy Compulsive | The compulsive numbers are 00, 01, 10 |
| Cc | Choleric Compulsive | The compulsive numbers are 80, 90 91 |

Looking at the WIDP scoring chart below, you will see there are dark colors in the four corners. This is where the compulsive numbers are, at the extreme corners farthest from the middle of the chart as possible.

It is essential to notice that P = Phlegmatic **has no compulsive numbers**. Reason being that it is in the centers of the chart. The Phlegmatic numbers are 44, 45, 54, and 55. There are only four of them. Although they do not have compulsive numbers, it's said that they are "compulsive" about not being compulsive. Phlegmatic as we have discussed in the Phlegmatic chapter is "middle of the road" and not excessive in any direction due to their having to protect their low energy level. Moderation is their motto.

Upper left the dark corner yellow, is the ISc, Introverted Sanguine Compulsive, with the compulsive numbers of 08, 09, and 19.

Top right-hand corner, dark green, is the Sc, Sanguine Compulsive, with the significant numbers of 89, 99, and 98.

Bottom left-hand corner, dark blue, is the Melancholy Compulsive with the compulsive numbers of 00, 01, and 10.

Bottom right-hand corner, dark red, is the Choleric Compulsive with the compulsive numbers of 80, 90, and 91.

WIDP is a groundbreaking temperament resource that, combined with a thorough understanding of WIDP and the dynamics of the interaction of the three domains of social/vocational, leadership, and relationship, WIDP identifies each's unique needs, desires, and possible behavioral responses. The compulsiveness is just another factor to consider in the overall understanding of people' temperament. It is not right or wrong; it is only part of their temperament that needs to be understood. Individuals with compulsive temperaments can, and most generally do, become an asset positioned in the right spot.

In general, the higher the differentiation between the demonstrated score and the desired score, the higher the chance that the individual is experiencing conflict in this area. Since WIDP provides a broad interpretation of these scores in the different printed profiles, numerical data supplied for clearer understanding. The WIDP comprehensive analysis is between fourteen to eighteen pages of data that represents your printed WIDP Profile temperament. Within each WIDP published profile assessment, an extreme amount of valuable data; data that will validate you as an individual, as a professional, and confirm those things that you know that now will be confirmed through WIDP. WIDP will validate who you are based upon how you know yourself, your true self. You see yourself on the written pages of your assessment. Whether it be as Founder/President at the Directors Board Meeting or communicating with your grandmother or your newly born family member; understanding the insight of WIDP is life altering. WIDP provides intellectual precision. self-determination .and laser guidance.

For those **"Big Decision Maker's"** who are interested in getting a competitors **$EDGE!$**
Contact: jwworley@widp.org

However, an individual can read their profile without debriefing and glean tremendous amounts of new knowledge about them. However, with a good debriefing from one of our associates, there is so much more clarity because of having a proper understanding of the dynamic functions of the three domains the three different profiles.

Worley's ID Profile describes temperament characteristics in individuals with specific score patterns. Because of variations within scoring ranges, a few details of WIDP may not apply precisely to the individual. However, the overall high reliability of WIDP is unparalleled in the field of assessment instruments. With a proper debriefing, the WIDP Profile data is exceptionally reliable. Most generally patterns will be around 96 to 98 percent stable and, in some cases, there have been many reports that WIDP is 100% reliable.

# CHAPTER 11

# WIDP Scores Graphically Represented

When we look at the graphic representation chart below of the WIDP Profile results of an individual's profile who happens to be:

Socially 27, leadership 12, and relationship 86:

It can be written or displayed in the following ways:

- **A Demonstrated Introverted (2) and Desired Sanguine (7) in their social profile**
- **A Demonstrated Melancholy (1) and the Desired Melancholy (2) in their leadership profile**
- **A Demonstrated Sanguine (8) and a Desired Sanguine (6) in their relationship profile.**

Alternatively, we can say the WIDP Profile results are:

**27 – Introverted Sanguine, 12 Melancholy, 86 Sanguine.**

Socially this profile is 27. Demonstrated score (2 in this profile) is **always** the first number, and the desired number (7 in this profile) is always the second number within each of the three sets of numbers identifying one's temperament when written as above, i.e., 27 12 86.

The first set of numbers (27 in this profile) is always the social profiles demonstrated (2) and desired (7) profile.

The second set of number (12 in this profile) is always the leadership profiles demonstrated (1) and desired (2) profile.

The third set of number (86 in this profile) is always the relationship profiles demonstrated (8) and desired (6) profile.

Alternatively, it can look like this:

**Demonstrated (Top) Number**    **2**
**Desired (Bottom) Number**    **7**

**Demonstrated (Top) Number**    **1**
**Desired (Bottom) Number**    **2**

**Demonstrated (Top) Number    8**
**Desired (Bottom) Number    6**

Alternatively, it can look like this: **27 12 86**

For all the illustrations above, look at the "WIDP Scores Represented Graphically Chart" below. There you will see the individual's WIDP results graphically represented with the profile results of 27 12 86. Here it is straightforward to see the six different facets or chessmen as we have referred to them, all listed in graphic form and quick read.

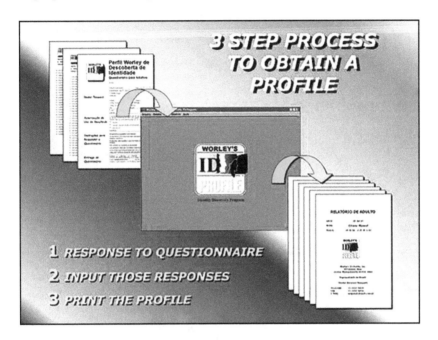

Now we will consider additional issues concerning graphic representation. How do we get to the graphics chart?

Well, the process is this—there are three steps involved:

- **Someone completes a WIDP questionnaire and gives it to you**
- **You enter the data from the questionnaire into the WIDP software**
- **The software generates a sixteen-to-eighteen-page profile for the individual.**

The WIDP questionnaire can be in one of the three languages of English, Spanish, or Portuguese. They can be adult or youth six to sixteen.

Individuals, institutions, or corporations have the choice of completing the WIDP questionnaire online at our website.

If an individual chooses to complete the WIDP questionnaire online, they can get their results back either in their web browser or have it sent to their email address or receive it both ways. Worley's ID Profile always gets a copy of every profile completed through the Internet. So, in case, someone should lose their WIDP Profile results, WIDP will still have a backup copy.

If you are completing the profile on the Internet, you can also select to have your profile sent to as many individuals as you want. All you have to do is when you come to the place where the person can put their e-mail address, enter a semicolon (;) not any spaces, and enter as many e-mail addresses as you would like, separated by a semicolon to receive a copy of that person's WIDP Profile results. This process takes only seconds, and once you have entered the data and hit the enter button, the result is in your web browser and e-mail within seconds.

So, realistically you can be anywhere in the world and have an individual complete a WIDP questionnaire in English, Spanish, or Portuguese, adult and youth (ages six to sixteen), and they can get their results immediately. The WIDP software is capable of handling 600 WIDP Profile questionnaires in a few seconds.

### WIDP Scoring Chart

Now, let's return to the graphics of the WIDP scoring chart below.

## PLOTTING YOUR WIDP PROFILE RESULTS

To accomplish this, you will need;

1. **Your WIDP PROFILE**
2. **The WIDP Scoring Chart Below**

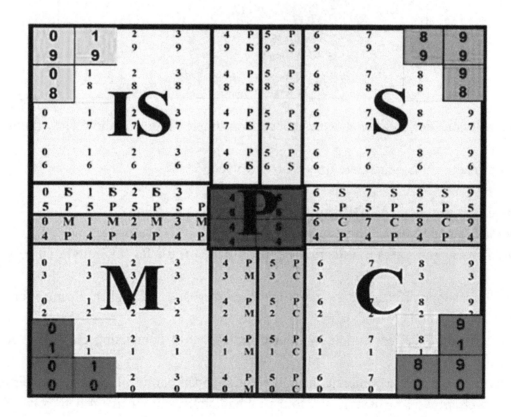

On the front of your WIDP Profile, you will see the following:

## CONFIDENTIAL ADULT PROFILE

**Date: 00/00/0000**

**Client: John Doe**

*Client ID: 012-34-5678*

**Client Profile: 27 12 86**

**WIDP User: Developing People, Inc.**

The information that is needed to plot on the WIDP scoring chart is the client profile. In this case, it is:

**Client Profile: 27 12 86**

The first set of numbers is the Social Profile 27.

So, you find the person's profile numbers and consider the first set of number. In this case, the numbers are 27.

We find 27 for John Doe, you find your first set of numbers "??" and find the same number on the WIDP scoring chart. Circle them and put an S beside it, indicating that this figure is the Social Profile results. It so happens that the number 27 falls into the section known as the Introverted Sanguine quadrant. Where do your numbers fall? Find it, circle it, and put an S beside it for social.

Now we go to the second set of numbers for John Doe 12, and you find your second set of numbers "??" then find the same number on the WIDP scoring chart. Circle it and put an L beside it, indicating that this figure is the Leadership Profile. It so happens that the number 12 for John Doe falls into section known as the Melancholy quadrant. Where does your second set of figures fit on the chart? Circle them and put an L beside them.

Last, we go to the third set of numbers for John Doe, 86, and you find your third set of the same number on the WIDP scoring chart and circle them and put an R beside it indicating that this figure is your relationship profile. It so happens that the number 86 belongs in the section known as the Sanguine quadrant. Where does your third set of number fall? Circle it and put an R beside it.

Now you have your WIDP Profile results plotted on your WIDP scoring chart. How do you accurately present your WIDP Profile to another person? Here is the proper way:

You say: My WIDP results are Social 27 Introverted Sanguine, Leadership 12 Melancholy, and Relationship 86 Sanguine.

So, whatever the results of your WIDP Profile are write them here:

    _____   _____   _____

    **Social**   **Leadership**   **Relationship**

Now you know what your WIDP Profile is and how to present your temperament correctly, and you have plotted your results on the WIDP Scoring Chart. Good job!

# CHAPTER 12

# TEMPERAMENT BLENDS

Now we need to consider the WIDP blends because some individuals have a WIDP Profile that falls into one of the blended areas of the WIDP Scoring Chart and asks the question "What is a blend?" Well, let's list some of the characteristics of a blend.

- The first thing to remember is that Phlegmatic is **the only** temperament that blends with the other four temperaments Introverted Sanguine, Sanguine, Melancholy, and Choleric. See the chart below for the various blend combinations. The Phlegmatic quadrant falls precisely in the center of the WIDP Scoring Chart and is composed of the numbers 45, 45, 54, and 55. The other four temperaments surround the Phlegmatic quadrant.

## WIDP Scoring Chart

| | | | | | | | | | |
|---|---|---|---|---|---|---|---|---|---|
| 09 ISc | 19 | 29 | 39 | 49 | 59 | 69 | 79 | 89 | 99 Sc |
| 08 | 18 | 28 IS | 38 | 48 P/IS | 58 P/S | 68 | 78 | 88 S | 98 |
| 07 | 17 | 27 | 37 | 47 | 57 | 67 | 77 | 87 | 97 |
| 06 | 16 | 26 | 36 | 46 | 56 | 66 | 76 | 86 | 96 |
| 05 | 15 IS/P | 25 | 35 | 45 | 55 P | 65 | 75 S/P | 85 | 95 |
| 04 | 14 M/P | 24 | 34 | 44 | 54 | 64 | 74 C/P | 84 | 94 |
| 03 | 13 | 23 | 33 | 43 | 53 | 63 | 73 | 83 | 93 |
| 02 | 12 | 22 M | 32 | 42 P/M | 52 P/C | 62 | 72 | 82 C | 92 |
| 01 | 11 | 21 | 31 | 41 | 51 | 61 | 71 | 81 | 91 |
| 00 Mc | 10 | 20 | 30 | 40 | 50 | 60 | 70 | 80 Cc | 90 |

- If you look closely at the WIDP Scoring chart above, you will find that right in the middle of the graph, horizontally and vertically, there are two rows of shaded areas that run from top to bottom and from side to side; directly in the middle of the chart is where the Blends exist. Moreover, they border all four areas of the Introverted Sanguine, Sanguine, Melancholy, and Choleric. The four temperaments in the four corners removed with only the blends left in the middle horizontally, and vertically.
- Whenever you see a blend of social/vocational, leadership or relationship think, "BALANCE" in the temperament section where the blends are located.
- Blends give the person a "softer" presentation of the temperament area with which they have blended.
- There are eight possible blend combinations. Remember the Phlegmatic is the only temperament who blends with the other four temperaments.

**The "Blends" are listed below:**

- Introverted Sanguine **Phlegmatic**   IS/P 0, 1, 2, 3 / 5
- **Phlegmatic** Introverted Sanguine   P/IS 5 / 0, 1, 2, 3
- Sanguine **Phlegmatic**   S/P 6, 7, 8, 9 / 6, 7, 8, 9
- **Phlegmatic** Sanguine   P/S 4,5/6,7,8,9
- Melancholy **Phlegmatic**   M/P 0,1,2,3/6,7,8,9
- **Phlegmatic** Melancholy   P/M 4,5/0,1,2,3
- Choleric **Phlegmatic**   C/P 6,7,8,9/4,5
- **Phlegmatic** Choleric   P/C 4,5/6,7,8,9

The blends are quite simple to understand. We will look at these one at a time and provide insight as we present each of these blends.

| IS | P |
|---|---|
| Demonstrated | Desired |
| **INTROVERTED SANGUINE**<br>People-oriented<br>Gentle<br>Diligent<br>Loving<br>Compassionate<br>Supportive<br>Loyal | **PHLEGMATIC**<br><br>Calm<br>Friendly<br>Objective<br>Diplomatic<br>Practical<br>Humorous<br>Dependable |

If the blend, like the first one listed here, is an Introverted Sanguine/Phlegmatic, then the Introverted Sanguine is the demonstrated (first number), and the Phlegmatic is the desired (second number). In other words, the first part of the blend is always made known and the second part is still the desired.

Also, in the blends, we have listed the primary characteristics of what the individual's preferences based on their temperament in those areas. What you can see in the first illustration below are the characteristics of the Introverted Sanguine:

**People-oriented**
**Gentle**
**Diligent**
**Loving**
**Compassionate**
**Supportive**
**Loyal**

We will not list all the Characteristics, as you need to know the basic functionality of each blend. **Introverted Sanguine/Phlegmatic: 05, 15, 25, and 35.**

So, the **horizontal** numbers of the Introverted Sanguine Phlegmatic are 05, 15, 25, and 35. The first numbers of each set are 0, 1, 2, and 3, are the **Demonstrated** numbers which are all introverted.

That means that they will not be demonstrating toward you and if they do, it will be just a little bit.

The second numbers, all 5s, are their **Desired** numbers, which means they are all introverted/extroverted. That means they can accept you demonstrating toward them in moderation. The desired quantity is 5, and they desire 5, and they will vacillate between being an introvert and then swing to be an extrovert. They are very comfortable with functioning either as an introvert or as an extrovert. Remember Phlegmatic is moderate in everything.

<table>
<tr><td align="center">**P**</td><td align="center">**IS**</td></tr>
<tr><td align="center">Demonstrated</td><td align="center">Desired</td></tr>
<tr><td>

**PHLEGMATIC**

**Calm**
**Friendly**
**Objective**
**Diplomatic**
**Practical**
**Humorous**
**Dependable**

</td><td>

**INTROVERTED SANGUINE**
**People-oriented**
**Gentle**
**Diligent**
**Loving**
**Compassionate**
**Supportive**
**Loyal**

</td></tr>
</table>

## Phlegmatic/Introverted Sanguine: 46, 47, 48, and 49

So, the horizontal numbers of the Phlegmatic/Introverted Sanguine are 46, 47, 48, 49.

The first numbers, all 4s, are the demonstrated numbers which are all introverted/extroverted. The demonstrated number is 4, and they demonstrate 4, and they will demonstrate and sway back and forth the between being an introvert and then swing to be an extrovert. They are very comfortable with functioning either as an introvert or as an extrovert. Remember, Phlegmatic is moderate in everything.

The second numbers—6, 7, 8, 9—are the **Desired** numbers, which are all extroverted. They will want you demonstrating high, very high, and sometimes compulsive toward them. Very outgoing individuals if they feel safe in the relationship.

| S | P |
|---|---|
| **Demonstrated** | **Desired** |
| SANGUINE | PHLEGMATIC |
| Outgoing | Calm |
| People-oriented | Friendly |
| Enthusiastic | Objective |
| Responsive | Diplomatic |
| Talkative | Practical |
| Loving | Humorous |
| Compassionate | Dependable |

## Sanguine/Phlegmatic 65, 75, 85, 95

So, the horizontal numbers of the Phlegmatic/Sanguine **are 65,** 75, 85, and 95.

The first set of numbers—6, 7, 8, 9—are the **Demonstrated** numbers, which are all extroverted. They will be demonstrating toward you high, very high, and sometimes compulsively. Very outgoing individuals if they feel safe in the relationship.

The second numbers, all 5s, are the **Desired** numbers, which means they are all introverted/extroverted. That means that they can accept you demonstrating toward them in moderation. The desired number is 5, and they desire 5, and they vacillate between being an introvert and then swing to be an extrovert. They are very comfortable with functioning either as an introvert or as an extrovert. Remember Phlegmatic is undemonstrative in everything.

| P | S |
|---|---|
| **Demonstrated** | **Desired** |
| PHLEGMATIC | SANGUINE |
| Calm | Outgoing |
| Friendly | People-oriented |
| Objective | Enthusiastic |
| Diplomatic | Responsive |
| Practical | Talkative |
| Humorous | Loving |
| Dependable | Compassionate |

**Phlegmatic/Sanguine 56, 57, 58, and 59**

So, the **vertical** numbers of the Introverted Sanguine Phlegmatic are 56, 57, 58, and 59.

The first number, all 5s, are the **Demonstrated** numbers which are all introverted/extroverted. The demonstrated number is 5, and they desire 5, and they will demonstrate and vacillate back and forth the between being an introvert and then swing to be an extrovert. They are very comfortable with functioning either as an introvert or as an extrovert. Remember Phlegmatic is modest in everything.

The second numbers, 6, 7, 8, 9, are the **Desired** numbers, which are all extroverted. They will want you demonstrate high, very high, and sometimes compulsive toward them. Very outgoing individuals if they feel safe in the relationship.

| M | P |
|---|---|
| **Demonstrated** | **Desired** |
| MELANCHOLY | PHLEGMATIC |
| Creative | Calm |
| Analytical | Friendly |
| Gifted | Objective |
| Self-sacrificing | Diplomatic |
| Compassionate | Practical |
| Perfectionist | Humorous |
| Disciplined | Dependable |

## Melancholy Phlegmatic 04, 14, 24, 34

So, the **horizontal** numbers of the Melancholy Phlegmatic are 04, 14, 24, and 34.

The first numbers of each set are 0, 1, 2, and 3, are the **Demonstrated** numbers which are all introverted. That means that they will not be demonstrating toward you; if they do, it will be just a little bit.

The second numbers are all 4s, the **Desired** numbers, which means they are all introverted/extroverted. That means that they can accept you demonstrating toward them in moderation. The desired number is 4, and they desire (4), and they sway back and forth between being an introvert and then swing to be an extrovert. They are very comfortable with functioning either as an introvert or as an extrovert. Remember Phlegmatic is reasonable in everything.

| **P** | **M** |
|---|---|
| **Demonstrated** | **Desired** |
| PHLEGMATIC | MELANCHOLY |
| Calm | Creative |
| Friendly | Analytical |
| Objective | Gifted |
| Diplomatic | Self-sacrificing |
| Practical | Compassionate |
| Humorous | Perfectionist |
| Dependable | Disciplined |

## Phlegmatic/Melancholy 40, 41, 42, 43

So, the vertical numbers of the Melancholy Phlegmatic are 40, 41, 42, and 43.

The first number, all 4s, are the **Demonstrated numbers** which are all introverted/extroverted. The demonstrated number is 4, they demonstrate (4), and they will demonstrate and sway back and forth between being an introvert and then swing to be an extrovert. They are very comfortable with functioning either as an introvert or as an extrovert. Remember Phlegmatic is moderate in everything.

The second numbers are all 6, 7, 8, 9 are the **Desired** numbers, which are all extroverted. They will want you to demonstrate high, very high, and sometimes compulsive toward them. Very outgoing individuals if they feel safe in the relationship.

**C**                        **P**

| Demonstrated | Desired |
|---|---|
| **CHOLERIC** | **PHLEGMATIC** |
| **Independent** | **Calm** |
| **Visionary** | **Friendly** |
| **Productive** | **Objective** |
| **Decisive** | **Diplomatic** |
| **Inspiring** | **Practical** |
| **Determined** | **Humorous** |
| **Strong Willed** | **Dependable** |

**Choleric/Phlegmatic 64, 74, 84, 94**

So, the horizontal numbers of the Choleric/Phlegmatic are 64, 74, 84, and 94.

The first set of numbers, 6, 7, 8, 9, the **Demonstrated** numbers, are all extroverted. Meaning they will be demonstrating toward you high, very high, and sometimes compulsive. Very outgoing individuals if they feel safe in the relationship.

The second numbers are all 4s, the **Desired** numbers, which means they are all introverted/extroverted. That means that they can accept you demonstrating toward them in moderation. The desired number is 4, and they desire (4), and they will sway back and forth between being an introvert and then swing to be an extrovert. They are very comfortable with functioning either as an introvert or as an extrovert. Remember Phlegmatic is moderate in everything.

**P**                        **C**

| Demonstrated | Desired |
|---|---|
| PHLEGMATIC | CHOLERIC |
| Calm | Independent |
| Friendly | Visionary |
| Objective | Productive |
| Diplomatic | Decisive |
| Practical | Inspiring |
| Humorous | Determined |
| Dependable | Strong-Willed |

## Phlegmatic/Choleric 50, 51, 52, 53

The first numbers, all 5s, are the **Demonstrated** numbers, which are all introverted/extroverted. The demonstrated number is 5, and they demonstrate 5, and they will demonstrate and sway back and forth the between being an introvert and then swing to be an extrovert. They are very comfortable with functioning either as an introvert or as an extrovert. Remember Phlegmatic is moderate in everything.

The second numbers 0, 1, 2, and 3 are the **Desired** numbers, which are all introverted. That means that they will not desire that you demonstrate toward them and if they do, that it be for just a little bit.

# CHAPTER 13

# GAP Theory

G = **Great**
A = **Anxiety**
P = **Present**

Going another level deeper in gaining knowledge of WIDP we have the **GAP** (Great Anxiety Present) that will give a further understanding of WIDP. Understanding this concept will enable you to define an individual's temperament further. Therefore, you will be more efficient in supporting that person. They will have a better understanding of themselves, and also your knowledge of GAP will fortify your circumstances with that person whether in a social, vocational, or a close relationship.

Looking at the results of a person's WIDP Profile, you must always be aware of the potential conflict with a profile G-A-P of four (4) or more point spread between their demonstrated score and their desired score within any of the three profile areas of; social/vocational, leadership, and relationship.

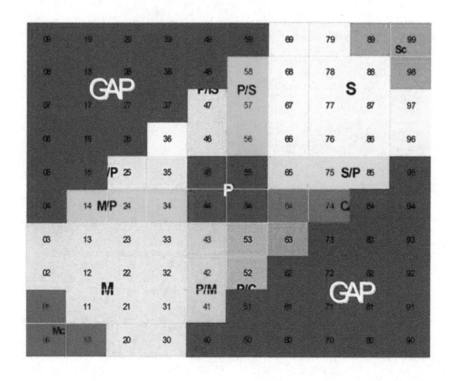

Looking at the GAP chart above, you can see that all the WIDP temperament numbers in the colored area do not have a GAP. However, all the numbers in the brown shaded part of the graph are all numbers that have a GAP of four or more.

As you can see, many GAP numbers are in either the Introverted Sanguine quadrant or the Choleric quadrants.

We now have a keen awareness in understanding that the Introverted Sanguine and the Choleric have a predisposition because of their temperament makeup to always be experiencing conflict with many of their relationships. Moreover, GAP numbers do also flow over into the blended areas of other temperaments.

The temperaments that **are not** within the GAP sector are listed below as the:

**Phlegmatic Sanguine 56, 57, 58**
**Phlegmatic/Introverted Sanguine 46, 47**
**Introverted Sanguine/Phlegmatic 25, 35**
**Melancholy Phlegmatic 14, 24, 34**

All the temperament profile designators above fall within the upper left-hand section of the WIDP GAP chart.

The GAP temperament That **is not** within the Choleric is listed below:

**Sanguine Phlegmatic 65, 75, 85**
**Choleric Phlegmatic 64, 74**
**Choleric 63**
**Phlegmatic Choleric 52, 53**
**Phlegmatic Melancholy 41**

All the temperament profile designators above fall within the bottom right-hand section of the WIDP GAP chart.

The widest GAP found in the WIDP scoring chart is 90, the Choleric Compulsive in the bottom right-hand corner, and 19 the Introverted Sanguine Compulsive in the top left-hand corner. So, the fuller the GAP, the more anxious, intolerant, insensitive, sensitive, stressful, blunt, stubborn, indifferent, cold, and driven the person will be.

Not only is this concept to be understood within your profile graph, but you must also consider that others you associate with might have a GAP of their own that you will have to compete.

What happens when others you associate with have a GAP, and you have a GAP in the same area of temperaments? As mentioned above, you will have to compete with the person having their GAP.

Using the Choleric Compulsive as an illustration let's say that you, a Choleric 90, have been promoted to a position where you must work with another Choleric 90 who has equal authority. Now we know that both Choleric wants to "run the show and be in charge." Do you think there will be a conflict between them? Of course, there will be conflict quite regularly. Why? Because both are very high in leadership and both want to lead the operations, and whatever that job is they will be jockeying for first place all the time.

Does this mean that they cannot work together as Choleric? No, it is not to say that. What it does say

is that the manager or director of that department who has the two Choleric under their supervision will have to know the temperament of each to have a positive impact on the two hard-driven Choleric.

It is prevalent to have more than one Choleric who is in the same department and both wanting to run the operation. However, if you know the temperament of the two individuals, then you can assign each of them their territory and gives them free rein run that section without interference from any other Choleric, coworker, peer, and in some cases, upper management.

Let me give you a side story of a former coaching client of mine to show you the power of a Choleric in conflict with another Choleric. For confidentiality let's call him Tom and the next manager under him who was running a significant facility in SW Arizona we will call Bill. Bill is the director of the facility. Now Tom is the number six person in the chain of command of a sizeable hi-tech firm in Massachusetts.

Tom has been telling me about having some issues with Bill about him not following his directives. Instead, Bill was creating his agenda as though Tom did not exist, and Tom stated that he was going to must deal with Bill.

I just figured that as a leader he would fly to Arizona and have a one-on-one with Bill and the corrections of the deficiency through proper leadership management would take place and things would move forward. The following week I did not see Tom, as he had to make the trip to Arizona. Now, remember what we have here is two very powerful Choleric who want their way and don't want to be controlled by anyone else. Independence for the Choleric is essential for them.

The following Week, Tom came in for his coaching Session. As soon as he walked into my office and before he even sat down, he said, "Well, I showed him who the boss was." I asked him what he did, and he said, "I closed his facility down and gave him a pink slip." Not having any idea of how large the facility was, I asked him, "So how big was his facility?" His reply: "Over seven hundred employees." I was stunned at his response. He just mumbled that he got even and would move on.

Now, that is a Choleric Compulsive in leadership, and they can make things happen. You never want to underestimate a Choleric when it comes to the issues of conflict. They are major contenders.

**Back to the GAP Theory!**

I want to show you a few graphs to illustrate the GAP theory. We will look at them in the following:

- The horizontal GAP within your temperament and another person
- The vertical GAP within your temperament and another person
- The cross-section GAP you're demonstrated to their desired and from their demonstrated to your desired

1. **Consider the horizontal view of your social profile with another person.**

   Here you put your temperament numbers on the designated line for demonstrated and your desire designator on the desired range. As you look at the graph below, you see the blank lines between the arrows. You put your social profile temperament numbers on the two lines: one for demonstrated and one for desired. Next, you put another person under the text "Other Person."

   For this exercise, I will be using the following temperament sets of numbers: your social profile is 80, and the social profile for the other person is 67.

Now looking at the **horizontal view** below of your profile compared to someone else's profile and considering the following:

- Do you see a GAP of four (4) or more between your demonstrated number 8 and the other person's 6? No, there is no GAP there, so these two individuals are OK in their social demonstrated numbers. No conflicts.
- Do you see a GAP of four (4) or more between your desired number (0) and their desired number (7)? Yes, we have a GAP here of seven, and that is a severe GAP. Will there be a conflict between them? Yes, there will be conflict.

The social GAP complex in graphic form.

# The Social "G-A-P" Complex

| Demonstrated | | | | |
| Desired | | | | |

SOCIAL   6    8

0    7

## HORIZONTAL VIEW OF YOUR SOCIAL PROFILE

YOU     OTHER PERSON

DEMONSTRATED \_\_\_\_ ⟷ \_\_\_\_\_

DESIRED      ⟷

2. **Consider the vertical view of your social profile and another person's profile.**

Here you put your temperament numbers on the designated lines for demonstrated and desired for both individuals.

- Do you see a GAP of four (4) or more between your demonstrated numbers of 8 and your demonstrated number of 0? Yes, there is a GAP of 8 there, so this indicates that you have an internal struggle as well as you are experiencing stress and anxiety with other individuals. Yes, there will be internal and external conflicts.

- Do you see a GAP of four (4) or more between the other person's demonstrated number (6) and their desired number (7)? No, we have only a GAP here of one, and that is not a problem for that person. No conflict within this individual.

# The Social "G-A-P" Complex

| Demonstrated | | | SOCIAL | 6 | | 8 |
|---|---|---|---|---|---|---|
| Desired | 0 | | | | 7 | |

## VERTICAL VIEW OF YOUR SOCIAL PROFILE

|  | YOU | OTHER PERSON |
|---|---|---|
| **DEMONSTRATED** | ____ | ____ |
|  | ↕ | ↕ |
| **DESIRED** | ____ | ____ |

- The cross-section GAP you are demonstrated to their desired and from their demonstrated to your desired.

    Here you put your temperament numbers on the designated lines for demonstrated and desired for both persons.

- Do you see a GAP of four (4) or more between your demonstrated number 8 and their desired number of 7? No, there is not a GAP. So, what you are demonstrating (8) and what they desire (7) are compatible. **No conflict here.**

    - Do you see a GAP of four (4) or more between the other person's demonstrated number (6) and your desired number (0)? Yes, there is a GAP of 6 there, so this indicates that you have an internal struggle as well as you are experiencing stress and anxiety with the other people. Yes, there will be internal and external conflicts.

# The Social "G-A-P" Complex

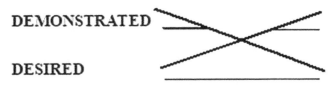

| Demonstrated | | SOCIAL | 6 | 8 |
| Desired | 0 | | 7 | |

## CROSS "X" SECTION OF YOUR SOCIAL PROFILE

YOU          OTHER PERSON

DEMONSTRATED

DESIRED

At this point, you complete the same exercise above and apply it to the leadership and relationship profiles and use a red marker for GAP's and a blue marker for the ones without a GAP. Then you will be able to see yourself and another person side by side from your temperament perspective, and you can immediately see potential problem areas between yourselves.

You can do this for several individuals at one time. It is beneficial for team development, matching people together that can work side-by-side in harmony. It is an excellent instrument for determining what person to use on marketing or sales assignment. Organizations can use it for new hire screening. WIDP a perfect conflict resolution tool and method in an environment where there are people. Apply the GAP Theory, and you will immediately see the potential conflicts and therefore be able to bypass them.

See if using the GAP Theory combined with your knowledge of WIDP Temperament determine who in situation identify the "team leader."

# Identify the team leader

|      | $\underline{S}$ | $\underline{L}$ | $\underline{R}$ |
|------|------|------|------|
| **Bob** | 21 | 81 | 25 |
| Tim  | 02 | 82 | 12 |
| John | 63 | 82 | 01 |

Using the Horizontal, Vertical, and Cross Section theory identify the team leader in this exercise. Okay, now determine:

# Who would make the best team leader and Why?

|      | $\underline{S}$ | $\underline{L}$ | $\underline{R}$ |
|------|------|------|------|
| **Joe** | 21 | 90 | 01 |
| Sue  | 02 | 45 | 54 |
| Tom  | 67 | 91 | 89 |

Using the Horizontal, Vertical, and Cross Section theory identify the team leader in this exercise. Decide who is the best team leader and why?

# Who is the best team leader?

|      | $\underline{S}$ | $\underline{L}$ | $\underline{R}$ |
|------|------|------|------|
| **Kim** | 26 | 34 | 02 |
| Barb | 31 | 20 | 12 |
| Jane | 01 | 12 | 05 |

Using the Horizontal, Vertical, and Cross Section theory identify the team leader in this exercise. These are real people in a real situation. Determine which one is the best leader and tell why you pick whom you do.

# Leaders Profiles

|  | S | L | R |
|---|---|---|---|
| John Doe | 10 | 50 | 25 |
| Mary Doe | 10 | 12 | 37 |
| Jim Doe | 36 | 70 | 46 |
| Don Doe | 50 | 80 | 55 |

# CHAPTER 14

# PSYCHOMETRICS OF WIDP

## Psychometric Evaluation Results
## of
## WORLEY'S ID PROFILE

This presentation of the psychometric properties of the WIDP temperament profile will begin with a discussion of the instrument and its structure, reliability, validity, and conclude with a general summary of its utility based on findings.

The **Worley Identity Discovery Program (WIDP)** a software system based on a sixty-item inventory developed by John W. Worley, Ph.D. I intended to produce an instrument that would yield a quick, but detailed, a summary of individual temperament to aid in the facilitation of an individual's development and self-understanding.

**Worley's ID Profile (WIDP)** interpretive reports, based on sixty simple questions answered on the computer program or the printed questionnaire for future computer entry by the user.

**Worley's ID Profile (WIDP)** provides a comprehensive identification of needs, desires, and interpersonal behaviors in three crucial areas of life (social, leadership, and relationship) and, those three sectors divided into two categories (demonstrated and desired). **Worley's ID Profile (WIDP)** consists of detailed temperament assessments in the following life areas:

| | |
|---|---|
| **Social Profile** | **Demonstrated** |
| | **Desired** |
| **Leadership Profile** | **Demonstrated** |
| | **Desired** |
| **Relationship Profile** | **Demonstrated** |
| | **Desired** |

This information enables the person to assess their individual's strengths quickly and weaknesses, potential target conflicts and develops sound beneficial strategies for future change. The person's understanding of self will be enhanced, increasing the possibility of a fulfilled and balanced life. With improved insight and self-awareness, they will enjoy greater success in interpersonal relationships.

## I. *Social Profile*

The social profile identifies the individual's temperament needs and desires for socialization, work/ school associations, and other superficial relationships. Requirements in this area may range from demonstrating and wanting minimal socialization, to showing and craving constant socialization. The social profile helps answer the question, **"Who is in or out of a relationship with this individual?"**

## II. *Leadership Profile*

**The leadership profile** identifies the individual's temperament needs and desires for influencing others, making decisions, and assuming responsibilities. Requirements in this area may range from independence to dependence. The leadership profile helps assess, **"Who maintains the power and makes judgments in a relationship with this individual?"**

## III. *Relationship Profile*

**The relationship profile** identifies the individual's temperament needs and desires in close relationships with family and friends. Requirements in this area range from emotional connections and expressions of relationships with many people to isolation from them. The relationship profile identifies, **"How emotionally open or closed to relationships is this individual?"**

**Worley's ID Profile (WIDP)** defines these varying needs and desires not as **"right"** or **"wrong"** but as individual differences and preferences. If the persons' life situation differs radically from their needs and desires in one or more of the areas, they will experience stress, conflict, and anxiety in relationships. By teaching the individual about their unique needs, they can use **(WIDP)** to help themselves restore balance and peace to their lives and relations.

Building any successful relationship involves moving through the three living areas, social, leadership, and relationship, in sequence. People typically begin relationships by setting social issues, to determine if the connection is safe. They then progress to leadership issues, establishing a mutually comfortable way, to handle power and control. If the first two areas resolve satisfactorily, people can move into a relationship, an area of emotional closeness with each other. Many interpersonal conflicts surface because social and leadership issues needing to be addressed, yet people are attempting to function in an area of personal relationships with each other.

# SCORING

The report generated for each of the three areas based on two scores: the demonstrated score and the desired score. Each rating may range from zero to nine. The individual's scores are recorded on the front page of **Worley's ID Profile (WIDP).**

**The demonstrated score** indicates how the individual prefers to act toward other people. This behavior can be observed: the image presented to others. The demonstrated score in each area is the level of action the individual feels most comfortable in using to bring people together (demonstrate socially), to get his/her way (demonstrate leadership) and to be close to others (demonstrate relationship). Scores are interpreted as follows:

## Demonstrated Score

| 0 – 1 | Very Low | | The individual rarely expresses this behavior and compulsively avoids this behavior |
|---|---|---|---|
| 2 – 3 | Low | | The individual may occasionally express this behavior |
| 4 – 5 | Moderate | | The individual tends towards expressing this behavior |
| 6 – 7 | High | | The individual characteristically expresses this behavior |
| 8 – 9 | Very high | | The individual compulsively expresses this behavior |

**The desired score** indicates the person's preferred behavior from others toward him/her. It is an indicator of the individual's inner needs and desires, which may differ significantly from their public images. The desired behavior in each area is the action the person prefers others use in their approach to get together with them (desired social), to get their way (desired leadership) and to be close to them (desired relationship).

## Desired Score

| 0 – 1 | Very Low | | The individual rarely wants this behavior demonstrated toward him/her by others, and compulsively avoids situations where it may occur |
|---|---|---|---|
| 2 – 3 | Low | | The individual may occasionally want this behavior demonstrated toward him/her by others |
| 4 – 5 | Moderate | | The individual tends towards expressing this behavior <br><br> The individual characteristically wants this behavior demonstrated toward him/her by others. |
| 6 – 7 | High | | The individual characteristically expresses this behavior |
| 8 – 9 | Very high | | The individual will compulsively seek this behavior demonstrated toward him/her by others |

In general, the more significant the discrepancy between the demonstrated score and the desired scores, the higher the probability that the individual is experiencing conflict in this area. Since **Worley's ID Profile (WIDP)** provides a comprehensive interpretation of these scores, numerical data is provided for your interest only.

**Worley's ID Profile (WIDP)** describes temperament characteristics found in individuals with specific rating patterns. Because of variations within scoring ranges, a few details of **Worley's ID Profile (WIDP)** may not apply precisely to the individual. However, the overall high reliability of **Worley's ID Profile (WIDP)** is unparalleled in the field of assessment instruments.

**Worley's ID Profile (WIDP)** includes the individual's temperament type, or temperament blends according to the theory first developed by Hippocrates and updated by contemporary professionals. These five basic types (Melancholy, Choleric, Sanguine, Introverted Sanguine, and Phlegmatic) and various blends (Melancholy-Phlegmatic, Phlegmatic Choleric, Introverted Sanguine-Phlegmatic and so forth) can accurately describe the individual's inner needs and desires. Two of the types, the Melancholy and the Introverted Sanguine, express along the continuum of shy behavior. The Choleric and the Sanguine both express as extroverts. The Introverted Sanguine demonstrates as a Melancholy, introvert, but desires as an extrovert. Listed below are the variations of the temperaments and temperament blends, and a list of the compulsive temperaments:

## FIVE TEMPERAMENTS:

IS    Introverted Sanguine
S    Sanguine
P    Phlegmatic
M    Melancholy
C    Choleric

## BLENDS:

P/IS    Phlegmatic/Introverted Sanguine
IS/P    Introverted Sanguine/Phlegmatic
P/S    Phlegmatic Sanguine
S/P    Sanguine Phlegmatic
MP    Melancholy Phlegmatic
PM    Phlegmatic Melancholy
CP    Choleric Phlegmatic
PC    Phlegmatic Choleric
IS/P    Introverted Sanguine/Phlegmatic
P/IS    Phlegmatic/Introverted Sanguine

## COMPULSIVE*:

ISc    Introverted Sanguine Compulsive
Sc    Sanguine Compulsive
Mc    Melancholy Compulsive
Cc    Choleric Compulsive

* **Compulsive** (Small "c" = compulsive)

In this context is not used in a negative sense like a fanatic, obsessive, uncontrollable, or unruly. **"Compulsive"** as used here indicates that the person's living patterns will focus on the various characteristics of that temperament need, whatever it may be within either of the three temperament areas of social/vocational, leadership, or relationship.

For example, individuals who are Melancholy compulsive in their Social/Vocational, very private, and they have a paramount need to maintain their privacy from other people. Melancholy people are timid in and around social settings. Likewise, Choleric compulsive people, in the area of leadership, focus on the control factor of control of themselves and others always.

This compulsiveness does not insinuate abysmal behavior. However, individuals who are compulsive in one or more areas of their behavioral makeup can be complicated people, especially in the instance of employers, leaders, managers, and close relationships.

**Worley's ID Profile (WIDP)** is an innovative temperament resource that, combined with professional communication skills, identifies individuals' unique needs, desires, and behavioral responses. This information becomes invaluable to everyone.

To assess the psychometric properties of the WIDP, I collected a database of 585 administrations of the instrument. The database evenly split between males and females (280 men and 305 women). The average age of the participants was 36 years (37.2 years men and 34.7 years female), with a mean education level of fourteen (14) years for all genders. Through psychometric evaluation, the Reliability and Validity was found to be trustworthy.

## Reliability

When defining the psychometric properties of an instrument, the term "reliability" is used in some ways. The most common use is the consistency with which an apparatus measures over time or occasions. This form of reliability, referred to as the coefficient *of stability or test-retest reliability*, is assessed by calculating the relationship between two or more sets of scores produced by the same group of individuals across a time interval. To assess WIDP test-retest reliability thirty-nine (39) people were given two administrations of the measure with a four-month interval between assessments. The normal relationships between scores on the six scales of the WIDP across the two administrations was found to be r.7 (Pearson Product Moment Correlation). The psychometric evaluation confirms that WIDP has excellent stability over time, and therefore, will provide consistent results between administrations.

Notes:  **The average test-retest reliability of similar types of instruments over one month is between .7 and .8. WIDP rating is - r.7 over four months is outstanding.**

Another measure of reliability used in assessing instruments properties is the *measure of internal consistency reliability.* On the individual scale level (the WIDP has six), this is an indication of how well the items in a scale measure the same thing. Because the elements on the WIDP six levels scored dichotomously (an article gave a value of one (1) or zero (0) based on specific response possibilities), the *Kuder-Richardson Formula 20 (KR-20)* was used. The average internal consistency of the six scales of **WIDP was KR-20 .54.** To put this result in perspective, consider that the average internal consistency of the 10 Minnesota Multiphasic Personality Inventory – 2 (MMPI-2) (the most widely used psychological measure today) Clinical scales and the three validity scale is .52.

Conclusions: The WIDP is very sound on instrument reliability.

# VALIDITY

How valid is WIDP? We can think of validity to the extent to which a test measures the characteristics it is designed to measure. Establishing the validity of WIDP was accomplished by two methods. The first of these methods (concurrent validity) was to compare the WIDP scores between individuals, not currently in counseling with those who have been diagnosed with specific psychological problems by clinical psychologists. Diagnosable issues carry known behavior patterns that should be demonstrated by mean scale scores found on the WIDP. Descriptions of the results presented by diagnosis:

## Major Depression:

Individuals with this diagnosis are typically withdrawn socially and lack the energy to pursue relationships actively. The WIDP profiles for this diagnosis indicate that they seldom initiate interaction with others, and they rarely want others to socialize with them. The average desired interaction score of this group is 0. Further, they report less than half of the willingness to make decisions or assume responsibility than that of nondiagnosed individuals (desired and demonstrated leadership low).

## Obsessive Compulsive Disorder:

Relationships for persons with this disorder are complicated. They typically lack intimacy in relationships and struggle in making decisions often to the point of wanting others to make decisions for them. WIDP scores for this diagnosis indicate that their desired relationship (what they desire from others) is much higher than that of the average person. Also, their demonstrated leadership scores show that they seldom want to make decisions and to take responsibility.

## Marital Problems

While not considered an actual psychological disorder, marital problems are a diagnosed condition. often, the question that couples face is of intimacy and control. Struggles over who makes decisions and who is responsible are every day. Blaming one another for what is missing in the marriage is the norms. The WIDP scores are consistent with these common issues. These individuals tend to desire relationships be demonstrated towards them much more than does the average person. WIDP results with higher than average levels of desired leadership score indicate that they would prefer their spouses to take on more responsibilities. Their low ratings demonstrated socially reflect the lack of desire to be socially involved and, a tendency to be withdrawn.

## Alcohol Dependence

Individuals who are alcohol dependent are often found to be lacking in their desire to be responsible and isolating from meaningful social situations. The WIDP profiles of this diagnosis indicate that their demonstrated social profile is less than half of the usual response style. They rarely express needs of desire for socialization. Their desired leadership scores (near zero) indicate that they do not wish others to make decisions for them or attempt to influence them. Their lower demonstrated leadership score further means that they do not want to make decisions.

**NOTE:** Even though the WIDP Profile is an analytical tool, the results of the comparison of mean responses with known characteristics of the established diagnoses above indicate that the scales have concurrent validity. That is, they measure what they intend to measure.

The second method of determining validity focuses on the position that the WIDP scales reveal different types of efficient functioning. If this were true, we would expect to find a broad range of response styles in the average population. During the sampling of individuals, I administered the Rosenberg self-esteem measure to eighty-two (82) of the participants. If the hypothesis is correct that healthy people can present many different scores on the six scales, then the scales will have little or no relationship with self-esteem. Results indicate that only desired leadership is related (marginally) with self-esteem. The other scales correlated zero (meaning no connection). Do not misinterpret this result to suggest that the WIDP is intended to present a complete profile that involves the interaction between the three areas of social, leadership, and relationships; also, between the demonstrated and desired elements of each of the domains. The results do indicate that self-esteem is not related to any of the temperaments found on any of the scales themselves, but as I have proposed, it is a product of, the difference between scales.

# CHAPTER 15

# CASE STUDIES USING
# WIDP TEMPERAMENT PROFILE

## Introverted Sanguine, Compulsive in Leadership
### "The Unwanted Promotion"

Michael now realizes he was a very successful assistant to the Director of Purchasing for a large university. The Purchasing Department was responsible for a $40,000,000 annual budget. Michael functioned very well in this position for fifteen years and was very active as the assistant. The reasons for his success were that his job neither required him to make many decisions or manage people. He was an assistant to the director and did what he was instructed to do by the director; which was primarily administrative. Since Michael's primary responsibilities did not require him to make a lot of crucial decisions or manage many people, Michael found himself comfortable with his job. (P.S. Introverted Sanguine finds it very challenging to make decisions and do not lead people well).

Everything was going great and then Michael's boss, the director of Purchasing, got promoted and relocated to the Southwest and Michael got a promotion to fill the vacant position of director of Purchasing! Immediate stress, anxiety, and frustration became apparent in Michael's life due to his promotion. Michael was in complete agony every day of his life, and his world turned upside down.

Along with the development came to the responsibility of managing twenty-seven staff and accountability for a $40,000,000 annual budget. After two years as director of Purchasing, Michael was exploring the possibilities of early retirement and a career change.

How could an Introverted Sanguine cope with all the decisions a Director of Purchasing would have to make, and how was he going to manage twenty-seven people? After struggling with the situation for two years and falling deeper and deeper into depression, Michael sought assistance from a business consultant. The business consultant administered the WIDP Profile to the results revealed that Michael was an Introverted Sanguine in leadership. Which means that Michael is a real second person, not the leaders, and he does not handle decisions well. How is he going to function as Director of Purchasing effectively?

With the insight provided by these WIDP results, Mike now realizes his areas of weakness as well as his strengths, and he has developed a strategy for coping with decision making and managing twenty-seven staff members. The group divided into thirteen teams with two members on each side. One member is the buyer, and one is the purchaser. The two of them assist each with decision-making issues. Each has its area of responsibility and are autonomous, thus eliminating the need for management. Only the decisions that they could not make as a team were taken to Michael. The extra person, the twenty-seventh, is a floater and fills in where needed when someone went on vacation or sick leave.

Michael's strategy has been working very well for five years and, years, and Michael is eligible for retirements but feels that he may stick around for a few years until his children graduate from college. Michael is very grateful for the WIDP. Success!

# Sanguine

## Stereotyped Female Attorney

Robin is a female attorney from Connecticut who had been practicing law for several years as the court-appointed attorneys for those that could not afford legal representation. Robin was very depressed with her profession as a lawyer and, with her lifestyle. Robin felt she was not the attorney type and that the occupation was stifling her personal growth. Robin felt obligated to dress and act the part, which made her attire feel out of place and unacceptable in the fashion world in which Robin worked each day. She was depressed and very distraught with her life and vocation and did not know how to change the situations. In desperation, Robin sought assistance from the Human Resource Department in hopes that they might provide some new insight into her condition.

On her first visit to the Human Resource Department, Robin was given the WIDP profile questionnaire to complete, which is standard procedure for everyone who seeks their assistance. Robin's profile results revealed that she is a Sanguine.

One of the greatest fears of the Sanguine is rejection by other people. Robin felt that she should model the appearance of the stereotyped attorney. Thus, she dressed to accommodate that look. Her dress was that of a **"schoolmarm."** Robin was single, 5' 9", well developed, tall, and wore her shoulder-length chocolate brown hair in a twisted bun on top of her head in a five-pronged pitchfork-style hair clip. She wore heavy black-rimmed glasses with the beaded chain attached to the lenses for hanging around her neck when not needed for reading. Robin wore no makeup. She wore a plain black pleated dress buttoned up to the throat, accompanied by black platform shoes. Her well-worn black briefcase carried the battle scars of many years of service. She could have posed with Mona Lisa as her sister. Except Robin's more inconspicuous than Mona in a dress.

Robin's counselor after reviewing her WIDP results exclaimed to her: "Robin, why don't you let your hair down, get yourself some new high fashion glasses, buy yourself a bright, flashy multicolored dress, some high-heeled shoes, and put on some makeup. Then become the friendly, outgoing woman that you are? Then go home, have a celebration, and burn all of the things you presently are wearing."

Robin started crying. Once she gained control of her emotions to the point she could speak, she asked this question: **"You mean I can dress like that?"** Robin was a stifled Sanguine wanting acceptance as an attorney but felt she needed to dress the part. Sanguine are very outgoing people who bring excitement and fun to the world wherever they find themselves. They are the life of the party kind of individuals. Sanguine make life tolerable for the other temperament types that are so serious and focused on accomplishing tasks. Her voluntary standards were unnecessary, unhealthy, and, violated her real personalities because they forced her into being someone other than herself. Guess what happened? Robin only needed one session with the Human Resource Department to transform her life. As it turned out, she did go home and have that celebration. Robin went back that day and burned the clothes she was wearing, purchased some makeup, new glasses, shiny new briefcase and, got a fashionable hair do-over! The results of the WIDP set her free to be the Sanguine she was intrinsically. Success!

# Phlegmatic

## Power versus Status Quo

Director of a nonprofit organization approached a consulting firm for assistance. He was trying to figure out a solution to a volatile situation over a parcel of land. The land had three buildings, was debt-free, and valued at $500,000 that belonged to his nonprofit organization if their personnel occupied the premises. Within three days, five leaders of the group had to hold these buildings to secure the property legally physically. The organization occupying the premises were part of his team, but they had allied with another group that had visions of taking over the property.

The director approached the consulting firm as an aggressive take-charge person who was able to make quick, intuitive decisions and go forward. He did not waver in conflict and was very direct and bold in his communications. However, after profiling the other four members of the leadership group, it was discovered that they were all Phlegmatic. Phlegmatic is very dependable, steady, task-oriented, and middle-of-the-road-type people. They rarely make quick changes to anything or anybody because they are **status quo** people. They do not like change unless it happens slowly over an extended period and everyone agrees to the modification. They have the mindset that **"if it worked for this long, then, why change it now?"** They do not like to take chances or expend any more energy than necessary to accomplish a task. They dislike conflict with a passion, and they will go to any extreme to avoid conflict, even to the point of sacrificing their values and morals. When it comes to making decisions, they want the unanimous vote to prevail. There must be a consensus, or this issue would be postponed indefinitely.

The director and the four leaders had been working together for two years. During this time, the aggressive, goal- and task-oriented director had encountered resistance from the other four members:

The four members did not like rapid change or an aggressive taskmaster approach to anything. They found themselves in a situation where they had to decide with three days to take possession of this parcel of property or lose it to another organization. The director is alerted to the issue by an anonymous phone call, and this is what he does:

Notified of the alert, the director arranges for personnel from his organization to occupy the property immediately. He also organized for a locksmith to put new locks on the buildings the following morning. Putting new locks on alone would have secured the property for his organization, but the major drawback: he had to get approval from the other four members of the board! After notifying them of an emergency meeting scheduled for the next morning, he felt everything was under control. Next morning the four members, all Phlegmatic, did not want to engage in any conflict or even question the integrity of the person who occupied the property. They could not believe that the other organization would also try to take over the property and would not permit the expense of changing locks on the buildings as a safeguard.

What happened? The other organization took control, changed the locks, and walked off with $500,000 worth of property. Why?

The Phlegmatic was right in their stand against the Choleric who wanted to jump in take over, and control the situation. In this situation, the Phlegmatic stood their ground based on what they felt was the right thing to do on this issue. The four Phlegmatic was an element of a larger parent organization, that also was run primarily by Phlegmatic. They were all quite comfortable operating as a **status quo** organization. The Choleric was out of place based on his temperament. He was too aggressive for the Phlegmatic. The Choleric resigned and, the Phlegmatic rejoiced. So, it was a success for the Phlegmatic.

# Melancholy

## A Manager of the Wrong Group

Barbara was a middle director of a more massive corporation on the East Coast. She had been in this assignment for five years when she sought assistance from her Human Resource Department. Barbara was experiencing extreme stress and depression. Human Resources referred her to her psychiatrist for the same therapy she had been under for twelve years. She did not want to return to her psychiatrist, as the past twelve years of therapy had provided little relief. Instead, she sought out Worley's ID Profile Counseling Center.

During her first visit with WIDP, she completed the WIDP Profile questionnaire, and the results revealed that she was a Melancholy Compulsive (on the MBTI she was an ISTJ) who was dealing with chronic depression and extreme anger. She was presently taking 150 mg of Trazodone per day for mental distress. Her medication record began in 1981 and continued until the day she arrived at the WIDP clinic. She had been on medication of Elavil 100 mg, Prozac, Zoloft 250 mg, and Wellbutrin 450 mg over the courses of thirteen years. Her mental condition diagnosed as having suicidal tendencies. According to Barbara, she only had two stable elements in her life: God and her husband.

After consulting with her psychiatrist, Dr. Worley recommends that all medication be eliminated and that her needs as a Melancholy Compulsive temperament type be addressed instead of just medicating what appeared to be a depressed and angry individual. The psychiatrist agreed, and the process of decreasing medication began immediately.

Barbara was unable to function at work, had a breakdown during a staff meeting, and broke out in a fit of rage. We immediately applied for STD (Short Term Disability), and it was granted. A treatment plan was implemented to reduce her medication to none as quickly as possible and see her three times a week.

For a clinical report, the following was established:

**Essential features:** Barbara is experiencing a reactive depression of severe proportions. She displays consistently and notably a depressed mood, and she reports a loss of interest in all vocational and social activities, including those that involve immediate family members. She is very sad, dissatisfied, angry, irritable, self-punishing, and very argumentative. Her emotional behavior is one of usually in tears and a state of despair and hopelessness.

**Associated features:** Additional symptoms include sleep and appetite disturbance, loss of energy, difficulties in concentrating, slowed thinking, periodic loss of memory, and thoughts of suicide or death.

**Social/vocational adjustment:** Barbara has withdrawn from friends and family members and prefers to avoid all interpersonal involvement whenever possible. Her situation was severe enough that she could not function socially or vocationally.

**Complications:** The most severe difficulty of her depression was suicide ideation combined with her melancholic temperaments and her codependency, which is cruel.

**Treatment recommendations:** Therapeutic intervention progressed from six to twelve weeks, will usually improve the client's condition. Self-recognition, behavioral modification, stress reduction, and stress management therapy and, focusing on the results of the WIDP Profile.

During the treatment process, it was revealed that she needed to transfer out of her vocation position. Her management position required her to interface daily with multitudes of people dealing with various issues. Barbara required regular employment; a place did not expect her to interface with people all day long. Transferring Barbara with an internal lateral move within the company worked. Within ninety days Barbara off medications, no longer angry, and in fact, happy with her new position. Therapy was no longer needed, a massive success for Barbara the Melancholy.

# Choleric

# A Leader out of Leadership

Renee was a twenty-six-year-old scientific engineer in a fast-growing company. She had been with the company for three years and was frustrated because she could not exercise her leadership skills in the enterprise. Her frustration caused her such extreme anxiety and such a sharp drop in her work performance that her supervisor strongly recommended therapy. Renee did not know that she had natural leadership abilities based on her temperament; she only knew of the internal anxiety and frustration she was experiencing in her profession, which also affected her marriage.

She scheduled an appointment with WIDP. Renee profiled with the WIDP, which revealed she was a Choleric in leadership and was codependent. At the time of her first therapy session, her primary focus was on the issue of wanting to divorce her husband. They had been married for nine months and had a seven-month-old daughter.

She also had a deep longing to reconnect with her mother. Her mother left her and her father to run off with another man when she was fourteen. Since that time, her mother had lived with fourteen different people and was now living with the fifteenth man in upper state, New York.

She also was interested in another man in the company for whom she worked. She had shared lunch with him a few times, but they were not yet actively engaged in a romantic relationship. Both desired a more intimate relationship.

She was very emotional and crying during her first three therapy sessions, but the tears diminished with each new session. The confusion was present in her thinking, and she was unable to make decisions or come to any conclusions without assistance from someone. She had no close friends that she could communicate with, so she spent most of her time in isolation as a very anxious and longing for her mother and wanting out of the marriage.

In her marriage, she felt that her husband wasn't acknowledging her abilities to participate in any decisions regarding their marriage, and he was intimidated by her success as a scientific engineer. She made more money than he did and had more education. So, he ruled the marriage by dominating her. These issues, combined with a longing for her mother, and the inability to realize her leadership potential in the corporate world, called for a total reorientation in her life. The following approach was taken:

A.   She had been encouraged to begin exercising her abilities as a leader in the marriage, and at work, and this gave Renee a sense of freedom she had never experienced.

B.   She was instructed to consider herself an equal individual, with equal opportunities, regardless of her gender. For Renee, this was a new and unexplored concept for her in her marriage and her profession.

C.   Regarding her marriage, it was recommended, that she first come to a better understanding of herself, based on the WIDP results, and then begin communicating this new understanding of to her husband. She was also encouraged to take a vacation together with her husband. The guidance for Robin reduced her anxiety and frustration level very quickly.

D.   She was advised to contact her mother by phone and then write to her a lengthy, detailed letter explaining how much she needed her mom in her life. Robin approaching her mother had never been considered by Robin before.

As she begins to implement these changes, her life began to change immediately. Within seven weeks, she started to feel free as a leader in her marriage and vocation. Robin and her husband spent a week together in Maine. During that time, she decided she did not want a divorce. Robin wrote her mother a letter. After completion of the letter writing, she felt like a new person just being able to express to her mother the love and longing for her she had in her heart. She even comments: **"Even if she will not visits with me or establish a relationship with me, I feel better, and I am no longer tormented over the issue."** She now is considering the possibility of completing her master's degree in engineering and receives encouragement from both her husband and her supervisor. All of this ended in seven sessions of using the WIDP profile. Success for the Choleric!

# Public School Second Graders
# Do Teachers and Students Always Connect?

An evaluation to determine the applicability and the effectiveness of Worley's ID Profile was conducted in a public school on the East Coast. Those participating in the assessment were as follows:

| | |
|---|---|
| **Students:** | Twenty-two students: twelve males and ten females |
| **Grade:** | Second grade |
| **Age:** | Seven years old |
| **Nationality:** | Mixed |
| **Teachers:** | One female |
| **Teacher Aides:** | Two females |
| **Special Education Teacher:** | One female |
| **Assistant Principals:** | Two (one from another school) |
| **Principals:** | One female |
| **School Counselors:** | Two females (one of them from another school) |
| **Consultant:** | One male |

## The contract completed in the following phases:

| | | |
|---|---|---|
| **Initial Meeting:** | Three (3) hours | Working with principals designing approach. |
| **Teacher Instructions:** | Four (4) hours | Instruction outside of the classroom in the interpretation of WIDP. |
| **Profiles:** | One (1) hour | Twenty-two (22) youth profile administered in the classroom. |
| **Review Profiles:** | Two (2) hours | This included one (1) consultant, one (1) principal, two (2) assistant principals, two (2) counselors, two (2) teachers, two (2) aides. |
| **Classroom Observation:** | Six (6) hours | Two (3 hrs each) observing in the classroom the interaction between teachers and students. |
| **Debriefing:** | Two (2) hours | all staff present. |

## Chapter 636 Information for this school district:

**K-8 Students:**

2000 - Special Education

3000 - Bilingual

4000 - Chapter 1 (Title One)

3000 - Mainstream

## Requirement needed from the school before the implementation of the project.

1.   Parental release form on each child.

(Example)

The children in Mrs. _____ & Mrs. _____ room will be working on a class project that will help children find helpful ways to solve problems and resolve conflicts. The teachers will be working with consultant _____, to learn some new methods about conflict resolution. As part of the plan, each child will be given a questionnaire to see how they presently solve problems, assumes leadership, and makes friends. The consultant and faculty to develop new methods for children and staff to work together to use this information. Please sign the permission slip below and return it to the school as soon as possible. Thank you for your attention to this matter.

### PERMISSION SLIP

I give my child permission to be included in this project.

_____

**Parent Signature    Date**

2.   Classroom seating arrangement diagram with each student identified.
3.   Diagnosis and Prognosis, from the counselor on each student who is presently seeing a counselor.
4.   Name of medication and dosage prescribed for each student.
5.   Identify any student who is or has been diagnosed with attention deficit disorder (ADD) or, attention deficit hyperactivity disorder (ADHD).
6.   Any other pertinent information relative to unusual classroom behavior, and known physical, mental, or sexual abuse.
7.   Approved and signed a contract with purchase order number.

### Findings during Testing:

The teachers and aides were worried as to whether the children could understand and follow the questions on the questionnaire and provide proper responses from the six different answers available to choose. The teachers developed three sets of **picture cards** and three **response clocks** as visual aids for the children to refer to when needed. The picture cards and clocks were placed strategically around the classroom.

The teachers also felt that it would be essential to allow the children more time to respond to the questions by providing breaks every ten questions. Time breaks would require an additional fifty minutes for testing as there are sixty questions on the questionnaire.

The teachers were amazed that the students did not refer to the **picture cards** or the **response clocks.** Neither did the children need breaks after every ten questions. They were provided one ten-minute break after completing half of the questions.

The children enjoyed the challenge of the project and participated without any complications. One of the male children became very anxious during the last fifteen minutes. This child was diagnosed with Attention deficit hyper disorder (ADHD).

During the debriefing session, the teachers and staff acknowledged that they were quite impressed with the reliability and predictability of the WIDP results. They were immediately able to identify how the effects could be very advantageous in many different applications with the children and with other peers and school staff.

One teacher realized when asked if she had trouble interacting with one child, related that she had a deep emotional dislike for this child. The WIDP results identified this inner conflict between, the teacher and this child. The teacher began crying and said she felt like a failure as a teacher because she did not like this child. The issues were corrected immediately by assigning the child to the other teachers in the same classroom who felt very comfortable with this child, and the problem was resolved.

Also detected was that individual students were more compatible with other students and would become more academically productive by just rearranging the classroom location of the students. The accommodation of the students were implemented, and the student behavior calmed down immediately.

The most important revelation was that the core participants realized how much more efficient they could relate to the students. Having a new understanding of the student's desires and needs, based on their individuality, gave them a deeper insight into the value of WIDP. Other applications of the WIDP that were identified by this group of teachers and staff as being needed in the academic institutions were:

1.  Leadership training
2.  Staff-to-staff relationships
3.  Staff-teacher relationships
4.  Teacher-to-teacher relationships
5.  Staff and teachers on how to relate to grandparents, and stepparents.
6.  The suggestion that all school counselors and educators receive training on the WIDP.
7.  Staff and teacher hiring process. Require completing the WIDP as a necessary part of the interviews, and evaluation process.
8.  All students tested upon entering the school system in the course of their enrollment processes. Then retest them every two or three years.
9.  WIDP Profile would be a tremendous asset for all high school students.
10. A class is instructing students on the value and application of their WIDP results.
11. Excellent for teaching conflict resolution, team building, determining a leader(s), project management.

The two public schools that participated in this project are delighted with the results. They are now in the process of applying for educational grants for further developing other programs within their schools.

# CHAPTER 16

# WORLEY'S ID PROFILE

## VS.

# TAYLOR-JOHNSON TEMPERAMENT ANALYSIS

## WIDP VS. T-JTA

The comparison of the WIDP to the T-JTA Regular Edition is so different that it becomes quite easy to understand their differences. The T-JTA is a diagnostic, counseling, and research instrument. T-JTA is primarily a marriage counselor's tool, used in identifying patterns of personality traits that represent the personal feelings and emotions at the moment. The T-JTA evaluation, however useful at that moment, is very temporary and subject to change within days, hours, or even minutes.

It serves as a convenient method of measuring essential personality traits, which influence personal, interpersonal, academic, and vocational functioning and adjustment. It is especially appropriate for premarital, marital, and family counseling purposes. The questions are constructed so the assessment cannot only be taken on yourself, but also by one person on another person in T-JTA **crisscross** fashion. Age range is thirteen to sixty-four, and there are 180 numbers of items to respond.

There is a T-JTA Secondary Edition that should be used only for self-testing with junior and senior high school students or adults who have attained a minimum fifth grade reading level, but less than eight grade level. Adult reading deficiency norms (ARD) developed for use with Secondary Edition, Form S Question Booklet. The age range is seven to twelve, and there are 180 numbers of items to respond.

For the T-JTA Regular Edition, the focus is on the **feelings** of individuals. This emphasis, as stated in the T-JTA training materials, is

**designed primarily to provide an evaluation in a visual form showing a person's feeling about himself/herself _at the time when he/she answered the questions._**

The word **trait** indicates a constellation of behavioral patterns and tendencies sufficiently cohesive to be used and measured as a unit. There are nine sets of traits in the T-JTA as follows:

## T-JTA TEMPERAMENT TYPE TRAITS

Trait A  Nervous vs. Composed
Trait B  Depressive vs. Lighthearted
Trait C  Active-Social vs. Quiet
Trait D  Expressive-Responsive vs. Inhibited
Trait E  Sympathetic vs. Indifferent
Trait F  Subjective vs. Objective
Trait G  Dominant vs. Submissive
Trait H  Hostile vs. Tolerant
Trait I  Self-Disciplined vs. Impulsive

This focus immediately differentiates the T-JTA from WIDP. The WIDP and the T-JTA are so different in their application of behavioral and temperament understanding that it's not even remotely close to try and compare them. For one, T-JTA is focused on **feelings of the moment,** and temporal, while WIDP is based on one's core temperament and is permanent.

### Worley's ID Profile Data

WIDP measures and determines individual intrinsic needs and desires relative to his/her base temperaments and gives you a detailed summary of people's social, leadership, and relationship.

I.   **Social Profile**          General social/work orientation
II.  **Leadership Profile**      Independence/leadership needs
III. **Relationship Profile**    Emotional involvement in close relationships

The report generated for each of the three areas based on two scores, the demonstrated score, and the desired score.

**The Demonstrated Score** indicates how the individual prefers to act toward other people. This behavior, the image presented to others, generally can be observed. The demonstrated score level in each area of action the individual feels most comfortable in using to

**Get together with others**    **Demonstrated social**
**Have their way with others**  **Demonstrated leadership**
**Be close to others**          **Demonstrated relationship**

**The Desired Score** indicates the preferred behavior from others towards them. This indicator of the individual's inner needs and desires may differ significantly from their public image. The desired behavior in each area is the action the person prefers others to use in their approach to

**Get together with them**      **Desired social**
**Have their way with him/her** **Desired leadership**
**Be close to them**            **Desired relationship**

In general, the **greater the distance** between the individual's demonstrated score and desired score, the **higher the probability** that the person is experiencing conflict in the measured/examined area.

## Additional data on the T-JTA

The T-JTA is a widely used diagnostic, counseling, and research instrument. It serves as a convenient method of measuring some essential personality traits which influence personal, interpersonal, academic, and vocational functioning and adjustment. It is especially appropriate for premarital, marital, and family counseling purposes, as the questions are constructed so the test cannot only be taken on self, but also by one person on another in T-JTA **crisscross** fashion.

The T-JTA **crisscross** fashion uses five profile combinations of two individuals. The five patterns would be:

1. Husband
2. Wife
3. Couple
4. Husband of wife
5. Wife of husband

The five profile patterns a complete T-JTA marital crisscross testing. The two top profiles depict the **husband** as he sees himself, and the **wife** as she sees herself. The center **couple** profile combines the two self-tests, to show the interrelationship between the two personalities. The two bottom profiles, **husband of wife** and **wife of husband**, again depict the two self-tests, but also portray the results of the tests that each spouse completed on the other. This set of profiles provide the counselor with vital information as to how each person see themselves, as well as how each person perceives the other. Similarities, differences, or areas of misunderstanding become clear. The T-JTA can also be administered in crisscross fashion between various family members.

The purpose of the T-JTA, to serve as a quick and convenient method of measuring some essential, and comparatively independent personality variables and tendencies. The test is designed primarily to provide an evaluation, in a visual form, showing a person's feeling about himself/herself at the time when he/she answered the questions. The T-JTA also makes possible the early identification of emotionally troubled individuals.

While the test was not designed to measure severe abnormalities or disturbances; it does provide indications of extreme patterns which require immediate improvement. There are four shaded zones on the T-JTA and clinical values for the zones are excellent, acceptable, improvement desirable, improvement needed. The profile is designed to indicate the standard range of individual differences and is in no way intended to be diagnostic in the case of psychotic states.

## Overview of the T-JTA Temperament Analysis Traits

The test is designed primarily to provide an evaluation in a visual form showing a person's feelings about himself/herself at the time when he/she answered the questions. It is also an indicator of a person's general patterns of reacting in his/her daily life.

The word **trait** indicates a constellation of behavioral patterns and tendencies sufficiently cohesive to be used and measured as a unit. There are nine sets of traits in the T-JTA as follows:

**Trait A**    **Nervous vs. Composed**

    **Nervous:**    A state or condition frequently characterized by a tense, high-strung, or apprehensive attitudes.

    **Composed:**  Characterized by a calm, relaxed, and tranquil outlook on life.

    Questions in this category are designed to measure nervousness, whether induced by internal or external stimuli, and whether it is experienced internally or manifested in external signs and symptoms. The items used include such indications of nervousness as the inability to concentrate, the presence of unnecessary worry or anxiety, excessive concern about health or physical well-being.

    Some of the more obvious external manifestations of nervous tension are excessive excitability, the natural loss of composure, excessive smoking, eating, drinking, indigestion or loss of appetite, the regular use of relaxant medications, and such nervous mannerisms as nail-biting, foot tapping, and restlessness.

    Composure, measured by a sense of calmness or serenity, freedom from excessive worry, and anxiety.

    **Nervous** appears to be more variable in its manifestation than most other traits. It is mostly a measure of anxiety, especially when combined with high scores in **depressive, subjective,** and **hostile,** and a low score in **self-discipline.**

    A high nervous score may be temporary when it results from immediate, acute stress.

**Trait B**    **Depressive vs. Lighthearted**

    **Depressive:**    Pessimistic, discouraged, or dejected.

    **Lighthearted:**   A happy, cheerful, and optimistic attitude or disposition.

    The items which directly measure depressive states or reactions include feelings of apathy, despair, disillusionment, or pessimism; depressive preoccupation with problems, or misfortunes; emotional exhaustion and the contemplation of suicide.

    The items which provide indirect indications of depression include feelings of being unwanted, of not belonging, of fearfulness, of being unimportant or unappreciated,

as well as a tendency to be easily disheartened by criticisms and discouraged because of a lack of self-confidence or a sense of inferiority.

    **Lightheartedness** is a sense of well-being and optimism.

    **Depressive** is found to correlate positively with **nervous**; improvement in either trait appears to improve the other.

    High nervous and high **depressive** scores are usually evident in persons seeking psychological assistance. While the cause of this pattern is frequently found to be subjective, medical examinations and cooperation may be advisable.

    When the **depressive** score is extraordinarily high and **self-disciplined** low, caution is indicated.

**Trait C**      **Active-Social vs. Quiet**

**Active-Social:**   Energetic, enthusiastic, and socially involved.
**Quiet:**          Socially inactive, lethargic, and withdrawn attitudes.
**Active-social** is a feeling of energy and vitality, the briskness of movement, keeping on the go, and being considered a go-getter, finding enjoyment in activity and excitement, being a tireless and industrious worker, enjoying a wide variety of activities and interests, and keeping in condition with regular exercise.

**Quietness** is a preference for a stable, restful, quiet life, for being alone rather than with people, and for little participation in social events or activities.

A high score in **active-social** usually indicates a liking for people and a need for companionship and group participation. High scores are considered admirable unless they are combined with a high **hostile,** high **nervous,** and a low **self-disciplined.**

A low, **quiet** score suggests a withdraw tendency.

**Trait D**      **Expressive-Responsive vs Inhibited**

**Expressive-Responsive:**   Spontaneous, affectionate, demonstrative.
**Inhibited:**              Portrayed by restrained, unresponsive, or repressed behavior.
**Expressive-responsive** is the ability to be friendly and responsive in contact with people, to be talkative and to express oneself with animation, enthusiasm, and gestures, to have many friends, and to be thought of by others as being an expressively warmhearted and outgoing person.

The items which measure more personal forms of expressiveness include, the ability to show affection without embarrassment, be warmly demonstrative with members of one's family, be able to express tenderness, sympathy, or pleasure, and be willing to share one's joys or sorrow with another person.

**Inhibited** is the inability to express tender feelings, and by a tendency to be reserved, restrained, repressed, and self-conscious.

The trait **Expressive-Responsive** is a measure of freedom to express the natural sense of warmth and affection and to respond to such feelings in others. It involves the desire to be liked.

**Trait E**      **Sympathetic vs. Indifferent**

**Sympathetic:** Empathetic, kind, compassionate, sensitive to the needs and feelings of others. Showing concern for the welfare of those who are less fortunate, aware of another's need for encouragement, kindness, or understanding, and fear for children, animals, and the elderly.
**Indifferent**: Is a lack of sympathetic interest in other people, a tendency to be strict, thoughtlessly inconsiderate, and slow to recognize the needs of family and friends.

Since sympathy involves compassion and concern for others; it is especially influential in creating healthy courtship, marriage, and parental relationships.

**Trait F**   **Subjective vs. Objective**

**Subjective:**   Emotional, illogical, self-absorbed.
**Objective:**   Fair-minded, reasonable, and logical in attitude.

The items include those indications of conflict or emotionality which tend to interfere with the ability to think objectively and impartially. Specific topics include tendencies to be overly sensitive, introspective, jealous, suspicious, or self-conscious, as well as the tendency to daydream, hold grudges, be easily embarrassed, or to misinterpret the motives of others.

**Subjectivity** when extremely high may indicate severe emotional disturbance. It seems to suggest that inner feelings tend to create bias and distortion of the ability to be logical in the appraisals of reality and life situations.

**The objectives are** the capacity to be analytical, impartial, dispassionate, not preoccupied with introspections or plagued by internal doubts and fears.

**Trait G**   **Dominant vs. Submissive**

**Dominant:**   Confident, assertive, and competitive. Indicated ego-strength, such as being influential with others or desiring to influence or change their thinking.
**Submissive:**   The tendency to follow, to rely too much on people, to give way to their wishes, to avoid complaining, to seek peace at any cost, and to be easily persuaded or taken advantage of by other people.

When interpreting the profiles of a married couple, an analysis of the interrelationship between the self-evaluation scores in **dominant** may be of more importance in counseling than the location of the ratings.

**Trait H**   **Hostile vs. Tolerant**

**Hostile:**   Critical, argumentative, and punitive.
**Tolerant:**   Accepting, patient, and humane in attitude.

The **hostile** tendency is to be superior, overbearing, impatient, sarcastic, argumentative, and unreasonable. As well, it shows contemptuous of weakness in others, quick to show temper, to tell others off, and to evidence a hostile reaction to people in general.

**Hostility** which is directed inward, against the self, is not exclusively measured by this one trait score but may be reflected in an inferior score in any one or more of the other categories.

**Trait I**   **Self-Disciplined vs. Impulsive**

**Self-disciplined:**   Controlled, methodical, persevering.
**Impulsive:**   Uncontrolled, disorganized, changeable.

Neatness, orderliness, and the ability to organize and plan. Have endurance and perseverance, the inclination to set goals, make plans well in advance, to be methodical and deliberate, to keep things in place, to budget, to think before acting, to avoid frequent shifts of interest and goals, and to have good self-control is self-disciplined.

The **impulsive** tendency is hastiness in making decisions, vacillation, reduced the ability to plan, a trend towards taking chances and easily tempted, to get into trouble because of hasty acts, as well as the inability to break bad habits.

A low level of self-discipline, (**impulsive**) indicates poor control and, in some cases, a tendency to act out. Such individuals tend to sway, seldom follow through on projects, even those of their choosing, and are prone to change jobs frequently.

**Impulsive** individuals find it difficult to persevere in counseling or therapy.

From the material presented, it is evident to see that the T-JTA and WIDP cannot be respectably compared due to the nature and natural makeup of each. However, it is clear that the more reliable and dependable of the two for measuring fundamental needs and desires that are foundational to the individual is WIDP.

# CHAPTER 17

# Myers-Briggs Type Indicator
# MBTI

The personality system presented here is known formally as **Jung's theory of personality type** (hereafter referred to as **personality type/types/typing**), first developed by Carl Jung in the early 1920s and more recently resurrected and re-designed into a useful instrument by Myers and Briggs. Sometimes, this system referred to as the **Myers-Briggs Type Indicator** (or MBTI), but in a rigorous sense, the MBTI is a test vehicle for personality typing.

Personality typing is not used nor studied in the psychiatric and research/academic, psychological community because it is, first, rejected by some schools of thought on fundamental philosophical grounds (e.g., cognitive psychology). Also, many counseling psychologists do not find it useful for their purposes for because it does not measure mental health. However, this does not mean that practicing doctors eschew personality typing. Many counselors do use this system for their patients/clients, particularly for helping people to **"find themselves"** and similar, nonmental health-related purposes.

Outside of the psychological community, however, personality typing (typified by the MBTI) is the most widely used model of human personality. It is used extensively in career counseling and development, business and education. Its penetration into these areas stems partly from the fact that does not touch upon the aspects of mental health, which are dealt with by trained counseling psychologists and psychiatrists.

In a nutshell, personality typing mostly assumes that our whole nature can be divided into four independent areas or scales: energizing, attending, deciding, and living (defined in detail below). Within each scale, we have a preference for one of two opposites that determine the range (also described below). A total of sixteen different combinations (2 x 2 x 2 x 2), each of which represents one particular and unique personality type.

This summary will cover the following subjects:

1. Description of the four scales
2. Preferred vocabulary for each of the four scales
3. A summary of the sixteen personality types
4. Correlation of personality typing to the four temperaments

The **four temperaments** comprise very well-known and often used models that divide human personalities into four major groups or temperaments. Hippocrates developed the first system in ancient Greece (where the four temperaments are better known as the four senses of humor). Recently, there have been more modern and refined **four-temperament** models, such as Keirsey and Bates, who found that the sixteen personality types can be summarized into four temperaments which parallel (if only approximately) the four Hippocratic senses of humor of Sanguine, Melancholic, Choleric, and Phlegmatic.

5.  Resource materials on personality typing
6.  Summary profiles for each personality type

## DESCRIPTION OF THE FOUR SCALES

In each of the following four scales, every person usually has a preference for one of the two different choices (designated by a letter). This does not mean that they do one to the exclusion of the other: most people go both ways depending on the circumstances. However, most people usually do have an overall preference. Where a person does not perceive of a clear and resounding choice, the letter X is used to designate this **"I don't know"** condition.

**Important note:** **The following scale descriptions are simplifications (and perilously close to oversimplifications) of quite complex, rigorous, deep and hard-to-understand reports presented by Jung (see recommended literature section for references).**

1.  **Energizing**    **How a person is energized:**

     **Extroversion**    **(E)**    Preference for drawing energy from the outside world of individuals, activities, or things.

     **Introversion**    **(I)**    Preference for drawing energy from one's internal world of ideas, emotions, or impressions.

         Note: In a deeper sense, energizing is only one facet of this scale; it is a measure of a person's whole orientation towards either the inner world (I) or the outer worlds (E).

2.  **Attending**    **What a person pays attention to:**

     **Sensing**    **(S)**    Preference for taking in information through the five senses and noticing what is actual.

     **Intuition**    **(N)**    Preference for taking in information through a **"sixth sense"** and seeing what might be. Jung calls this **"unconscious perceiving."**

3.  **Deciding**    **How a person decides:**

     **Thinking**    **(T)**    Preference for organizing and structuring information to decide in a logical, objective way.

     **Feeling**    **(F)**    Preference for organizing and structuring information to decide in a personal, value-oriented way.

**4.** **Living Lifestyle a person adopts:**

| | | |
|---|---|---|
| **Judgment** | **(J)** | Preference for living a planned and organized life. |
| **Perception** | **(P)** | Preference for living a natural and flexible life. |
| | | Note: An alternative definition of this scale is **"Closure whether or not a person likes an open-ended lifestyle."** |

## PREFERRED VOCABULARY FOR EACH OF THE FOUR SCALES

There seems to be a specific vocabulary associated with each preference for the four scales. By reading the word list on the left and the right for each scale and determining which list you like the sounds and meanings of the phrase better may indicate your preference for that scale. This vocabulary list will also help you to understand better what the four scales measure or denote.

Also included with each scale is the percentages of the total population (in Western culture) who hold that preference; studies have shown the four scales to be substantially independent of one another.

## EXTROVERSION INTROVERSION PREFERRED VOCABULARY

| **Extroversion (E) 75% of Population** | **Introversion (I) 25% of Population** |
|---|---|
| sociability | territorial |
| breadth | depth |
| external | internal |
| extensive | intensive |
| interaction | concentration |
| expenditure of energy | conservation of energy |
| interest in external events | interest in internal reaction |
| multiplicity of relationships | limited relationships |

## SENSING INTUITION PREFERRED VOCABULARY

| **Sensing (S) 75% of Population** | **Intuition (N) 25% of Population** |
|---|---|
| experience | hunches |
| past | future |
| realistic | speculative |
| perspiration | inspiration |
| actual | possible |
| down to earth | head in clouds |
| utility | fantasy |
| fact | fiction |
| practicality | ingenuity |
| sensible | imaginative |

# THINKING FEELING PREFERRED VOCABULARY

| Thinking (T) 50% of Population | Feeling (F) 50% of Population |
|---|---|
| objective | subjective |
| principles | values |
| policy | social values |
| laws | extenuating circumstances |
| criterion | intimacy |
| firmness | persuasion |
| impersonal | personal |
| justice | humane |
| categories | harmony |
| standards | good or bad |
| critique | appreciates |
| analysis | sympathy |
| allocation | devotion |

# JUDGEMENT PERCEPTION PREFERRED VOCABULARY

| Judgment, J (50% of Population) | Perception, P (50% of Population) |
|---|---|
| settled | pending |
| decided | to gather more data |
| fixed | flexible |
| plan | adapt as you go |
| run one's life | let life happen |
| closure | open options |
| decision making | treasure hunting |
| planned | open ended |
| completed | emergent |
| decisive | tentative |
| wrap it up | something will turn up |
| urgency | there's plenty of time |
| deadline! | what deadline? |
| get the show on the road | let's wait and see... |

## A SHORT SUMMARY OF THE SIXTEEN PERSONALITY TYPES

The two preferences for each of the four scales give sixteen different combinations (2 x 2 x 2 x 2). If one includes the X preference (which means either the person has no clear-cut choice, or that they do not know it yet), there can be as many as eighty-one different combinations. However, each X choice is usually handled by blending and carefully studying the two associated preferences. The order of designating the letters is:

## Energizing, Attending, Deciding, and Living

Here's a summary of the overall personality for each of the sixteen types as determined from various studies:

**ENFJ:**      **"Pedagogue"** Outstanding leader of groups. Can be aggressive at helping others to be the best that they can be. Five percent (5%) of the total population.

**INFJ:**      **"Author"** Strong drive and enjoyment to help others. Complex personality. One percent (1%) of the total population.

**ENFP:**      **"Journalist"** Uncanny sense of the motivations of others. Life is an exciting drama. Five percent (5%) of the total population.

**INFP:**      **"Questor"** High capacity for caring. Calm and pleasant face to the world. High sense of honor derived from internal values. One (1%) of the total population.

**ENTJ:**      **"Field Marshall"** The basic driving force and need is to lead. Tends to seek a position of responsibility and enjoys being an executive. Five percent (5%) of the total population.

**INTJ:**      **"Scientist"** Most self-confident and pragmatic of all the types. Decisions come very easily. A builder of systems and the applier of theoretical models. One percent (1%) of the total population.

**ENTP:**      **"Inventor"** Enthusiastic interest in everything and always sensitive to possibilities. Nonconformist and innovative. Five percent (5%) of the total population.

**INTP:**      **"Architect"** Greatest precision in thought and language. Can readily discern contradictions and inconsistencies. The world exists primarily to be understood. One percent (1%) of the total population.

**ESTJ:**      **"Administrator"** Much in touch with the external environment. Very responsible. Pillar of strength. Thirteen percent (13%) of the total population.

**ISTJ:**      **"Trustee"** Decisiveness in practical affairs. Guardian of time-honored institutions. Dependable. Six percent (6%) of the total population.

**ESFJ:**      **"Seller"** Most sociable of all types. Nurturer of harmony. Outstanding host or hostesses. Thirteen percent (13%) of the total population.

**ISFJ:**      **"Conservator"** Desires to be of service and to minister to individual needs and is very loyal. Six percent (6%) of the total population.

**ESTP:**      **"Promotor"** Action! When present, things begin to happen. Fiercely competitive. Entrepreneur. Often uses shock effect to get attention. Negotiator par excellence. Thirteen percent (13%) of the total population.

**ESFP:**      **"Entertainer"** Radiates attractive warmth and optimism. Smooth, witty, charming, clever. Fun to be with. Very generous. Thirteen percent (13%) of the total population.

| ISTP: | "Artisan" Impulsive action. Life should be of impulse rather than of purpose. The action is an end in itself. Fearless, craves excitement, master of tools. Five percent (5%) of the total population. |
|---|---|
| ISFP: | "Artist" Interested in the fine arts. Expression primarily through action or art form. The senses are keener than in other types. Five percent (5%) of the total population. |

## CORRELATION OF PERSONALITY TYPING TO THE FOUR TEMPERAMENTS

There are other systems developed to model human personality. The most well-known and often used ones are those that divide human personality into four major groups or temperaments. Hippocrates in ancient Greece described the first four-temperament system, also known as the **Four Humours:** Sanguine, Melancholic, Choleric, and Phlegmatic. More recently, Keirsey and Bates took the sixteen personality types and categorized them into four recognizable temperaments based on certain combinations of three of the four scales: SJ, SP, NT, and NF. Also, they named each temperament after a Greek god. Mythological legends best exemplify the personality attributes of that temperament: Epimetheus (SJ: **"Hindsight"**), Dionysius (SP: **"Let's Drink Wine"**), Prometheus (NT: **"Foresight"**), and Apollo (NF: **"Reach for the Sky"**).

There are some correlation and overlap between the Hippocratic Humour and the Keirsey-Bates temperaments, but the fit is nowhere near perfect. To complicate matters, the understood definitions of the Hippocratic humour have themselves changed over time; there is no generally agreed-upon definition. Thus, I will focus on the Keirsey-Bates system and try best as I can to correlate it to a modern description of the four Hippocratic Senses of humour (as defined in the book **Personality Plus** by Florence Littauer).

The Keirsey-Bates system is summarized as follows:

> **(Note: The lists of focus/needs/beliefs/behaviors for each temperament are aggregated listing; this means that any one person of that temperament will exhibit or have only some of these attributes. The other two scales play a role in this.)**

**SJ:   DUTY/COMMERCE/ECONOMIC (Epimetheus)**
**Key Focus/Emotional Need: Responsibility, Tradition, and To Maintain Order**
**Beliefs/Behaviors**

1.   Conserves heritage and tradition or establishes new ones.
2.   Can be very analytic (especially T types).
3.   Belief in the hierarchy: subordination and superordination.
4.   Rules: compelled to be bound and obligated.
5.   My duty is to serve, give, care, save, share.
6.   "Shoulds" and "oughts"; "be prepared".
7.   Fosters and creates social units: clubs, church groups.
8.   Management style: traditionalist, stabilizer, consolidator.
9.   Most likely Hippocratic Humour (modern usage): Melancholic.
10.   Spiritual Style: St. Ignatius.

**SP:  JOY/ARTISTRY/AESTHETIC (Dionysus)**
**Key Focus/Emotional Need: Freedom, Independence, Spontaneity, and To Have Fun**
**Beliefs/Behaviors**

1.   Impulsive.
2.   Can be very expressive (esp. if an E).
3.   To do what I want, when I want.
4.   Action to fulfill my current needs, impulses, not an investment for long-term need.
5.   Works dramatically and quickly in a crisis.
6.   Hungers for action without constraints.
7.   Tremendous stamina.
8.   Management style: troubleshooter, negotiator, fire fighter.
9.   Most likely Hippocratic Humour (modern usage): Sanguine.
10.  Spiritual Style: St. Francis of Assisi.

**NT:  SCIENCE/THEORETICAL (Prometheus)**
**Key Focus/Emotional Need: Competence, Knowledge, and To Lead and Control**
**Beliefs/Behaviors**

1.   Tries to understand the "whys" of the universe (especially if a P).
2.   Very demanding of selves and others.
3.   Goal setter.
4.   A driver (especially if a J).
5.   "Should have known" and "Should have done better."
6.   Coolly objective; straightforward and logical in dealing with others.
7.   Reluctance to state obvious; little redundancy in communications.
8.   Work is for improvement, perfection, and proof of skills.
9.   Love of knowledge.
10.  Management style: visionary, architect of systems, builder.
11.  Most likely Hippocratic Humour (modern usage): Choleric (esp. if a J).
12.  Spiritual Style: St. Thomas Aquinas.

**NF:  SPIRIT/ETHICS (Apollo)**
**Key Focus/Emotional Need: Search for Self, and Peace and Harmony**
**Beliefs/Behaviors**

1.   "How do I become the person I am?"
2.   Value relationships.
3.   Harmony with others can be very amiable.
4.   The desire to inspire and persuade.
5.   Need to live a life of significance.
6.   Search for unique identity.

7.   Tend to focus on the good in others.
8.   Especially abhors "evil" if it violates cherished values.
9.   Management style: catalyst, spokesperson, energizer.
10.  Most likely Hippocratic Humour (modern usage): Phlegmatic.
11.  Spiritual Style: St. Augustine.

# CHAPTER 18

# TEMPERAMENT VS. PERSONALITY

The development of a person's temperament, character, and personality based on the following three steps:

Step One: Genetic **temperament** makeup is determining while you are in your mother's wombs: that is, **inborn or genetic**.

Step Two: Then comes the formation of the individual's **character**, which they have shaped and designed, affected by your family of origin, and the influence of people, learned behavior and your environment.

Step Three: Finally comes the formation of the individual's **PERSONALITY**, which is self-selected, and a mask, you only reveal what you prefer others to see, the standard presentation people present to those around them.

Personality is the focus of the DiSC Profile. The DiSC only reveals what the real side (observable) of the person's personality, that is not the real person. Personality is a chosen mask presented to you based on what the person wishes to reveal to you about them.

Temperament, the persons' intrinsic, subjective inner self is Worley's ID Profile focus. Temperament is not alterable or fluid-like personality. A person's temperament is static despite their environmental focus. Therefore, an individual who understands their temperament can understand themselves and others. Each is extraordinary and unique based upon their genetic/ inborn makeup. God uniquely designs people.

**An Overview of Personality:**

**PERSONALITY**

**PERSONALITY:** They design personality training to identify individual styles of personality in, a setting or environmental focus, which means that your personality **changes** depending upon your environments.

They develop the personal profile system (DiSC) to increase understanding, acceptance, and respect for individual differences in the work or social environment. Their system based on the DiSC model of behavior as developed by William Moulton Marston and John Geier. This model identifies four distinct types of personality people use to meet their needs and desires. All people could use all four of these tendencies. However, individuals use some behaviors more than others.

We briefly define the four behavioral tendencies as:

**D    DOMINANCE:** People with a high **D** behavioral tendency seek to meet their needs by controlling their environment through direct, forceful action, often overcoming opposition in hostile or antagonistic situations.

**i    INFLUENCING:** People with a high **I** behavioral tendencies seek to meet their needs by persuading others to work with them to accomplish results. They function effectively in favorable, supportive environments.

**S    STEADINESS:** People with a high **S** behavioral tendency seek to meet their needs by cooperating with others to carry out their respective tasks. They function effectively in favorable, supportive environments.

**C    CAUTIOUSNESS:** People with a high **C** behavioral tendency seek to meet their needs by working with existing circumstances to provide quality and accuracy. They strive to achieve their standards for results, even in hostile environments.

Personality Training focuses on the real side of the person based on an environmental focus during evaluation. Persons answering the behavioral profile will respond one way

- as an employee
- as a spouse
- at the family picnic
- in a conflict situation
- In an intimate relationship

The DiSC assessment process will give you five different personality profiles for the same person. Nevertheless, each requires the individual to fill out another separate questionnaire to evaluate each of the environmental focuses that can be many. In the examples above, the individual can be different in the five areas of employee, spouse, family picnic, conflict, or intimate relationship.

The DiSC is the **masked** approach, which always creates a situation where people only see what the other person wants them to see. The DiSC is the self-selected self the individual wants you to see, and, they do not understand the real temperament of the individual.

# CHAPTER 19

# The Contrast between WIDP Profile and Tim LaHaye's Temperament Assessment

The probable strengths in the *WIDP Profile by Dr. Worley* (the "Profile") are that it can be used in the business place to help assess the people that you employ. This tool assisted me in dealing with my boss and other business associates. You can take this assessment and use it for the hiring of new employees; all companies need help in this area. Using WIDP enables you to hire positive people, people who will make a difference and take you to new heights and make your business shine.

After attending the seminar, the information I acquired helped me resolve quite a few conflicts, which made my business environment a better place for everyone to work. We all have different temperaments. Therefore, I took the tools that Dr. Worley gave us and put them to use. Everyone now thinks that I am a temperament genius, but I know that I had much help.

The WIDP profile also has a test in the handbook for building low self-esteem. With this, I was able to help others come out of a small place, with the aid of the Holy Spirit of course. He is the real teacher. He tells me what to say, and when to say it, in love.

Anyone can take this test, which is excellent because then, no one can make excuses that it is too hard, or that they comprehend it. It is simple, and it does not take long at all to apply. It brought much light to my temperament type. It caused me to pick up on little things that go right in line with my temperament descriptions. I discovered that I must get the timber out of my eye before I can get it out of someone else's eyes. I now can respect people more and can understand their weak areas as well as my own. However, we should not use this information to make people uncomfortable.

The Profile is designed to benefit us and to help us overcome weak areas that we have. We need to work on these areas together so that we can be more of a blessing to our families. The overflow will be a benefit to the casual relationships that we have and will also be a blessing to us. It will make you a better person. We all need someone to talk with and share ideas that we have. The WIDP Profile was very confident in this area and enlightened me a great deal. As I stated before, it is an essential reference tool. When you obtain useful information like this, it should be shared with others who want to learn.

*Transforming your Temperament by Tim LaHaye* (the book) is somewhat of a contrast to the WIDP Profile. The test in the book was good, but my conclusion is that it did not go into as much depth as the WIDP Profile did. The book does enable you to examine yourself, as the WIDP Profile does, but it does not allow you to get down to the core of a person.

The test in the book shows you how to evaluate yourself. You must, however, give the test to two people who know you so that they can assess you. You must also evaluate yourself. Once the evaluations have been completed, you can mail them to Mr. LaHaye, and he will send you your profile description. His profile descriptions are like the WIDP Profile, but there are some significant differences. Mr. LaHaye's temperament descriptions imply that the four temperament descriptions that exist may overlap. He feels that a person can have more than one temperament type, they can overlap, and there could even be multiples.

For example, you could have the traits of a Melancholy Choleric who are Sanguine Choleric or are Phlegmatic Melancholy.

Mr. LaHaye's chart is broken down in certain parts where I couldn't understand them, so it would be tough for me to explain these to anyone, and you could not market this in the business arena. Also, another setback is that part of the test you must hand out to your friends to let them examine you. This part I do not agree with that your friends will not grade you from a truthful standpoint, but friends could classify you because they are your friends, and not be accurate so this can harm you from this perspective. You can use this test, but it would not be an excellent hiring tool either, because you have too many people playing a significant role in your results. Therefore, I would not recommend this test as stated in the book to anyone. The foundation is very vague, and it does not minister to me at all.

For instance, when you are taking any test, it should be able to see what you know, not to confuse you. Mr. LaHaye's Profile does not get to the point as the WIDP Profile does. Mr. LaHaye's temperament charts are not broken down and simple to understand. His profile was hard to retain and some parts of the book I did not understand. Time's a significant factor in everything that we do, and I believe that his tests should be shorter. It also doesn't have an excellent example of how long or short his exam is. There were other areas in the book that are very good, but this area needed significant work. Anyone who reads the book would feel that there should be a better way of getting the results of their temperament type.

Before the creation of WIDP Profile, there was nothing out there that was respectable enough for me to critique as far as being good or bad in identifying the real person's fundamental needs and desires. They all focus on personality, behavior, or character. The WIDP Profile assessment is the best resource I have seen so far, focusing on your temperament.

I do feel that getting carried away with the results of WIDP Profile could be self-destructive. I could give anyone a temperament test to see what their numbers are and just totally let that control the way I think about everything. That is how powerful this profile is. We do have to be careful who we let see the test results. Someone who has low self-esteem could be taken to an all-time low after taking this test. We need to remember who we are in Jesus Christ. I believe the WIDP Profile will revolutionize the way the whole world thinks because the Profile will make a believer out of you. The information is so fulfilling that it just helps you to change instantly. It will even work on those of us who like to pretend that things are all right all the time and are just outstanding actors. The Profile can penetrate the surface of and make you take a good and hard look at yourself.

One good example that Mr. LaHaye gave was that some people use this as an excuse to act a certain way. He broke down the temperament types and provided examples that we sometimes will do anything to play with Jesus Christ. Sometimes I believe we do not think God knows everything; that is the way we act. Both profiles touch on some good ideas that will help you in your daily walk with the Lord.

Some people may envy you and don't like anything about you. They may set out to harm you, so it is crucial that we understand all the different types of temperaments and allow ourselves to people whether they like us or not. The Bible does not say like; it commands you to love your brother and sister. We must be standing in the gap for each other and learn how to love one another as Christ loves us. The Profile strategy is meant for you to improve yourself. We need to have compassion for each other and not criticize each other when we find out what each other's temperament type is. Try to lift each other no matter what.

The book also has a standard IQ test that you can take. I am not sure if the accuracy rate is good, and I do not think it is vital at all. It has thirty different vocations, and that's a lot to pick and choose. They are vocations that you can use to work inside of the church. However, I believe you should take the gifts you have and be good at them.

Mr. LaHaye's book states that we have weaknesses and then gives you suggestions on how to bring them in control. The WIDP Profile does not emphasize strengths or weaknesses; it only provides you with the probable strengths and potential weaknesses that someone might have. The book does not say how you can, or suggest what you could do, to be in control of your temperament.

The factor that separates the two profiles is that the WIDP Profile offers immediate results, and the Profile in Mr. LaHaye's book does not. Mr. LaHaye's Profile gives you suggestions after you take the test the WIDP Profile breaks everything down, which is very simple to understand. Mr. LaHaye's Profile is, not a far contrast from what I can tell. However, I have not seen his test or taken it.

From what I know, the only thing Mr. LaHaye's Profile does is give a direction for some people who have no idea what they should do with their gifts. As I said, I am not sure how you would apply the results of your Profile once you receive them, because I have not taken the test.

The overall view of both profiles is really to help people. Not to say whose results are better or worse because the foundation of both is outstanding. It is undeniable that a lot of time and research has been put into both. Overall, on Mr. LaHaye's personality profile versus WIDP assessment: I would have to say that, the WIDP Profile provides more efficient and reliable information. More areas covered, and explicitly pinpointed. **It lists social, relationship, leadership, and demonstrated desires.**

The WIDP Profile can help you with your relationships because when it comes down to it, the way you respond to things/people is key. Personally, it enhanced the foundation of my marriage and made my wife, and I take a whole different approach to the way we respond to each other and solve disagreements. It enabled us to counsel each other and do what the Bible says as far as not letting the sun go down before we resolve any problems or conflicts that we may have. My relationship with my wife is significant to me, so whatever I can do to help us to grow, I will do it.

I also understand that before I have a relationship with anyone, I have first to love myself so that I can give that love to someone else. **When you find out that you need help in this area, some people may not want to admit that they have problems at one point or another.** Your relationship scores in the WIDP Profile will let you know if you need love or to give love. It can also let you know if you want more respect than you are providing. Sitting down with your spouse and finding out if any of their needs are not met will also help you in getting your needs met.

My wife and I made personal vows to the Lord when we were married. I vowed that I would love her as Christ loves the church and that we would be sensitive to each other's needs. With the training that we received in the classroom, I took it and started making it a part of our daily lives. It enabled me to overcome much bad behavior that I was exhibiting in my marriage. I stopped being selfish and started loving her for who she is, not trying to change her to be something that I want her to be. That was one of the things I know I was doing wrong. The Holy Spirit was already ministering to me about them, and then the WIDP Profile came along with confirmation in those areas. It has helped my relationship a great deal, and the conflicts that we had just immediately did a 360-degree turn for the better and made our household a very loving home. It is great to go back again, and our relationships are given a new beginning. The WIDP Profile helps me with communicating socially with others. My numbers were 00, which means that I do not like to socialize, and I do not need confirmation from people. I realize that I must be able to talk to people no matter how much I do not like it at times. I can't miss my blessing by not wanting to have a conversation with someone who wants to talk. I must be able to relate to everyone because I am in a management position, so it is essential to be social. I need to be able to talk to my employees. I cannot go into the office first thing in the morning and not speak to no one. Even though many people do act like that, it is still wrong.

Several years ago, the 00-temperament description would have described me, but I am now an approachable and talkative person once I get to know a person. When I first meet someone, we will break the ice and continue from there. To have friends, you need to be friendly. I do not agree with the WIDP Profile where it states that my temperament profile type needs acceptance and approval from people. If I work unto the Lord and do the best I can unto him, then I have done an excellent job. If we get our approval from people, we have already received our reward.

The WIDP Profile also states my temperament type needs time to be alone to counter the interaction with people. I disagree because I preach in the prison ministry and to minister in that capacity, you must want to be around people. I don't go to every social event I hear about because I realize that everyone is not where I am spiritually, and some engagements can be disappointing. We must be careful because we can easily create cliques and cults, misery loves company.

The WIDP Profile also states that I must have low self-esteem. In my case, that is not possible because I think highly of myself and try not to worry about what people say. There will always be people who will do something to get you hot under the collar. This Profile tells you socially how you interact with people and how to have a good perception of yourself. The way others are perceiving you is always going to be very different; know who you are in Jesus Christ, and everything else will take care of itself.

Depression is a big problem in this country. We have much work to do in the church because there are too many people hurting. Mr. LaHaye's breakdown of our temperaments regarding depression lacks from his standpoint. Many people do not like to face their problems, so they have much self-pity to do it because they did not get enough attention when they were children. None of us has had great childhoods. We need to quit blaming things for the way you were raised. That excuse is no good anymore.

The flesh will make you do some wild stuff. When I was practicing sin, my will was so loud when I wanted to get high or go party. Once my mind was made up, that was it. Since God chose the old man, the carnal nature part of me has passed away, the same will that I had then I have now.

In Mr. LaHaye's book, he talks about how to overcome your weaknesses and gives an x-ray of your temperaments. It is broken down into strength, weakness, spiritual weakness, and other temperaments types. It does not help you resolve anything as far as depression goes. That chapter was pretty good. There were good examples but no proper foundation to back them up. Ministering to someone and helping them overcome depression, for instance, is a real challenge and there is nothing there that jumps off the pages and supports them. There is nothing to assist them in their behavior, so this chapter was not effective at all. It had no immediate impact on me and wouldn't on anyone if they had never heard of temperament types. They would not get anything out of this chapter that would make it clear and understandable. If I were depressed, then I would continue to stay in that state of mind. There is nothing to build on, so I could not recommend this to anyone who wanted to overcome a compulsive behavior. This particular chapter did not minister to me, but it might someone else though.

The WIDP Profile and Mr. LaHaye's book did an outstanding job in talking about the different temperaments. They help you identify yourself and enable you to understand yourself. It let you know how your leadership skills compare to what you think of yourself as a leader if you are correct. Some individuals believe they are leaders when they are followers. Both books are excellent and objective to our profile. It evaluates the strengths that everyone has, and how to use them to help you be beneficial. It also gives way that we have a perception of others. At times, all of us are still self-centered and get in our world. It helped me immensely in my weak areas and, gave me one of the most excellent tools to use in the workplace. It changed so many things around and, gave me peace of mind to look at people, and know how they act. In the relationship, it was beneficial to both of us. We talk to each other even more about our temperaments, and, we work on the weak areas to see if we are getting our needs met.

If she does not get her needs met or I do not get my needs met, we will look elsewhere to get them fulfilled. The profiles give much information to help you explain to others if they need help in any area. They both have a foundation that you can build. It is just a tool that's part of our everyday life. I do not have children, but it would be useful on kids, and you get the immediate return on your investment for new hires; this is most effective because there is no better way to hire new associates. The profile results enables you to hire individuals who will make an immediate impact on the business, and you won't have as much turnover because it allows you hire the right ones the first time and not lose time and money in training them. If organizations do not know about the profile, they should because this could take their company to another level and, feature positive feedback. Within hours of the test, you can see the result instead of taking a chance on bad investments, which we all do. The discovery program is doing excellent work and will continue to do so in my life and others around me. We need this in a world that we all must live in, to make it a better place.

Temperaments influence everything that we do in our day-to-day lives. It is crucial that you have it under control and work on areas that need improvement. Mr. LaHaye's book also touches briefly on eating that may be out of control. His book states that we sometimes judge people by some of their quirks.

In everything you do, your temperament plays a significant role because you must know how people are and continually try to see the best in people. It does not matter how they are acting because we all have our shortcomings, and we have areas that need work. Not just our temperaments but the attitude has a lot to do with it.

Remember that you must bring your temperament in line with the Holy Spirit and also be willing to work with all kinds of people. Wherever you go, there are people. You must be able first to recognize their essential temperament. Once that is done, you must be ready to accept where they are with their spirituality and begin to minister to them accordingly. It could be an employee, which could make the workplaces more peaceful, or a personal relationship, which could make your home a more pleasant place to come home to after a gruesome day.

The methods described in LaHaye's book could work some areas of your personal life, and it can improve your relationship with Jesus Christ if you follow the instructions. Everyone should be striving to do that, and once we get our will lined up with His, there will be nothing, including any temperament, that we cannot change. I am a living witness to that. Once I came to Jesus and meant that I wanted to change my life and stopped playing church, I became a better person.

Let's talk about Melancholy. They are very bright, outgoing, fun to be around people, and not afraid of a challenge in any area. One thing that I disagree with as far as the Melancholy temperament description is that I do not agree with his statement that Melancholy doesn't like to give people praise or recognition. I give praise where praise is due, and I believe that we express love in a very excellent manner. If that individual deserves praise, then he will get his recognition. We know how to show appreciation.

His statements imply that Melancholy live under rocks and have enormous egos. I deal with people every day and if someone does me wrong or vice versa, then, first I must repent and ask them for forgiveness, and they should ask the same from me. Once we do a case study or a profile description of people, we look at them in just one way. People do change, but it seems like the foundation of test and patterns in these books are never-ending.

I believe Mr. LaHaye, or anyone who reads his book, should spend time with all the different temperament types because everybody is not going to be the way we think they should be.

Mr. LaHaye gives good illustrations on how the temperament influences the way we act, and he touches on all the temperaments, just as the WIDP Profile does. He stated that Sanguine is very loud and hard to get along with but, I know some individuals who have this temperament and they are entertaining loving people. I do have to agree with him that, some of them are overly expressive and that they take a little fish story and turn it into one of the largest you have ever thought of or heard.

Do opposites attract, a straightforward chapter to understand? It made me realize that you and your mates both, should be willing to work things out. You cannot just get only the surface of a problem; you must understand the rest of the subject matter at hand.

Anytime, you are with the other sex, and there is going to be an adjustment. First, the two of you are not staying together in the same household. It does not matter what your personalities are "clashing" about, you still must be able to handle any problem with a level head, and you also must be willing to communicate with each other. If the communication is not happening, then there is nothing you can do because you are not talking. There will be no way that you can solve problems. You must be able to complement each other and know that we all have weaknesses, and you can get through it together with God's help. Agape love is not instantaneous; we experience it over a period. We must live with the things that we do not agree with about each other.

Any relationship is given and take; you just can't be controlling all the time. God must be the author of your contacts, and as Mr. LaHaye stated, the one thing myself and my wife agree upon was never to get a divorce, and I was always to treat her as Christ loves the church. It is hard sometimes, you better believe it is, but we must keep God in the center of our will. The WIDP Profile goes along this. The Profile is right in front of you, and there is no excuse; it helps us not to destroy one another because as individuals we are very selfish—it is always me, I, and you are not worried about your mate or family. The Profile helps us get beyond just ourselves all the time and see the big picture of people. We can all learn from each other and help build each other up. If we take the investment and the foundation that both profiles have, you will be happy with yourself and other people, so this helps you illustrate love and not talk about it. Anybody can talk about how they are going to love their wife more and then don't put it into action, or the plan is not okay at all.

Another significant area was explaining the demonstrated score in the WIDP Profile, which indicates how the individual acts toward other people. If your demonstrated score was meager, which my number was, it means you do protect the private environment that you have around you because that is what's most important once you get off from work. Anything I like to come back and be comfortable around the people I love, and it also shows if you have a wide gap between your demonstrated score and your desired score, you are going to have some conflicts with working things out. You might need a reality check with yourself.

The WIDP Profile shows based on just those two scores, and the desired score tells what you want back from an individual. You must be careful: it is a perfect concept to understand, but it will not matter because you will not know if that person has the GAP complex. A gap complex described as someone needing more love than they are willing to give in return. Mr. LaHaye's book, in contrast, does not have any of these examples and the GAP area in WIDP Profile shows this conflict.

The WIDP Profile has real objectives from which you can evaluate behavior. Mr. LaHaye has examples on the temperament, but it's not broken down, as I said earlier. His chart is tough to understand, and you should have a straightforward and not a complex profile that can be appreciated. Your profile should minister life to you, and that is what you need, not just another profile.

Mr. LaHaye did an excellent job with his chart. He has broken down into smaller areas, or should I say, more regions, based on my opinion, and I have shown people both profiles. More people showed more interest in the WIDP Profile, and it has improved a lot of people's understanding of temperaments or mood swings whatever you want to call it. They cannot change.

Many people didn't know what each profile was about at first, but with the help of the Holy Spirit, I showed them where they were if they want guidance from the Holy Spirit through me. It does not matter what your background is and what area you lived in; Jesus can work it out if you let him. Get your mind out of the way and let the WIDP Profile minister to you because with the profile you can touch a city, and this can be very enlightening to someone's life.

Temperament influences everything that you do. It is essential to find out what temperament type you are. It plays a significant role in everything that's about us in our lifestyles as we live it today. In Mr. LaHaye's book it broke down each area; first was our eating habits. He stated that he could tell your temperament type by how and what we eat. I believe I will give him a run for his money. He says that Melancholy are very picky eaters and it takes us forever to make up our minds. I do not believe that at all. He talked along the lines of our driving skills, which at times we are all crazy drivers in that area where you have much research. One point he stated was that Melancholy always leave home well prepared, but I love to get up and say we are going here or there and then we are off. I am quite the opposite. The other area that I do not agree with is that we are tough to please, and I believe this is wrong. I am not a perfectionist, but I do want you to give me your all then I have no problems with anything.

In closing, let's use the Melancholy temperament, for example. I believe all temperaments are a blessing as if we are seeking God. Then and only then will everything be all right—but back to my temperament evaluation. If you go through the Bible, some great people will be of this temperament, including Moses, Daniel, and Ezekiel, to name a few. I want to think that I am sensitive too and appreciative of the more extraordinary things in life.

I push myself to higher standards every day. I try to do better in everything that I accomplish or strive. My greatest enemy is myself, so I compete with me. I like to outdo myself. I would like to believe that I am a nice person. We all have gifts; it is just up to us to turn those gifts and make it work. I enjoy success by my standards, not other people's. If you go by other people's standards, you can set yourself up for a fall. That is just a little preface of myself. I could write a book that would sell. Getting back to the topics that are at hand, I am delighted that Dr. Worley came to Atlanta to enrich us with his teaching in the WIDP Profile. It changed my thinking in many areas of my life. I thank God for the power of his Holy Spirit that flows through us. We should not be selfish with our gifts but bless others with it. I use the tools I learned, to be a blessing to everyone I meet, not to abuse it but be a real blessing. I do not walk around just picking people apart anymore. I know individuals who have taken this course, and they take the information and use it as a sword. I don't mind taking something healthy and running with it, but when I see this happening it bothers me.

I would recommend these books to anyone, who is willing to be changed, and filled with excellent teachings that would carry them for a lifetime. These lessons are simple and include useful formulas that are conducive to the development of people. It is a suitable material that gives formal instruction on what the Holy Spirit wants to do in our lives. I thank both, for their time and efforts and the work they have put into these projects. They were well worth the time it took to read them. It will help anyone who reads them spiritually because they are both excellent for individual and corporate development.

## The Contrasts and Parallels of

# LaHaye's Approach
# and
# WIDP

*After attending the Worley ID Profile Seminar and reading the book "Transforming Your Temperament" by Tim LaHaye, the significant difference I have seen is that Dr. Worley defines three different areas of temperament, not just a blend of two as in LaHaye's approach.*

It has been beneficial taking the WIDP to find out that my temperament is not just a smooth blend of two personality types but a trio consisting of areas such as social, leadership, and relationship. Understanding that a person may have a different temperament in each of these areas would explain why we do not act the same way at work as we do at play or home.

I want to talk about my temperament that I operate in socially, which is Phlegmatic Melancholy (40). It is beneficial to have the essential characteristics of the adult social profile to know which ones stick out the most. The top three for myself are friendly, dependable, and disciplined. There have been several occasions during review time on my job that these three areas have been mentioned. With LaHaye's approaches, it is a lot more general. He does break it down to strengths and weaknesses, but it is hard to understand because it does not go into as much depth as the WIDP. The flaws don't seem to line up with my social temperament. I guess this means I don't have any (like self-centeredness) ha! But seriously, I do see stubborn, self-protective, and sarcastic humor as a defense. Overall, I would have to agree with my social profile.

In the area of leadership, my temperament score was a (70) which, is Choleric. My line of work positively reflects my leadership profile as a Choleric. My needs and desires line up almost word for words with WIDP in the area of my job. "Transforming Your Temperament" does not address the area of needs and desires in the manner that WIDP does. It is imperative for me to know my strengths and weaknesses in leadership capabilities so that I may continue to improve.

In the relationship area of WIDP, I scored as a Melancholy (23). I was a little confused when I first read my relationship needs and desires concerning the characteristic of "expresses the minimal amount of love and affection in close relationships" because I am not that way with my wife. But as I continued to read, as I am famous for stopping too short, it began to make sense to me. I am very faithful, and committed to my wife, and she is the only one whom I want to have a close relationship with, next to God, of course. This is another example of why it is necessary to have the depth that WIDP provides to understand more entirely vs. general information.

In closing, my overall comparison is that the WIDP delivers a lot of information about who you are, and allows you to understand more in depth, why you are the way you are. It goes to the core of your makeup to find what God put inside of you. A personality can be formed, but temperament is who you become at conception—your intrinsic design.

WIDP does not address personality type, which is refreshing compared to a lot of other assessments around. It may be a little confusing at first when you take WIDP if you have already experienced different types of evaluations, but I have found that it seems to be pretty accurate. Don't get me wrong: LaHaye's book is not entirely off the mark; it just is not quite as in-depth as WIDP. The more information you can find to help understand yourself and others more accurately, the better off you are. It makes sense to break it down into the three different areas of temperament because you don't feel like a hypocrite thinking that you act one way at work, and another way at home. It's OK!

The only area that I see that would make WIDP more complete would be a list of careers that were best suited for each type of temperament.

Michael Brock

# PARENTAL/ADULT VS PEER DEPENDENCY IN HIGH SCHOOL STUDENTS' FEEDBACK PREFERENCES AND AGREEMENT RELATING TO

# WORLEY'S ID PROFILE TEMPERAMENT INFORMATION

## RESEARCH DESIGN

# CHAPTER 20

# HIGH SCHOOL PROJECT

## This project was conducted by a college senior

**Parental/Adult vs. Peer Dependency in High School Students' Feedback Preferences and Agreement Relating to Temperament Information**

*Abstract*

The studies conducted to determine if freshman/sophomore and junior/senior high school students sought parental/adult feedback or peer feedback, concerning the information they received from a temperament assessment instrument, as well as, whether students agreed more with a parental/adult rating of assessment accuracies or with peer evaluation of assessment accuracy. Data raises questions about and suggests further research around issues of, adolescent development including identity formation, parental vs. peer dependency, and handling of, nonsocial information.

*Introduction*

Temperament, as a general construct, refers to a broad array of behavioral traits that are thought to be biologically rooted and first appearing (Bates, Dodge, Pettit, & Ridge, 1998). Temperamental characteristics are present early in life, are stable over time, and are related to biological factors (Capaldi & Rothbart, 1992 and Thomas & Chess, 1977, both as cited in Stice & Gonzales, 1998). Temperament is purported to be the foundation for personality (Buss & Plomin, 1984, as mentioned in Stice & Gonzales, 1998).

Worley's ID Profile, or WIDP, assesses an individual's temperament based on an update of Hippocrates theory while retaining his basic terminology, including Sanguine, Phlegmatic, Melancholy, Choleric, and the most recently discovered classification Introverted Sanguine. Each temperament type or derived blend defines a person's unique needs, desires, differences, and preferences. Dr. Worley, the developer of the WIDP, describes temperament as an individual's inborn subjective self—his/her unique desires and needs—who one is. Personality defined as the aspects of a person's temperament chosen to present to society. In this model, demonstrated behavior (personality) is only one aspect of a person—desired behavior (temperament) is the part of a person that cannot be observed—it can solely be determined by testing the individual (Worley, 1998).

The Health Examination Survey (HES) (Wells, 1980, as cited in Katainen, Raikkonen, Keskivaara, & Keltikangas-Jarvinen, 1999), is a questionnaire designed for use by nonprofessionals. To screen children for potential behavioral problems, it measures particular behavioral components that relate conceptually to the temperament dimensions described by Buss and Plomin (1975, as cited in Katainen et al., 1999). This instrument assesses an individual primarily through observed behavior (personality), equating personalities with temperament, even though the research on which this assessment is based asserts that temperament is the basis for personality. Much research, utilizing the term 'temperament,' looks for the underlying 'nature' factors of negative behavior (Rothbart & Ahadi, 1994; Tarter, Kabene, Escallier, Laird, & Jacob, 1990; Thomas & Chess, 1977; Watson & Clark, 1993; Kochanska, 1991; Gray, 1987; all as cited in Stice & Gonzales, 1998).

The WIDP is particularly unique in the category of temperament assessments. WIDP distinguishes between temperament and personality and does not represent any temperament type as 'right' or 'wrong,' or desirable (Worley, 1998).

The developmental theory states that stable identity formation is the primary task of adolescence, according to Erikson (1959/1980, as cited in Kerpelman, Pittman, & Lamke, 1997). Resolving the identity vs. identity confusion stage depends on repeated explorations, and commitments in the context of an individual's emotional development, close relationships, and current societal norms (Marcia, 1966, and Kroger, 1989, both as cited in Kerpelman et al., 1997). Young adolescents, indicate family to have more importance than other relationships, but this family influence diminishes in older adolescents. Parents are viewed as less relevant than peers as teenagers become independent adults (Furman & Buhrmester, 1985, 1992; and Cotterell, 1992, all as cited in O'Koon, 1997). A case can be made that high school juniors, seniors will seek feedback more frequently from their peers than parents/adults about their WIDP, and that high school first-year students and sophomores will find input more often from relatives/adults than peers about their WIDP. (Hypothesis 1).

Findings indicate that in issues relating to morals, values, education, occupation, and other nonsocial matters, adolescents overall are more strongly influenced by parents and other adults than by peers (Richardson, Abramowitz, Asp, & Petersen, 1986 and, Sebald, 1984 and Phelan, Yu, & Davidson, 1994. All as cited in Wilson & MacGillivray, 1998). Since the WIDP assesses temperament, a personal aspect of an individual, it's expected that high school students will be more in agreement with parents/adults than with their peers about the accuracy of their WIDP profile results. (Hypothesis 2)

Friendship is considered a critical part of adolescent development and may even be the most significant relationships for a teen during the transition from child to adult. Contributing importantly to the emergence and development of ego identity (Berndt, 1982 and Youniss, 1980 and Youniss & Smollar, 1985, all as cited in Akers, Jones, & Coyle, 1998). Many similarities between young friends have been documented including grade level, age, gender, religion, ethnicity, specific behaviors (i.e., substance use), school attitudes, college plans, and academic achievement (Kandel, 1978a, and Epstein, 1983, both as cited in Akers et al., 1998). Combining Youniss and Smollar's assertion, it is by way of interpersonal relationship and social construction that an adolescent develops their social sense of self, with the similarities between friends in psychological and behavioral characteristics (Kandel, 1978 a; 1978 b as cited in Akers et al., 1998). For the relationship between mental, behavioral, and identity characteristics (Bourne 1978a, and 1978b, both as cited in Akers et al., 1998), a possible conclusion is those young friends share similarities in identity development. Therefore, contrary to Hypothesis 2, a position can be taken in that high school students will be more in agreement with peers than parents or adults about the accuracy of their WIDP. (Hypothesis 3).

## *Method*

# Subjects

The subjects for this study consisted of 42 students in grades 9–12 drawn from the high school population of a private Christian school in rural New England. The sample included 28 females, 14 males, 20 first-year students/sophomores, and 22 juniors/seniors; 21 of the students lived in campus dorms, and 21 lived at home and commuted to school. After the principal had permitted to conduct the research, project information with an attached permission slip provided for distribution to the parents of each high school student.

Convenience sampling was the basis of the choice of school; this was necessary due to time constraints of the project, and the difficulty of finding high schools willing to participate in the project. The participating schools were selected based on proximity, and willingness to engage. The subjects, not randomly chosen since all students could participate. Students without signed permission, absent, or prefer not to attend were not included. Sampling bias was evident because participants were voluntary, and only recruited from one high school; therefore, they are not representative of the general high school population.

## *Materials*

Each high school student who chose to participate and had a signed permission slip received a copy of the initial questionnaire packet, which, included, a cover sheet (A) and two questionnaires: a preassessment form (B), and the WIDP questionnaire (C), all of which were attached. The cover sheet included the title of the project, "WIDP Project," as explained in the informational sheet given to the parents. The preassessment form was a self-report of temperament attributes; the WIDP, a 60-item inventory relating to social, leadership, and personal relationship preferences.

Each participant had their WIDP generated a personal profile, which was returned to students one week ahead, along with a brief explanatory note (D). One additional week later, a follow-up questionnaire was administered to the subjects. Each student who participated in the first phase was given a follow-up packet. The package included a cover sheet (A) their original preassessment form with the results of their WIDP profile; recorded at the bottom (B) a page listing the temperament types and characteristics for references (E) and the follow-up questionnaire relating to the perceived accuracy and usefulness of the WIDP profile (F).

## *Research Design*

The research design of this project used attitude tests in questionnaire format. The WIDP is a 60-item inventory that generates a detailed summary of individual temperament. The items are divided into six scales, corresponding to demonstrated and desired behaviors for social, leadership, and relationship assessment categories. However, they appear on the form as 33 questions regarding frequency and 27 questions relating to quantity. A frequency or number choice from 1 (low) to 6 (high) is chosen to answer each of the 60 items, which can be answered directly on the computer program or a printed questionnaire and entered into the computer later. The questionnaire takes approximately 10 minutes to complete. After the computer scores it, an interpretive report is generated for the individual.

A test-retest administration assessed the instrument's reliability with a *four*-month interval between two assessments. The test-retest yielded a reasonable relationship between scores on the six scales of the WIDP across the two administrations of r = .7 (Pearson product moment correlation). This score compares very favorably to average scores for similar instruments, which usually fall between .7 and .8 over *one* month. Also, a measure of internal consistency was performed, yielding an average internal consistency score for the six scales of KR-20 = .54 (Kuder-Richardson formula 20) comparing quite favorably to the MMPI validity score of .52.

Comparing the WIDP scores of people not in counseling with those of people diagnosed with specific psychological problems by clinical psychologists assessed the concurrent validity of the WIDP. Behavior patterns recognized by the psychological community for diagnosable issues were demonstrated by mean scale scores found on the WIDP. Problem diagnoses included: major depression, obsessive-compulsive disorder, alcohol dependence, and marital problems. While the WIDP is not to be used as a clinical diagnostic tool, the results of the comparisons indicate that the scales have concurrent validity. Also, the Rosenberg self-esteem measure was administered to a sample of healthy (non-counseling, nondiagnosed) individuals who also took the WIDP. Dr. Worley's contention that individuals can present many different scores on the six scales was supported by 5 of the scales correlating at almost zero, indicating no relationship, and only the desired leadership scale, relating marginally to self-esteem. The lack of correlation means that the scales measure different types of efficient functioning and that self-esteem is not tied to any of the temperaments found on any of the scales themselves.

The follow-up questionnaire (F) included nine questions. A 4-point Likert scale was used to score the first three questions; the remaining issues, included two closed, two open-ended, and two modified Thurstone-type questions. Only items 2 and 3 were utilized in this study. Three pieces of information were gathered from these questions: how much each student agreed with their profile; whom else (if anyone) the students showed their profile information to; and how much each other person agreed with the student's profile. The range of responses rated the amount of agreement from, "not much" to "almost all." Due to time constraints, a pre-study administration of the questions was not conducted. Descriptive information regarding the results of items 2 and 3, as well as the, provided demographic data, was obtained. A frequency analysis was performed to compare the persons to whom first-year students/ sophomores showed their profiles and the persons to whom junior/senior showed their profiles.

Further comparisons were made between dorm and town students, like accessibility to parents, was an essential factor in assessing parental and peer dependency. The amount of subject agreement with the profile was measured using the score from question 2; the sum of others' agreement with the profile was measured using the score from question 3. An analysis of variance was completed to determine whether subjects' perception of WIDP accuracy was more in agreement with parents'/adults' or peers' assessment of WIDP accuracy.

## *Procedure*

Subjects were obtained by calling local high schools. Two granted informational interviews; one agreed to allow testing. The school set the dates for the administration of the two-wave research surveys, each wave conducted in one morning. Each grade was studied each time individually.

The researcher did not contact individual teachers before the administration of the surveys, but estimates of the time required (30 minutes for the first wave, 15 for the second) were given to the principal. Participation from the entire high school (70 students) was sought; 53 permission slips were obtained. The experimental mortality was 11; 3 did not complete the first wave due to absence; 1 chose not to participate; 5 did not complete the second wave due to lack; 1 student did not receive a personal profile due to researcher oversight, and one student skipped the questions pertinent to this project. 42, subjects remained in the study.

Efforts were made to avoid response bias by standardizing the administration of the surveys to each class. After survey packets had been distributed, a brief, prewritten explanation regarding the general purposes of the research and step-by-step instructions were read at each administration of the questionnaires to each class. Subjects were asked to respect the privacy of other students by not looking at other papers and by not talking. Participants were thanked for their participation at the end of each session.

Since this study was conducted in a naturalistic setting, and without random sampling, it is believed essential to note variables that may affect the results. All subjects participated between 8:00 AM and 11:30 AM on each of the two days. Some were given at the beginning of class, while others were done at the end of class. While the first wave, was administered on a regular midweek school day, the second wave, was administrated on the Friday after a late-night formal banquet, and on the morning of the final half-day before a traditional holiday concert and dismissal for semester break. Teachers in whose classes the surveys were administered were, equally gracious on each administration day.

## *Ethics*

Informed consent obtained through parental/guardian permission forms distributed to each high school student before the surveys. The permission slip informed the parents/guardians that, a Fitchburg State College student carried out the study and, that the project included the WIDP and a follow-up survey about the accuracy and usefulness of the profile.

The directions read to each class, before participating in the study, informed them that participation was voluntary and that they could stop participating in the project at any time. The subjects were advised, that some questions could potentially be upsetting. However, all questionnaires, as well as sample profile results, were reviewed by the course professor, a Ph.D. researcher, and clinician; the practicum supervisor and developer of the WIDP, a licensed psychologist; the school principal—all deemed the materials appropriate for the students.

Confidentiality was established by the use of a cover sheet on each survey packet, returning the profiles to students in sealed envelopes, and removing the names from questionnaires before the data was read and analyzed. Anonymity was a more complex issue. Because the research was conducted in two waves, and the second wave was dependent on the subjects referencing the questionnaires they had completed in the first wave; it was necessary to have the participants put their names on the surveys.

The completed questionnaire sets were subsequently matched, numbered 1-49; moralized subjects were dropped, titles removed, and only then was the raw data read and analyzed.

Some mild deception was employed. The subjects were not informed of the focus of this study: to whom they showed their results and how accurate the students believed their profiles were compared to how sure others thought their profiles were. We thought this was necessary so that the students are not overly concerned about whom they showed their profiles to or how much in agreement they agreed with the profile, and therefore tried to obtain feedback that the researcher might consider desirable or undesirable. In a general information sheet that accompanied the results of the profile, one sentence encouraged the respondents to share their findings with people who knew them well, but this suggestion was not especially emphasized and constituted an appropriate recommendation for minors dealing with personal information.

### Results

While the participants in this study were all high school students, the demographic information obtained indicates that they are not representative of all high school students specifically regarding the type of secondary school attended, residential status, and regional distribution. The high school is private and Christian; some students live at home while others live in campus dorms; most student families live in New England.

A descriptive analysis of the data obtained from the portion of question 3 relating to whom subjects showed their WIDP profile was done using a frequency distribution in cross-tabulation form. Subjects' possible choices included; 'no one,' 'mother,' 'father,' 'sibling,' 'friend,' 'adult.' (See Appendix F). ('Sibling' was dropped from analysis due to very few responses, and lack of relevance to this study.) Subjects were encouraged to list additional people who they showed their profile if insufficient spaces were designated on the form. Table 1 compares all first-year students/sophomore students to all junior/ senior students. The freshmen and sophomores showed their profiles most to their "friends only" or "parents/adults and friends." These two categories captured 40% of their respondents. Distant third group was "no one" at 15%, and lastly, was "parents/adults only" at 5%. Jr/Sr showed their profiles most frequently to 'no one' at 36%; the second category was 'friends only' at 32%; third was 'parents/ adults and friends,' at 18%, and last, was 'parents/adults only,' at 14%.

Table 2 compares town first-year students/sophomore to town junior/senior, and Table 3 compares dorm first-year students/sophomore to dorm junior/senior. Because most dorm students did not have access to their parents between the survey dates, 'parent' and 'adult' categories were combined for all statistics, and the descriptive data was separated into the dorm, and town student groups to highlight any differences between the groups. The data distributions, for both the town and dorm students, were very similar to the combined group, the notable exception being that none of the dorm students showed their profiles exclusively to parents/adults. Table 4 compares first-year students/sophomore and junior/senior ranking of persons shown their profiles. Differences in classification and percentages were observed between subject groupings; the first-year students/sophomore ranking most closely resembled the overall classification.

A chi-square test was done using data from the portion of question 3 relating to the people subjects showed their WIDP profile. The categories of first-year students/sophomore and junior/senior were compared to whom they showed their WIDP results to parents/adults *and* friends, friends only, and a combination cell of parents/adults just and no one, yielding a 2 x 3 contingency table. All cell frequencies were over 5, but the chi-square value was not significant at the .05 probability level, failing to support hypothesis 1.

# TABLES

## Table 1

**Frequency and Percentages of Persons Shown**
**WIDP Profile Results by High School Freshmen/Sophomores and Juniors/Seniors**

| Persons showed profile | Freshmen and Sophomores | | Juniors and Seniors | | Total | |
|---|---|---|---|---|---|---|
| | N | % | N | % | N | % |
| Parents/adults and friends | 8 | 40 | 4 | 18 | 12 | 29 |
| Friends only | 8 | 40 | 7 | 32 | 15 | 36 |
| Parents/adults only | 1 | 5 | 3 | 14 | 4 | 10 |
| No one | 3 | 15 | 8 | 36 | 11 | 26 |
| **Totals** | **20** | **100** | **22** | **100** | **42** | **101** |

*Note:* Percentages may not add to exactly 100% due to rounding.

## Table 2

**Frequency and Percentages of Persons Shown WIDP**
*Profile Results by High School Town Freshmen/Sophomores and Juniors/Seniors*

| Persons showed profile | Freshmen and Sophomores | | Juniors and Seniors | | Total | |
|---|---|---|---|---|---|---|
| | N | % | N | % | N | % |
| Parents/adults and friends | 4 | 45 | 2 | 17 | 6 | 29 |
| Friends only | 3 | 33 | 3 | 25 | 6 | 29 |
| Parents/adults only | 1 | 11 | 3 | 25 | 4 | 19 |
| No one | 1 | 11 | 4 | 33 | 5 | 24 |
| **Totals** | **9** | **100** | **12** | **100** | **21** | **101** |

*Note:* Percentages may not add to exactly 100% due to rounding

# Table 3

**Frequency and Percentages of Persons Shown WIDP**
**Profile Results by High School Dorm Freshmen/Sophomores and Juniors/Seniors**

| Persons showed profile | Freshmen and Sophomores | | Juniors and Seniors | | Total | |
|---|---|---|---|---|---|---|
| | N | % | N | % | N | % |
| Parents/adults and friends | 4 | 36 | 2 | 20 | 6 | 29 |
| Friends only | 5 | 46 | 4 | 40 | 9 | 43 |
| Parents/adults only | 0 | 0 | 0 | 0 | 0 | 0 |
| No one | 2 | 18 | 4 | 40 | 6 | 29 |
| **Totals** | **11** | **100** | **10** | **100** | **21** | **101** |

*Note:* Percentages may not add to exactly 100% due to. rounding.

# Table 4

**Ranking and Percentages of Persons Shown**
**WIDP Profile Results by High School Freshmen/Sophomores and Juniors/Seniors**

| Rank | Freshmen and Sophomores | % | Juniors and Seniors | % | Total | % |
|---|---|---|---|---|---|---|
| 1 | Friends only (Tie) | 40 | No one | 36 | Friends only | 36 |
| 2 | Parents/adults and friends | 40 | Friends only | 32 | Parents/adults and friends | 29 |
| 3 | No one | 15 | Parents/adults and friends | 18 | No one | 26 |
| 4 | Parents/adults only | 5 | Parents/adults only | 14 | Parents/adults only | 10 |
| | **Totals** | **100** | | **100** | | **101** |

*Note:* Percentages may not add to exactly 100% due to rounding.

A descriptive analysis of the data obtained from question 2 and the portion of question 3 that reported the amount of agreement with the WIDP profile subjects as well as those who read their profile had with the profile was done using measures of central tendency and measures of variability. (Table 5) In question 2, the three sections of the profile were each scored on a scale ranging from 'not much,' 'some,' 'a lot,' to 'almost all.' The choices were assigned a numerical value, 2, 4, 6, or 8, with 2 corresponding's to 'not much,' up to 8 corresponding's to 'almost all.' The numerical values chosen for the three sections were averaged, yielding one score for the overall perceived accuracy of the WIDP to the subjects themselves. In question 3, the subjects also reported the amount of agreement other people had with the subject's profile, on the same scale with the same corresponding numerical values. The three sections of the profile were not scored individually in this question; rather, the perceived accuracy of the entire profile was rated once. Multiple scores within the parent/adult or friend categories for each profile was averaged to obtain one score for each group. There was a possible high score of 8 and a possible low score of 2. High scores indicate that the individual or group was more in agreement with the WIDP profile results. This data was broken down into several measures of central tendency and variability analyses as follows:

All profiles,

Table 5: profiles rated by subjects, parents/adults, and friends,
Table 6: profiles rated by subjects and friends,
Table 7: profiles rated by subjects and parents/adults,
Table 8: profiles rated by subjects only,
Table 9: profiles rated by subjects and any other group(s),
Table 10: Mean accuracy score for subjects was highest on the profiles that only parents/adults reviewed; the subjects' mean accuracy score was lowest on the profiles that were not shown to anyone else.

A one-way ANOVA of the data from question 2 and the portion of question 3 that reported the amounts of agreement with the WIDP profile subjects as well as those who read their profiles were done. Profiles shown to both parents/adults and friends (Table 6) were included in this analysis. The amount of agreement with the WIDP profile as reported by the subjects, parents/adults who reviewed their profiles, and friends who examined these same profiles were analyzed for significant variation. The F ratio was not statistically significant at the .05 probability level, failing to support either hypothesis 2 or hypothesis 3.

# Table 5

## Measures of Central Tendency and Variability in Agreement Scores for All Profiles

| Profile raters | Mean | Median | Mode | Range | SD |
|---|---|---|---|---|---|
| Subjects N = 41 | 5.1 | 5.3 | 6 | 6 | 1.6 |
| Parents/Adults N = 15 | 5.8 | 6 | 6 | 6 | 1.9 |
| Friends N = 26 | 4.7 | 4 | 4 | 6 | 1.7 |

*Note*: N indicates the number of PROFILES rated by rating group, NOT the number of persons who rated profiles; only in subjects group does some persons an equal number of profiles.

# Table 6

## Measures of Central Tendency and Variability

### In Agreement Scores for Profiles rated by Subjects, Parents/Adults, and Friends

| Profile raters | Mean | Median | Mode | Range | SD |
|---|---|---|---|---|---|
| Subjects **N = 11** | 5.9 | 6 | 6 | 4.7 | 1.3 |
| Parents/Adults **N = 11** | 5.5 | 6 | 6 | 6 | 2.1 |
| Friends **N = 11** | 5.1 | 5.3 | 4 | 6 | 1.6 |

*Note*: N indicates the number of PROFILES rated by rating group, NOT the number of persons who rated profiles; only in subjects group does several persons an equal number of profiles.

# Table 7

## Measures of Central Tendency

### Variability in Agreement Scores for Profiles rated by Subjects and Friends

| Profile raters | Mean | Median | Mode | Range | SD |
|---|---|---|---|---|---|
| Subjects **N = 15** | 4.9 | 5.3 | 2.6 **5.3** **6** | 5.4 | 1.5 |
| Friends **N = 15** | 4.4 | 4 | 4 | 6 | 1.7 |

*Note*: N indicates the number of PROFILES rated by rating group, NOT the number of persons who rated profiles; only in subjects group does several persons an equal number of profiles.

# Table 8

## Measures of Central Tendency and

### Variability in Agreement Scores for Profiles rated by Subjects and Parents/Adults

| Profile raters | Mean | Median | Mode | Range | SD |
|---|---|---|---|---|---|
| Subjects **N = 4** | 6 | 6.3 | 6.6 | 2 | .8 |
| Parents/Adults **N = 4** | 6.5 | 6 | 6 | 2 | .9 |

*Note*: N indicates the number of PROFILES rated by rating group, NOT the number of persons who rated profiles; only in subjects group does several persons an equal number of profiles.

## Table 9

### Measures of Central

### Tendency and Variability in Agreement Scores for Profiles rated by Subjects Only

| Profile raters | Mean | Median | Mode | Range | SD |
|---|---|---|---|---|---|
| Subjects | 4.4 | 4 | 3.3 | 6 | 1.8 |
| **N = 11** | | | **5.3** | | |

*Note*: N equals the number of profiles AND number of persons who rated profiles

## Table 1. Scores for Subjects Whose Profiles Were Rated by Others

| Profile raters | Mean | Median | Mode | Range | SD |
|---|---|---|---|---|---|
| Subjects | 5.4 | 6 | 6 | 5.4 | 1.5 |
| **N = 30** | | | | | |

*Note*: N equals the number of profiles AND number of persons who rated profiles

*Summary and Discussion*

The goals of this study determine how high school students handled the personal information generated by the WIDP temperament assessment, specifically by noting with whom they shared that information, and by measuring with whom they agreed more, were met to some extent. Having ascertained the presence of parental/adult vs. peer dependency issues, and the shifts during adolescence through referrals to theory, and earlier studies, this research emphasized frequencies with which parents/adults or peers were sought and measurements of agreement with parents/adults or peers. While data obtained, indicated that some shifts in dependency might be present, and a deal was possibly influenced by whom subjects showed their profiles to, no statistically significant relationships were found to exist.

This study was limited by several factors that need consideration when discussing the data obtained. Time restrictions affected the setting of the survey and therefore, the composition of the sample; in the short times available, only one high school agreed to allow the research to be conducted. Time was also a factor in obtaining signed consent from parents/guardians. The school distributed and collected the slips; however, quite a few were not returned, and so some potential subjects did not participate in the study. Time was an essential factor in the scheduling of the two sessions required to complete this study. It had been hoped that the first wave could have been conducted in mid-November, which would have allowed for the profile results to be returned to the subjects before Thanksgiving vacation, giving an opportunity for dorm students to share the results with parents/adults.

Although the school contacted parents and permission for the study was granted in plenty of times; administrative circumstances were such that scheduling could not start until the first week of December. Because of the time required for profiles to be generated by the subjects and the need to allow them time to read and share them if desired, the second wave of the research could not be scheduled until right before semester break. Unfortunately, the only option for this second wave was the morning after a late-night school event and on the last day of classes before semester breaks. Also, this was a half-day that included a vocal concert to be given by the high school soon after the administration of the survey. Subject mortality was already evident, as several students had left for the airports; the remaining students were noticeably tired and anxious to leave school as soon as possible. While the first wave was administered to students who appeared rested and happy for a break from their regular classes, the second wave confronted students who were exhausted and less than thrilled about yet one more task to be completed before they could go home. Since the research project was mainly dependent on the responses to the second wave questionnaire, the circumstances noted on the days in question may have affected the results.

The absence of reliability and validity for the follow-up questionnaire implies that the tool of measurements used may not be an accurate indicator of to whom subjects showed their profiles and the perceived accuracy of the profiles. It should be noted that all responses were self-reported; it was not within the parameters of this study to obtain independent checks on perceived accuracy from the parents, adults, or friends, to whom the profiles were shown. With more time, a valid and reliable tool for measurement could have been designed, but since this was a preliminary survey, relating to a unique research area, with a meager budget, the information gathered should be viewed as leading to further research.

The data relating to who the subjects showed their profile results reveal some interesting patterns. For all students, and breakdowns (Tables 1–3), the 'friends only' and 'parents/adults and friends' categories were the overwhelming first or second choices for all freshmen/sophomore. In the full sample, these options tied; in the dorm sample, 'friends only' won out slightly (by 10%) and in the town sample, 'parents/adult and friends' won slightly (by 12%). The results are not surprising since town students had easier access to parents, and other adults they would have known for a long time, while dorm students have less access to parents, and long-term adult friends, accounting for the difference. These differences offset each other, in the overall sample, leaving the top two categories even.

The complete sample and the dorm sample for freshmen/sophomore both rated 'no one' and 'parents/ adults only' as distant third and fourth places, respectively; town students' ratings of these same categories tied as least attractive options. Again, the dorm and town students' ratings were consistent. It is notable that none of the dorm students chose 'parents/adults only'; this is not surprising considering that they had less access to parents and adults they would have known for a long time. While some of them did show results to friends *and* adults, none chose feedback exclusively from a group that, given the timing of the research surveys, could primarily be drawn only from adult school personnel. The research suggests that while high school students develop close friends quickly in a new setting, parents are not as easily 'replaced' by other adults.

Patterns also emerge from the junior/senior data. For all students and breakdowns (Tables 1–3), the 'no one' and 'friends only' categories were overwhelmingly the first or second choices for all junior/ seniors. In the dorm sample, these options tied; in the town sample, 'no one' won out by 8%; in the complete samples, 'no one' won out by 6%. In both the complete sample and the dorm sample, 'parents/ adults and friends' and 'parents/adults only' were ranked third and fourth choices, respectively. In the town sample, 'friends only' and 'parents/adults only' tied for second and third positions; 'parents/adults and friends' was ranked last. Junior/senior town and dorm students' ranking were similar, though not as consistent as the first-year students/sophomore rankings. No junior/senior dorm subjects chose 'parents/ adults only' like the freshmen/sophomore dorm subjects.

Comparisons of ranking and percentage data for each class grouping suggest differences between younger and older high school students (Table 4). Very noticeable is the difference in ranking the category 'no one' as third and 15% for freshmen/sophomore and the ranking of the same category as first and 36% for the junior/senior. 'Parents/adults and friends' went from the first rank and 40% for underclassmen to third ranks and 18% for upperclassmen. "Friends only" dropped in prominence from the first rank and 40% for freshmen/sophomore to second rank and 32% for the junior/senior. 'Parents/adults only' was rated fourth by each both class groupings, but the freshmen/sophomore was 5% while the junior/senior was 14%. While the underclassmen's rankings were like the complete rankings, the upperclassmen's percentages per rank were more like the total percentages per class.

The drop in percentage points in the category 'parents/adults and friends' were almost the same as the increase in percentage points in the category 'no one,' as categories are compared, from underclassmen to upperclassmen. Additionally, 15% of underclassmen sought feedback only from themselves, 45% from self and one group (friends or parents/adults), 40% from all groups. In comparison, 36% (over twice the percentage) of the upperclassmen sought feedback only from themselves, 46% (the same percentage) from self and one group, 18% (less than half the percentage) from all groups. (This suggests a shift in dependencies for feedback from 'everyone available' (self, friends, parents, and adults) for underclassmen towards increasing dependence on self for upperclassmen. Further research to determine if this shift from 'everyone' and towards 'no one' (self) continues into young adulthood and beyond, as well as whether the dependency on 'everyone' increases down into childhood, is needed before present data differences could be considered trends.

The data relating to the agreement on WIDP accuracy between subjects and the persons who were shown the profiles raises more questions than it answers. It is important to mention that the accuracy ratings were self-reported by the subjects; no independent checks were made with the parents, adults, or friends who also looked at the profiles.

In the measures of central tendency and variability tables, subjects' means were only higher than parents/adults' means once out of three times. Parents/adults' means were higher than subjects' means for all profiles and the group of profiles rated exclusively by subjects and parents/adults. This group of profiles was unique in that the means for both subjects and parents/adults were the highest in the whole study. It could also be because the profiles for these subjects were exceptionally accurate. Also, these subjects knew themselves and were known so well by their parents/adults that the match between profiles and subjects were recognized. Alternatively, these subjects and parents/adults could have a relationship where another or both parties strongly influence one party to think similarly, or the interaction between subjects and parents/adults particularly increased subjects' accuracy perception. The evaluation with such a small group cautions against anything more than possible implications.

Another unique profile group was those subjects who did not share their results with anyone else. In contrast to the subjects who showed their results only to parents/ adults, the 'no one' else subjects had the lowest subjects' mean for profile accuracy. Also, this could be because the profiles for these subjects were especially inaccurate. Alternatively, it could be that these subjects did not know themselves as well as other subject groups, and did not recognize the match between their profiles, or it could be that a lack of interaction with at least one other person about the profile somehow lowered accuracy perception.

The changes in the subjects' means depending on which co-raters they shared their information with raises the possibility that there is a relationship between the subjects' perceived accuracy of their profiles and to whom they showed their profiles. The two profile groups that included parents/adults as co-raters (Tables 6 & 8) yielded the highest and virtually identical subject means for accuracy. The friends' highest mean was in the group that included parents/adults, as seen in (Table 6). However, the subjects' means in each group differed by only .1 in mean value. The parents/adults' mean in Table 8 (6.5) was almost exactly as much *higher* than the subjects' mean that it was *lower* than the subjects' mean in Table 6 (5.5). Therefore, it appears that if a relationship does exist, it may be the experience of feedback (albeit positive in both cases) from parents/adults who supported the high and consistent subject means rather than the actual levels of parents/ adults' profile agreement.

The two profile groups that included friends as co-raters (Tables 6 & 7) yielded the second highest subjects' mean (5.9) in the group that also included parents and the next to lowest subjects' mean (4.9) in the group that included only subjects and friends. Friends' means, were not only less than the subjects' means but also consistently the lowest in every group in which they appeared. While peer dependency is often considered a fact of teenage life, it is worth noting that subjects' means were always higher than friends' means. The subjects' and friends' feedback group (Table 7) did coincide with a higher subjects' means than for subjects who sought no comments. However, the consistently higher subjects' means could indicate that friends either did not know the subjects, as well as subjects, knew themselves or that their friends did not take a firm stance on the profile information. From lowest to highest, the means for subjects ranked:

**4.4** - subjects only, Table 9;
**4.9** - subjects and friends, Table 7;
**5.1** - all profiles and raters, Table 5;
**5.4** - all profiles rated by subjects and others, Table 10;
**5.9** - profiles rated by subjects, parents/adults, and friends;
**6** - profiles calculated by subjects and parents.

The increase in the subjects' mean for profiles rated only by subjects and at least one other person was one full mean point. Similarly, the increase in subjects' mean for profiles rated by subjects and friends and those rated by subjects, parents/adults, and friends, was also one full mean point. If a relationship does exist between the experience of feedback and increased subject means; all feedback may contribute to an increase of the means of issue and parents/adults' feedback may mainly contribute to an increase of the means an issue.

The noticeable differences in the subjects' means invite speculation as to how they chose co-raters. Were their choices made because of their temperaments being extroverted or introverted, self-reliant or dependent? Alternatively, is it because they thought the profile was very accurate and they did not want to reveal parts of themselves to others? Alternatively, maybe they were too unimpressed with the information to bother. Alternatively, perhaps their relationships with friends and parents/adults were strained or friendly, or were there special personal circumstances that either discouraged or encouraged them to share information; had they just outgrown the need for a significant amount of feedback or did they still desire as much input as possible? Subjects' choices and no doubt the results of this study would have been affected by testing at a different time of year under different circumstances.

*Conclusion*

An additional study would be necessary to attempt to meet the goals of this research project, indeed. A larger and more representative sample of the high school students in this area, including sex-linked response comparisons, the development of a reliable and valid measurement tool, independent checks, and attention to ruling out confounding variable issues around consent forms and schedules might result in more accurate and well-rounded information. After a revised administration of this study, it would be essential to contrast these results with similar studies of persons older and younger than high school age.

*References*

Akers, A.F., & Jones, R.M., & Coyl, D.D. (1998). Adolescent Friendship Pairs: Similarities in Identity Status Development, Behaviors, Attitudes, and Intentions. Journal of Adolescent Research, 13, 178–201.

Bates, J.E., Dodge, K.A., Pettit, G.S. & Ridge, B. (1998). Interaction of Temperamental Resistance to Control and Restrictive Parenting in the Development of Externalizing Behavior. Developmental Psychology, 34, 982–995.

Giordano, P.C., Cernkovich, S.A., Groat, H.T., Pugh, M.D., & Swinford, S.P. (1998). The Quality of Adolescent Friendships: Long Term Effects? Journal of Health and Social Behavior, 39, 55–71.

Greenberger, E., Chuansheng, C., Beam, M. (1998). The Role of "Very Important" Nonparental Adults in Adolescent Development. Journal of Youth and Adolescence, 27, 321–343.

Katainen, S., Raikkonen, K., Keskivaara, P.& Keltikangas-Jarvinen, L. (1999). Maternal Child-Rearing Attitudes and Role Satisfaction and Children's Temperament as Antecedents of Adolescent Depressive Tendencies: Follow-up Study of 6- to 15-year olds. Journal of Youth and Adolescence, 28, 139–163.

Kerpelman, J.L., Pittman, J.F., Lamke, L.K. (1997). Toward a Microprocessor Perspective on Adolescent Identity Development: An Identity Control Theory Approach. Journal of Adolescent Research, 12, 325–346.

O'Koon, J., (1997). Attachment to Parents and Peers in Late Adolescence and Their Relationship with Self-Image. Adolescence, 32, 471–482.

Stice, E. & Gonzales, N. (1998). Adolescent Temperament Moderates the Relation of Parenting to Antisocial Behavior and Substance Use. Journal of Adolescent Research, 13, 5-31.

Van Beest, M., Baerveldt, C. (1999). The Relationship between Adolescents' Social Support from Parents and Peers. Adolescence, 34, 193–201.

Vondracek, F., Silbereisen, R., Reitzle, M., Wiesner, M. (1999). Vocational Preferences of Early Adolescents: Their Development in Social Context. Journal of Adolescent Research, 14, 267–288.

Wilson, J.D., & MacGillivray, M.S. (1998). Self-Perceived Influences of Family, Friends, and Media on Adolescent Clothing Choice. Family and Consumer Sciences Research Journal, 26, 425–443.

Worley, Ph.D., John W. (1998). Psychometric Evaluation Results.

# Appendix II

## Statistical Analyses of the Survey Data

### (Form A)

### PROJECT PARTICIPATION SLIP

Dear Parent,

The high school students at DCA will be participating in a research project to determine the benefits of **Worley's ID Profile (WIDP)** to high school students. As part of this study, each student will be given a questionnaire as to how he/she presently assumes leadership, makes friends302 and interacts socially. This information will generate a personal temperament profile for your child that he/she may keep. Also, a brief temperament preassessment questionnaire and a follow-up questionnaire about the accuracy and usefulness of the profile will be given to each student. This information will be used to help determine the most beneficial time to assess students with the **WIDP**.

## WHAT IS WIDP?

**Worley's ID Profile** provides a comprehensive assessment of needs, desires, and interpersonal behaviors in three significant areas of life: social, leadership, and relationship. This temperament assessment is drawn from the individual's responses to the 60-item **Worley's ID Profile** questionnaire. The **Profile** is a psychometrically approved questionnaire and based on the premise that social, leadership, and relationship scores can assist in understanding and predicting a person's behavior.

Dr. Worley defines temperament as a person's God-given (Ps. 139:13–15) subjective self—an individual's unique desires, needs, and ways of relating to the world—and identifies five basic temperaments: Introverted Sanguine, Sanguine, Phlegmatic, Melancholy, and Choleric. Dr. Worley believes that temperament and personality are **not** the same personality is the 'mask' that an individual present to society, often including aspects of one's temperament, but only the elements are chosen to show. Worley's ID Profile gives a detailed summary of an individual's three major life areas: social, leadership, and relationship.

1. **SOCIAL PROFILE:** General social/work orientation

   The social profile identifies the individual's needs and desires for socialization, work/school associations, and other superficial relationships. Requirements in this area may range from demonstrating and desiring minimal socialization, to demonstrating and desiring constant socialization. The social profile helps answer the question: **Who is in or out of relationships with this individual?**

2. **LEADERSHIP PROFILE:** Independence/leadership needs

   The leadership profile identifies the individual's needs and desires for influencing others, making decisions and assuming responsibilities. Requirements in this area may range from independence to dependence. The leadership profile helps answer the question: **Who maintains the power and makes decisions in relationships with this individual?**

3. **RELATIONSHIP PROFILE:** Emotional involvement in close relationships

The relationship profile identifies the individual's needs and desires in intimate relationships with family and friends. Needs may range from emotional relationships and expressions of love with many people to isolation from loving relationships. The Relationship profiles helps answer the question: **How emotionally open or closed to the relationship is this individual?**

**Worley's ID Profile** defines these varying needs and desires, not as **"right"** or **"wrong,"** but only as individual differences and preferences. If a person's life situation differs dramatically from his/her needs and desires in one or more areas, he/she is likely to be experiencing stress, conflict, and anxiety in relationships. The **WIDP** does **not** measure intelligence, ability, maturity, or identify mental disorders. Additionally, it is not designed to 'change' people. Rather, the positive contributions of each's temperaments are emphasized, and possible limitations will be stated in a nonjudgmental manner. Any of these potential barriers can be overcome provided the person is willing and can learn the required new skills.

**Worley's ID Profile** assumes that any individual can use a temperament style, introversion or extroversion, to meet the requirements of any role or situation (Eph. 2:10). Still, each person will find some behaviors easy to use and others very uncomfortable. The interpretive reports are intended to provide enough information about a person to enable them to make informed choices about personal and professional development.

*PERMISSION SLIP*

I give my child, _____, permission to be included in the WIDP project.

Parent signature _____ Date _____

## (Form B)

### WIDP - Preassessment

**Name** _____ **Grade** _____

**School** _____ **Gender F___ M___**

## Here is a list of some temperament characteristics—circle as many as you think to describe the 'real you':

| | | | | |
|---|---|---|---|---|
| People-oriented | Angry | Diligent | Loving | Determined |
| Supportive | Loyal | Dependent | Sensitive | Manipulative |
| Indecisive | Introverted | Enthusiastic | Responsive | Talkative |
| Extroverted | Creative | Sympathetic | Emotional | Disorganized |
| Exaggerates | Decisive | Controlling | Humorous | Fun-loving |
| Unemotional | Friendly | Objective | Diplomatic | Practical |
| Dependable | Easygoing | Procrastinate | Frugal | Stubborn |
| Dislike change | Moody | Perfectionist | Organized | Analytical |
| Self-sacrificing | Negative | Critical | Independent | Productive |
| Inspiring | Kind | Strong Willed | Adventurous | Impulsive |
| Holds grudges | Calm | Sarcastic | Demanding | Gentle |

### Please do not write below this line

**Social:** _____     **Temperament:** _____

**Leadership:** _____     **Temperament:** _____

**Relationship:** _____     **Temperament:** _____

## (Form C)

## WIDP Questionnaire

## (Form D)

# WIDP Results

Dear Student,

Thank you *very* much for taking the time to fill out the WIDP questionnaire. Dr. Worley and I hope that the information in this profile is helpful to you. We appreciate your participation in this research project and highly value your feedback about this assessment. You will have the opportunity to give your reactions and suggestions in a follow-up survey in about a week.

On occasion, a person does not agree with their profile results. Dr. Worley offers three explanations:

1.    You may not have answered the questions based on your legitimate inner needs and desires. Instead, you might have responded to the questions with the viewpoint of "whom I think I should be" or "how I should answer."

2.    You might be the exact temperament the WIDP report indicates, but you may have been molded to act and respond in ways different than your temperament.

3.    You may have matured in areas so that your behavior is different in some respects from your temperaments.

Whether you, agree or disagree, with your profile results, getting some feedback about this report is recommended. People who know you well, and care enough to be honest with you, such as parents, other relatives, and close friends, are good choices for additional discussion about your profile. Remember—ALL temperaments bring significant strengths to life; you have a unique opportunity to impact your world in an unusual and meaningful way!

## (Form E)

### WIDP—Follow-Up

**Name** _____

**Grade** _____

**School** _____

**Gender    F ____   M ____**

**Please put an X in front of each answer.**

1. **How well did your pre-assessment temperament choices match your WIDP?**

   Social:        ____ not much ____ somewhat ____ a lot ____ most or all
   Leadership:    ____ not much ____ somewhat ____ a lot ____ most or all
   Relationship:  ____ not much ____ somewhat ____ a lot ____ most or all

2. **How much do you agree with your WIDP?**

   Social:        ____ not much ____ somewhat ____ a lot ____ most or all
   Leadership:    ____ not much ____ somewhat ____ a lot ____ most or all
   Relationship:  ____ not much ____ somewhat ____ a lot ____ most or all

3. **What other people did you show your WIDP results to and what did they think? Check all that apply.**

   ____ No one
   ____ Mother       ____ agreed     ____ disagreed
   ____ Father       ____ agreed     ____ disagreed
   ____ Best friend  ____ agreed     ____ disagreed
   ____ Friend       ____ agreed     ____ disagreed
   ____ Sibling      ____ agreed     ____ disagreed
   ____ Relative     ____ agreed     ____ disagreed
   ____ _____     ____ agreed     ____ disagreed
   ____ _____     ____ agreed     ____ disagreed

4. **What section of the profile results was the most helpful to you? The least?**

   **Most:**                    **Least:**
   ____ Social                  ____ Social
   ____ Leadership              ____ Leadership
   ____ Relationship            ____ Relationship

5.   **In what ways do you think your WIDP will be helpful to you? Check _all_ that apply.**

_____ Understanding myself
_____ Understanding other people
_____ Other people understanding me
_____ Job/career choices
_____ Choosing classes/course of study
_____ Relationships with people at school/work/social contacts
_____ Relationships with close friends and relatives
_____ Leadership and decision-making style and preferences
_____ Solving problems
_____ Conflict resolution
_____ Other: _____

6.   **At what times do you think the WIDP would be helpful? Check _all_ that apply.**

_____ In elementary school
_____ Start of junior high/middle school
_____ End of junior high/middle school
_____ Start of high school
_____ End of high school
_____ Start of school after high school
_____ Start of job/career
_____ While engaged to be married
_____ At no time
_____ Other: _____

7.   **What did you like about WIDP?**

8.   **What didn't you like about WIDP?**

9.   **Would you like to have a WIDP Seminar at school on how to use your WIDP results in relationships, career decisions?**

_____ Yes _____ No

## (Form E Modified)
### WIDP—Follow-Up

**Name** _____ **Grade** _____

**School** _____ **Gender F___ M___**

**Please put an X in front of each answer.**

1. **How well did your preassessment temperament choices match your WIDP?**

   Social: ____ not much ____ somewhat ____ a lot
   Leadership: ____ not much ____ somewhat ____ a lot
   Relationship: ____ not much ____ somewhat ____ a lot

2. **How much do you agree with your WIDP?**

   Social: ____ not much ____ somewhat ____ a lot
   Leadership: ____ not much ____ somewhat ____ a lot
   Relationship: ____ not much ____ somewhat ____ a lot

3. **What other people did you show your WIDP results to and how much did they agree with your WIDP? Check _all_ that apply.**

   ____ No one
   ____ Mother ____ not much ____ somewhat ____ a lot
   ____ Father ____ not much ____ somewhat ____ a lot
   ____ Best friend ____ not much ____ somewhat ____ a lot
   ____ Friend ____ not much ____ somewhat ____ a lot
   ____ Sibling ____ not much ____ somewhat ____ a lot
   ____ Relative ____ not much ____ somewhat ____ a lot
   ____ _____ ____ not much ____ somewhat ____ a lot
   ____ _____ ____ not much ____ somewhat ____ a lot

4. **What section of the profile results were the most helpful to you? The least?**

   **Most:**                    **Least:**
   ____ Social                  ____ Social
   ____ Leadership              ____ Leadership
   ____ Relationship            ____ Relationship

5. **In what ways do you think your WIDP will be helpful to you? Check _all_ that apply.**

   ____ Understanding myself
   ____ Understanding other people

_____ Other people understanding me
_____ Job/career choices
_____ Choosing classes/course of study
_____ Relationships with people at school/work/social contacts
_____ Relationships with close friends and relatives
_____ Leadership and decision-making style and preferences
_____ Solving problems
_____ Conflict resolution
_____ Other: _____

6. **At what times do you think the WIDP would be helpful? Check _all_ that apply.**

_____ In elementary school
_____ Start of junior high/middle school
_____ End of junior high/middle school
_____ Start of high school
_____ End of high school
_____ Start of school after high school
_____ Start of job/career
_____ While engaged to be married
_____ At no time
_____ Other: _____

7. **What did you like about WIDP?**

8. **What didn't you like about WIDP?**

9. **Would you like to have a school seminar have a WIDP Seminar in your school on how to use your WIDP results in relationships, career decisions?**

_____ Yes _____ No

# CHAPTER 21

# WIDP TESTIMONIES

To whom it may concern,

I've had the pleasure of knowing and working with Dr. John Worley for almost nine years. During those times, Dr. Worley helped me with numerous assignments and has also helped several of my friends and business associates with their personal – business issues. He has time and again helped me to resolve crucial business and personal matters. These include discussions relating to my creating and leading three national companies to address organizational issues to personal growth issues. John's advice and support have been precious to me.

My early involvement with John included his development of several of my senior staff - from an "Executive Coaching" capacity. He excelled in that task. Later, he was engaged to conduct organizational development activities, spending time with each senior leader and doing the remarkable Worley ID Profile assessment system and debriefing each. That assignment challenged the company management to better understand each person's natural temperament, which later facilitated team building and improved communications. As an HR advisor, John is a precious resource.

I have sought John's advice many times over the years to help me sort out and resolve personal, family and business challenges. I have never been disappointed with John's support, advice, or direction. Further, I find John to be quite direct and to the point. That is a refreshing change from most HR or counselor types who seem to like to create "dependent" relationships. (Those where you always need to spend more time & money before a direction is finalized).

John has my unqualified endorsement for anyone needing an executive coach or strategic advisor. On a personal level, I find John to be one of the most brilliant, insightful, and personable and compassionate people that I know.

Sincerely,

Greg Wing
President
Bedford Capital Corp.

As President of an information technology consulting company, I have found Worley's ID Profile to be a valuable Human Resource assessment tool used to identify individual strengths and providing critical input to successful team building. Worley's ID Profile, combined with the expertise of working one-on-one with the companies' highly trained staff, has provided greater personal insight and enabled personal improvements. The results are higher productivity and improved business and personal relationships. I highly recommend engaging Worley's ID Profile for personal growth, corporate management coaching, and team building initiatives.

*Stephen Engman*
*President*
*ITC Consulting Group, LLC*

---

Time and again, I've witnessed WIDP's unique power, speed, and efficacy to improve business performance using WIDP coaching services substantially. When executives adopt it as their primary focus for executive development, or as a standard for their HR Management and HR related problem solving, they will experience impressionable results. Worley's ID Profile, Inc., is true to its commitment, delivers excellent executive coaching, whether one-on-one or in workshops, and I'm delighted to represent it in Brazil.

*Vera Cristina Fonseca*
*Director, Human Resources*
*Stratus*
*Rio de Janeiro, Brazil*

---

Having spent many years working with Personality Assessment tools such as the MBTI, DiSC, & FIRO-B, I was just amazed at the powerful and all-encompassing results provided by with WIDP. Within minutes, WIDP provided me with an individual's basic needs, desires & motivations in three key life areas. It also offered in-depth sight into the persons Desired and Demonstrated Behaviors. Having applied this Temperament Assessment tool for many years now, I find myself in awe of its essential application value during Hiring, Team Building, Conflict Resolution, Position Strengthening, Leadership Development, and Individual Enrichment. It has helped my various teams understand the true meaning of Diversity, as this tool provides a strong message of Acceptance, Inclusion, and Tolerance. Finally, for the individuals who are assessed, resounding results are achieved time and again.

*Mario di Girolamo*
*Medical Services Operations Manager*

---

Regardless if one hires, manages, coaches or commands, WIDP is the ultimate tool which ensures complete temperament assessment of potentially new, or existing, personnel. WIDP allows an organization to put their people in the proper roles to maximize efficiency, production, and management. I know of no other tool which delivers such consistent, accurate analysis of the human psyche.

*Peter Dunnington*
*OSP Fios Engineering*
*Project Manager*

---

*After being unemployed 14 months, I signed up with a career coach to help me shift to new professional status, and it is a career decision that has propelled me further than I could have imagined. He has evaluated me through a unique personal discovery profile and is coaching me on how to unify my personalities with my new career. If anyone wants help transitioning to a new career (or to a new job), please let me know, and I can give you more information. He is indeed a unique and gifted coach that also provides professional coaching services to all levels of executives.*

Peter Thompson
Real Estate Broker

---

Worley's ID Profile has helped us recognize our temperament as well as their strengths and potential weaknesses. This WIDP Profile has proved to be of great value to our family as well as our venture as new business owners. Once we correctly perceived our temperaments, then the solutions to life issues were tackled positively. My family has taken the WIDP Profile, and a better understanding of each other has ensued. The basic seminar has taught us how to recognize and deal with different temperaments healthily.

As future business owners, our employees will be taking the WIDP Profile. I know that this will help us recognize the motivations, needs of our employees as well as real management of them.

Thanks, John & Barbara for the kind words and support during a crucial time in our lives.

Dennis & Rebecca Michaud
Franchise Owners
Drama Kids of Merrimack Valley

---

You are in our prayers. Thanks for praying for us. I'm excited about your meeting in St. Louis. I pray God will open huge doors for you and John. The Worley ID Profile is, in my opinion – pure genius – share it with the world.

Its fun building His kingdom together.

Jim Charron
Executive Director of Sharing Way
Atlanta, GA

---

I have been a WIDP Representative since attending Dr. Worley's WIDP Training Seminar in 1997. I have been using WIDP in my Christian Counseling practice since that time. I consider it an indispensable tool in assisting individuals, couples, families, and congregations. It is the most effective and detailed profile I have found in over 20 years of ministry. I highly recommend WIDP!

Don C. Stevens, L.P.C.
Burton, Texas

---

Dr. John Wayne Worley is my friend. He lovingly helped me to go through and successfully deal with one of the worst crises in my life. The incident happened about two decades ago when I lived and worked in the U.S. in an official assignment for the Brazilian Government. I do not exaggerate when I say that his support was paramount for my family and me at that moment, and, for those who share my worldview and my faith, that coming to know him was indeed a gift from God.

At center stage of his praxis was his fantastic psychological self-discovery tool, Worley's Identity Discovery Profile, which very rapidly and precisely pinpointed my temperamental traits that contributed so markedly for the condition that led me to seek for his professional counsel, as well as potential and actual aspects of my family's interpersonal dynamics that demanded improvement.

Dr. Worley is my friend. I miss the long conversations we had in his beautiful office and the wisdom contained in his specific recommendations.

I wish you the very best, Doc. May your book reach and dramatically improve the lives of every human being in need of WIDP, the same way it did for me.

Jurandyr de Souza Fonseca, M.Sc., Colonel Aviator (Retired)
Brazilian Air Force

---

Worley's Identity Discovery Profile was a life-changer for our family. My father assessed me when I was 12 and found out that we were both natural born leaders. He immediately knew how to speak with me in a way that saved our relationship, one that continues to flourish to this day. Several years ago, I started my own Behavioral Consulting business that uses the WIDP as a fundamental tool to have conversations and resolve/prevent conflict in every environment. Knowing that organizations, churches, orphanages, families, and relationships, to name a few, are all merely the people within them, the WIDP allows a person to enter into any conversation or situation on a shared understanding and to love each other as each needs to be enjoyed. It was this tool that allowed me to see that God's design for me is intentional for the work He has for me to do. This instrument will enable me to point others to their calling and to hear God's voice in their life, experiencing His will being carried out on each one's unique design! It is vital that we understand God's intention and see others through His eyes, and that's what the WIDP reveals! What a powerful tool to help get our needs met and meet the needs of others in love and humility!

**Sam Stevens**
**Owner/Founder**
**Humble Pie Solutions**
*Giving Over Gain!*

A testimony to the Worley's ID Profile. Dr. Worley and I grew up in the same small town in Southeastern, OH. I have known him all his life. Our families are close friends.

I have had a profile done by Humm and Worley ID. Both were very thorough. Worley's the most recent. WIDP is a straightforward profile to take. The research provides many results to us or for our employees. It covers Social, Leadership, and Relationship also includes personal needs and desires, and more. I worked at an Alloy Corporation for 22 years from the Furnace Department to Personnel Director of over 1,200 employees Union and Non-union. Also, I took and administered the Humm/Woodworth Profile. The WIDP gives a thorough profile of who, what, and why we are who we are. May be of some help to you if considered. I was owner/operator of several family restaurants-catering for 34 years with 49 employees. Wish I would have had this WIDP Profile then. The profile will help you to understand yourself or an employee. An excellent asset to any company to realize who, what, and why we are who we are as an individual. The superb advantage when using this profile, you will benefit tremendously personally and professionally.

**Lewis Charles Burckholter**
**Papa Chucks Restaurant**
**Owner**

---

John W. Worley, Ph. D. introduced me to the WIDP evaluation tool many years ago to assist me in my pastoral counseling responsibilities. As a Licensed Clinical Pastoral Counselor with Advanced Certification, I am always looking to improve my evaluation tools. I started by taking the assessment myself to determine how comprehensive the WIDP would be in helping the counselee to have a better understanding of their strengths and weaknesses. I was amazed at how accurately it described my essential traits and where weaknesses could be turned to powers when you let God take control.

I began using the WIDP with all my counselees and repeatedly heard from them, "How can this short test know so much about me." With God's help and a willingness to work on making the changes needed to improve their lives through the insights of the WIDP and other assessments, lives were transformed into being productive.

Thank you, Dr. John W. Worley, for helping me to be a better counselor through WIDP assessment. I would recommend the WIDP evaluation tool to all who want to improve their counseling skills.

Arthur E Burke Ph. D.

---

One day, my father, Dr. John W. Worley decided to give the whole family an assessment. Once all the members had taken the test, I had a chance to go over the new data Daddy had printed out about me. He embraced me in a big hug and said, **"Oh honey, I wasn't aware of how different you are from the rest of the family, and I will do my best to be sensitive to your needs."**

That day changed my life. Growing up in a household of strong temperaments, I learned about who I was and how it's OK to be me and to wait for the right timing to approach others in the family. Years later and now have a family of my own, we have all taken the profile and studied ourselves, and each other and live in unity, acceptance, and understanding of who each of us is deep down inside. My relationship with my husband is stable and secure, and we live daily with the knowledge of each other based on our temperaments. We appreciate and respect each other and give each other space and consideration when approaching delicate subjects.

I can easily see when outside of our home when other people misunderstand each other based on their different temperaments, and it saddens me. Everyone should understand who they are and how they can be the best version of themselves, and that can only be thru the application of WIDP.

Sincerely, the third John W. Worley daughter.

Melaney Michelle Worley Fodera
Lynnfield, MA

---

Hi.

So, I must share this with you.

I had a conversation with the director of my program today that left me feeling unsettled and a little depreciated.

I sat and thought about it for a while, and then thought about the WIDP results that talked about my tendencies to let things fester rather than relying on more direct communication.

So, when next we spoke, I said, hey, can we chat for a moment about our last conversation?

And we had a good, honest back and forth about it. Tensions were eased, and work continued more productively.

Thanks! I'm a believer.

June
June Peoples Mallon

---

I have personally known Dr. Worley, for close to 20 years. I have found him to be a man of integrity, one who is highly qualified, and one who cares genuinely for people.

His expertise in counseling, coaching, and training along with his patience and a willingness to work with people, has had an extraordinary impact on my life and the life of many others that I am personally aware.

I have used **WIDP** in a variety of settings, as a Pastor in Counseling Pre-marriage sessions and post marriage conflicts, I have also used WIDP in a professional business context, resolving Personnel issues. In addition to a host of personal development scenarios. I have found this instrument to be precise in its detail and extraordinarily useful on every occasion.

I highly recommend it

**Pastor Ken Reed, Radio Host**
**New Covenant Perspectives and**
**co-Pastor of New Creation Christian Church**
**Worcester, MA**

WIDP has made a profound impact on my life, personally and professionally. I have used other assessment tools in psychometrics before, but none of them created as linear of a baseline and dimensional understanding of the human temperament as WIDP.

On a personal level, my level of self-understanding became more in-depth, more granular, thereby helping me to be able to explain who I am to those I am in a relationship.

Conversely, can understand those closest to me better than ever before.

On a professional level, my team building skillset has become more highly advanced through the use of WIDP. Employee coaching, conflict resolution, and task assignment have all become more efficient.

People can have a more accurate picture of who they were created to be and enjoy much fuller relationships through the greater understanding of the human expression that WIDP affords.

In the 25 years I have known John Worley, his teaching, along with WIDP, have forever changed and enhanced my life. But not only mine but also the countless people who have been mentored using WIDP through my life professionally and in ministry. Each coaching session and seminar using WIDP have always brought the same reaction, uplift, and enlightenment. And for that, we are all forever grateful.

**Richard Henry**
**Pastor and Entrepreneur**

---

WIDP is such a valuable tool for a multitude of audiences. Both professional, family, and social atmospheres will benefit from a device that is designed to assess the temperament of individuals. While often differences in personalities can cause disagreements and misunderstandings, knowing the causes of behaviors and reactions can eliminate these misunderstandings. For example, while we might tag an individual as being a controlling personality, the WIDP might show us that this person isn't trying to control others but merely trying to make their world function appropriately. In understanding the human psyches better, we can be at peace and more successful in our daily endeavors.

The WIDP is an asset for the family and businesses as it teaches about individual differences. Whether it's a marriage, parent/child relationship, or professional relationship, WIDP assesses needs, desires in a way that is constructive and useful to the often very dynamic functions of a family workforce. The WIDP is also the perfect length, it is fast enough to answer promptly and thorough enough to come up with an accurate conclusion. I highly recommended this valuable tool for anyone who wants to improve their positions in life.

Charles J DiMatteo, Jr., CPA

ACTS Inc.
A NON-PROFIT COMMUNITY ACTION ORGANIZATION
ELIZABETH DORRIS PRESIDENT | LIBBYDORRIS19@GMAIL.COM

Endorsement John W. Worley, Ph.D., WIDP

**To Whom It May Concern:**

I have known John Worley in both a professional capacity and personal capacity for 30 plus years. I have used and will continue to use his brilliantly easy yet comprehensive Temperament Identity Profile (WIDP). It offers versatility like none other on the market today. It has proven timeless in its simplicity to pinpoint personal temperament identity, and hence their strengths and weaknesses.

I have a consulting business and found it useful when dealing with organization clients and their employee's interpersonal relationships as well as bringing clarity to individual's temperaments helping them to understand themselves and their strengths and weaknesses. I found that identifying the temperament of employees and co-workers optimizes productivity in the work environment as co-workers begin to understand each other and work better together and the human resource department can better manage personnel placement maximizing the best and highest use of their personnel.

In conclusion, WDIP is essential in all interpersonal interactions such as pre-marital counseling, marital counseling, group training seminars. WIDP is an asset in personal identity discovery and development, employment counseling, and family counseling.

Respectfully,
Elizabeth Dorris
President ACTS

---

There are lots of personality tests out there, but none compare to the accuracy and validity of WIDP. This tool has enabled me to live a more freeing lifestyle. Granting me the ability to understand myself and others on a deeper level; thus, increasing my interpersonal relationships and connection with them.

After taking the WIDP questionnaire and reviewing my profile with the help of my loving Grandfather; John W. Worley, I have learned SO much about myself. It has given me a sense of freedom and liberation from situations that I would shy away from before. Being an Introverted Sanguine Socially it can be hard putting yourself out there. However, once I understood my emotion, I was able to finally overcome these obstacles with a sense of confidence and reason.

In my opinion, WIDP is the key to understanding people and the psychology that drives every one of us.

Thank you so much, Dr. Worley, for not only helping me understand myself and others - but learning to live 'in the jet stream.'

**Joshua Fodera**
Consultant

Being a product of a broken home, I had a hard time identifying with anyone in my family, especially since half of my family was unknown to me. Once I got into the business world and introduced to different personality types through sales training seminars, I started to understand some but not all of who I was. These other personality profiles could not explain everything and would leave me confused in particular areas. It was not until I met Dr. John Worley and introduced to WIDP was I able to really understand temperaments and how God uniquely wired me. The Worley's Identity Discovery Profile explained everything about me in detail and was able to bring clarity to my life. Over the last four years of using this tool, I have been freed to be who I was always meant to be, and it has also given me the insight to understand others around me. Things that used to befuddle me in relationships now make perfect sense. I live and walk in a newfound understanding and freedom both personally and professionally.

**Dorothy Henry**
**LegalShield**
**ID Shield**
**Independent Associate**
**Executive Director**

# Frequently Asked Questions About WIDP

**What are the applications that Worley's ID Profile can be applied?**

Clinical
Corporate
Educational
Ministry
Family
Individual

**Has a psychometric evaluation been done on the WIDP?**

Yes!    The assessment and the results are very favorable in construct validity as well as reliability. A formal report is available upon request and can be a review of our website.

**Is there a comparison of the WIDP temperament profile to other similar instruments?**

Yes!    At the hyperlink, you will find several comparisons of other tools, such as the MBTI DiSC, PPS, FIRO-B, FIRO-B/C, TAP, T-JTA, and Temperament by LaHaye.

**Does Worley's ID Profile produce a mental diagnosis?**

No!    WIDP does not diagnose mental disorders but can determine if the individual is emotionally stable enough to complete the questionnaire accurately. The interpretive report will verify, whether, the person competently answered the question. Through clinical interpretation, the interpretative statement can be used as an assessment instrument for checking and balancing the validity of the results of the profile.

**Does Worley's ID Profile measure intelligence?**

No!　However, WIDP assesses the behavior modality of the individual, which does identify whether the person is analytical and or intellectual. If the person is systematic and rational, they would naturally have the potential to increase their intelligence.

**Does Worley's ID Profile measure one's ability?**

No!　WIDP does not measure one's ability but does assess and identify their needs and desires, which will complement their potential skills for learning new skills.

**Does Worley's ID Profile measure maturity?**

No!　WIDP does assess one's perception of self and their emotional orientation, which can determine how well they accept their temperament composition as well as the temperament structure of others. Therefore, WIDP does verify and identify one's competence to be untroubled with themselves and with others.

**Does Worley's ID Profile measure self-esteem?**

No!　WIDP does not evaluate self-esteem currently. However, there is factored data within the present questionnaires that will provide data for future research and development of a self-esteem section of the current interpretative report.

**Does Worley's ID Profile measure anger?**

No!　WIDP does not evaluate violence currently. However, there is factored data within the present questionnaires that will provide data for future research and development of a section on anger that will be available in a later version.

**Does Worley's ID Profile interface with the ICD 10 (International Classification of Diseases) or the DSM-V (Diagnostic and Statistical Manual of Mental Disorders-Version V)?**

No!

**Is Worley's ID Profile like the MBTI?**

No!　The MBTI is a scientific behavioral instrument that classifies individuals within one of sixteen categories of behavior. Worley's ID Profile is an objective and subjective temperament tool that reveals the individual's needs and desires in three areas: Social, Leadership, and Relationship. Further, it shows how the three sectors interface with each other. There are 55,488 possible combinations of the WIDP temperament profile.

**Does the program build a database of individuals profiled?**

Yes!　The Internet WIDP Software Program is fully automated and creates a database of profiled individuals that can be printed out, and the system will also print out index cards. Names in the database can be printed with any of the following items in print out:
First Name, Middle name, Last name,

Address 1
Address 2
City, State, Zip Code
Phone Number
Fax Number
Email Address
Sex
Birthday
Education
Race
Nationality
Profile Date
Profile Results and Profile Type (Adult or Youth—Age 6–16), and in your choice of languages of English, Spanish, or Portuguese.

You can choose which item you want in the printout in your Profile Summary.

**Can an individual be profiled more than once?**

Yes!    Each time you profile the person, the date profiled is on the information screen of that individual. Therefore, you highlight the previous time and year of their last profile you want to reprint, or you can enter the present date to reprofile for comparison of earlier patterns.

**Can the profile be taken "on the computer"?**

Yes!    Individuals can choose the adult or youth profile on the computer screen, or you can print a paper questionnaire for people to fill out and then enter their responses manually.

**How long does the questionnaire take to complete?**

Seven to ten (7–10) minutes!

**Can you skip questions and leave them blank?**

No!    Every question must be complete, or the profile is invalid.

WIDP interpretive reports based on sixty simple questions, which are answered on the computer software program or a printed questionnaire form for future entry into the computer. Individuals or groups of individuals preparing to complete WIDP questionnaire need instructions on the following guidelines before completing the questionnaire:

**WIDP Profile Questionnaire Instructions:**

-    Fill out the information at the top of the questionnaire sheet; name, address, email, and sex are required. Date of birth, education, and race are optional.
-    Please answer the questions carefully.

- **Do not analyze or compare** the items!
- Answer each question as though it is a standalone question.
- Your first response is the best response.

All questions must be answered, in the boxes or circles, legibly. It should take about seven to ten (7–10) minutes to answer all sixty (60) questions.

## Can it be used with an audience?

Yes! If the individuals have the intelligence and reasoning abilities to be able to understand the questions and respond appropriately. However, there may be cultural differences in the meaning of words, and this obviously would affect the results.

## Can an individual answer Worley's ID Profile questionnaire incorrectly?

Yes! There are two possibilities should one not agree with their profile.

1. Learned behavior. The person is the correct behavior as Worley's ID Profile report indicates, but they were **"tampered with"** or **"molded"** into someone else. The negative learned behavior would create a tremendous amount of stress, anxiety, unhappiness, and even anger in the individual's life.
2. The individual did not respond to the questions honestly. It is possible that they were answering the items from the premise of **"whom they think they should be"** and **"how they should answer."**

## FAQs ABOUT SOFTWARE TRAINING

### Can anyone access the Worley's ID Profile?

Yes! The WIDP Profile is available to everyone.

### Does the professional use Worley's ID Profile software program require formal training to use?

Yes! There are four different certification training programs available for those who desire an in-depth understanding of WIDP: certified individual, certified associates, certified affiliates, and certified affiliate manager.

- **Certified Individuals.** A certified person must have a background of high-level experience at stand-up platform speaking or training skills. Step one is to sign a confidential agreement, and participate in a two (2)-day certification training program sponsored by WIDP or an associate or affiliate. All certification activity shall be under the oversight of a WIDP representative. Certified individuals are responsible for the quality of WIDP related training conducted by authorized representatives for certified individual clients.
- **Certified Associates.** The certified associate is qualified to purchase the WIDP software and sell profiles. Associates are responsible for the person/organization that trained them. Associates will buy all products through the person or organization that taught them.

- **Certified Affiliate.** An affiliate must have a background of high-level selling experience, stand up speaking or training skills, and ideally, sales management experience. Step one is to sign a confidentiality agreement and participate in a three (3)-day certification training program sponsored by WIDP, or WIDP associate or affiliate. All affiliate and associate activities shall be under the umbrella of WIDP.
- Affiliate is responsible for the quality of WIDP-related work conducted by authorized representatives for affiliate clients. Each associate of an affiliate with access to the WIDP materials will be required to execute a confidentiality agreement.
- **Certified Affiliate Manager.** WIDP affiliate managers must have five (5) or more WIDP affiliates under their structure, own their WIDP software, and WIDP PowerPoint presentation, and conduct WIDP seminars, basic and advances, train new associates and affiliates under them, and they get reduced rates on profiles.
- All associates and affiliates are required to pay their annual renewal fee directly to WIDP.
- Anyone trained by WIDP will be under WIDP agreements and responsible for WIDP only.
- There are no provisions for "geographical or organizational protection," just because you have a client from Walmart within your geographical area does not give you exclusivity to all Walmart stores unless you have a contract with Walmart headquarters to provides services to all their Walmart stores.
- No WIDP associate or affiliate may transfer to another person's structure.

**Is there any category of persons not required to complete the certification training for clinical recognition?**

**Yes!**   There are three classes of people that are not obliged to complete the certification training. However, they can only be certified individuals. If these individuals want to be certified as associates or affiliates, they must complete the three-day certification training program.

The three exempt categories are:

1.   If you are a licensed professional counselor and have a current state license from the state you reside in, you are free from the certification training. The following category of licensure are exempt: psychiatrist, psychologist, mental health clinical counselor, marriage and family therapists, licensed social worker, licensed independent social worker, licensed pastoral counselors, and any individual holding active state licensure.
2.   If you hold a master's degree in psychology, counseling, or any related field and have completed graduate studies in psychometry or testing and measurements, you are exempt. Certified copy of the transcript required as proof of course completion.
3.   If registered as a C-level psychological instrument user with any of the original psychological publishing houses, i.e., Consulting Psychologists' Press (CPP), Western Psychological Institute (WPI), or other publishing houses, you are exempt from the certification training. Proof of registration is required.

**Are there training and seminar programs available to teach the process, theory, and application of Worley's ID Profile Software System?**

Yes! WIDP, Inc. provides training depending upon the needs of the end user. There are one-, two-, three-, and four-day workshops designed for individual, group, or organizations. Call for programs of training and financial quotes.

**Are there any credentials that I am required to obtain before I can be certified to use Worley's ID Profile Software System?**

No! You can become a certified individual, associate, or affiliate.

To successfully install and operate Worley's ID Profile (WIDP), you need:

- Microsoft Windows* compatible computer with minimum 640K memory.
- Microsoft Windows
- Hard disk drive with 10 MB of space available
- 4 MB RAM (8 MB recommended)
- Color or monochrome VGA monitor
- Attached printer
  * TM is a trademark of Microsoft Corporation

**Is there a size or model of printer required to print the profiles?**

No! The program will print on any printer. The speed of the printer will determine the print.

**Can the software be installed on more than one computer?**

Yes! However, you are required to register with Worley's ID Profile and purchase the program each time the application's installed on a new machine(s). Alternatively, you can buy the multiuser system that can accommodate unlimited stations at one time.

## FAQs ABOUT SOFTWARE

**Can profiles be taken on the Internet now?**

Yes! Visit our Internet site at www.WIDP.org and click on the black and white WIDP logo of the male and female, this will take yours directly to the WIDP questionnaire. Your profile can be returned to you electronically and will always be available to you in the future.

**What profiles does the WIDP program produce?**

Adult and youth (ages 6–16) profiles are available.

**What type of media does Worley's ID Profile software come on**

The software is provided in a PDF format as an attachment in an email and then executed on your computers.

**Will the software ever be available over the Internet?**

**Yes!**     WIDP is fully functional on the Internet.

**What is the difference between objective and subjective temperament?**

**Objective Temperament:**

Objective behavior is the behavior one displays depending upon the environment they find themselves in which is self-selected, also known as **"masking"** or **"personality."**

**Subjective Temperament:**

Subjective behavior, which Worley's ID Profile identifies, is the inborn or genetic temperament one has inherited from birth. The individual will always revert to and be more comfortable when they are functioning from their temperament style. Their temperament style is steady, stable, and consistent regardless of the environment.

**What temperament, psychological, behavioral, or personality classifications does Worley's ID Profile use?**

Worley's ID Profile uses the standard ratings of other instruments: Introverted Sanguine, Sanguine, Phlegmatic, Melancholy, and Choleric. The blends of the five temperaments are Introverted Sanguine Phlegmatic, Phlegmatic Introverted Sanguine, Sanguine Phlegmatic, Phlegmatic Sanguine, Melancholy Phlegmatic, Phlegmatic Melancholy, Choleric Phlegmatic, and the Phlegmatic Choleric. It is possible to have temperament blends in all three of your temperament's areas of; Social, Leadership, and Relationship.

Your identification in each of the three areas of social, leadership, and relationship is determined by where your temperament falls on a continuum of zero (0) introvert to nine (9) extrovert. Each of the three areas of social, leadership, and relationship evaluated in the two regions of demonstrated and desired behavior.

**What are the demonstrated score and desired score?**

In each of the three areas Social, leadership, and Relationships there is a linear bar graph representation like this:

**Demonstrated**

| 0 | 1 | 2 | 3 | 4 | 5 | 6 | 7 | 8 | 9 |
|---|---|---|---|---|---|---|---|---|---|
| 0 | 1 | 2 | 3 | 4 | 5 | 6 | 7 | 8 | 9 |

**Desired**

An individual's scores will be reflected twice in each of the three areas of; social, leadership, and relationships; one demonstrated score, and one desired score for each of the three regions. The demonstrated score indicates how the individual prefers to act toward other people. The desired score shows the persons preferred behavior from others toward them.

**Can Worley's ID Profile be used in non-English speaking countries?**

Yes!     If there is someone to interpret the questionnaire for them. There is a danger of losing the meaning of some words, and the results could be negatively affected, thus rendering unpredictable results.

**Will Worley's ID Profile be available in other languages?**

Yes!     The WIDP will be designed as various communication needs, and languages are identified. WIDP now is presently translated into English, Spanish, and Portuguese for the adult and youth (ages 6 -16). However, within time the WIDP Profile System will be available in most languages world-wide. Check the Internet for your current language needs. www.WIDP.org

**What do I do if I have problems with my software program?**

Worley's ID Profile software program has a built-in error log that records any errors that occur within the system. Once an error has occurred, we request that you print out the error log and send it to WIDP. We determine the failure and correct it or send you new software.

**How many profiles can I purchase at one time?**

As many as you would like prepaid! They come in lots of ten (10) profiles.

**Is the program copyrighted?**

Yes!     Worley's ID Profile software program was copyrighted in 1995 and registered with the Copyright Office in Washington, D.C.

**How many pages in the printer profile?**

The printed profiles are fifteen to eighteen pages in length.

**Are there different formats of the profile to be printed?**

Yes!     There are two, enhanced and unenhanced. The enhanced version has borders around each page plus new graphics. The unenhanced version has no boundaries on each page and fewer graphic borders. Both have a left-hand margin designed for putting the profile in a nice binder, spiral or three-hole, for presentation to the recipient.

## FAQs ABOUT ORDERING

**Can I purchase the training and profiles with a credit card?**

Yes!     We accept Pay Pal, Venmo, Cash App, Square, Cashier Checks, Visa, MasterCard, Discover, and American Express.

**Can I purchase the software with a personal or business check?**

Yes!     There is a five workday hold to ensure checks clear.

**Can I become a distributor of Worley's ID Profile?**

Yes! You would be required to complete at least associates' certification training and sign a nonexclusive independent contractor agreement. You would need to provide Worley's ID Profile with a description of your marketing experience and the audience you would be targeting along with the geographical territory you intended to focus on marketing. There are no private markets available.

**How often is the certification training offered?**

Please contact our office for the training schedule dates, locations, and fees.

**Where can I contact WIDP?**

Worley's ID Profile
190 Bishop Road
Fitchburg, MA 01420
info@WIDP.org

# REFERENCES AND ADDITIONAL READING

## BOOKS

- **An Introduction to Theories of Personality,** B.R. Hergenhahn. Prentice-Hall, New Jersey, 1990.

- **An Empirical Investigation of the Jungian Typology,** by Leon Gorlow, Norman R. Simonson, and Herbert Krauss. In Theories of Personality, Primary Sources, and Research, editors: Gardner Lindzey, Calvin S. Hall, Martin Manosevitz, Robert E. Krieger Publishing Company, Florida, 1988.

- **Dichotomies of the Mind: A System Science Model of the Mind and Personality,** Walter Lowen (with Lawrence Miike). John Wiley, 1982 ISBN 0471083313. A bizarre, but intriguing attempt to "correct" the MBTI's inherently 'F' focus to a 'hyper-T' perspective.

- **Facing Your Type,** George J. Schemel and James A. Borbely. Published by Typophile Press, Church Road, Box 223, Wernersville, PA 19565.

- **From Image to Likeness A Jungian Path in the Gospel Journey,** W. Harold Grant, Magdala Thompson, and Thomas E. Clarke. Paulist Press, 545 Island Road, Ramsey, NJ 07446. ISBN: 0809125528, 1983. This book deals with people's spiritual growth vis a vis personality type.

- **Gifts Differing,** Isabel BriggsMyers (with Peter Myers). Consulting Psychologists Press, 1980 ISBN 0891060111 (PB) 0891060154 (HB).

- **LifeTypes,** by Sandra Hirsh and Jean Kummerow, ISBN 0446388238 USA and ISBN 0446388246 Canada. Warner Books, Inc., 1989.

- **Manual: A Guide to the Development and Use of the Myers-Briggs Type Indicator,** by Isabel BriggsMyers and Mary H. McCaulley. Consulting Psychologists Press, 1985.

- **Please Understand Me, An Essay on Temperament Styles,** by David Keirsey and Marilyn Bates. Prometheus Nemesis Book Company, P.O. Box 2748, Del Mar, CA 92014 (6196321575). One of the more widely known books describing the Myers-Briggs Type Indicator. It includes a self-test (many do not consider it to be as good as the "real" MBTI test).

- **People Types and Tiger Stripes,** Gordon Lawrence. Available from Center for Application of Psychological Type, Gainesville, Florida. ISBN 0935652086. This book is written primarily to help teachers counsel students but is applicable for other related uses.

- **Portraits of Temperament,** David Keirsey. Prometheus Nemesis Book Company, P.O. Box 2748, Del Mar, CA 92014 (6196321575), 1987.

- **Prayer and Temperament,** by Michael and Morrisey. Other bibliographic information not known at present.

- **Personality Types and Religious leadership,** by Oswald and Kroeger. Available from the Alban Institute, 4125 Nebraska Ave NW, Washington, D.C., 20016. Phone 18004572674. Other bibliographic information not known at present.

- **Psychological Types,** C.G. Jung, H.G. Baynes (Translator). Bollingen Series, Princeton U.P., 1971 ISBN 0691018138 (PB) 0691097704 (HB). This book (originally written in the early 1920's) inspired Briggs & Myers to create the MBTI test. If you have only read, Please Understand Me, then you will have some trouble making the correlation.

- **The real Please Understand Me**, from the horse's mouth (i.e., the daughter in the original mother/daughter pair). A good bridge between Jung and PUM, but no self-test included.

- **Type Talk**, Otto Kroeger, and Janet M. Thuesen. Bantam Doubleday Dell Publishing Group, Inc. (Tilden Press also mentioned.) ISBN 03852982859. An easytoread a book that gives profiles for all sixteen personality types.

- **Type Talk at Work,** Otto Kroeger, and Janet M. Thuesen. ISBN 038530174X.

- **Type Watch,** Otto Kroeger, and Janet M. Thuesen.

- **The leadership Equation,** Lee Barr, and Norma Barr. Eakin Press, Austin, Texas. 1989.

- **The Measurement of Learning Style: A Critique of Four Assessment Tools,** Timothy J. Sewall, University of Wisconsin, 1986.

- **Using the Myers-Briggs Type Indicator in Organizations,** Sandra Krebs Hirsh. Consulting Psychological Press, Inc., Palo Alto, CA. 1985.

- **Working Together,** Olaf Isachsen and Linda Berens. New World Management Press, Coronado, CA. 1988.

# Periodical Literature

- **Journal of Psychological Type,** the official research journal of the Association for Psychological Type, 9140 Ward Parkway, Kansas City, MO 64114.

- **The Type Reporter,** Susan Scanlon, editor. For Subscription information, mail to 524 North Paxton Street, Alexandria, VA 22304. (703) 8233730. It comes out roughly eight times a year and costs $16 for a year's subscription. Recent topics include "Mistakes When Teaching Type," "Spending and Saving," and "Making Love."

- **Mental Measurements Yearbook (MMY).** Has lists of references to articles in peer-reviewed journals in which the MBTI test is used. Anthony DeVito gives an excellent review of MBTI in the 9th MMY, and two additional studies in the 10th MMY. The recently published 11th MMY does not include these. The MMY are available in the reference section of most college and university libraries.

# GLOSSARY OF TERMS

**Character**    Our family of origin, culture, and the environment in which we were raised, determines character. Our character is defined between the ages of, two to middle/late teens.

**Choleric**

The **Choleric** is quick to receive the information and process it. They devour the facts and are swift to conclude. Their fast action must not be confused with **"jumping to conclusions"** for they have handled the available data. This characteristic can cause other temperaments much agitation and frustration. If not carefully the Choleric merely overwhelm those around them.

### I.    Potential strengths of Choleric

A.    Very determined and strong-willed.
B.    Very independent.
C.    They are visionary and are adventurous to the point of leaving secure positions.
D.    Are practical and happiest when engaged in a worthwhile project.
E.    Are productive and will usually work circles around the other temperaments.
F.    Is decisive and can quickly appraise a situation and devise/determine solutions.
G.    Has strong leadership tendencies.

### II.    Potential weaknesses/shortcomings of the Choleric

A.    Usually cold and unemotional and the least affectionate.
B.    Very self-sufficient and independent.
C.    Is very impetuous, tends to start projects that he later regrets.
D.    Domineering.
E.    Is usually unforgiving and will carry a grudge forever.
F.    Can be very sarcastic, blunt, and cruel.
G.    Can be angry and cause pain to others and enjoy the experience.

## Demonstrated

Demonstrated is the temperament a person expresses toward others and is observable. The demonstrated score indicates how the individual prefers to act toward other people. This temperament can be observed and constitute the image presented to others. The demonstrated score in each area is the level of temperament the individual feels most comfortable using to:

| | |
|---|---|
| Get together with others | Demonstrated socializing |
| Have his/her way with others | Demonstrated leadership |
| Be close to others | Demonstrated relationship |

## Desired

Desired is the temperament that a person desires from others toward them. The desired score indicates the individual's preferred temperament from others toward him/her. It is an indicator of the individual's inner needs and desires which may differ significantly in from his/her public image. The desired temperament, in each area, is the temperament the person prefers others to use in their approach to:

| | |
|---|---|
| Get together with him/her | Desired socializing |
| Have their way with him/her | Desired leadership |
| Be close to him/her | Desired relationship |

## Extroverts

Extroverts are the outgoing, social people who enjoy being around people most of the times and have a need and desire to be with people frequently if not always.

## GAP

A GAP (Great Anxiety Present) is the theory of the distance between the demonstrated temperament score and the desired temperament score.

Always, be aware of the potential conflict with a profile G-A-P of four (4), or more, in any of the three profile areas.

The wider the G-A-P, the more anxious, intolerant, insensitive/sensitive, stressful, blunt, indifferent, cold, and driven the person will be.

Not only is this concept to be understood within your graph but also consider the G-A-P between yourself and others in each of the three areas of social, leadership, and relationship.

## ID

In simple terms, ID (**WIDP**) is the subjective side of human temperament, part of the person's original design at conception that is within us from birth and will remain constant throughout one's life.

ID The division of the psyche associated with instinctual impulses and the satisfaction of fundamental needs and desires.

## Individual

Is the person taking the questionnaire.

## Introvert

Introverted individuals are very rational people who need very little socialization, and spend most of their time thinking out issues.

## Introverted Sanguine Temperament

The **Introverted Sanguine** will process the facts and then not do anything with them unless others ask them. This temperament will also set about questioning those they trust to see if the information and situation are correct from their perspective. This inaction is entirely in line with the other aspects of the Introverted Sanguine. They are not dense in cognitive skills, just unable to initiate action.

### I. Potential strengths of the Introverted Sanguine.

A. Highly relational but must be personally invited.
B. The most naturally gentle and kind of all temperaments.
C. Have a real servant's heart.
D. Is a very diligent worker if praised or recognized.

### II. Potential weaknesses/shortcomings of the Introverted Sanguine.

A. Appears withdrawn, and downbeat, like introverts, yet desires to be an extrovert.
B. They are often alone, and isolated, because of own no assertiveness.
C. Is dependent on others to take care of them and to tell them what to do.
D. Becomes severely anxious when lack of recognition causes bitterness and resentments.
E. They are often depressed and are very sensitive to rejection.
F. Can be very manipulative and will use much indirect temperament. Will usually check out all counseling advice with someone else.

## Introvert/Extrovert

These people can function well in either environment as an introvert or extrovert.

## Leadership Profile

The leadership profile identifies the individual's needs and desires for influencing others, making decisions and assuming responsibilities. Needs may range from independence to dependence. The leadership profile helps answers the question: **Who maintains the power and makes decisions in relationships with this individual?**
**Leadership:** The next area of the temperament is called the **leadership profile.** Leadership deals precisely with what the title implies. How we control people and situations and how we allow individuals and conditions to control us is demonstrated in the area called leadership. It is the decision part of our temperament which dictates whether we will be a leader or a follower (in general) in our life. Depending on which temperament we are, leadership will dictate how we make decisions and who will be dominant in the relationships. The temperament needs in leadership can range from total dominance of an individual to being dominated by the other party in the connection.

**Melancholy Temperament:**

    The **Melancholy** needs time to detail the incoming facts. They will retreat into their private worlds and analyze the situation. After this assimilation time, they are ready to make up their mind and usually have a clear understanding of the situation.

### I.    Potential strengths of the Melancholy

A.    Usually very gifted—more so than any other temperament.

B.    Is very analytical and is a hound for detail.

C.    Is self-sacrificing and will work hard to meet deadlines will work around the clock.

D.    Extremely self-disciplined.

E.    A faithful friend and the most dependable of the temperaments.

F.    They have strong perfectionist tendencies.

G.    Is the most sensitive of all the temperaments.

### II.    Potential weaknesses/shortcomings of the Melancholy

A.    Tends to be moody, gloomy, and depressed.

B.    Are naturally the most self-centered of the temperaments.

C.    Is prone to pessimism, causing indecisiveness, for fear of being wrong.

D.    Melancholy is the most critical of temperaments.

E.    They are touchy, and thin-skinned, usually need to be handled with kid gloves and expect to be appreciated.

F.    Is generally unsociable and needs time to warm up to people.

G.    Is a negative person.

**Phlegmatic Temperament:**

    **Phlegmatic** will take their time and weigh it all out, dissect it, and ponder the situation. After scrutiny, it, they will make the necessary decisions and be quite capable of doing so. This process will be less lengthy than that required for the Melancholy.

### I.    Potential strengths of the Phlegmatic

A.    Is usually calm and quiet, rarely becomes agitated.

B.    Is easygoing—most likable of the temperaments.

C.    Phlegmatic are very consistent and dependable; is not prone to sudden change.

D.    Are usually objective, kindhearted, and sympathetic. Seldom conveys real feelings.

E.    Is usually humorous and enjoys a good joke.

F.    Efficient, organized, practical, and pragmatic.

G.    Are born diplomats.

## II. Potential weaknesses/shortcomings of the Phlegmatic

A. Phlegmatic often appears to be unmotivated.

B. Tends to procrastinate more than the other temperaments.

C. Has a strong tendency to be selfish, and few people know it without the ability to recognize the trait in self.

D. Usually the stingiest of the temperaments.

E. Tends to be the most stubborn of all temperaments; cannot change their mind (when unblended).

F. Is indecisive in many areas because of not wanting to become involved.

G. Has a fearful heart that keeps them from confrontation and decisions.

## Sanguine Temperament:

The **Sanguine** will not bother processing the information unless it is in simplified form. They cannot be bothered with that sort of activity no will their short attention span allow them the opportunity. They will be off to other people and situations quickly.

## I. Potential Strengths of the Sanguine.

A. Is outgoing and is a super extrovert.

B. Is responsive and likes to give hugs and handshakes.

C. Is warm and friendly and is a people person.

D. Is talkative and is a good conversationalist.

E. Is enthusiastic, and has no problems starting projects.

F. Is compassionate and cries easily.

## II. Potential weaknesses and shortcomings of the Sanguine.

A. Tends to be disciplined, to a fault.

B. More emotional than everyone else except the Melancholy.

C. Be very impractical, and disorganized.

D. Can become obnoxious, by dominating conversations.

E. Tend to exaggerate; Sanguine invented fish stories.

## Social Profile

The social profile identifies the individual's needs and desires for socialization, work, school, and other superficial relationships. The social profile helps answer the question, **Who is in or out of relationships with this individual?**

**Social Profile:** The first area of temperament is called social, or perhaps it would be easier to think of it as socialization. The social profile is the area which dictates how you will interact with the world in general, in those situations such as parties, career, neighbors, and other circumstances, which bring you into contact with people. The area of the social profile does not involve the deep, intense emotions of intimate relationships (these are in the area called relationship). The social profile deals with the surface relationships we encounter in our daily social situations. The temperament needs of the social profile can range from involvement with many people to relationship with only a few selected individuals.

Another aspect of the social profile is the cognitive or intellectual functions of the temperament. Why do we process the information we receive the way we do? Our temperament in the social profile is the answer to this question. Each temperament treats information in different ways. These are consistent with other aspects of each temperament.

## Personality

Personality is the self-selected mask that people present to others. The mask is what they want you to see and is not who they are. The personality changes with each environment. The circumstances, and who the audience is, will determine what personality the person wants to present.

## Profile: Corporations/Businesses

Corporations and business organizations; Worley's ID Profile is competitive in human resource ingenuity. The state-of-the-art software gives organizations the tools to bring the psychological temperament assessment of its corporate members into harmony with organizational missions, goals, and corporate visions.

WIDP has **_unlimited_** applications in a corporate setting. Corporations can realize the return on their investment within days. Corporate executives, human resource directors, training consultants, corporate advisors, and business management consultants, are profiting from the breakthrough benefits of WIDP.

## Profile: Professional Counselors

Worley's ID Profile software enables the counselors to quickly assess the individual's strengths and weaknesses, target potential conflicts, and develop sound therapeutic strategies for future counseling sessions. WIDP can help people achieve new levels of self-awareness, maximize their potential for fulfilled and balanced lives, and enjoy greater success in their interpersonal relationships.

## Profile: Educational Institutions

Educational Institutions: Worley's ID Profile software brings new meaning and perspective to all relationships founded in an educational setting. Immediate tangible strategies can be assessed (or available) for addressing dynamics of temperament differences. WIDP provides highly effective approaches for even serious temperament problems. Training is available for audiences ranging from one student to large groups of principal's teachers, and school counselors.

By providing clarity and understanding of emotional and psychological needs and desires, WIDP brings together the evaluation process for teacher-teacher and teacher-student relationships.

## Profile: Ministries/Clergy

Worley's ID Profile software will assist pastors, youth leaders, elders, lay counselors, Sunday schools superintendents, and teachers to effectively counsel members of their congregations. WIDP, after identifying an individual's personal inner needs and desires, provides new revelation and understanding of oneself. WIDP will enable the individual as well as the congregation to capitalize on temperament strengths and strengthen areas of weaknesses. Although WIDP is not a spiritual or religious evaluation, overall improvement of life will occur from understanding the results of their profile.

## Profile: Family Insights Relationships

Worley's ID Profile designed for families interested in improving their understanding. Family members use WIDP for, adding insight to their knowledge of themselves, and their loved ones, and for further development of their people awareness skills. These skills contribute significantly to, improved marriages, enhanced communication, and heightened awareness of the needs and desires of others, conflict resolutions, relationship restorations, bridging generation gaps, and many other interpersonal situations.

## Profile: Personal Insights

Personal Information/Affirmation: Worley's ID Profile designed for individuals who want to improve their understanding of self and to maximize their potential for a fulfilled, and, balanced life.

With increased insight and self-awareness, these people enjoy greater success in interpersonal relations.

## Relationship Profile

The relationship profile identifies the individual's needs and desires in close relationships with family and friends. Needs may range from emotional intimacy with expressions of love with many people to isolation. The psychological profile answers the question, **How emotionally open or closed to the relationship is this individual?**

**Relationship:** The third area is called the relationship profile. Again, this is very clear by the title given. This area of the temperament determines how we want to love and receive affection from others and how we will provide love and devotion to others. The relationship profile is the area of the temperament where the focus is one-on-one. The relationship is not a group function as are the social profile and the leadership profile. This area deals with the more in-depth relationships, which we have in our life as opposed to the general social situations covered by the social profile.

In a nutshell, the social profile determines who is in or out of the relationship; leadership profile determines who maintains the power and makes the decisions in the relationship, and the relationship profile defines how emotionally close or distant the relationship is.

## Temperament

Temperament is the inborn genetic makeup of who we are from birth and does not change like one's character and personality.

## Temperament Blends

Temperament blends occur when some person's temperament response renders any score that has a four or five in the combination of their profile numbers. See the examples below, which lists ALL the blends.

There is only one temperament that blends with the other temperaments, and that temperament is the Phlegmatic.

There are eight (8) different temperament blends of temperaments:

| | | |
|---|---|---|
| Melancholy Phlegmatic | (MP) | 04, 14, 24, 34 |
| Phlegmatic Melancholy | (PM) | 40, 41, 42, 43 |
| Phlegmatic Sanguine | (PS) | 56, 57, 58, 59 |
| Sanguine Phlegmatic | (SP) | 65, 75, 85, 95 |
| Choleric Phlegmatic | (CP) | 64, 74, 84, 94 |
| Phlegmatic Choleric | (PC) | 50, 51, 53, 54 |
| Introverted Sanguine/Phlegmatic | (IS/P) | 05, 15, 25, 35 |
| Phlegmatic/Introverted Sanguine | (P/IS) | 46, 47, 48, 49 |

**WIDP**  **Worley's Identity Discovery Profile (W I D P)**

| | | |
|---|---|---|
| W | Worley's | |
| I | Identify | Identify Your Inner Needs and Desires |
| D | Discovery | Dare to Become All You Can Be! |
| P | Profile | |

## WIDP Profile

A temperament assessment report (16–18 pages) generated by the WIDP software program from the 60 questions questionnaire responses of an individual.

## WIDP User

WIDP user is the person administering the WIDP software program.

| 3,449 Combined Spreadsheet | | | | | | | | | | | |
|---|---|---|---|---|---|---|---|---|---|---|---|
| | **Social** | | **%** | **Leadership** | | **%** | **Relationship** | | | **%** | |
| C/CC | 50 | / 0 | 1.45% | 415 | / 175 | 17.11% | 16 | | 0.46% | | |
| C/P | 39 | | 1.13% | 36 | | 1.04% | 41 | | 1.19% | | |
| IS/ISC | 202 | / 13 | 6.23% | 82 | / 26 | 3.13% | 243 | | 7.05% | | |
| IS/P | 91 | | 2.64% | 64 | | 1.86% | 334 | | 9.68% | | |
| M/MC | 1355 | / 303 | 48.07% | 1084 | / 839 | 55.76% | 800 | / 22 | 23.83% | | |
| M/P | 164 | | 4.76% | 142 | | 4.12% | 482 | | 13.98% | | |
| P | 133 | | 3.86% | 65 | | 1.88% | 318 | | 9.22% | | |
| P/C | 94 | | 2.73% | 194 | | 5.62% | 27 | | 0.78% | | |
| P/IS | 120 | | 3.48% | 17 | | 0.49% | 223 | | 6.47% | | |
| P/M | 274 | | 7.94% | 249 | | 7.22% | 265 | | 7.68% | | |
| P/S | 152 | | 4.41% | 12 | | 0.35% | 176 | | 5.10% | | |
| S/SC | 345 | / 55 | 11.60% | 26 | / 4 | 0.87% | 362 | / 71 | 12.55% | | |
| S/P | 59 | | 1.71% | 19 | | 0.55% | 69 | | 2.00% | | |

| 3,449 Combined Spreadsheet | | | | | | | | | | | |
|---|---|---|---|---|---|---|---|---|---|---|---|
| | **Social** | | **%** | **Leadership** | | **%** | **Relationship** | | | **%** | |
| C/CC | 50 | / 0 | 1.45% | 415 | / 175 | 17.11% | 16 | | 0.46% | | |
| C/P | 39 | | 1.13% | 36 | | 1.04% | 41 | | 1.19% | | |
| IS/ISC | 202 | / 13 | 6.23% | 82 | / 26 | 3.13% | 243 | | 7.05% | | |
| IS/P | 91 | | 2.64% | 64 | | 1.86% | 334 | | 9.68% | | |
| M/MC | 1355 | / 303 | 48.07% | 1084 | / 839 | 55.76% | 800 | / 22 | 23.83% | | |
| M/P | 164 | | 4.76% | 142 | | 4.12% | 482 | | 13.98% | | |
| P | 133 | | 3.86% | 65 | | 1.88% | 318 | | 9.22% | | |
| P/C | 94 | | 2.73% | 194 | | 5.62% | 27 | | 0.78% | | |
| P/IS | 120 | | 3.48% | 17 | | 0.49% | 223 | | 6.47% | | |
| P/M | 274 | | 7.94% | 249 | | 7.22% | 265 | | 7.68% | | |
| P/S | 152 | | 4.41% | 12 | | 0.35% | 176 | | 5.10% | | |
| S/SC | 345 | / 55 | 11.60% | 26 | / 4 | 0.87% | 362 | / 71 | 12.55% | | |
| S/P | 59 | | 1.71% | 19 | | 0.55% | 69 | | 2.00% | | |

# Scriptural References to the Five Temperaments

## INTROVERTED SANGUINE

Proverbs 30:10 "Do not slander a servant to his master, or he will curse you, and you will pay for it." (NIV)

Proverbs 30:10 "Accuse not a servant unto his master, lest he curse thee, and thou be found guilty." (KJV)

## SANGUINE

Proverbs 30:13 "Those whose eyes are ever so haughty, whose glances are so disdainful." (NIV)

Proverbs 30:13 "There is a generation, O how lofty are their eyes! And their eyelids are lifted up." (KJV)

## MELANCHOLY

Proverbs 30:11 "There are those who curse their fathers and do not bless their mothers." (NIV)

Proverbs 30:11 11 "There is a generation that curseth their father, and doth not bless their mother." (KJV)

## CHOLERIC

Proverbs 30:14 "Those whose teeth are swords and whose jaws are set with knives to devour the poor from the earth, the needy from among mankind." (NIV)

Proverbs 30:14 "There is a generation, whose teeth are as swords, and their jaw teeth as knives, to devour the poor from off the earth, and the needy from among men." (KJV)

## PHLEGMATIC

Proverbs 30:12 "Those who are pure in their own eyes and yet are not cleansed of their filth." (NIV)

Proverbs 30:12 "There is a generation that are pure in their own eyes, and yet is not washed from their filthiness." (KJV)

CPSIA information can be obtained
at www.ICGtesting.com
Printed in the USA
LVHW061939290919
632568LV00001B/1/P